An Anatomy of Power

Michael Mann is one of the most influential sociologists of recent decades. His work has had a major impact in sociology, history, political science, international relations and other social science disciplines. His main work, *The Sources of Social Power*, of which two of three volumes have been completed, will provide an all-encompassing account of the history of power from the beginnings of stratified societies to the present day. Recently he has published two major works, *Fascists* and *The Dark Side of Democracy*. Yet unlike that of other contemporary social thinkers, Mann's work has not, until now, been systematically and critically assessed. This volume assembles a group of distinguished scholars to take stock, both of Mann's overall method and of his account of particular periods and historical cases. It also contains Mann's reply where he answers his critics and forcefully restates his position. This is a unique and provocative study for scholars and students alike.

JOHN A. HALL is Professor of Sociology at Dartmouth College. His books include *Powers and Liberties* (1985), *Liberalism* (1989), *Coercion and Consent* (1994) and (with Charles Lindholm) *Is America Breaking Apart?* (2001).

RALPH SCHROEDER is a Research Fellow at the Oxford Internet Institute at the University of Oxford. His books include *Max Weber and the Sociology of Culture* (1992) and, as editor, *Max Weber, Democracy and Modernization* (1998).

An Anatomy of Power

The Social Theory of Michael Mann

Edited by

John A. Hall

Ralph Schroeder

CAMBRIDGE UNIVERSITY PRESS
Cambridge, New York, Melbourne, Madrid, Cape Town, Singapore, São Paulo

CAMBRIDGE UNIVERSITY PRESS
The Edinburgh Building, Cambridge CB2 2RU, UK

Published in the United States of America by Cambridge University Press,
New York

www.cambridge.org
Information on this title: www.cambridge.org/9780521615181

First published 2006

Printed in the United Kingdom at the University Press, Cambridge

A catalogue record for this book is available from the British Library

ISBN-13 978-0-521-85000-1 hardback
ISBN-10 0-521-85000-2 hardback
ISBN-13 978-0-521-61518-1 paperback
ISBN-10 0-521-61518-6 paperback

Contents

Figures

Contributors

ROBERT BRENNER is Professor in the Department of History at the University of California, Los Angeles

JOSEPH BRYANT is Professor in the Department of Sociology and the Department for the Study of Religion at the University of Toronto

RANDALL COLLINS is Professor of Sociology at the University of Pennsylvania

STEPHAN R. EPSTEIN is Professor of Economic History at the London School of Economics and Political Science

JACK A. GOLDSTONE is Virginia E. and John T. Hazel Professor of Public Policy at George Mason University

PHILIP S. GORSKI is Professor of Sociology and Director of the Center for Comparative Research at Yale University

JOHN A. HALL is Professor of Sociology at Dartmouth College

JOHN M. HOBSON is Professor of Politics and International Relations at the University of Sheffield

EDGAR KISER is Professor of Sociology at the University of Washington

DAVID LAITIN is James T. Watkins IV and Elise V. Watkins Professor of Political Science at Stanford University

MICHAEL MANN is Professor of Sociology at the University of California, Los Angeles

GIANFRANCO POGGI is Professor of Sociology at the University of Trento

RALPH SCHROEDER is Research Fellow at the Oxford Internet Institute, Oxford University

JACK SNYDER is Robert and Renée Belfer Professor of International Relations at Columbia University

FRANK TRENTMANN is Senior Lecturer in the School of History, Classics, and Archaeology at Birkbeck College, University of London

LINDA WEISS is Professor in the Department of Government and International Relations at the University of Sydney

1 Introduction: the IEMP model and its critics

Ralph Schroeder

This volume brings together essays that critically assess Michael Mann's sociology. The major works discussed here are *The Sources of Social Power, Volume I: A History from the Beginning to 1760 AD* (1986) and *Volume II: The Rise of Classes and Nation-States, 1760–1914* (1993). We shall have to wait for Volume III, which will take us to the present day, because Mann has concentrated for the last decade on another project: two volumes which have just been published entitled *Fascists* (2004) and *The Dark Side of Democracy: Explaining Ethnic Cleansing* (2005). *Fascists* is a comparative historical sociology of the six main fascist regimes, and the companion volume, *The Dark Side of Democracy*, covers the main modern instances of ethnic cleansing. He has now returned to working on the third volume, to be called 'Globalizations'. Still, we already have some indications of what is to come in the third volume from various articles (see the list of his publications at the end of this book) and from his recent book *Incoherent Empire* (2003), an analysis of America's role in the world today.

This introduction is intended for orientation. In the first part, I provide a brief introduction to Mann's sociology. In the second, I will give an overview of the contributions to the volume.

Mann prefers historical narrative to sociological model-building, but in the opening chapter of the first volume of the *Sources of Social Power* he puts forward what he calls the IEMP model, named after the four sources of social power: Ideological, Economic, Military and Political. In my exposition, I will concentrate on modern Europe, and especially on Volume II, or what Mann calls the 'age of popular modernity', from 1780 onwards (2000: 16), because that is where his IEMP model ties up most closely with contemporary debates in social theory.

Three of the four sources of social power – economic, ideological/cultural, and political – will be familiar to students of social theory. This is the way that Marx, Weber, Durkheim and most contemporary theorists analyse society. The most distinctive part of Mann's model is that he conceptualizes militarism as a fourth and separate source of social power.

From our vantage point after the end of the Cold War, it may be easy to overlook the importance of militarism, which has recently been very much neglected in sociology. Mann, however, treats it of equal weight with the other three sources, and we will see later that his separation of military power from political power is contentious. Moreover, we will need to wait until Volume III, when Mann covers the two World Wars, which he has labelled the period of 'citizen warfare', and the Cold War's 'nuclear age' (1988: 166–87), to find out how he analyses war on a global scale. It can be anticipated, however, that these periods of mass mobilization, and what he has called the 'deterrence-science' militarism of nuclear warfare, which almost put an end to history altogether, will go some way towards vindicating his separation of military power from the other forms of power.

Mann argues that militarism – along with economic power – was one of the primary determinants of social change in modern Europe up to the period ending with the Napoleonic Wars (1993: 251). The resources devoted to preparing for and making war in Western societies peaked at the end of this period, both in fiscal extraction and manpower (1993: 215), not to be matched again, as Mann is fond of pointing out, until present-day Israel and Iraq. This peak in military power coincided with the state's greatest relative size *vis-à-vis* civil society (1993: 504).

Apart from its role as a dominant power organization, the importance of militarism – and here Mann is in agreement with a school of thought which includes Theda Skocpol, Charles Tilly and Jack Goldstone (see Collins 1993) – is that up to and including the French Revolution, the function of the state was primarily military and geopolitical (1986: 511). His break with this 'state-centred theory', in which the power of the state is determined from the outside in (i.e. from the relations between states to internal state power), comes mainly, as we will see below, in the nineteenth century with the growth of the infrastructural and collective power of the state.

But militarism shares determining the relations between states with a different type of power, the outward-facing side of political power which he labels 'geopolitical diplomacy'. For Mann, there are two types of political power: outward-facing, or how the relations between states are governed depending on whether these powers are more equal or highly unequal, and inward-facing political power, power within the state, which will be discussed in a moment. The outward-facing form of political power organization, outside the bounds of territorially centralized units, alternates between hegemonic empires and multi-state civilizations. These two constellations have quite different 'rules of the game', rules by which relations between states are governed *apart from* the military strength with which they are enforced. This, the level of the most 'macro-' relations of power, also partly falls outside what can be theorized in sociology, as it seems that Mann wants to allow for a degree of contingency here (hence Mann's dotted rather than solid causal arrow in his diagram of the IEMP model, 1986: 29). One example is the 'over the top' – over the top of all four sources – slip into World War I (1993: 740–802).

The importance of geopolitical diplomacy is that it may prevail over militarism when it is controlled by the shared norms of transnational elites. Examples are the middle of the nineteenth century (1815–1880) when transnational capitalism plus British 'near hegemony' and a balance of power allowed the shared norms of diplomats to maintain relatively pacific geopolitical competition. Another possible example is today's 'soft geopolitics' after the Cold War (see Mann 1997). On the other hand, when, as often in modern times, militarism is autonomous and beyond the control of (civilian) political elites, and/or when society – the 'nation' – is mobilized for war, military power prevails over geopolitical diplomacy.

This brings us to the most well-known part of Mann's work, his analysis of political power *within* the state, and in particular his distinction between despotic and infrastructural power, or power 'over' as against power 'through' society (1993: 59–60). Pre-modern imperial and European absolutist states had much despotic power *over* a – laterally insulated – civil society, but little infrastructural power to penetrate civil society or implement its control on the ground. Feudal states had little despotic *or* infrastructural power. Authoritarian states – such as Nazi Germany and the Soviets – had *both*. The key question is: how do we arrive at today's 'bureaucratic–democratic' state, which is low on despotic power and high on infrastructural power?

Mann identifies several stages en route: after the puny feudal 'coordinating state', political power expands with the rise of the 'organic state' from the Reformation to the Napoleonic Wars. During this period, militarism and geopolitics centralized the state and added to its despotic power, but also deepened its reach down into civil society – infrastructural power. But militarism and geopolitics, and not domestic politics, remained the major causes of state-building into the nineteenth century.

This is the first part of the story, to borrow from the title of one of his essays, of 'the rise and rise' of the state: the organic state (up to 1780) expanding and reaching downward. The next period, from 1780 to 1815, as mentioned earlier, saw the high point of the state's power *over* civil society as well as a peak in military power. After this period, in the middle of the long nineteenth century, there was a further 'rise' with the 'tightening' of the state–society relationship, 'caging social relations' (1993: 61). This was the advent of the 'polymorphous' state: 'polymorphous' in the sense that the scope and the functions of the state expanded, but also in as much as it is no longer possible to speak of *the* state in the singular, but only of its 'crystallizations', the state's functioning in different capacities.

The tightening of the state–society relationship, slowly replacing despotic state power over civil society, means that the power of different groups in civil society can crystallize *in* the state. Put differently, the infrastructural power of the polymorphous state – in contrast with the power of the organic state – reaches not just downward but upward. Again, this is a form of power 'through society'. When deciding which groups are dominant in society, or which distinctive paths the state thereby takes, Mann looks to 'higher level crystallizations' (1993: 76) which prevail among the various functions of the state. Thus the state becomes much more powerful during this period, but also 'morphs', develops in different directions, and loses its coherence (1993: 79). Losing coherence means both taking on a variety of new functions (1993: 79) and no longer being subject to the control of a single autonomous regime.

This is an evolutionary view of the state and political power – the state has become ever more powerful – but it has also become less autonomous from, more entwined with and more promiscuous with the other sources of social power. And its size *relative* to civil society *declined* over the course of the nineteenth century, even while its scope increased (1993: 504).

States were more diverse at the end of the nineteenth century with their different 'higher level crystallizations' than they are today, after being 'compromised': some regime types were, according to Mann, defeated by two World Wars. Thus we have arrived at 'bureaucratic–democratic' state, low on despotic and high on infrastructural power, or at 'democratic-party states, routinely controlled by civil society' (1993: 61), or at the 'age of institutionalized nation-states' (1995). Northern states after World War II have converged on liberal-democratic and social democratic norms (2000: 48). They are more homogenous as they all have 'democratic party' regimes, and their coherence has increased – even while new functions have been added and there are more inputs from civil society.

Political power is thus the most complex part of Mann's IEMP model. But the main point here is simply that Mann puts much more weight on political power than any other classical social theorist with the possible exception of Weber, and than any other contemporary school of social theory apart from the 'state-centered' school – though this school professes comparative history rather than 'theory'.

So we can move on to ideological power or 'culture'; Mann seems to think that either term can be used. There are two types of ideological power, which Mann calls 'sociospatially transcendent' and 'immanent morale'. Here it is best to give some key examples: the 'sociospatially transcendent' ideology of Christendom and its 'normative pacification' was 'necessary' for the rise of modern Europe (1986: 506–7), but its role was gradually replaced by the shared norms of the state-system in a multistate civilization (1986: 512–13) which played such a decisive role, as we saw above, by the middle of the nineteenth century. 'Immanent morale' is a less autonomous form of power, strengthening existing social organizations. The street-level organizations of the fascist paramilitary social movements, as we shall see in a moment, are a prime example.

The place where comparative historical sociologists would most expect ideological power to play a decisive role is in relation to the world-religions. The foremost thinker associated with this view is Weber. But in the chapter on the world-religions in Volume I (1986: 341–72), Mann is sceptical towards assigning a key role to the world-religions in social development, and a comparative approach to world-civilization also falls outside his – narrowly evolutionist – narrative of power. The second place where we might expect a major role for ideology is during the French Revolution. But again, while acknowledging its local morale-boosting role, Mann is doubtful about its transcendent role in subsequently spreading the impact of the revolutionary message beyond France.

Ideological power provides a good opportunity for a brief digression from the IEMP model to discuss Mann's ideas about networks and power. The most famous statement in Mann's sociology is that 'societies are constituted of multiple overlapping and intersecting networks of social power' (1986: 1). Networks are thus the 'containers' (my word, not Mann's) of the four power sources. In relation to ideological power, this means that ideology must be contained in an organizational form to have an impact. As has just been mentioned, Mann distinguishes between two types of ideological power, 'sociospatially transcendent', covering a larger territory in a diffuse manner, and 'immanent morale', which is more intensive than extensive. And we have already encountered two types of political power, 'despotic' and 'infrastructural'. The other sources of social power also come in different types, so that in addition to 'intensive' and 'extensive' types of power, Mann distinguishes between authoritative and diffused power, and between collective and distributive power. The various combinations of authoritative/diffused and intensive/extensive yield four combinations of what Mann calls the 'organizational reach' of networks (1986: 9). We will also come back shortly to the zero-sum or A over B nature of authoritative power, which can be contrasted with Mann's notion of collective power, adopted from Parsons, 'whereby persons in cooperation can enhance their joint power over third parties or over nature' (1986: 6). At this point, we should merely note that Mann has described his approach as 'organizational materialism', which means – again, in my interpretation – (a) that power always has to be contained in an organizational form, it is never free-floating, and (b) that the types of power are not ideal types in Weber's sense, constructs that are imposed on reality, nor are they a reality separate from human beings and imposed upon us, but they are rather, to use Mann's term, 'emergent'.

We can now return to Mann's scepticism about the ideological reach of the French Revolution. He is willing to concede that ideological power played a world-historical role on this occasion, but the wider ideological ramifications of this event were limited because the organizational networks could not carry this ideology very far in practice, which was in any case hemmed in by France's geopolitical defeat in 1815 (1993: 246). As the contributions to this volume will make clear, ideological power is where Mann is at the receiving end of the strongest criticisms, but I would point out here that this organizational materialism, the idea that ideology, like the other sources of power, is always contained within the reach of networks, is also an excellent tool for eliminating excessive claims for the power of ideology or culture: briefly put, if it is not in a network or in an organization, it can't *do* anything.

The only other place in Mann's sociology where the power of ideology comes into the foreground as a determining source of social power is among the fascists. In this case, ideology took the form of providing the immanent morale for a social movement, which boosted authoritarian statists' parties into power and ultimately, in the Nazi case, aimed at the transcendence of their national cages. Mann makes an important though highly contentious contrast with the role of ideological mobilization in the other authoritarian statist surge of the twentieth century – communism – which, he argues, was primarily oriented to transforming everyday life (and failed partly for not delivering on this aim), and not towards transcending its borders. Again, we see ideological networks, some sociospatially transcendent and others providing immanent morale, some seeking to transform other power networks, others being contained within them.

When it comes to economic power, the faultline in social theory has been between those whose analysis focuses on capitalism and those who prefer the label 'industrial society'. Capitalism in Marxist thought means the economic determinism of classes and their conflict. For liberal social thought, on the other hand, capitalism often consists of a frictionless plane of atomized market relationships. The alternative 'industrial society' view is that economic growth is produced by science and technology and the division of labour – without the state's developmental assistance.

The IEMP model goes along with Marxism in defining classes in relation to capitalism and economic power. Yet 'commercial' and 'industrial' (1993: 250) capitalism consists of diffused rather than authoritative power, and therefore does not fundamentally reorganize other power relations, including distributive – class – relations (1993: 219). Mann's downplaying of social change as a result of modern capitalism brings to mind Ernest Gellner's comment that the concept of capitalism is much overrated (for some comparisons between Mann and Gellner, see Schroeder 1998).

This distinction between capitalism and industrialism in Mann's account of the nineteenth century – and his bracketing industrialism together with the increase in collective (rather than distributive) power – makes all the difference in setting his position apart from that of Marxists. But it also sets him apart from liberal social thinkers, who argue that markets or civil society provide an important balance *against* the modern state – after the increased productivity of the industrial revolution and the division of labour in the market has made possible the transition from a pre-modern (despotic and Hobbesian) state to the modern liberal state of Locke, Tocqueville and the pluralists. Instead, we need to recall the 'promiscuity', as Mann calls it, of political power that was mentioned above: the economy bolsters the collective/infrastructural power of the state, and the state, in turn, 'tightens' its relationship with the economy/civil society.

In going beyond the use of 'industrialism' or 'capitalism' as master concepts, with the respective ramifications of each, Mann is in line with an emerging consensus among economic historians that looks more closely at the different phases of the two industrial revolutions and at regional variations in industrialization during the long nineteenth century. Without going into this complexity, it is possible to say that Mann provides a response to the question of the relation between economic power and the other forms of power in society, or a response to what has been possibly *the* key question in social theory – the *primacy* of capitalism or industrialism in the transition to modernity. His answer is both, neither, and more: *both*, inasmuch as he wants to use both concepts to argue that the increase in collective power that was made possible by the industrial revolution and by capitalism was such that it revolutionized the other sources of social power, and especially the infrastructural/collective powers of the state; *neither*, in so far as capitalism and the industrial revolution did not fundamentally transform distributive power, and that although industrialism was transnational and uniformly imposed changes on society, it was also adapted by nation-states to their own ends. And *more* than these two concepts are needed since this transition was also determined: (1) up to 1820, by geopolitical diplomacy and military power which remained in the control of an elite; and (2) thereafter by political power because the state, in the form of the strategy of dominant regimes which controlled it, and by means of its increasing scope and infrastructural power, was central to how the relations between citizens/classes were institutionalized (see 'Ruling Class Strategies and Citizenship', Mann 1988: ch. 7). Thus the state is also gaining infrastructural strength as it becomes democratized by incorporating citizens/classes.

This last argument is also the key to the transition to 'popular modernity'. This transition is a product not of economic but of *political* power, conceived not as 'power over' or despotic power, but 'power through' or infrastructural power. This allows Mann to avoid a one-sidedly economic determinist explanation which relies on the combination of class and power, and a one-sidedly political or 'elite theory' explanation whereby the ruling elite forces social change from above. Further, it allows him to propose that there is variation in the paths to 'popular modernity' – a variety of state forms or state 'crystallizations' – within an overall pattern towards an increase in infrastructural/collective power.

Perhaps 'popular modernity', power from below as opposed to elite power, will thus turn out to be a more important concept than capitalism or industrial society for Mann's theory. If so, it will cement the dominant place of political as opposed to economic power in his social theory, at least on the question of the transition to modernity, and set him apart from most major modern social thinkers – the closest perhaps being (the relatively neglected) Carl Schmitt, whom Mann discusses at length in *Fascists*.

Yet there remains – and this is why the focus on the age of popular modernity (or the transition to modernity/capitalism/industrial society) is so central to an assessment of Mann – a question which leads to a potential criticism: what is the *lever* of this transformation? Mann seems to argue that it is (a) a much longer-term process (at least in the crucial case of England/Britain) reaching back to long before this transition (1993: 214). But then (b) he also does not want to downgrade the revolutionary character of the two industrial revolutions (1993: 94, 597) in enhancing collective power – but in this case, the burden of the explanation lies on science and technology which are extra-social forces (see also Goldstone's chapter in this volume), and part of the traditional explanation of 'industrial society' theorists. Or finally it is (c) a chain of factors – a state with stronger despotic power gained from militarism enables state-led economic development, which allows economic growth, which, in turn, enhances the infrastructural collective power of the state (1993: 251). Yet such a chain of causes, though it comes closest to

Mann's view and may be closest to the truth, fails to satisfy in the sense that it does not allow us to go from history to a theory of society, where theory supplies both the analytical tools as well as an explanation of 'how we got here'. Put differently, this 'chain' puts Mann among the multi-factorialists or multi-causalists like Gellner (1986) or neo-Weberian institutionalists, rather than among theorists of power who identify 'primacy' in the course of history.

Mann often insists that he uses and needs all four sources to explain social change, but his aim is still 'primacy' (Mann, 1986: 3–4). For the long nineteenth century, which is covered in the second volume, this becomes very complex. If there is nevertheless an overall pattern, then, as we have seen, it is the 'tightening' state–society relationship. There is also a broader pattern that can be discerned with the help of his recent series of lectures entitled 'Modernity and Globalization' (2000), which is the shift from elite to popular modernity. With *Fascists* and *The Dark Side of Democracy: Explaining Ethnic Cleansing*, Mann has now extended both patterns into the twentieth century. He argues that the democratization of the state of 'popular modernity' has a 'dark side', the violence used in the name of 'the people' – in some cases by colonial settlers, but increasingly centred on the state, to suppress and eliminate others who are not part of 'rule by the people'. 'Tightening' and 'caging' can therefore be positive – a democratization of power from below whereby power becomes laterally shared or compromised (even here, there is a negative side – 'others' may need to be displaced or eliminated 'sideways'). Or it can be negative, as when the pressures of war and from below squeeze 'statists' upwards into the tops of their national cages such that they coerce and remove 'others' in the cage below – at the extreme murdering them – or in their aggressive outward expansion. In his *Fascists* and *The Dark Side of Democracy*, political power thus constitutes the most important part of Mann's explanation of the twentieth century's (non-war) atrocities. If political 'caging' and 'popular' democratization are also the master trends – outside war when militarism trumps the other sources – of the third volume, as they are for the nineteenth century and for *Fascists* and *The Dark Side of Democracy*, then it can be anticipated that this volume will go strongly against the congratulatory self-image – the end of history and the global triumph of democracy and markets – of our age.

Overview of the contributions

The volume is divided into four parts. The first two cover Mann's theoretical background, method and the four types of power. In the third part there are three essays that assess Mann's view of the rise of the West. And in Part IV, there are three contributions which discuss the prospects for analysing contemporary change in the light of Mann's sociology.

Collins sketches how Mann's theory fits in with and advances upon some key findings of contemporary sociology. Mann's central contribution, he says, is to trace how one power network – the state – crystallized more strongly in modern Europe than did the other power networks. This process, for Collins, culminates in today's states as the targets of social movements. Collins anticipates Mann's Volume III in suggesting that today these social movements are not, as in classical social theory and in Mann's second volume, classes and nations, but rather gender, ethnicity, environmentalism, religion and many more. Even in this cacophonous struggle, Collins argues, the key aim of social science must be to continue along the lines Mann suggests: to find the major cleavages in politics-centred struggles that define contemporary social change. Here I would remind the reader of a point I made earlier: that Mann's focus during 'popular modernity' is above all on political power.

Hall begins by contrasting Mann's view with the disenchantment thesis held by Weber and Ernest Gellner, whereby modern society does not allow for all-embracing political ideologies – regrettably for the Nietzschean Weber, thankfully for the Popperian Gellner! Mann's early empirical research on the British working class, Hall points out, made him, too, stay clear of the ideological fervour of the social sciences in the 1970s, and put him close to a pragmatic and reformist version of democratic socialism. But Hall also suggests that Mann underplays the ideological implications of different regimes: socialism, in Hall's view, often took a more statist form than Mann allows, and ideology on the right, rather than being merely technocratic (Mann's view), did in fact have a strong – anti-statist – appeal. Hall worries about Mann's failure to analyse some of the drawbacks of socialism; in Hall's view, entrenching the rights of some social groups may be at the expense of other groups (for example curtailing the rights of immigrants) and may also foment industrial conflict. At the same time, he notes the absence of alternatives to the liberal American post-war political order – even if he also recognizes its shortfalls. Hall thus follows Collins' highlighting of state-centred struggles with a different argument: there may be illiberal consequences if state struggles permanently entrench the rights of some social groups to the detriment of others.

The program of the multi-dimensional conflict sociology that Collins advocates, I would argue, is above all Weberian in inspiration, even if Collins also detects the ghost of Marx. The next two contributors concentrate on Mann's method. Kiser, who also argues for a Weberian sociology, is more interested in method than content. Kiser's preference is for an 'analytical Weberianism' which can steer between a 'verstehen'-based cultural Weberianism and a macro-'structural' Weberianism that gives no room to agency. Kiser's analytical Weberianism meshes with a rational choice agenda in social science, in which the rationally maximizing actor is the basic unit for causal analysis. And while he concedes that Mann's social actors often follow *broadly* rational goals, they do not always do so. For Kiser, then, Mann only partly lives up to the scientific aim of rational choice historical sociology, which is to find causal explanations in the light of pre-specified goals of individual actors.

Bryant, like Kiser, notes that the building blocks of Mann's theory at the micro-level are minimal; actors pursuing their well-being. Yet the main criticisms that have been directed at Mann's method in the past have not attacked these foundations as such, but have rather come from positivist and Marxist epistemology, charging him with too much theory (or too little empiricism) from the positivist side and too little materialism from the side of Marxist theory. Bryant defends him against both charges and points out how theory and evidence discipline each other as much as they can in Mann's historical narratives. Yet he also faults Mann for paying insufficient attention to ideology, using early Christianity as an example. He argues that the beginnings of Christian belief were less uniform and they had a more insecure appeal than Mann allows, and that to cope with this he could have paid more attention in this case to the complex *content* of ideology or culture.

Gorski also wants to put more emphasis on ideological power. To do this, he reviews Mann's explanation of the rise of the West; the normative (ideological) pacification achieved by Christianity in the Middle Ages, the growth of state muscle with military competition from the sixteenth century onwards, and the subsequent increase of the state's infrastructural capacity in the nineteenth century. In place of this, Gorski offers a religion-centred explanation not, as in Weber's case, of economic change, but rather of patterns of state-formation; and more specifically, of religion's society-organizing capacity or Mann's 'infrastructural power'. Further, Gorski argues that ideological power played a role for longer, and more forcefully, than Mann allows, including its entwining with secular ideologies like nationalism, right up into post-war welfare states. Finally, he suggests that many forms of ideology – religion and its substitutes in the form of everyday transcendences and rituals – still play a role today, against Mann's implicit argument, shared by many contemporary social thinkers, that modernization entails secularization.

Hobson and Weiss both also criticize Mann's downplaying of the bottom-up capacity of civil society at the expense of the increasing top-down capacity of the state. Weiss does this by arguing that the state can gain power from the coordination of economic relations, while Hobson suggests that 'realist' power between states can be softened by the civil societies within states. Hobson begins by making the case against the static 'billiard ball' logic of realist international relations theory, but he also thinks that Mann shares some of its faults. Geopolitics is too much of a separate arena for Mann, Hobson argues, which consists only of power interests. Hobson's alternative is to recognize that states sometimes shape the international arena as well as being shaped by it. And like several other contributors, Hobson thinks that Mann pays insufficient attention to ideology, in this case the norms and shifting identities of the actors in the international arena. Still, Hobson thinks that there are considerable payoffs for an international relations theory informed by historical sociology.

Weiss addresses the topic of state power and economic globalization. She highlights Mann's point that 'transnational and national interaction has surged together' (Mann 2000: 44) in the twentieth century, instead of being two zero-sum processes as they are for most others in the debate about globalization. What she criticizes is that Mann still sees the state as constrained by globalization, and proposes instead that states' enabling role, and especially industrial governance, has grown and made states stronger in the face of globalization. The state has not only become a top-down regulator – Mann's view – but also in Weiss's view a coordinator of economic activity which is responsive to civil society. This is an important challenge not only to Mann's ideas, but also to current thinking about globalizing economic forces.

Poggi challenges Mann's separation of military power. The political implication of Mann's argument that Poggi wants to avoid here is that a separate source of military power can override the democratic accountability of the state. This is also an empirical issue: military elites are not separate, he says. They are, with a few isolated empirical – not theoretical – exceptions, subordinate to political elites. Poggi may be suggesting good reasons against separating military power and sticking to the holy trinity of economy, ideology/culture and politics. Yet I cannot help briefly intervening here to argue that there is, to my mind, an unassailable argument in Mann's sociology for keeping military power separate: first, as Mann shows, the idea that the domination of the South by the North was due to economic exploitation is one that the evidence forces us to abandon (see also O'Brien 1997). It seems that even at the height of colonialism in the late nineteenth century, geopolitical interests far outweighed economic ones. If this is so, then we *must* have military power as a separate source of power to explain this domination, since clearly political power won't do (the legitimate monopoly of power *within* states), and cultural/ideological power, as Mann shows in *Modernity and Globalization* and *The Dark Side of Democracy*, also cannot explain the colonialist domination of the South. (It can be added that international relations theory also does not help us here since it cannot explain *systematic* relations of domination. The only international relations theory which *could* explain this domination is world-systems theory, which was ruled out under economic power above.) Logic combined with evidence may therefore force us to treat military power separately – that is, of course, *if* we do not want to abandon the idea of Northern or Western domination altogether.

The political implications of the next section, 'European Exceptionalism?', are more oblique, though they are most obvious in Brenner's Marxist attack. Brenner revisits some key debates in the transition from feudalism to capitalism and restates the case for economic primacy. He argues for the mutual dependence of – or overlap between – the propertied and ruling elites. This ruling class, he argues, was critical to the economic-cum-political transition from feudalism to capitalism. He agrees with Mann on the importance of political power and inter-state competition, but contends that he ignores the economic dimension of this factor. According to Brenner, 'warfare was, for the lords of medieval Europe, a great machine for economic aggrandizement'. With this argument, he puts economic exploitation at the centre of social change, in contrast with Mann's (and Tilly's) emphasis on state-formation and militarism.

Two further chapters challenge Mann's account of European exceptionalism, Goldstone from a comparative perspective (as we will see in a moment), and Epstein on the European turf itself. In the place where Mann emphasizes the Christian ideological or normative umbrella fostering economic exchange, Epstein stresses trade beyond this normative zone. He also adds a role for religion which Mann overlooks: the corporate form of the early modern church, which ultimately lent itself to the institution-alization of property beyond the religious sphere. He further questions Mann's argument (though from a different perspective than Brenner's) that the state's economic power was driven by military competition. Instead, Epstein argues, there was a delicate balance between the state's economic and political power such that the most successful states were those that could overcome prisoners' dilemmas and coordination failures; where elites were not entrenched in zero-sum rent-seeking *and* the state could efficiently gather taxes.

Epstein's chapter provides an interesting example using rational choice theory in historical sociology. But while Kiser's chapter in this volume (discussed earlier) advocates rational choice as a method, Epstein's argument is an application of the method: he charts European states' ability to extract taxes in terms of 'transaction cost analysis' (a concept that lies broadly within the rational choice paradigm) about the costs of coordinating economic activity by different types of institutions.

For Goldstone, the strength of Mann's method, the focus on networks of power rather than reified 'societies', is also its weakness. Mann must trace these networks over time, rather than being able to compare them synchronically as bounded units. In Goldstone's view, this handicaps Mann's account of the rise of the West: in place of Mann's narrative of England's emergence as the leading edge of power, Goldstone presents evidence that Holland had more impressive economic growth than England up to 1750. Even more importantly, China's economic growth was more powerful and, according to recent scholarship, China also had higher levels of consumption than England up to roughly the same period. The explanation for the breakthrough to modernity must therefore be located after 1800, when a divergence in economic growth, uniquely high in England/Britain, took place. Goldstone thinks that the crucial factor here is knowledge, and in particular the technologies of the steam engine and coal, thus suggesting a further source of social power that must be added to Mann's four-fold schema.

Whatever the role of England/Britain in the rise of the West, its liberal path to modernity has a special place in Mann's theory. Trentmann thinks that Mann treats this case as too top-down, with an old regime elite reluctantly ceding some political power to the middle and later the working classes in the nineteenth century. In correcting this picture, Trentmann does not deny elite power, but he argues that this leaves out pressure from below, which shifted the ground among all political actors, not just the elite. Thus over the course of a series of crises in the nineteenth century, the very terms in which political conflict was negotiated were transformed, a change in the political culture which came to consist of an increasingly well organized and vocal civil society. Again, there are implications for contemporary politics since Trentmann refers to Mann's resigned – almost fatalist and certainly 'determinist' – dissection of the decline of British power. Yet Mann's refusal in his most recent work, *Fascists* and *Ethnic Cleansing*, to overlook the 'agency' of the perpetrators even if his explanation remains 'structural' is perhaps a sign that, as he gets closer to the present day, he will be able to rectify his relative neglect of our power to shape – rather than be shaped by – our social cages.

Snyder proposes that it is impossible to separate 'is' and 'ought' in the study of ideology. Although he couches his analysis in utilitarian and economistic language – supply and demand, competitive advantage, salvation premiums, etc. – he in fact argues that ideology rests on non-utilitarian commitments and constitutes an attempt to surmount practical realities. And while ideology on occasion plays a decisive role in Mann's work,

Snyder thinks that he provides no convincing explanation of why this is so. His own view is that they are successful because groups infused with the force of beliefs are demonstrably stronger than those who are not. Snyder uses a number of examples, especially early Christianity, to illustrate his alternative view of the power of ideology. And while early Christianity is Snyder's main example, there are clearly implications of his view for today's ideologically riven world, with further implications for international relations, Snyder's home discipline.

Laitin takes Mann to task for his main thesis about ethnic cleansing, that 'murderous cleansing is modern, because it is the dark side of democracy' (Mann 2005: 2). In Laitin's view, Mann does not establish this link and in fact often presents evidence that goes directly against it; what Mann often *does* show is that ethnic cleansing is an abomination of the democratization process. Further, Laitin questions whether Mann's identification of genocide as the worst form of murderous violence is justified: this allows Mann to put cases with proportionately fewer killings into a category that is worse than more systematic killings in many instances of warfare, ethnicide and the elimination of enemy political classes. For Laitin, the value of Mann's recent work lies more in his subordinate theses and in empirical accounts of political violence.

Laitin's contribution brings us back to fundamental debates about theory and method. Yet what is remarkable about Mann's reply to his critics is the extent to which the debate remains on the terrain of substantive empirical issues, rather than theoretical or methodological ones – as with so many contemporary debates among social scientists. Put differently, there is much common ground here, and agreement that the way forward is by weighing the evidence. *The Dark Side of Democracy* also leads us back to the heart of today's most serious political conflicts, the civil wars of the post-war period in which all four sources have been blamed as root causes. Mann's focus on the infrastructural power of states in particular (or the lack thereof) will no doubt provide him with the tools to chart the strengthening of twentieth-century democracies as well as their continuing weaknesses and failures. He has synthesized an enormous amount of material to allow historical analysis to stay abreast with contemporary social change. We look forward to his third volume and to continued critical engagement with him as he tracks the sources of social power into the twenty-first century.

Acknowledgements

The editors would like to thank Dominic Lieven and Patrick O'Brien for helpful comments during the workshop at the LSE where some of the chapters in this volume were first presented. Thanks go also to Odul

Bozkurt for help with arranging the second workshop for the volume at UCLA, and Sophia Bengtsson at Chalmers University for assistance in preparing the final manuscript.

References

Collins, R. 1993. Maturation of the State-Centered Theory of Revolution and Ideology. *Sociological Theory*, 11.

Gellner, E. 1986. *Plough, Sword and Book – The Structure of Human History*. London: Collins Harvill.

Mann, M. 1986. *The Sources of Social Power, Volume I: A History from the Beginning to 1760 AD*. Cambridge: Cambridge University Press.

  1988. *States, War and Capitalism*. Oxford: Basil Blackwell.

  1993. *The Sources of Social Power, Volume II: The Rise of Classes and Nation-States*. Cambridge: Cambridge University Press.

  1995. As the Twentieth Century Ages. *New Left Review*, 214.

  1997. Has Globalization Ended the Rise and Rise of the Nation-State? *Review of International Political Economy*, 4(3).

  2000. 'Modernity and Globalization'. Unpublished, given as the Wiles Lectures at Queen's University, Belfast.

  2004. *Fascists*. Cambridge: Cambridge University Press.

  2005. *The Dark Side of Democracy: Explaining Ethnic Cleansing*. Cambridge: Cambridge University Press.

O'Brien, P. 1997. International Trade and the Development of the Third World since the Industrial Revolution. *Journal of World History*, 8(1).

Schroeder, R. 1998. From Weber's Political Sociology to Contemporary Liberal Democracy. In R. Schroeder (ed.), *Max Weber, Democracy and Modernization*. Basingstoke: Macmillan.

Part I

Theory, practice, method

2 Mann's transformation of the classic sociological traditions

Randall Collins

Michael Mann's ongoing work is as close to classic sociology for our own day as anything one can find. This is so in several senses. It has the scope of classic themes: the major conditions and processes which shape the relatively stable social structures of each historical period, and propel their changes. Mann's work is also classical in a sense that connects it with what we have come to see as the main stream of macro-sociology; he sets forth that which we have learned from Marx and Weber that is worth preserving, and displays the state of our knowledge on Marxian and Weberian themes. This is not to diminish the considerable originality which is found in Mann. A living classic contains a balance of what is old and what is new; it gives a sense of continuity from the great issues of the past and the concepts that frame them, and a sense of growing intellectual sophistication. Scholarship is a collective enterprise; much of what makes Mann's work a contemporary classic is his exemplary statement of lines of research that have been pursued by many scholars. But this is true of any great classic. Weber was selected out by his successors from a large and sophisticated scholarly community doing related work in what we would now call historical sociology; he too was a packager and crystallizer of the work of that larger community.

The main analytical innovations in the later twentieth century have come from the part of the scholarly field where there is a strong admixture of Weberian and Marxian concepts in the research enterprise of historical sociology. We have been in a new Golden Age of historical sociology from the mid-1960s onwards, centred on such topics as the comparative sociology of revolutions (Barrington Moore, Skocpol, Goldstone, and others); social movements (Tilly, McAdam, Tarrow, and others); the development of the modern state (Mann and others); the capitalist world economy (Wallerstein, Abu-Lughod, Frank, Chase-Dunn, Arrighi, and others). The common focus on these world-determining, centrally important phenomena has brought Marxian and Weberian scholars into fruitful interchange, and into blending many conceptions.

In the last third of the twentieth century, a hybrid Marx/Weber conflict sociology came to dominate a large field of scholarship. Its home ground has been historical sociology, the wide-ranging kind of history that I have called 'macro-history'; in contrast to the more limited specializations of many disciplinary historians, historical sociologists have used the wide scope of long-term change, and the leverage of comparison among partly similar but differing world regions, to build a general theory. A common ground among Marx and Weber has proven fruitful: that examining conflicting social interests is the best way to understand the patterns of social change; and that stable patterns of social structure exist when those conflicts are demobilized, held latent or in tension, by the dominance of one set of interests over others. These patterns of conflict in Mann's terminology are called 'sources of power'; their stable formation in a particular historical period are called 'crystallizations'.

In what follows, I will review Mann's work as our contemporary standard of knowledge on four points: the expansion of class conflict theory into the four-dimensional model of economic, ideological, military and political power networks; globalizing the unit of analysis and dissolving the bounded society into a set of overlapping territorial networks; the military-centred theory of the modern tax-extracting and society-penetrating state; and the state-centred theory of conflict mobilization in the modern era.

From Marxian class conflict to Weberian three-dimensional stratification to Mann's four power networks

Mann's big synthetic work, *The Sources of Social Power*, has the feel of a contemporary classic, because it gives perhaps the best current statement of what sociologists have developed from the synthesis of the Marxian and Weberian traditions. By the 1970s, there was already considerable convergence between the camps that stratification has three aspects; Marxian theorists were largely concerned with the issue of the relative autonomy of ideological and political structures which made for flexibility in defence of class interests, for instance by the politically motived reforms of the welfare state which preserved rampant market capitalism from itself. Mann's early work dealt with just these issues; his 1970 paper 'The social cohesion of liberal democracy' demonstrated that the upper and upper-middle classes are much more mobilized politically than the working and lower classes, and thus are ideologically committed to democracy without sacrifice of their class interests.

Mann built explicitly on the Marx/Weber synthesis which treated all three dimensions as versions of struggle over social power: i.e. the left-Weberian position which takes all forms of stratification as extensions or analogies to class conflict. Mann's major innovations were two: to split the political dimension into two further dimensions; and to conceptualize each dimension as a social network. Mann refers to this as the IEMP model, a convenient acronym for Ideological, Economic, Military and Political. Turning these back into the Weberian terminology, we have economic class, status group as cultural or ideological communities, and the dimension of 'party' or political power split into military power and political power *per se*. As Mann notes, although Weber defined the ideal type of the state as an organization monopolizing legitimate political force upon a territory, this is an abstraction from history; much of the time states lacked a monopoly of force, and mililtary units of marauders, *ad hoc* coalitions, rebels, or bandits could build up outside states and shape new ones; states sometimes crystallized from military organization but were not coextensive with it. By the same token, the political dimension of power has its own organizational locus and its own forms of action; we get a more refined theory of politics when we separate it out for special consideration.

Like Weber at his best, Mann does not make these distinctions merely for the sake of taxonomic clarification; they are working tools by which he builds an *histoire raisonné*, a narrative history of social institutions. Mann is more of a historical sociologist than Weber, in the sense that Mann shows the sequences by which the structures of power emerged in world history, and what went into their specific blends and crystallizations in particular places and times. Weber, by contrast, was primarily a comparativist using historical materials; although the comparisons are meant to contribute to explaining the crucial divergence in world history which gave rise to modern capitalism, Weber rarely gives much of an account of how processes of change actually worked themselves out. (The main exception to this is in *Ancient Judaism* (Weber 1952), which gives more of a sense of the series of political struggles that shaped Judaic religion than Weber does for any of his other studies of the world religions.) Mann thus gives more of a payoff to the Weberian style; whereas Weber provided a toolbox for analysing world history, Mann actually does the historical analysis.

Mann's move to separate military and political dimensions opens the way for a more systematic theory of both, and of their interaction. Geopolitical relations among states now come into their own. There has been a tradition of geopolitical analysis, to be sure, since the turn of the twentieth century; but it was for a long time a distinct, even segregated speciality. The nationalist and bellicose ideological predelictions of some of its earlier practitioners gave geopolitics a nasty reputation in liberal and left circles; and even after the analysis of military 'international relations'

or 'interstate relations' became respectable in political science departments after mid-century, geopolitical research remained largely distinct
from sociology, even though it had an undertone of resonance with
Weberian historical sociologists. Mann's elevation of military power to
a distinct dimension of the expanded Weberian model is a signal of the
legitimation of geopolitical theory. The modern state developed from the
ramifications of the military revolution of early modern times; this shows
that the importance of the military involves not only the external relations
among states – their geopolitics – but also the internal structuring which
happens on a state's territory as it builds infrastructure to support its
military forces. The sphere of politics, independent of the military, grows
historically because of the institutionalization of the Weberian, force-
monopolizing territorial state. As the state develops an administrative
and tax-extracting apparatus, it becomes a target for social groups who
attempt to control it; the state itself becomes a prize to be captured, and a
tool to be used for the agendas of all politically mobilized groups. Thus
the sphere of politics, which Mann has pulled out for consideration
separate from military power, is emergent, increasingly autonomous
from military power; this happens in an historical sequence in which
military configurations are the crucial first steps.

Here is a further significance in the fact that Weber's 'Class, Status and
Party' was a subsection within his chapter on 'Political Communities'.
For Weber, classes, status groups, and 'parties' or political factions are all
contenders for control of the state; one could define politics narrowly, but
in an historically useful way for the modern era, as action to get control of
the state apparatus, either as an end in itself or in order to use it to further
one's ideologies and interests. But as Mann shows, only after the historical rise of the military-centred state could political interest groups of this
sort become mobilized to contend over it. By separating the dimensions
of military and political power, Mann generalizes them to lines of action
which can occur in all historical periods and whether or not the state in
any specific sense actually exists. As a result, we can see how various
forms of power create structures, as well as operating within existing
structures. Weber's analysis, with its tendency towards comparative sta-
tics, in Mann's hands becomes fluid and dynamic.

Each of the IEMP dimensions is a social network: which is to say, a
chain of connections linking people together. One advantage of this
conception is that power is never free-floating; we are never tempted to
treat it merely as an abstraction, somehow existing inherently in the
'system', or in the 'logic' of social form, as in the tendency for scholars
influenced by semiotic post-Marxism to talk about the logic of capitalist
reproduction, or of feminist theorists to talk about the logic of patriarchy.

Networks do not have logics; they are real connections among people, empirically observable as to where they spread out in space. It is always possible, in principle, to examine the shape of a network of power; ideological power, for example, is not simply at one time in history the workings of religious belief, but has a structure of priests, monks, missionaries, people participating in religious ceremonies. Similarly with economic power; this is not simply a matter of the abstract logic of capitalism, but can be studied as the networks which exist among entrepreneurs, merchants, customers; among upstream and downstream flows through business organizations; and as specific circuits of capital which exchange particular currencies in particular kinds of transaction. Mann's conception of power networks, in the case of economic networks, resonates with the new economic sociology promoted through such work as Harrison White (2002), Viviana Zelizer (1994), and others. Networks are inherently processual; they exist as long as and to just the degree that action flows through them. They are emergent, but also ephemeral; they come into existence, expand by adding new links and intensifying the flow through them, but also contract, die down, fade out. In current economic sociology, markets (which economists theorize as following an abstract logic of competition) are seen more realistically as webs of connections through which non-competitive niches are established, regions of profits are constructed and sometimes defended against intruders. Mann's conception of economic power networks thus meshes with another currently flourishing theoretical research enterprise. Economic sociologists are building a distinctive, empirically grounded theory of how economic networks operate; connecting this with Mann's conception promises a way of seeing how the dynamics of economic networks interacts with the other three kinds of power networks: ideological, military and political.

Globalizing the unit of analysis

The concept of power networks leads us to another respect in which Mann's work exemplifies the leading conceptions of contemporary scholarship. There is a strong tendency to dissolve boundaries, to see structures as fluid, contingent, or at least historical constructions. Mann makes this abundantly clear in the case of the state. States in the Weberian sense, monopolizing force over a territory with clearly marked boundaries, came into being gradually between the seventeenth and the nineteenth centuries; earlier states were often a thin layer of military aristocrats, moving from place to place, maintaining alliances through feudal ties or dynastic marriages. Even the more centrally organized states that existed from time to time (the late Roman empire; some Chinese dynasties) had a thin layer of bureaucracy that interfered little with local powers. Boundaries and jurisdictions of states were generally vague. In still earlier periods, proto-states consisted in ceremonial centres which sometimes amassed military as well as ideological power; but prehistoric peoples repeatedly evaded these crystallizing power centres by migrating away, as Mann shows in one of the stellar chapters of the first volume of *The Sources of Social Power*. The construction of states with boundaries, and with identities of people inside them as belonging to a particular state, occurred only because of special historical conditions (which we will come to below).

The example of states as contingent, historical constructions is important for social theory because it underlies a major scholarly misconception up through the mid-twentieth century. The unit of analysis was typically and unreflectively taken to be the 'society', a bounded system with a shared identity, culture, and economic and political institutions. The 'society' was a concept abstracted from the nation-state, the result of successful state-building culminating in the late nineteenth or early twentieth century. Functionalist and cultural anthropologists projected it onto tribal societies, disregarding or minimizing their relationships with other tribes; nationalist historians, even in parts of the world where states were clearly riven with ethnic and other divisions, projected the ideal backwards in picking out a clear channel of national development leading up to the unified society even if it were still a future project.

Mann's conception of power networks provides a way of reconceptualizing the units that social scientists work with. It is not useful to go to the opposite extreme, after the fashion of some poststructuralist thinkers, declaring all structures to be mere labels of equal dubiousness; for in some historical periods units do become more bounded, not only more state-like but more society-like, with sharper cultural identities, more segregated economic institutions, a more intense circuit of local political action. The issue is to be able to see the scope of the social unit as a variable. Mann solves this problem by treating the four kinds of power networks as of varying and overlapping geographical scope. Each network spreads out in space, and has its own intensity of flows and exchanges. But the different networks need not have the same extensiveness, nor the same intensity.

Mann discusses this problem in posing the question of what is the leading or pattern-setting power network at a particular historical epoch. In the first millennium CE, ideological power networks were generally the most extensive and most dynamic, i.e. religious missionaries spread out widely beyond the boundaries of existing military and political agglomerations: Christian missionaries spreading into northern Europe, and Buddhist monks spreading from India into China, and later into Japan, and within those places from royal courts and capital cities into the countryside; Islamic movements spreading, at one period along with military forces, but later in peaceful movements of Sufis and other popular religious organizations. This should not be regarded simply as the spread of belief, since indeed belief in these periods was often shallow, compromising and syncretist; more fatefully, it was the spread of ideological organization, of the structure of monasteries, lay religious orders, patterns of spreading rituals and texts, and the linking of these together into long-distance communities bound by pilgrimages and contributions.

We could multiply such examples. Some parts of the world, such as India, were much more structured by religious networks than by their regional and usually ephemeral state structures. One way of intepreting Weber's theory of religious influences on the growth of capitalist market economy is to see this as the development of religious networks which expanded their material component into a market economy; at the point where the economic character of the exchanges came to outweigh the religious exchanges – an event which I have argued took place several times in world history, in medieval Christan Europe, as well as in Buddhist China and Japan (Collins 1999) – a large-scale economic network cut loose from the ideological network, ushering in a different kind of leading edge of power and a different dynamism of historical change. One of the things we see from this illustration is that some historical power networks are larger and more expansive than others; but also that the leading network provides a way for other networks to piggyback upon it, to follow its geographical expansion, and at some points in time to become autonomous from it, outstripping the earlier power network in scope and dynamism.

What then is a 'society'? Better to say, what is it that sociologists, historians, and other scholars are studying? It is the shifting networks of military, political, economic and cultural action across the world landscape, and their degree of overlap. World-system theorists, like Chase-Dunn and Hall (1997), have been studying these processes in a similar way, looking at what they call (with a neo-Marxian tone) bulk goods networks (economic), prestige goods networks (ideological), political networks and geopolitical networks. There are considerable variations in patterns of relationship among such networks, but some generalizations also are emerging. Among these are the conditions which allow one network to break out of local bounds set by other types of networks – where religious networks can leapfrog the economy; and conversely where one type of network is a facilitator for the expansion of another. In the contemporary world, we see this in the expansion of ideological networks of popular entertainment culture flowing from a few world production centres into mass world distribution; here a cultural network is also a component of the global economy, selling cultural products.

Mann and other scholars have documented that so-called globalization is not a distinctively recent process mainly characteristic of the late twentieth century. Globalization or world-system has always been a central process throughout history, in the sense that local units of social organization are typically structured 'from the outside in' by their relationship with long-distance networks of one kind or another. The problem isn't to explain the global networks so much as to explain the conditions which determine the kinds of local units crystallizing within them. There is no simple trend towards omni-globalization, since the predominance of long-distance processes have at various points in time shifted towards more intense, locally bounded units. Here states have been crucial, and are likely to continue to be so; precisely because modern states crystallized as organizations marshalling an escalating level of military resources, they had to penetrate deeply into local communities, with the result that they mobilized cultural and political networks that reinforced the focus upon the bounded state. Modern states generated a very strong zone of overlap, or coincidence, among cultural and political networks with units of military action; and although economic networks have often overlapped these states as parts of a world economy – indicating that the capitalist economy is less locally bounded than politics – states remain very engrossing centres for social action. Political mobilization is the most immediately practical way of trying to get what one wants; it generates high levels of emotional commitment because it shapes collective antagonisms, whether directed towards domestic rivals or foreign enemies; and these political mobilizations make people identify as cultural communities, thus countering the trends of the world cultural economy. Military links separate as well as connect; a geopolitical network is in an analytical sense causally connected together, but its outcomes often are to keep local state units tightly bounded and in place.

Even in a palpably global economy, and with a great deal of cultural flows across state borders, state units are too important as centres of action for them to fade away. The particular states which exist, of course, can change their forms; the European Union may well become a powerful federation, which given the right geopolitical conditions could conceivably become a strong state superseding the activities and loyalties of the older states which made it up. But these are changes in the distribution of borders among networks, not in the nature of the beast. There remains the potential for all of the different power networks to expand, contract and overlap in various ways, into the foreseeable historical future. But a crystallized state, with its local overlap and mutual reinforcement of several if not all power networks, is too powerful an attractor of social action, too useful as an organizational resource, to be easily superseded. Whatever comes after, if anything does, is bound to have some state-like characteristics.

The rise of the military-centred, tax-extracting, society-penetrating state

The fully fledged ideal type of the force-monopolizing territorial state gradually developed from 1500 in the West, although there have been variations along this continuum elsewhere in world history. Mann is one of the spearheads of a movement of contemporary scholarship (along with Tilly 1990; Parker 1988; and others) focusing on the military revolution which drastically increased the size and expense of armed forces. State organization began to grow in order to extract resources to support current military expenses and past debts, above all by creating a revenue-extraction apparatus. This was the pathway towards bureaucratization and centralization. State penetration into society brought a series of effects in economic, political and cultural spheres. State apparatus now could increasingly regulate the economy, provide infrastructure, compel education and inscribe the population as citizens in government records.

Mann's account of the rise of the modern state is congruent with Weber's theory of the rise of bureaucracy. Considered in Weberian terms and on the level of organization, the rise of modernity is best characterized, not as a move from feudalism to capitalism, but from the patrimonial household to bureaucratic organization. What Weber called patrimonial organization exists where the basic unit of society is the household, and larger structures are built up as networks of links among households. It is important to note that the household mode of organization is not the same thing as the family mode of organization, although they are related. The household typically had at its core a family, the head of household with his wife (or wives) and children, perhaps with some other relatives; and thus property and authority were hereditary. But households could never be very large if the only people they included were family members. Patrimonial households were full of pseudo-familistic relationships; a household of the upper classes would include servants, retainers, guards, guests, hostages and others, all supported from the household economy, and all expected to provide some resource: work, loyalty or military force. An important house contained within it enough armed force to be powerful; it was a fortified household. Links to other households of lesser or greater power constituted the political structure of the society; under certain legal arrangements, these might be called properly 'feudal', but a variety of other structures were possible. The economy too was organized in patrimonial households or their linkages; the labour force consisted of servants and apprentices under familistic protection and discipline rather than independent wage relationships. To refer to a great 'house' was both literal and metaphorical; the aristocracy and the great burghers or merchants were the possessors of the largest household units with the most retainers.

The rise of bureaucracy was the dismantling of the patrimonial household. Workplace was separated from home, private force was superseded by professional military and police units belonging to the state. The physical separation among buildings where production, consumption, politics and administration took place was also the creation of the divide between public and private spheres. Bureaucracy was the creation of offices separate from the persons who held them, the creation of a sphere of interaction apart from family ties and pseudo-familistic relationships of loyalty and subordination. The impersonality of bureaucratic organization depends upon paperwork, codifying activities in written rules and keeping count of performance in files and records. Bureaucracy is thus the source of modern ideologies: the rule of law, fairness, justice, impartiality; the previous practices of loyalty to the patrimonial household, and the consumption of organizational property became condemned as nepotism and corruption. Bureaucracy is the source of individualism since the unit of accounting and responsibility is the individual who can be appointed, promoted, moved from one position to another, paid, reprimanded and dismissed, all with reference only to a personal dossier rather than family and household connections.

Weber's explanation of the transition from patrimonial to bureaucratic organization has usually been interpreted as a series of material preconditions (existence of writing, long-distance transportation, a monetary system, etc.) or as a functionalist argument that bureaucracy arises because it is the most efficient way to coordinate large-scale and complex activities. Mann provides a more dynamic and better-rounded historical picture of the process. The state is a project, an attempt to control and coordinate force in as definite a manner as possible. Bureaucratization was a move in the struggle between whoever was the paramount lord at any particular moment and his allies and rivals among the other great patrimonial households. A crucial condition was the geopolitical configuration. Decentralized chiefdoms and hereditary feudal lineages raised less military resources for their paramount lords and thus tended to be conquered, or were forced to imitate the bureaucratizing manners of the more successful states. Dynastic states proved geopolitically weak because farflung marriage ties produced scattered states, in effect subject to the effects of logistical overextension. History of course is more complicated than a simple winnowing out of non-bureaucratic states by bureaucratic ones; resource advantage is not the only geopolitical principle, and some states favoured by marchland positions might survive with more quasi-patrimonial structures (as Britain did down through the nineteenth century); and bureaucratizing states might nevertheless fail to expand their territorial power because of logistical overextension. Nevertheless, the long-run trend is towards the victory of the bureaucratizers. The successive waves of the military revolution were steps in the development of bureaucracy, first within the military itself (especially logistically intensive branches such as artillery), then in the revenue-extraction service. State penetration was largely bureaucratization at the expense of the patrimonial household. Extensive market capitalism and especially its industrial form prospered under particular versions of state penetration and military mobilization; in this way bureaucracy spread from government into the economic sector; and this in turn fed back into still further government bureaucracy.

The mobilization of modern social conflict

The process of state penetration into society, in Mann's terms, which is also the Weberian shift from patrimonial households to bureaucracy, via the intermediate phase of patrimonial bureaucracy, made possible modern mass politics: ideologically, it fostered the conception of the individual's rights to democratic representation and legal status apart from the jurisdiction of the household head; structurally, it made it possible for workers, women and youth to mobilize in their own places of assembly and their own cultural and political movements. Overt class conflict became possible in the modern era because penetration by the revenue-extracting state created a centralized arena for political action; a complementary reason was that class and other conflicts were mobilized by being freed from the constraints of patrimonial household organization (a point also developed by Tilly 1978; 1995).

State penetration mobilized people's collective identities into social movements operating at a national level: in part because the state itself now constituted a visible target for demands from below; in part because state penetration provided the mobilizing resources of communication, transportation and consciousness-raising. State penetration thus fostered both its own support and its domestic opposition; as Mann has demonstrated, both nationalism and class conflict were mobilized as part of the same process. The modern state became a breeding-ground for social movements; and whenever a social movement has been successful, it has institutionalized its victories by creating new laws which are administered by the bureaucratic state.

Social movements became possible in the modern era in a way that they were not possible before the rise of the modern state. The nearest equivalent to social movements in a society organized around patrimonial households would have been religious movements; sometimes these had political ramifications, but in general they could only be aimed at attacking or reforming existing religious centres, or at setting up new religious centres; or sometimes such religious movements took the form of proselytizing groups spreading religious networks further into the hinterlands. Such religious movements typically connected more patrimonial households into a religious network; or drew out a few individuals to leave their households and become full-time religious specialists, usually by becoming monks living in their own self-contained communal households.

The modern era is a time of social movements, ranging from electoral party politics through single-purpose reform and protest movements, and out into revolutionary, breakaway utopian, and lifestyle movements. We live in an era of social movements because state penetration and the dissolving of the patrimonial household makes individuals available to be mobilized, without having to break away from constraining social structures on the level of everyday life. Unlike premodern monks or religious proselytizers, individuals do not have to radically break away from 'the world' of everyday life in order to participate in social movements; for most people, these are part-time activities that break no social ties and challenge no social authorities that live in close proximity to them. Consider the contrast with premodern households where servants, younger sons, and women, would have had little chance to participate in a conflictual collective activity mobilizing others of their own position, and apart from the full participation of the household and the community in which it was embedded.

Mann shows that all the major political movements were mobilized at the same time and by the same process. Class conflict movements and nationalist movements often got in each other's way, and sometimes fought each other violently, as in the left/right struggles of the early twentieth century; yet both were equally modern movements, reflecting complementary aspects of modern social organization. The rise of the bounded, population-inscribing, society-penetrating state could become an object of group loyalty, at the same time that it mobilized classes into a national arena where they could fight to subdue their class enemies and to seize the state apparatus to carry out their reforms. In the late twentieth century and into the next, these forms of group mobilization have not been superseded, but they have been joined by many more movements: race and ethnicity (construed in various ways), gender, sexual preference, student, environmentalist, animal rights, anti- and pro-religious movements. All these operate under the umbrella of the overarching, society-penetrating state, and thus make an appeal to the same large public consciousness and to state enforcement of their demands.

This is why the late twentieth century has the character of political gridlock; there are too many movements, cutting across each other in too many ways for grand victorious coalitions to emerge; and even the attempts at grand protest coalitions (e.g. the 'rainbow coalition') are artificial constructs with little coherence. If we add into the mix the various kinds of entertainment movements which attract people's loyalties and enthusiasms, it is apparent that contemporary society is both highly mobilized, and in some sense highly conflictual, yet lacking in clear lines of politically organized conflict. A high degree of mobilization along multiple lines produces a situation which is not exactly static – indeed viewed locally in close detail there is always considerable ferment – but in which at the aggregate level conflict groups tend to cancel each other out. In trying to characterize this situation, it is not surprising that many observers have adopted the terminology of 'postmodernism', of a world of infinite perspectives, without grand narratives of historical change. The nihilistic epistemology that sometimes goes along with this rhetoric is oblivious to a rather clear sociological picture on the level of what has brought about this situation. It is not because we live in a postmodern society that there is a high level of group mobilization, resulting in a cacophony of ideological voices and for the most part blocking each other on the level of coherent political action. This high level of mobilization of conflict groups is a direct extension of the main political trend of modernization, the continuing penetration of state into society pulling individuals into framing their conflicts at the level of the largest public arena. That arena has become increasingly crowded.

Big dramatic confrontations, like the showdown of class war that Marxians once envisioned coming up on the horizon, are rare, not because economic class conflict isn't real, but because it is just one of many possible lines of conflict which become mobilized. The story that Mann tells is in a sense a continuation of the story of class conflict; but the later chapters of the story are not the victory of the working class (or even its defeat) that Marx would have comprehended. They are closer to what is implied in Weber's additional chapters, that conflicts go on in several dimensions. Yet Weber still has a rather tidy conception of class, status and party, which can indeed on occasion mutually reinforce each other. The chapters that Mann adds, nearly a century later, tell us that the main trend of modern era, state penetration, mobilizes an increasing variety of conflicts. The class conflict model is on the right track; it is the heading of the story. The later generations of scholars telling the story, Mann prominent among them, multiply the lines of conflict analogous to class.

Extrapolating this trend into the future is a safe bet. But here we come up against the horizon of theoretical questions for the future. How many lines of conflict can possibly be mobilized? Are there not situations – wars, geopolitical strains, economic crises, organizational transformations not yet envisioned – which can simplify or superimpose lines of conflict, making some of them much more fateful than others? In this sense the classic macro-historical question, if not the classic answer, belongs to Marx. Mann represents how far we have travelled on the multi-dimensional path; and this is the pathway of scholarly complexity and theoretical sophistication. But if the formations of power crystallize in particular historical periods, at times so do lines of conflict. On the agenda for future sociology is a theory of the crystallization of major conflicts.

References

Chase-Dunn, C., and T. D. Hall. 1997. *Rise and Demise: Comparing World-Systems*. Boulder, CO: Westview Press.
Collins, R. 1999. An Asian Route to Capitalism. Chapter 7 in *Macro-History: Essays in Sociology of the Long Run*. Stanford, CA: Stanford University Press.
Hall, J. 1986. *International Orders*. Oxford: Polity Press.
Mann, M. 1970. The Social Cohesion of Liberal Democracy. *American Sociological Review*, 35.
Parker, G. 1988. *The Military Revolution: Military Innovation and the Rise of the West*. Cambridge: Cambridge University Press.
Tilly, C. 1978. *From Mobilization to Revolution*. Reading, MA: Addison-Wesley.
   1990. *Coercion, Capital and European States, AD 990–1990*. Oxford: Basil Blackwell.
   1995. *Popular Contention in Great Britain, 1758–1834*. Cambridge: Harvard University Press.
Weber, M. [1917–19] 1952. *Ancient Judaism*. New York: Free Press.
White, H. C. 2002. *Markets from Networks: Socioeconomic Models of Production*. Princeton, NJ: Princeton University Press.
Zelizer, V. 1994. *The Social Meaning of Money*. New York: Basic Books.

3 Political questions

John A. Hall

> No sociological enterprise of this magnitude has ever been undertaken
> that was not animated by some – tacit or implicit – political passion. One
> waits absorbed to see what that will prove to be.
>
> (Anderson 1986: 176)

Great treatises do indeed contain images of good and evil, of limits to our
options given the constraints of social structure. So the central question at
the heart of this chapter is that of Perry Anderson. Mann certainly has
political views, and one contribution of this chapter is to complement
Randall Collins's general picture with specific information about the more
politicized British background from which Mann came. Of course, strongly
held political views can be dangerous for scholarship: hope can replace
analysis – as it did, for example, for Hobhouse and Ginsberg, sociologists
at the London School of Economics long before Mann taught there. Let me
say immediately that I do not think this is so for Mann. Rather he has
followed empirical trails in directions he found unpleasant, and has quite
often changed his mind as the result of substantive work. This gives me my
subject matter. I suggest that there are tensions between his central political
values, discovered early and maintained today, and his substantive discoveries. I seek to push him, in ways that might be uncomfortable, to confront
ambiguities and lacunae. This should not be misunderstood, especially in
light of an occasional personal comment. My affection for the human being
has no limit, and I revere the scholar; further, my own political preferences
are similar, even if I am a little more pessimistic about their realization. More
to the point, I do not mind being wrong, should that prove to be the case, for
that is something from which we can all learn.

I begin with a comparison to Max Weber, and then turn to the British
background. Attention thereafter focuses on popular politics – but on the
nation as much as on class, as well as on the interaction between them.

Max Weber and Michael Mann

Fred Halliday once remarked that Mann wished to be Max Weber. Whilst
sense might be given to the notion that Mann is our Weber, matters are in

fact rather complex. In a nutshell, Mann obviously differs from his German forebear but he is closer to him than one might think. It makes sense to consider three points.

On the first point – that of the rise of the West – little time needs to be spent. Mann did indeed take this half of Weber's *Problematik* more or less for granted, albeit the solution he proposed had a great deal to do with power rather than belief, anyway seen in Durkheimian rather than Weberian terms. Several authors in this volume take up this theme, some supporting, others disputing Mann's position – and many more argue that his notion of ideological power is deficient precisely because it ignores Weber's concern with the content of doctrine.[1] It will be interesting for me to see Mann's replies to issues on which it seems to me that he is – or, if he has changed his mind, was! – very largely correct (Hall 2001).

A second element here is his desire to respect the autonomy of different sources of power. It is here that he is most obviously Weberian, albeit he differs in three ways: in his insistence on the autonomy of military power; in his view of ideology; and in his attempt to replace Weber's view that there is no pattern to the interaction of power sources with a systematic account of why particular sources gain salience at particular points of the historical record.[2] An early generalization exemplifying this last point was that ideological power, in the form of the world religions, changed the pattern of history – but thereafter lost significance, as is demonstrated by the inability of the Reformation to change political boundaries in Europe (Mann 1986: 470). Collins describes Mann's position well, whilst many of the authors in the volume debate particular claims. Two points can usefully be added.[3] First, Mann has changed his mind at key points. Most important of all, perhaps, is the realization in *Fascists* that the twentieth century was an age of great – and transcendent – ideologies. Secondly, one should take care to locate the real suggestiveness of Mann's work. There is some justification to Barrington Moore's charge, at least for those of us wedded to multicausal explanation, that there is sometimes more sense than absolute originality in Mann's explanation of events in terms of his IEMP model.[4] Mann's greatest strength may well lie in his middle-range theories. There is, to begin with, the challenging question at the start of *Sources* as to which society one belongs – the point of course being that social theory has so reified the nation-state that it is incapable of understanding most of the historical record. Equally important are the emphases on 'interstitial emergence' and the 'promiscuity' of power sources, together with the continuing insistence that social movements gain their character from the nature of the state with which they interact. The most striking contribution is that of the notion, ever more amplified, of 'caging'.

There is an obvious sense in which the emphasis on the autonomy of different sources of power is germane to the theme of this chapter. (Less obvious is the fact, to be discussed, that a crucial element of the first purportedly 'Eurocentric' view has relevance for politics too.) Mann is well aware that citizens need to be protected from the powerful as much as from the rich, for at least sometimes these two categories do not overlap. Further, he shows consistent awareness of the need for settled geopolitical frames, for it is the absence of such that occasions zero-sum trade rivalry leading to wars in whose aftermath social revolution can all too easily occur.[5] Finally and more specifically, interesting arguments about gender suggest that women's movements are best advised to take on the state since it is there rather than in social relations as a whole that progress can be made.

Nonetheless, much more central for the purposes of this chapter is a third level, best referred to as the Nietzschean feeling of power so often present in the work of Max Weber. Donald MacRae, in an otherwise wholly irresponsible book about Max Weber, interestingly described the great German thinker as a failed existentialist (1974). Certainly Weber admired those who 'marked' the world, whilst being well aware – at least, for most of the time – of the constraints within which we live. Very much a part of this vision is the insistence that modernity has an opportunity cost, that is that the increase in technical power provided by modern science undermines moral certainty, thereby leaving us in a disenchanted world. This is of course the other side of Weber's *Problematik*, perhaps even more influential on social thought than the better-known thesis about religion and the rise of capitalism.[6]

The obvious initial point that must be made is that Mann's world, descriptively and prescriptively, feels entirely different. He is instinctively democratic, and has, as we shall see, particular understanding and sympathy for the achievements of the British working class. In my opinion, this makes him write better about collective power than about distributive power.[7] Further, he is opposed in formal terms to the view that modern life is bereft of meaning. One element of this is appreciation of the richness and decency of the lives of ordinary people.[8] At least as important is the view, stated in a powerful but little-known early essay, that capitalism *is* based on a particular ideology, that of possessive individualism – albeit that ideology is not endorsed or even fully appreciated by all members of the societies in question (Mann 1975).

In the final analysis these views do *not* take one that far from the disenchantment thesis. The most striking follower of Weber's central vision seems to me to have been Ernest Gellner – who endorsed the disenchantment thesis whilst appreciating the prosaic virtues of affluent liberal democracy.[9] This was essentially because the operating ideology of such societies was so thin: possessive individualism does not warm the heart like wine, nor can much mileage be found in the call for consumers of the world to unite. Hence Gellner in effect preached a good deal of political passivity for liberal democracies. Let the public world be cold and efficient so that warmth can flourish in the private realm! Down with all attempts to run complex modern societies as ideocracies, for every attempt at public re-enchantment of modernity has led to disaster!

Mann should be and to some extent is deeply troubled by the disenchantment thesis. Most obviously, the political transition that Mann desires, that of democratic socialism, will only be possible if an alternative vision of society, that is a general ideology, is both available and widely embraced. Has realization of the horrors perpetrated by the great ideologies of modernity now made him a little nervous about the demand for renewed ideological transcendence? Attention here will focus most, as noted, on the tension between his political hopes and his sociological analysis. But there is a second consideration of at least equal weight. Mann's instinctive democratic sentiments rest upon a sense of fundamental human decency. However, he has recently discovered that there can be a dark side to democracy, that ethnic cleansing, even mass murder, can be popular. Mann has thought through political strategies needed to cope with the national side of the drive to modernity, but one still wants to know whether his moral vision as a whole has been shaken. But before turning to these matters, and to a crucial way in which they merge, let me provide some basic details of the British background from which he derives.

An English social democrat

The 'new critics' of the 1950s made much of the 'pathetic fallacy'. It was held to be a terrible mistake to concentrate on the teller rather than the tale. There is a good deal of truth to this, but sin may be justified on this occasion. Some simple biographical information *does* cast light on his intellectual trajectory. Still, something of a mystery will remain. For the rise of historical and comparative sociology has often been linked to immediate political events. What might be termed Theda Skocpol's generation in the United States became aware of the state because it exhibited its powers, above all in conscription (Hall 1989). British scholars have no such immediate political experience, although most do have national decline clearly at the forefront of their minds. Still, there seems a direct connection between politics and scholarship in the cases of Mann's rivals: Perry Anderson's hatred of his own class surely has something to do with his Irish background, whilst Garry Runciman is one of Britain's 'great and good'. In contrast, Mann's intellectual journey seems to lack any prime mover.

Mann was born in Stretford, one of Manchester's outlying towns, in 1942, and spent his childhood in the same area, first in Sale and then in Rochdale. His father was of lower-middle-class background – an 'organization man' in the words of his son, who began his career as a salesman and ended it as a sales director.[10] His mother – whose household accounts he refers to in his book (1993) – came from a more solidly middle-class background, placing him in a cross-class family; she remained at home caring for all three children.[11] He attended a local primary school, before then going to Manchester Grammar School – at that time a state school with a prodigious record of academic achievement. This non-elite background may help explain Mann's democratic sensibility. But the background was in no way working-class. To the contrary, the father tended to vote Liberal, and the mother perhaps Conservative. The cooperatives that were so important in Rochdale were, moreover, organized by the Liberals rather than by Labour. In consequence, the town had a long tradition of sending Liberals to Westminster. Hence it was not perhaps surprising that Mann himself was a devoted Liberal for at least two years, serving as a volunteer campaign worker for Eric Lubbock – whose success in gaining entry into parliament in 1961 seemed at the time to herald one of many purported Liberal revivals.

Mann gained entry to University College, Oxford where he studied history – a course then requiring attention to the whole run of British history and to political theory. No particular intellectual influences stand out from this period, but a commitment was clearly made to socialism. Perhaps in consequence he began to train as a social worker in Barnett House upon the completion of his degree. But he never completed the formal degree, the CQSW, allowing him to practise as a social worker. For he was approached by Patrick Collinson who suggested that he apply for a grant to study the relocation of a Birds factory from Birmingham to Banbury. Thus the move into academic life – for this Oxford doctoral thesis became his first book, *Workers on the Move* (1973a) – was essentially accidental. It is important to note too that the initial entry into the profession was thoroughly empirical: a British doctorate at that time had no general courses, and so was based entirely on research.

As Mann did his initial doctoral work whilst at Nuffield College, it is not surprising that the views of Alan Fox, the leftist theorist of industrial relations, had some impact upon Mann. But before the doctorate was finished Mann was appointed to the Department of Applied Economics at Cambridge University. The formative figure at the time was John Goldthorpe, although he moved to Nuffield College within a year of

Mann's arrival. Still, Goldthorpe was the chief investigator of a research project on levels of working-class militancy in different European countries. The project failed to attract large-scale funding, and so folded within a very short period, but it did lead Mann to deal with French theories of class, notably those of Touraine and Mallet. These were apparent in his second book, the short but highly stimulating *Consciousness and Action in the Western Working Class* (1973b). But his actual work for the DAE was on a local labour market survey in Peterborough conducted between 1969 and 1972. This became *The Working Class in the Labour Market*, co-authored with Bob Blackburn in 1979. The detailed empiricism of this volume is, again, very noticeable. But by that time Mann had moved to a regular academic position in the Department of Sociology at the University of Essex. This was one of the best departments in the country, headed by David Lockwood and with a series of important young scholars, amongst them Howard Newby and Colin Bell. His teaching responsibility included that of a general course on the Enlightenment, and it was this that gave the empiricist a taste for general ideas. Mann was particularly close to Lockwood, whose intellectual formation had been at the London School of Economics – not least in a study group, together with Ralf Dahrendorf, which sought to replace the consensus theory of Talcott Parsons with an invigorated appreciation of social conflict.[12]

A coherent general picture emerges from Mann's early work. An initial element can be seen in Mann's first, oft-reprinted article on 'The Social Cohesion of Liberal Democracy' (1970). Various data sources are held to demonstrate that there is no consensus within liberal democracy, that is neither a 'dominant ideology' nor any sort of Parsonian shared set of values – let alone any 'end of ideology'. This led Mann to suggest that social cohesion results from some combination of force, fraud and resignation – as well as that produced by the benefits of sharing, unequally, in a growing economy. Very closely related to this is the research on the working class. *Workers on the Move* (1973a) had noted the pragmatic way in which workers calculated their best options when faced with a move, and how they maintained connections with friends and family remaining in the initial location. *The Working Class in the Labour Market* (1979) went further in the same direction, showing rational adaptation to a wasteful world in which internal promotion, demonstrated to be the only real source of mobility, effectively depended upon sucking up to management. But it is a 1976 essay which best captures Mann's general view – and which makes one realize that it is very much based on British material. The British working class is seen as an estate of the realm, too ensconced in society to really dream of changing it.[13] Its great historical achievement is held to have been that of 'working less hard than the workers of any other major industrial power'.

This may not be economic efficiency, but it is undoubtedly civilization. Britain still has a very peaceful, pleasant social climate. For this we can thank the working class. Of all working classes, the British is one of the least violent. This is because it has built the best, the most civilized defences for its community against the exploitation that is capitalism. Eventually those defences may prove inadequate. Its own political party is beginning to use the power of the state against the old compromises, and is asking that further sacrifices be made. It is very doubtful whether, in response, the core of the working class can generate alternative solutions. (1976: 29)

The last sentence of this passage neatly encapsulates the main thesis of *Consciousness and Action in the Western Working Class* (1973b). Capitalism on its own generates mere trade union consciousness on the part of working classes. An alternative socialist vision does occasionally develop, but this was held to be the case only when conflicts are layered or superimposed on top of each other, as Dahrendorf had argued powerfully in his *Class and Class Conflict in Industrial Society* (1959).[14] Mention is made of working-class political consciousness being created when religious conflict is layered on top of class disputes, and hints are given of the impact not just of aggressive employers but of the impact of exclusionary authoritarian regimes. This is the origin of much that Mann will have to say later, but the ideas are as yet hunches more than fully developed theories.

How should all this be taken in political terms? One's first impression is of determined leftist radicalism. Consider this judgement about the impossibility of reforming the labour market:

We do not believe that alienation can be remedied merely by reforms, even compulsory ones, located within the firm. Political reforms would also be necessary, principal among which would be the guarantee of economic security to every citizen whether he was in employment or not. That, of course, means the abolition of wage labour, and of capitalism itself. (Blackburn and Mann 1979: 294)

Mann's reputation in this regard so to speak soared when an investigation by Lord Annan – the greatest of Great Britain's 'great and good' – into student troubles at Essex named Mann as leading troublemaker. Further, at this time he was attracted to French ideas, being in fact the first person to bring Nicos Poulantzas to England. Most importantly, his central claim was really that of Lenin – that workers left to themselves would never gain political consciousness. This was remarkably close to the spirit of *The New Left Review* of the time, scornful of 'pseudo-empiricism' and piecemeal social reform, keen to elevate the thoughts of the masses by means of the introduction of continental theory.

Mann was distinctively not of this company. He found Poulantzas, for instance, to be more interested in Marxism than in the world. This is not to say that Marxism, especially in its *structuraliste* form, was ignored. But the questions that it raised were considered by means of his deep-rooted commitment to empiricism. Above all, awareness of the importance of war, and of its centrality to state finances, stands behind such early essays as 'States, Ancient and Modern' (1977).[15] His mild marginality was increased, I suspect, by his liking of British life, of the decencies, the compromises and meaningfulness, of the lives of ordinary people. The theme of a marvellous essay of this period went so far as to say that anti-capitalism of theorists had more to do with their own ills, placed by modernity in the interstices of the market, than with the condition of workers (Mann 1975). The elitism of Lenin's call for a vanguard party and of *The New Left Review*'s demand for intellectual leadership made no sense to an instinctive democratic socialist.[16] Above all, of course, was the presence of the Labour Party, of a potential mechanism for social change.

Several of Mann's views made him somewhat at odds with the Labour Party. He had little time for the anti-Europeanism prevalent at the time, and his appreciation of basic material goods must surely have made him suspicious of the anti-industrial ethos – wittily named 'Hobbit socialism' by one critic – to which it was often related. As it happens, I think that he does not quite understand the party, given that he has emphasized its secular nature. This is surely not correct, essentially because it is too English a view. There is much to Halevy's view that the British working class had methodism rather than Marx, especially in the Celtic fringes upon which Labour has always depended. Still, what is noticeable is the view that Labour could be reformed – towards genuine democratic socialism. The key text in this context is his 1985 Fabian Society pamphlet *Socialism Can Survive: Social Change and the Labour Party*.[17] This interestingly distinguished three groups of potential Labour voters. The unionized working class provided reliable Labour voters. Those increasingly disadvantaged by life in declining inner cities tended not to vote heavily, but appeals could at least be made to them. In contrast, Labour was in danger of losing non-unionized workers outside large industry. Two striking claims were made in this context. First, Mann insisted that the right had no ideology capable of general appeal. Second, Labour could survive only if it moved beyond the provision of a mere shopping list of policies towards the creation of a genuine ideology, that is of a transcendent vision capable of uniting different groups towards a common purpose.

There is undoubted logic to Mann's position, both in itself and as an extension of some of the central categories of his work. But I interpret his position differently, then and now. Mann considers himself to be a rather optimistic democratic socialist. It seems to me that his central point about Britain – that the working class is unlikely to be able to generate an alternative vision – must suggest pessimism about social change that we both deem progressive. In that sense, Mann forcefully undermines the hopes of the left. And a further critical point must be made immediately. It seems to me wholly wrong to say that the right had no ideology: Thatcherism set the agenda – and not just in Britain! – to a very remarkable extent.

These points will be developed in the rest of this chapter, by turning away from the peculiarities of Britain to the more general substantive findings of his major works. But before doing so, it may be useful to briefly complete the biographical material with which this section began. In 1972 he wrote a paper on 'Economic Determinism and Structural Change' designed 'not only to refute Karl Marx and reorganize Max Weber but also to offer the outlines of a better general theory of social stratification and social change' (1986a: vii). This did not lead to a single volume for Methuen, instead becoming his ongoing *The Sources of Social Power*. But the ambition of the project was impressive enough to get him to the London School of Economics in 1977, as a reader in sociology with particular reference to research methods – albeit his main teaching was in sociological theory.[18] The connection of Lockwood with Dahrendorf (at that time the school's director) perhaps helped him get the job, but the enthusiasm of Ernest Gellner for historical sociology also played a role in the appointment.[19] In 1986 the first volume of *The Sources of Social Power*, purportedly dealing with agrarian society with two further volumes (on industrial society and on theory) to follow, appeared to very great acclaim. But in that year Mann was refused promotion at the London School of Economics, albeit this was offered a year later, and he moved, perhaps partly in consequence, to UCLA – where he has stayed, despite misgivings and consequent soundings to British universities, ever since. Of course, the character of his project has changed, with the second volume that appeared, to a rather more mixed reception in 1993, essentially covering the long nineteenth century. By necessity this means that the historical trajectory of *The Sources of Social Power* must now involve at least three volumes – and possibly four, if the intent remains that of closing the project with a volume on theory. Research for that volume has of course led to the production of important volumes on fascism and on ethnic cleansing, as well as a lecture series at Queen's University Belfast on 'Modernity and Globalization' (2000). In addition, important work has been done on the persistence of national differences within capitalism and on the 'incoherence' of the American empire (Mann and

Riley 2002; Mann 2003). All of these works make use of the IEMP model, but at least two of them have immediate significance for his politics. I suspect that the discovery of a dark side to democracy is – or perhaps ought to be – of particularly great importance to his basic moral preconceptions.

Negative critique: the theory and practice of socialism

The tension in Mann's political views about Britain has already been made clear. But much more is involved than a single, slightly odd case. Classical socialism had joined together a theory with practical means ensuring that it would be realized. What Marx put together, Mann sets asunder. This needs elucidation, with attention given to the fullest and latest statements. Once that has been done, reflections on Mann's position can be offered.

The discovery that matters here concerns the patchiness of support for socialism. A continual theme in all of Mann's work has been that civil society left to itself will manage by itself, with popular movements arising only in response to state demands. When recruiting officers and press gangs take young men away, it breeds reactions, as do demands for taxation. There is no doubt at all but that this general account of social movements is as firmly established a sociological law as any that we possess. But I am interested here in something that goes a little bit beyond this, namely the way in which the degree of radicalism of social movements results from the nature of the political regime with which they interact. Let me rehearse the core of Mann's argument by noting the situation of working classes before 1914.[20]

Russian workers proved themselves to be genuinely revolutionary in 1917, when they seized power, thereby creating the situation of dual control so brilliantly analysed by Trotsky. Of course, Russian workers were not always revolutionary. In the early years of the century trade unionist 'economism' was prevalent, and Lenin did indeed capture its character in 'What Is to be Done?' Variations in intensity of feeling are best ascribed to changes in the policies of the regime. Roughly speaking, people hate being killed on the barricades, and only take on the state when they are absolutely forced to do so. Differently put, moments of liberalization are likely to decompress, to allow activists to seek reform rather than revolution. When the autocracy of the Romanovs shot strikers, it bred revolutionaries; when reforms were promised, more moderate, economistic politics gained ground.[21] The same sociological mechanism is at work in a rather different regime type, the authoritarian capitalism of Wilhelmine Germany. A short period of anti-socialist laws led to the

creation of a worker's movement with a political wing as well as an industrial wing. Max Weber argued that this was a regime blunder, that workers
would have had no political consciousness other than national loyalty had a
more generous policy been pursued (Weber 1978). A word of caution is
due at this point. The early presence of citizenship in the United States and
the relative ease with which workers were incorporated in Great Britain
does go a long way to explaining the absence of socialist political consciousness in those countries. (Britain developed a Labour Party, of course, in
large part because of a moment of near exclusion – when the *Taff Vale* case
suggested a legal attack on trade union rights.) But Mann's complete
theory about the social cohesion gained by liberal capitalist regimes entails
quite as much a rather different consideration. Both Britain and the United
States in fact experienced moments of genuine worker radicalism. If political opening did much to defuse the situation, vicious repression imposed
in each case by a united dominant class played a considerable role in
destroying challenges from below. Mann's analysis here is brilliant, powerfully undermining naïve liberal self-congratulation.

This substantive sociology is surely disturbing for a democratic socialist. The key source of left popular movements has been that of citizenship
struggles – rather than of any logic of response to capitalism *per se*. This
suggests that liberal machiavellianism, that is giving rights whilst removing the state from responsibility for social and economic affairs, might
well allow for political stability without economic justice. This position
was well argued by Alan Gelb and Keith Bradley (1980) when discussing
the early years of Mrs Thatcher's political economy. 'Beer and
Sandwiches' in Downing Street during periods of Labour government
had led to militancy, precisely because this was seen as a sign of state
responsibility for employment, welfare and the state of the economy. In
contrast, leaving everything to the market – albeit, taking care to provide
schemes to distract the young – disoriented and debilitated quite generally, with the consequence that the opposition to high levels of unemployment was very muted.[22] Perhaps this example misleads, in that it suggests
some large move from one political economy to another. In fact, institutional foundations for tripartite social contractual bargaining were never
very strong in the Anglo-Saxon world, making the move to unfettered
neoliberalism relatively easy. The fact of path dependency, of our being
trapped – bar the disruptions of major defeat and subsequent collapse in
war – by our past, stands right at the front of much of Mann's most recent
work.[23] This has enormous implications for his political views, as is made
clear in his most recent defence of socialism.

'After Which Socialism?' is a response to the claim, made particularly
clearly by Dan Chirot, that the socialist project had failed once and for all

(Mann 1992a). For Mann the death of state socialism has nothing to do with the essence of socialism. For a regime that was totalitarian and bureaucratic fundamentally betrayed democracy – which does stand at the heart of socialist beliefs. In this context, Mann makes two claims. First, a good deal of the move towards democratic accountability has resulted from the actions of working classes.[24] Second, he sees no reason to believe that societies that have achieved elements of social democracy are necessarily bound to lose out in the face of intensified international economic pressures. A distinction is drawn at this point between different elements – nationalization, economic planning, redistribution and social welfare – that comprise social democracy so that finer distinctions can be drawn. Mann recognizes that nationalization has lost its appeal, and he further allows that some types of economic planning are under threat – albeit he insists (without much evidence) that greater European unity might allow a concerted stand against international capitalist pressure. Mann often stresses the need of any particular model to change its emphases, but – with that proviso – he argues that the other elements of social democracy remain in place. Hints are given, however, of a recognition that socialism has a poor record in the underdeveloped world – although this admission is allied to an insistence that liberal doctrine has been no more efficacious.

It is as well to highlight immediately change in Mann's position. Bluntly, a good deal of radicalism has gone. Realism and moderation reign in a discussion that concerns less the replacement of capitalism than softening of life within it – for that is, surely, what social democracy means in comparison to democratic socialism. Further, Mann's very recent work demonstrates that many of the checks against the market are present not just in Nordic social democracy but quite as much in European conservative corporatist regimes – that is, in the social formation established after World War II by Christian Democrats. Beyond this basic consideration, three further points need to be considered.

The first must trouble everyone on the left. The softening of capitalism in Europe has not been the result of any inevitable process of social evolution. Very particular circumstances created the farmer–worker alliances of Northern Europe (Esping-Andersen 1985). Further, social progress resulted as much from promises given to peoples involved in conscription war as it did from popular movements from below. Finally, Christian Democracy gained its power on the back of the military destruction of radical right political movements. It was less endogenous than imposed. Social democracy too was given a boost by American determination to act against communist movements in Europe after World War II. All of this leads to a general analytic point. To Mann's hesitancy about the radical potential of working classes must now be added awareness that much progressive social change has been conjunctural. Lucky accidents have mattered more than any long-term beneficial trend. Luck is not generally available – thank goodness, one must add, given that a part of the luck in question was that of major war. In a nutshell, one can praise social democracy and think its heartland secure, but it is hard to be optimistic as to its spread.

Secondly, Mann's comments about state socialism are worrying. One certainly misses any sustained analysis of what was by any standards a world historical change. More to the point, such an analysis would likely raise interesting points about Mann's own position. For one thing, his celebrated schema of state autonomy never really compared levels of state strength (Mann 1984b).[25] This is a complex matter. Still, there is much to be said for the view that constitutional states have greater strength than despotic states in the industrial era, that is when both possess key infrastructural means. For what is astonishing about much – but certainly not all – of the history of actually existing socialism is that the leviathans involved were desperately puny. Even in the industrial era, voluntary cooperation of citizens with their state – that is a state that they trust because they have a measure of control over its actions – matters enormously. Differently put, legitimacy enhances the infrastructural reach of the state. For another, the ease with which state socialism is considered as something utterly distinct from the core of socialism is disturbing. It is certainly true that Bolshevism had its peculiarities. It was militarism incarnate and a model for development. Still more importantly, more than half of the first Bolshevik cadre was non-Russian, with a significant section of this group having Jewish backgrounds – whose experiences with the nationalisms of the Russian periphery had turned them into (radical) empire savers.[26] Nonetheless, the heroic appeal of these socialists, the belief that a new moral world was being created, surely has something to do with socialism. Did not very many socialists in the West believe this to be so?

Finally, reference should be made to an important essay in which Mann analyses variations of working-class consciousness after World War I (1995). A principal argument of this essay is that the right fought back against socialism and communism with very great effectiveness. By and large Germany's social democrats were unable – at once too respectable and convinced that agrarian life was both backward and bound to end – to recruit in the countryside. There was no peasant–worker alliance in this case but rather genuine ideological innovation on the right – at its least in technocracy and rationalization, at its most powerful in fascist ideology. The central point of Mann's work on fascism is that it had genuine moral appeal. Whilst the horrors of that ideology have been revealed, much caution should surely be shown – as already suggested – to the notion that the right lacks capacity for ideological innovation and moral appeal.

The general argument of this section is simply that the substantive evidence provided by Mann must make our hopes for social democracy, and especially for its spread, both muted and limited. It may well be worth fighting for and the fight may not be in vain; but it will scarcely be easy. Two final considerations can round out the argument. First, I have not in fact presented all of the substantive considerations raised by Mann that curtail hope. For instance, he makes much throughout his work of the capacity of upper classes to outflank those beneath them. This has scarcely diminished in contemporary circumstances, thereby at the least adding difficulties to working-class movements that are so much more nationally caged. Second, serious thought about the well-being of the vast majority of mankind makes one realize just how difficult progressive politics can be. If all human beings count, that is if we consider the welfare of the members of poorer societies than our own, then it behoves us to introduce as much free trade as possible. How can the Caribbean prosper if the European Union insists on consuming its own expensive sugar beet rather than accepting the sugar cane which is the region's only element of comparative advantage? Advocating such openness means condemning some of my fellow citizens to the vagaries of change and probably to the necessity for harder and certainly newer work. I do so, but less than gladly.

Positive critique: nationalism and liberalism

The best way of highlighting Mann's achievements, descriptive and prescriptive, in the field of nationalism is by means of a comparison with the very familiar view of Ernest Gellner. A fine essay by Mann (1992b) critically assailed what many think the central link in Gellner's theory, namely the notion that the coming of the industrial era bred nationalist politics. The core of Mann's argument was that nationalism in France and England pre-dated the industrial era, emerging in the eighteenth century largely because of the intensification of geopolitical competition. As it happens, Gellner was not worried by this attack: it mattered little in his view if the cultural homogenization he felt was required by modernity was created by states in a few specialized cases (Gellner 1996: 536). One might go further and add to Gellner's defence an insistence that the combination of social inequality and ethnic marker did often matter in the history of nationalism. But my general sympathies in this whole matter go with Mann. Nationalist mobilization pre-dates industrialism in varied places essentially because nationalism is above all the result of exclusionary politics of states.

But I do not think that Gellner's most important insight has to do with the needs of the industrial era. What is absolutely central to Gellner's view is that nationalism is about homogenization: roughly speaking, get your own state or try to assimilate – and pray that you find yourself in a country in which the dominant group will let you in. This viewpoint has been subjected to much criticism. One line of argument suggests that the politics and practices of forcible homogenization have been so destructive that it makes nonsense of his view that cultural unity was a precondition for economic success (Laitin 1992: 159–63). There is some truth to this – which is not to deny that a pre-existent homogeneity may encourage economic success. Another line of argument intermingles prescription with description. Is homogenization in fact inevitable? Is it not possible for us to do better? Can arrangements not be made allowing multiculturalism, even multinationalism, to flourish? Will not inclusion and recognition of minorities allow for varied combinations of cultural diversity within shared political frames? Differently put, is there not reason to believe that just as nationalism (understood as secession) is caused by the desire to exit consequent on the lack of voice, so too might the loyalty of cultural minorities be secured by political liberalism? No scholar has made these points more cogently than David Laitin, whose work is represented in this volume. It is worth recording his comment that Gellner – whose work he admires despite the bite of his attack upon it – was describing his own life and calling it sociology (Laitin, 1998).[27]

My claim is that Mann stands exactly between these two poles, and that he is right to do so. He certainly has none of the absolutism and pessimism so characteristic of Gellner's account, as can be seen if we consider the two sides of his portrait in turn.[28] On the one hand, he stands close to Gellner's critics, albeit in novel ways. Full-blooded nationalism was not inevitable: several thresholds had to be crossed before murderous ethnic cleansing occurred. Crucial to this account is a concern with geopolitical insecurity. One way in which this corrects Gellner is in its view of Czechoslovak history: the multinational entity in which Gellner grew up was destroyed by geopolitics rather than the logic of industrialism. More generally, however, Mann is suggesting that the heights of nationalism are linked to the intensity of geopolitical competition. This allows for an initial prescription, namely that geopolitical security may allow for more liberal arrangements – and so for the maintenance or creation of multinational states. Mann of course favours the introduction of liberal arrangements of all sorts, typically varied combinations of federalism and consociationalism, and he thinks that they have had some success. Finally, he notes that many new states, notably in Africa, have such varied ethnic composition as to make it unlikely that any one ethnic group will dare to play the ethnic card: differently put, the history of Europe may not be repeated elsewhere.

But there is a pessimistic side to counter this initial optimism. Laitin's jibe at Gellner's expense might well not appeal to Mann – for did not Gellner's life exemplify the twentieth century of Europe, whose importance in world history can scarcely be in doubt? Further, Mann is well aware that liberal policies do not always work, as has often been the case with federalism in East Africa. In this context, it behoves us to realize that liberalism in much of Europe came after vicious ethnic cleansing – that is after deep divides in society had been 'removed'. Most importantly, Mann is at one with Gellner in stressing that forcible homogenization is – at the least – a temptation of modernity. For Mann of course the pressure for homogenization does not come from the needs of industrialism, but from nothing less than democracy itself. It seems to me to be intellectually brave to stress that murder can be popular, and it leads me to suggest that Mann stands close to Gellner in two final ways. First, *The Dark Side of Democracy* shares a measure of Eurocentrism with Gellner. Northwestern European development, in which class came before nation, is judged as a lucky precondition for liberalism – the argument being that skills of conflict regulation developed in the area of class were then used so as to domesticate nationalism. Secondly, Mann does not subscribe to the view, so present in the foreign policy of the contemporary United States, that multinational arrangements, being purportedly ever possible, should thereby always be encouraged. I suspect that he would agree that, given demography and recent history, recognition should be given to an independent and rather homogeneous Kosovo.

Let me finish this section as I did the last by underscoring that the national question poses great difficulties for political judgement. To say that one ought to encourage liberal arrangements *ab initio* but drop them once politicized national self-consciousness has been created is difficult enough. Still more problematic is the near contradiction between the demands of intervention and liberalism. Intervention tends to work best if it is early, forcible and decisive. But the liberal arrangements that do much to make foreign policy making less adventurist depend upon delay – crucially upon subjecting policy to sustained evaluation by committees and cabinets. This is a very difficult circle to square at all times; it is at present well beyond our institutional capabilities.

Decency and sympathy, Europe and America

The general issues raised can be taken a little further by briefly commenting on an interaction between class and nation that has relevance when judging

Mann's admiration for social democracy and his increasing frustration towards the United States. I suspect that there is a little simplification and exaggeration in Mann's view. To advance the argument, four points on an imaginary circle need to be distinguished (Hall 2002). The dangers of ethnic nationalism, standing so to speak at the north of this circle, are well known, as are the attractions of civic nationalism standing at the east. But civic nationalism can be repulsive, as Mann has stressed: 'join us', perhaps – but quite as much 'join us or else'. Further, most civic nationalism is based on an ethnic core, whose culture has firm rules that those wishing to get in must accept. A wholly more desirable position, that of civil nationalism, is that at the south of the circle. This is the world in which multiculturalism and/or multinationalism is allowed and in which national identities can be redefined and loosened – in which, most important of all, genuine entry into the society can be seen in key indices such as that of high rates of intermarriage between different ethnic groups. The character of civil nationalism can be seen in the fact that ethnicity is a choice rather than a cage. The fear of many commentators – a fear it should be stressed rather than an omnipresent reality – is that multicultural policy could stand to the west of the circle in question, so caging ethnicities as to encourage vicious competition. Such competition could fuel demands for ethnic nationalism.

We have some understanding of Scandinavian social democracy, both as a general model and in terms of important differences within that model, and are particularly well informed, as noted, about the role played by cross-class alliances between peasants and workers (Esping-Andersen 1985). But a key characteristic of the regime type is that of very high levels of social homogeneity – in terms of nation, class and religion. There is decided truth to the notion, very well explained by Peter Baldwin (1990), that high levels of welfare spending rest upon the willingness to give generously to people exactly like oneself. It may be philosophically regrettable that there are limits to sympathy, to respect for 'the universal stranger' – Hume and Smith did not think so, but I do – but it is something that has to be taken seriously when considering social democracy. Note that contemporary Denmark, a country dear to my heart, has established harsh regimes restricting both entry into the country and the attainment of citizenship and welfare rights for immigrants. This is not, one has to say, the end of the Danish system but rather its very logic: this is national socialism. I suspect that rates of intermarriage between Danes and immigrants are low. Certainly, the country is so homogeneous that it is hard for newcomers to gain acceptance. Consider the United States in contrast. Mann has made us aware that the country was founded in hideous acts of ethnic cleansing, and it is all too obvious that the tenor of American civic nationalism has the permanent potential of becoming illiberal. Still, American identity has in quite a few regards been less fixed than that of most European states, and a great achievement of the society as a whole is that of very high rates of marriage between members of different ethnic groups. This does not apply at all, of course, to the position of African Americans within the United States: racial discrimination remains the hideous horror that it has always been.[29] Nonetheless, some of the admiration shown towards social democracy ignores its limited social preconditions. Many who admire its achievements would be uncomfortable living within its confines.

A final comment is in order about the external policy of the United States. One of Mann's continuing, most forcefully argued points is, as has been seen, that of the varied impact of geopolitics. Since 1945 a great deal of international stability has been provided by the United States. There is very strong evidence that this has been of enormous benefit to the advanced world, but of more questionable value to the rest of humanity – whilst there can be no doubt that the engagement of the United States has been very much in its own, at times predatory, self-interest. By what standards should one judge the American empire? Whilst it is not hard to imagine better policies, the partial stability provided – together with the fact that its non-territorial character means that American imperialism has killed far fewer than did the imperialism of Great Britain – ought to place some limit on condemnation. A part of the reason for that relatively benign history is that of incoherence, lack of interest in the world – for who is to say that coherence would be of the right kind? Indeed, we have had the most radical sort of coherence imaginable in the last years, as Mann (2003) himself stresses in contradiction to the title of his book, and it is such – for I agree with Mann's arguments – as to threaten the stability of world politics. Beyond that, however, I suspect that there is a difference between us. I have long wanted a European presence to balance the power of the United States (Hall 1986: Conclusions), so as to create better policy. But that is very unlikely: Europeans prefer to be supine yet whining, and certainly are not prepared to pay the vast amounts needed to gain geopolitical autonomy. Further, I doubt that the euro will replace the dollar as a currency in which world commodities can be traded, thereby believing that the United States will retain considerable benefits from seigniorage. There is plenty to criticize, but perhaps one's hopes have to be for a restoration of moderation in Washington given that it is very hard to envisage any alternative.

Conclusion

Max Weber made us well aware of some of the difficulties that face academics when they deal with the political. For one thing there is the question of time, the fact that politicians have to act – without the benefit of a seminar beforehand. For another, politics involves coercion. Aron made much of the fact, as he had it, that politics is not moral, not least when trying to distinguish himself from his generation; it led him to a strict consequentialist position in which condemnation was only held to be acceptable when a workable alternative could be specified.[30] In general, when one sees the mess that intellectuals have often made of politics, one is tempted to say leave well alone – do not, so to speak, rush in where angels fear to tread. For that very reason I am somewhat nervous about raising the subjects of this chapter at all. I am entirely happy to see Mann producing substantive sociological results. If his work does amount to analytic history, then I want more of it. And one thing can be stated firmly: our primary loyalty must be to the truth. There is no question but that Mann seeks the truth. The intellectual bravery of his account of fascism – at the heart of which is the reconstruction a genuine moral appeal – is wholly meritorious.

Still I have made three arguments for him to consider. First, his substantive findings seem to me – and despite his own protestations – to undermine rather than to support his political hopes for socialism. In contrast, secondly, there is much greater fit between his hopes and his analysis when dealing with nationalism – whose varied characters he has, in my view, done much to successfully explain. Thirdly, there seems to be a touch of (accurate, desirable) Eurocentrism in his work. What I have in mind here is less debates to do with the rise of the West, than the fact that the sequencing and speed of social changes matter a great deal. Northwestern Europe has a social portfolio that privileges liberalism because class did, as he stresses, come before nation, and over a very long period at that. In general, I am a little more pessimistic than Mann. But this is not to say that there are no political developments that can raise one's spirits. Three cheers can surely be raised for the enlargement of the European Union, and for the vast improvement in European politics more generally. Something less than that level of enthusiasm must be given to the extension of the market principle. This is not so much because the principle is wrong, as because geopolitical logic – seen most clearly in the appalling agricultural protectionism of the United States and the European Union – looks set to make its application so very biased.

Notes

1 I coined the term 'organizational materialism' with Mann's work in mind in *Powers and Liberties* (1985: 21), and have been amused to see that this has been much used – not least by Mann himself. Guenther Roth told me in 1986 that the *Politbureau* of Weberian scholars had discussed Mann's work when it first

appeared, and had decided that it was not fully Weberian precisely because of its negative view of Weber's account of ideology.

2 On the last point, see Mann (1986a: 523–4) and Chapter 16 *passim*. It may be of interest to record Mann's own assessment of his relation to Marx and Weber. When responding in an interview to a question posed by Wayne Hudson – in an in-house journal, *c.* 1988, the reference for which cannot now be found – asserting that he had returned to Weber he replied:

> It is Marx's questions that I really go back to. I think Marx helps us most when he is clearest, and therefore most materialist. I don't like the fashionable Marxism, which sophisticates Marxism, while removing his materialist emphasis. Weber's weakness was his persistent tendency towards idealism. You could say that I rework Weber's project from a more materialist but not a reductionist standpoint, and that I owe the cutting edge of that standpoint to Marx.

3 A third point could be added. Mann has taken considerable attention to get his history right – so much so that each volume he produces covers a smaller historical range albeit with massive detail. One notes that the first volume of *Sources* received enormous attention, whereas the second volume elicited few reviews of significance. Is the price of fastidious empiricism that of being ignored? Must books offer simplistic views – rather than complexity, difficulty, even ambivalence – in order to gain success? Or, is it the case that Mann has been so overwhelmed by historical material that he has in fact ceased to be a sociological theorist, becoming an analytic historian instead? Of course, this is as much a question about the status of historical sociology as it is about the work of Mann himself.

4 Moore (1988).

5 Another place where an appreciation of the logic of geopolitics is apparent is in 'Nationalism and Internationalism in Economic and Defence Policies' (1984a). This politically engaged essay in fact stood some way apart from much of the left in Britain at the time because it took for granted that defence against the Soviet Bloc was necessary, albeit not by the means envisaged by the military establishments of the time.

6 Weber is of course the ghost haunting the minds of members of the Frankfurt School; his fears are quite as much at the back of the mind of communitarian thinkers such as Charles Taylor.

7 I differ here from Stewart (2001) who argues that Mann fails to understand the collective face of power. Joseph Bryant makes the same point in this volume, when considering Mann's treatment of the early Christianity.

8 In this context, it is worth noting that he has little time for the full-blown secularization thesis that derives from Weber, according to which the era of religious belief is quite simply over and done with.

9 This point was made, with characteristic brilliance, by Anderson (1992). One should note, however, that Gellner did more or less accept the secularization thesis.

10 The basic facts of this section were provided by Michael Mann in an interview in June 2001.

11 Some of the dynamics of such families are analysed in McRae (1986).

12 Mann's *Sources of Variation in Working Class Movements in Twentieth Century Europe* was written to honour Lockwood on the occasion of his retirement. Mann acknowledged a debt (1995: 15) not just to Lockwood's appreciation of differences in working-class behaviour (which he sought to explain, however, in a rather different way) but 'even more to his constant example and injunction to pursue a form of sociology that is simultaneously theoretical, empirical, comparative, historically and socio-politically relevant'.

13 Cf. McKibbin (1990).

14 It should be noted that Mann makes no specific mention of Dahrendorf's work – but the idea seems to me to have been his.

15 Awareness of the importance of war allowed Mann to distinguish himself from the historical sociology of Perry Anderson: he noted the way in which military explanations – especially when explaining the trajectory of East Central Europe – were introduced in an *ad hoc* manner. This general viewpoint was absorbed by a group of graduate students – including Roland Axtmann and John Hobson – at the London School of Economics in the late 1970s and early 1980s.

16 My own experience in a local branch of the Labour Party in the late 1970s and the early 1980s suggests that he had a point. The introduction of discussions of Foucault led the working-class members, almost immediately, to protest – by voting with their feet.

17 Also important is 'Nationalism and Internationalism in Economic and Defence Policy' (1984a). This argued for an alliance of democratic socialist states in the face of international capitalist pressures. A notable feature of that essay, developed at greater length in later work, was the realization that the advanced core of capitalist society did not depend upon the exploitation of the developing world – that, to put it differently, imperialism was unnecessary, for all that it was all too present. He urged at the time that 'class be taken out of geopolitics'.

18 His concern with methodology led to the interesting 'Socio-logic' (1981).

19 For several years Mann ran, with Gellner and the author, a seminar on 'Patterns of History' in which very distinguished lecturers were quizzed for references for the books on which the organizers were at work.

20 The discussion that follows draws on Mann (1993), chs. 15, 17 and 18.

21 This is made particularly clear in McDaniel (1988). This is one of the sources on which Mann relies.

22 The most striking account of the stability of capitalist society, when freed from government, is that of my former colleague Michael Smith in his classic *Power, Norms and Inflation* (1992). I compared Mann and Smith in 'A Curious Stability' in my *Coercion and Consent* (1994).

23 The fullest statement is Mann and Riley (2002).

24 Mann cites and endorses the argument of Rueschemeyer, Stephens and Stephens (1992).

25 Mann's 'The Autonomous Power of the State: Its Nature, Causes and Consequences' (1984b) is the most cited of all his essays.

26 I rely here on the data of Riga (1999).

27 Several chapters in this volume make the critical points noted.

28 I draw here of course on Mann (2005).
29 The points alluded to here receive fuller treatment in Hall and Lindholm (1999).
30 This logic lay behind my criticism of Mann's view of America. There is much to condemn, but how heavy should the condemnation be given that an alternative is not readily available?

References

Anderson, P. 1986. Those in Authority. *Times Literary Supplement*, 12 December.
  1992. Science, Politics, Enchantment. In J. A. Hall and I. C. Jarvie (eds.), *Transition to Modernity: Essays on Power, Wealth and Belief*. Cambridge: Cambridge University Press.
Baldwin, P. 1990. *The Politics of Social Solidarity: Class Bases of the European Welfare State*. Cambridge: Cambridge University Press.
Blackburn, R. M., and M. Mann. 1979. *The Working Class in the Labour Market*. London: Macmillan.
Dahrendorf, R. 1959. *Class and Class Conflict in Industrial Society*. Stanford: Stanford University Press.
Esping-Andersen, G. 1985. *Politics against Markets: The Social Democratic Road to Power*. Princeton, NJ: Princeton University Press.
Gelb, A., and K. Bradley 1980. The Radical Potential of Cash Nexus Breaks. *British Journal of Sociology*, 31(2).
Gellner, E. A. 1996. Reply to Critics. In J. A. Hall and I. C. Jarvie (eds.), *The Social Philosophy of Ernest Gellner*. Amsterdam: Rodopi.
Hall, J. A. 1985. *Powers and Liberties*. Oxford: Basil Blackwell.
  1986. *International Orders*. Oxford: Polity Press.
  1989. 'They Do Things Differently There' or, the Contribution of British Historical Sociology. *British Journal of Sociology*, 40(4).
  1994. *Coercion and Consent*. Cambridge: Polity Press.
  2001. Confessions of a Eurocentric, *International Sociology*, 16(3).
  2002. Disagreement about Difference. In S. Malešević and M. Haugaard (eds.), *Making Sense of Collectivity*. London: Pluto.
Hall, J. A. and C. Lindholm. 1999. *Is America Breaking Apart?* Princeton: Princeton University Press.
Laitin, D. D. 1992. *Language Repertoires and State Construction in Africa*. Cambridge: Cambridge University Press.
  1998. Nationalism and Language: A Post-Soviet Perspective. In J. A. Hall (ed.), *The State of the Nation: Ernest Gellner and the Theory of Nationalism*. Cambridge: Cambridge University Press.
McDaniel, T. 1988. *Autocracy, Capitalism and Revolution in Russia*. Berkeley: University of California Press.
McKibbin, R. 1990. *Ideologies of Class*. Oxford: Oxford University Press.
MacRae, D. G. 1974. *Weber*. London: Fontana.
McRae, S. 1986. *Cross-Class Families: A Study of Wives' Occupational Superiority*. Oxford: Clarendon Press.

Mann, M. 1970. The Social Cohesion of Liberal Democracy. *American Sociological Review*, 35(3).
1973a. *Workers on the Move*. Cambridge: Cambridge University Press.
1973b. *Consciousness and Action in the Western Working Class*. London: Macmillan.
1975. The Ideology of Intellectuals and Other People in the Development of Capitalism. In L. N. Lindberg, R. Alford, C. Crouch and C. Offe (eds.), *Stress and Contradiction in Modern Capitalism*. Lexington: D. C. Heath.
1976. The Working Class. *New Society*, 4 November.
1977. States, Ancient and Modern. *European Journal of Sociology*, 18.
1981. Socio-logic. *Sociology*, 15.
1984a. Nationalism and Internationalism in Economic Defence Policies. In J. A. G. Griffith (ed.), *Socialism in a Cold Climate*. London: Allen and Unwin.
1984b. The Autonomous Power of the State: Its Nature, Causes and Consequences. *European Journal of Sociology*, 25.
1986. *The Sources of Social Power, Volume I: A History from the Beginning to 1760 AD*. Cambridge: Cambridge University Press.
1992a. After Which Socialism? A Response to Chirot's 'After Socialism, What?'. *Contention*, 1.
1992b. The Emergence of Modern European Nationalism. In J. A. Hall and I. C. Jarvie (eds.), *Transition to Modernity: Essays on Power, Wealth and Belief*. Cambridge: Cambridge University Press.
1993. *The Sources of Social Power, Volume II: The Rise of Classes and Nation-States*. Cambridge: Cambridge University Press.
1995. Sources of Variation in Working Class Movements in Twentieth Century Europe. *New Left Review*, No. 212, 25.
2000. 'Modernity and Globalization'. Unpublished, given as the Wiles Lectures at Queen's University, Belfast.
2003. *Incoherent Empire*. London: Verso.
2005. *The Dark Side of Democracy: Explaining Ethnic Cleansing*. Cambridge: Cambridge University Press.
Mann, M., and D. Riley. 2002. Globalization and Inequality: The Enduring Impact of Macro-Regional Ideologies and Nation-States. Unpublished paper.
Moore, B. 1988. Review Essay. *History and Theory* 2.
Riga, L. 1999. Identity and Empire: The Making of the Bolshevik Elite, 1880–1917. Unpublished Ph.D Dissertation, McGill University.
Rueschemeyer, D., E. H. Stephens and J. D. Stephens. 1992. *Capitalist Development and Democracy*. Chicago: University of Chicago Press.
Smith, M. 1992. *Power, Norms and Inflation*. New York: Aldine de Gruyter.
Stewart, A. 2001. *Theories of Power and Domination*. London: Sage.
Weber, M. 1978. Parliament and Government in a Reconstructed Germany. In Weber, *Economy and Society*. Berkeley: University of California Press.

4   Mann's microfoundations: addressing neo-Weberian dilemmas[1]

Edgar Kiser

Most historical sociologists study macro-level outcomes, explain them using macro-level causes, and test their arguments using macro-level data. Although all of these scholars realize that individual action brought about these outcomes, and few believe that these individuals are either just bearers of social structure or cultural dopes, explicit discussions of individual motivation and action are rare in historical sociology.

One obvious reason for the lack of focus on micro-level causal mechanisms is that it is especially difficult in historical sociology. When actors are more distant from us in time and space, it is harder both to theorize (make assumptions) about their motives and to get any empirical data about them. The classical sociologist who most explicitly addressed the difficult issue of the motives of historical actors was Max Weber, and contemporary neo-Weberians (along with a handful of rational choice theorists) have been most likely to follow his lead. This chapter explores the microfoundations used by one of the most prominent and accomplished neo-Weberian historical sociologists, Michael Mann.

Weberian historical sociologists who address the problem of microfoundations face two dilemmas. First, how can they use multiple micro-level causal mechanisms (Weber's four types of social action or something similar) without making their arguments tautological? The problem here is the same as that of tautology in rational choice models that do not specify preferences *a priori* – with many different microfoundations allowed, any action can be 'explained' after the fact. This problem can be resolved by either denying the importance of theory testing, or by specifying the conditions under which different microfoundations will be important.

The second dilemma is whether to specify micro-level causal mechanisms theoretically (*a priori* assumptions) or empirically (*verstehen* using rich, usually primary, data sources). The theoretical strategy works best when general, shared motivations are important and large groups of people are involved, while its greatest cost is oversimplification. The empirical strategy works best when rich data are available (more likely for elites and contemporary societies) and the motivations to be explained are particular (specific elites or culturally different societies).

This chapter will outline and assess various solutions to these two dilemmas in Weberian historical sociology. After quickly reviewing microfoundations in Weber's work, and different approaches taken by contemporary Weberians, I focus on Mann's Weberian microfoundations. Mann is explicit and detailed in specifying microfoundations, and makes important progress towards specifying the conditions in which different motivations will be operative. However, the complexity of his microfoundations does sometimes produce *ad hoc* arguments. His use of *verstehen* to specify microfoundations has increased significantly in his more recent work, and it has been coupled with an increasing focus on non-instrumental motivations.

The Weberian heritage: multiple microfoundations from both theoretical and empirical sources

The foundation of Weber's approach to causal analysis is methodological individualism. By this he means that all complete explanations must include an analysis of individual motives and actions (the same argument has been made recently from a rational choice perspective by Hechter (1983) and Coleman (1990)).[2] Weber ([1922] 1978: 11) defines motives as 'a complex of subjective meaning which seems to the actor himself or to the observer as an adequate ground for the conduct in question'.

Weber's four types of social action are different orientations to action. Weber's *instrumental* action is consequentialist. People are motivated instrumentally whenever they choose a course of action which they believe is the most effective means of attaining their goals in a given situation. His other three orientations to action are non-consequentialist. Action may be determined by a conscious belief that it must be done because of duty, right, or merely for its own sake, regardless of its consequences – Weber's *value-oriented* action. *Emotional* action, determined by the actor's specific affects, is likewise non-consequentialist. Finally, action can be purely *habitual* – determined by reflex rather than calculation or impulse.

As an empirical summary, Weber's use of multiple micro-level causal mechanisms is reasonable – people certainly act in many different ways for many different reasons. However, it is problematic as a theoretical approach *unless the conditions under which different motivations for action will be dominant can be specified*. In other words, it is necessary to specify the scope of these different micro-level causal mechanisms. This is a difficult theoretical task (its difficulty is one of the strongest arguments in favour of using simpler microfoundations). In the absence of a theoretical specification of their interrelations, arguments using different microfoundations to explain different actions will be *ad hoc*.

Weber makes some progress toward addressing this issue by giving analytical primacy to instrumental rationality. He (1978: 5) argues that '[t]he interpretation of such rationally purposeful action possesses, for the understanding of the choice of means, the highest degree of verifiable certainty'. He ([1903–06] 1975: 186) goes even further to claim that '[i]t is incontestable that the degree of "self-evidence" attained by this sort of understanding is unique'. Hence, by assuming instrumental motivation, the analyst can most easily derive models that yield *empirical implications* for any set of circumstances. Weber (1975: 186) notes that 'the relation between "means" and "ends" is intrinsically accessible to a rational *causal account which produces generalizations*, generalizations which have the property of "nomological regularity"' (emphasis in original).

Weber did not believe that all action could be explained instrumentally. He (1975: 190) stresses the fact that 'the ideal typical constructions of economics – if they are correctly understood – have no pretensions at all to general validity'. Instrumental microfoundations are used as ideal types (1975: 188), and as such they often clearly reveal anomalies. 'For the purposes of a typological scientific analysis it is convenient to treat all irrational, affectually determined elements of behavior as factors of deviation from a conceptually pure type of rational action' (Weber 1978: 6; see also 1975: 190).

Although this provides a clear starting point for the analysis and a way to address anomalies, it does not fully resolve the problem. In the absence of precise arguments about the conditions in which non-instrumental microfoundations will be important, they can still be used in *ad hoc* ways. As a consequence, it becomes very difficult to test arguments or to adjudicate between competing accounts stressing different microfoundations. This is the first dilemma of Weberian microfoundations: how is it possible to use complex microfoundations and still be able to test (even in a rough sense) particular arguments?

The second Weberian dilemma concerns the proper method for figuring out the motives of actors – should it be theoretical (by assumption) or empirical? Weber's method of *verstehen* combines theoretical assumptions (there are four types of social action, we can begin by assuming instrumental motivations) with empirical analysis (using historical sources such as diaries, letters and memoirs) to get a detailed picture of what and how historical actors thought.

We would always prefer to use the most realistic motivations in our explanations, but our ability to do so is limited by the availability of appropriate evidence. In some cases, we have detailed information about the goals of action, but it is rare to have such good data in historical work. Weber notes that '[m]any ultimate ends or values toward which experience shows that human action may be oriented, often cannot be understood completely, though sometimes we are able to grasp them intellectually. The more radically they differ from our own ultimate values, however, the more difficult it is for us to understand them empathetically.' When empirical evidence is unavailable or unreliable, the only choice (other than ignoring microfoundations) is to make assumptions about motives. It is always preferable to make these assumptions explicit, but this is often not done in historical sociology.

Contemporary forms of neo-Weberian microfoundations

Contemporary neo-Weberians have attempted to deal with these dilemmas in very different ways. At the risk of oversimplification, we divide them into three broad groups (see Collins's essay in this volume for a more detailed summary). Cultural Weberians (Bendix 1977; Hamilton and Biggart 1980, 1984; Gorski 1993) have attempted to retain complex microfoundations and *verstehen* while downplaying the importance of testability, whereas structural Weberians (Gerth and Mills 1946; Skocpol 1979; Ertman 1997) and Weberians influenced by rational choice theory (Adams 1996; Swedberg 1998; Kiser and Hechter 1998; Kiser and Baer Forthcoming; Norkus 2001) have preserved testability at the cost of forgoing *verstehen* and analytically simplifying microfoundations.

Cultural Weberianism

For much of this century, cultural Weberianism was the dominant form. Until a few decades ago, Parsons's (1937) interpretation of Weber was still dominant – *The Protestant Ethic and The Spirit of Capitalism* ([1904–05] 1930) was seen as his most important work, and as a result he was understood mainly as an idealist counterpoint to Marx who advocated an interpretive methodology (*verstehen*). Cultural Weberians (Bendix 1977; Hamilton and Biggart 1980, 1984; Gorski 1993) have provided rich and detailed analyses of the cultural (especially religious, elaborating on Weber's argument about Protestantism) and historical factors affecting many aspects of society. These arguments are often based on data from primary sources that document changes in culture and individual motivations over time.

Contemporary versions of cultural Weberianism do not claim value rationality is the only (or even main) micro-level causal mechanism, but use it as part of an explanation employing multiple microfoundations. For example, Hamilton and Biggart's (1980, 1984) work on policy implementation looks at both instrumental interests and incorporates values. They stress the fact that different types of agents are controlled in different ways. The personal staff are selected on the basis of personal ties and loyalty, they are usually dependent on the governor, and if all else fails they can be sanctioned severely and arbitrarily. Compliance of cabinet heads is maintained less by personal ties than by philosophical and ideological similarity (Hamilton and Biggart 1984: 55–66). Since cabinet heads have a great deal of autonomy from the governor, monitoring is difficult, so a similarity of fundamental values is important to ensure that they usually act in the interests of governors. Professional experts are controlled by a combination of monitoring and sanctions typically used for civil servants and by drawing on their professional loyalty.

Gorski (1993) develops an argument about the 'disciplinary revolution' in early modern politics, by applying Weber's main thesis in *The Protestant Ethic and the Spirit of Capitalism* to the state. He claims that instrumental motivations cannot fully explain the efficiency of state administration in Holland and Prussia. Internalized religious values and religious monitoring mechanisms also motivated state officials. Gorski argues that one of the main causes of the efficiency of administration in Prussia and Holland was that rulers selected agents on the basis of religious affiliation, since these agents had religious values that inhibited corruption. Gorski's stress on value rationality, without denying the importance of instrumental motivations, illustrates the use of complex microfoundations in cultural Weberianism.

The main limitation of cultural Weberianism is an inability to construct general, testable models. This is the consequence of using multiple micro-level causal mechanisms without specifying the scope within which each will be important. Some have avoided this criticism by denying the necessity for general, testable theories, and instead develop arguments about unique times and places.

Structural Weberianism

The most radical movement in the other direction (and in line with most contemporary historical sociology) is to avoid the dilemmas of Weberian microfoundations by avoiding the micro-level entirely, focusing instead on the macro-level aspects of Weber's work. This rough category can be labelled structural Weberianism (see Gerth and Mills 1946; many of the essays in Tilly 1975; Skocpol 1979; Ertman 1997). The foundation for this move was a new interpretation of Weber's work, based more on

Economy and Society (1978) than on his work on the religious foundations of capitalism (Gerth and Mills 1946; Collins 1986).[3] This interpretation sees Weber as a primarily materialist conflict theorist who usually (but certainly not always) used instrumentalist microfoundations, rather than as a *verstehen*-based cultural sociologist.

The main limitation of this work is its neglect (in some cases explicit rejection (Skocpol 1979)) of human agency. Although they rarely provide any explicit, general discussion of microfoundations, they are implicitly specified using a fairly simple process: (1) loose instrumental microfoundations are assumed (rationality, but usually without goal specification); and (2) the interests of actors are then specified as a direct reflection of their structural positions. When their actions do not seem to fit their structural interests, other factors are introduced (usually cultural factors assuming value rationality).

This sort of rough materialism, amended when necessary, is the most common form of specifying microfoundations in contemporary historical sociology (not just among Weberians). It works well either when the micro-level is not very important (for example when strong selection mechanisms are present) or when the link between structural position and interests is fairly clear and unmediated. However, the lack of explicit focus on the micro-level has two negative effects: (1) since microfoundations are unclear and underspecified, they often change throughout the argument in *ad hoc* ways; and (2) more specific features of microfoundations – risk, discount rates, information availability – are usually not addressed.

Analytical Weberianism

A third type of Weberianism is emerging. Just as Analytical Marxism (Elster 1985; Roemer 1986) attempted to blend structural arguments from Marxism and rational choice microfoundations, analytical Weberianism provides a bridge between structural Weberianism and rational choice theory. It is made possible by the conjunction of a more materialist interpretation of Weber and a broadening of rational choice theory.[4] Analytical Weberianism begins with instrumental rationality, but unlike most rational choice approaches it also assumes that other types of motivations (values, emotions) are sometimes important (Adams 1996; Kiser and Hechter 1998; Norkus 2001). It then attempts to specify the conditions under which non-instrumental motivations are likely to be important. Its goal is to produce both general propositions with abstract scope conditions and concrete analyses of particular historical events and outcomes.

To take just one example, Adams (1996) begins with standard rational choice microfoundations, then uses agency theory to model the relationship between metropolitan principals and colonial 'company men'. She (1996: 14) assumes that 'both principals and agents tend to act in intendedly rational fashion, and opportunistically, to advance their own individual gains'. In the conclusion of the paper, Adams (1996: 26) broadens the microfoundations of her argument by briefly exploring the possibility that motivations such as family honour were also important.

The main problem Analytical Weberianism faces is the difficulty of specifying the scope of different micro-level causal mechanisms (including both non-instrumental motivations and different goals within instrumental rationality). Analytical Weberianism is in this respect more difficult than Analytical Marxism, since the latter does not have to address the problem of multiple microfoundations.

Mann's solutions

Michael Mann's work does not fit cleanly into any of the types of Weberianism outlined above. His solutions to the Weberian dilemmas are often novel, and worth exploring in some detail.

Like Weber, Mann is a methodological individualist. Mann (1986: 4; see also 15, 29) argues that 'these human characteristics [his assumptions about motivations and action] are the source of everything. They are the original source of power.' *Fascists* (2004) makes it clear that the book is about understanding the motivations and actions of individuals. The first sentence reads: 'This book attempts to explain fascism by understanding fascists – who they were, where they came from, what their motivations were, how they were organized, how they rose to power.'[5]

Instrumental microfoundations are also primary for Mann. He (1988: 59) begins an early essay with what he calls a 'crude materialist psychology'[:] 'mankind is restless and greedy for more of the good things of life, and that essentially this is a quest for greater material rewards'. He opens *The Sources of Social Power* (1986: 4) with a similar description of his view of human nature: 'human beings are restless, purposive, and rational, striving to increase their enjoyment of the good things of life and capable of choosing and pursuing appropriate means for doing so'. He (2005: 25) later argues that instrumentally rational action 'is obviously important in human affairs'. This indicates that for Mann this assumption is not just analytically useful as it is for Weber, but a reasonable (albeit rough) summary of the empirical world, as well. Mann thus accepts instrumental microfoundations more fully than Weber, empirically as well as analytically.

Echoing Weber, there is also a strong focus on the role of mistakes and unintended consequences throughout Mann's work. This is most prominent in the second volume of *Sources of Social Power* (1993: 3–4). He outlines a 'foul up' theory of the state (1993: 53–4), and although he does not fully support it, it provides an important part of his argument at the end of the volume (1993: 740–802) about the causes of World War I (in which he claims that 'actions taken were objectively irrational'). His argument (2005) about ethnic cleansing also relies heavily on mistakes and unintended consequences. Mann (2005: 26) argues that ethnic cleansing is in part based on irrational microfoundations. His (2005) discussion of the unintended consequences of a series of interactions yielding escalation toward ethnic cleansing reads like an informal game theoretical analysis – in fact, this section could benefit from the explicit use of those theoretical tools. This focus on imperfect information and unintended consequences is very different from rational choice models used in traditional neoclassical economics, but it is quite similar to those developed in contemporary institutional economics (see North 1991).

Mann's use of multiple microfoundations

Unlike rational choice theorists who argue for the necessity of *a priori* specification of the goals of actors, Mann (1986: 30) says that 'what the goals are, and how they are created, is not relevant for what follows'. Rational choice models that do not specify goals *a priori* tend to become unfalsifiable tautologies – so is Mann able to avoid this problem? In general he does so by implicitly assuming fairly general goals, such as wealth and power. However, his introduction of other more specific goals is often *ad hoc*.

Although Mann relies heavily on instrumental microfoundations, it is not fair to judge his work using the standards of rational choice theory, since he does not view it as a form of rational choice theory. In fact, he does not provide any extended discussion of rational choice theory until his most recent book, *Murderous Ethnic Cleansing*, and his conclusions there are primarily negative. After noting that he uses causal mechanisms developed by rational choice theorists (among others) to explain ethnic cleansing, Mann (2005: 25) makes the fairly standard criticisms that the actors in these models are 'too stable' and too few, and that emotions are ignored. His (2005: 26) conclusion is that 'Rat. theory demands a level of rigor and simplicity not found in the real world.' He then supports a Weberian approach relying on multiple microfoundations (Weber's four types of social action) and a *verstehen* methodology. The argument for multiple microfoundations is developed further in a later section (2005: 26–30).

Mann creates a complicated list of nine different types of killers, most with mixed microfoundations.

The main source of non-instrumental microfoundations in Mann's arguments is his discussions of ideological power. For Mann (1986: 22–4), ideological power encompasses concepts and categories of meaning, norms, and aesthetic and ritual practices. He divides it into two types: transcendent autonomous organizations and immanent ones that intensify morale in other power organizations. Mann pays special attention to the material foundations (infrastructure) of ideology – the technologies, organizations, and networks that create and spread ideas and values.

Ideology plays an important part in some of Mann's arguments. He (1993: 31) suggests that interests alone cannot explain class action – 'norms and passions' are also important. Mann's (2000: 13, 19, 28, 50–3) discussion of globalization often concentrates on identities and values. Mann (2005: 25) argues that 'we must also study how norms, values, and social identities arise and help define our sense of our own interest' (see also 1993: 50). One of his most extended arguments about ideological power is his (1986: 300–80) discussion of the role of religion in shaping historical trajectories, including the rise of the West. The main argument is that the different 'world religions' that develop between BC 600 and 700 AD initiate a branching process in which clusters of societies go down different paths. In addition to this, he sees religion as important to the rise of the West, although not in the standard Weberian 'Protestant ethic' sense. Basically, he argues that Christianity provided the normative pacification necessary for capitalism to flourish. Mann (1986: 342, 363) sees religion not as epiphenomenal, but as an important 'tracklayer of history'.

However, just as non-instrumental microfoundations play a smaller role in Weber's substantive analyses than they do in his theoretical typology, ideology often plays a lesser role than other sources of power in Mann's arguments. In the preface to his *States, War, and Capitalism* (1988: ix) Mann notes that ideology is 'for the moment omitted' in this volume.[6] Mann (1993: 1–2) later argues that ideological power becomes less important and more immanent in the eighteenth and nineteenth centuries (economic and military power are dominant in the first, economic and political in the second). He (2005: 6, 32–3) argues that political power relations are most important in ethnic cleansing, but that ideology also plays some role.[7] Mann does not follow Weber in stressing the importance of legitimacy for states, but focuses on the more material aspects of Weber's model (1988: x; 1986: 7). He (1988: 65) also rejects Weber's argument about rationalization because it relies too much on 'ideological factors'. Although the role of religion is discussed very briefly, his 'caging' argument about the origin of states uses purely instrumental microfoundations (1986: chs. 2 and 3). His (1986: 130–57) discussion of the development and dynamics of 'empires of domination' based on 'compulsory cooperation' also relies on instrumental microfoundations almost exclusively (primarily military power).

Mann's theory of ideology is basically materialist, and thus reliant on instrumental microfoundations. His use of ideology does not indicate any link to highly constructivist or interpretivist cultural theory. He treats ideology concretely and materially, as a definite type of power organization, inhabited by personnel who have interests. One recurring theme in Mann's discussions of religion is its role in providing cohesion and unity to ruling classes. This is its main effect in Mesopotamia (to some extent), Rome and Persia (a lot), and throughout Europe with medieval Christianity. Chapters 4–7 of the second volume of *The Sources of Social Power* (1993) trace the ways in which ideological power shapes the development of the bourgeoisie as a class, including shaping its passions. Mann's argument about the success of various religions is a reflection theory, or, as he puts it, 'recognizably materialist'. He (1986: 306–7) suggests that Christianity responded to the contradictions of the Roman empire and satisfied some basic needs of converts. Mann (2004: 2) makes basically the same argument about the success of fascism: 'since fascists did offer plausible solutions to modern social problems, they got mass electoral support and intense emotional commitment from militants'. It is not rare for Mann to provide material foundations for values. He (1986: 19) argues that the success of Flemish and Swiss pikemen was due to the high morale and trust created by their egalitarian communal life. His discussion of hoplite armies is similar. He (1986: 201) argues that their battle formation (close, with interlocking shields) produced high morale and commitment to 'common good for the city and all the people'.

One of the most 'Analytical Weberian' aspects of Mann's project is his attempt to specify the conditions under which ideology (and thus values and sometimes emotions at the micro-level) is important. His (2004: 78) most general argument is that times of crisis lead to the breakdown of existing routines, which induces people to seek new ideas and routines. In his conclusion to *Fascists* (2004: 357), Mann specifies the limits of instrumental rationality thus: 'When multiple crises generate multiple goals among collective actors who overlap and intersect in complex ways, ensuing actions rarely follow narrow interest group rationality.' He applies this argument to both the rise of world religions and the rise of fascism. In another example, Mann (2005: 26) argues that emotions are one important source of ethnic cleansing, and he specifies the stage in the process in which they arise – they become especially important when ethnic hostilities escalate. These are both very helpful specifications of the scopes of alternative micro-level causal mechanisms. Perhaps Mann's theoretical conclusion to *The Sources of Social Power* (Volume IV) will elaborate on them.

Mann's use of verstehen

Mann's early work did not employ the methodology of *verstehen*. Direct quotations or other forms of detailed empirical evidence of motives are rare. Instead, Mann relies on broad information about structural and (to a lesser extent) cultural conditions, and assumptions about motives (e.g. 1986: 380–1). This combination of somewhat loose assumptions (specifying instrumental rationality but not specific goals/preferences) and broad historical empirics is by far the most common mode in contemporary historical sociology. Readers generally trust this approach only in the hands of scholars who know the history well and have few theoretical biases. Since Mann excels on both criteria his version of this methodology often produces impressive results.[8] This is not true more generally – this is a case in which the type of practice that can be used effectively by exemplary scholars is not advisable as a norm for all.

Mann's most recent work, on the twentieth century, does begin to employ *verstehen*. In *The Dark Side of Democracy* (2005: 26), Mann outlines his method: 'We should attempt to reconstruct the preferences of variable and changing actors, including values, traditions, and emotions, as well as instrumental goals, amid broader and changing contexts of power.' He (2005: 212 ff.) goes on to use extensive detailed data on microfoundations, including biographies of 1581 German perpetrators. This is also true of *Fascists* (2004: 3): 'To understand fascism, I adopt a methodology of taking fascists' values seriously. Thus each of my case-study chapters will begin by explaining local fascist doctrine, followed, if possible, by an account of what ordinary fascists seem to have believed.' The book relies on both *verstehen* and assumptions about the structural determination of interests and preferences, but Mann has a clear preference for the former. He (2004: 9, 12–13) prefers direct evidence of fascists' beliefs to deducing these beliefs from fascists' social characteristics.[9] However, Mann is aware of the fact that *verstehen* is very difficult even in fairly contemporary societies. Even in the twentieth century, Mann (2005: 212) concludes that 'it should be frankly admitted that we cannot penetrate far into the characters of most perpetrators, since we lack reliable psychological data'.

What explains the increasing reliance on *verstehen* and non-instrumental microfoundations in Mann's later work? It could be a period effect – like many others, he could have been affected by the recent historical and cultural 'turns' in the social sciences (McDonald 1996). Or it could be a different type of period effect, a consequence of the focus on more contemporary societies in his current work. Not surprisingly, the increased use of *verstehen* in Mann's later work is coupled with a larger focus on non-instrumental microfoundations. For example, Mann (2004: 25) defines fascists' behaviour as irrational: 'for they greatly exaggerated the threats and neglected safer means of avoiding them which were prevalent across the northwest. They over-reacted, reaching for the gun too abruptly, too early. Explaining this puzzle – of class behavior which seems somewhat irrational – is one of the principal tasks of this book.' He (2004: 63–4) later argues that the answer to the puzzle is to be found in individuals' emotions (fear, hatred) and values (nationalism, statism, militarism). Mann (2004: 357) concludes that 'goals were displaced away from a narrow instrumental rationality calculating about economic interest to a broader "value rationality" in the sense of Max Weber's sense of the term'. It is obvious that *verstehen* is easier as we get closer to the present (as well as closer culturally), but there is also a general tendency to include more details in studies closer to the present (witness the tendency for multi-volume historical works to focus on shorter time intervals as they approach the present). One of those details seems to be complex, non-instrumental microfoundations.

Conclusion

Like Weber, Mann's microfoundations derive from a mix of assumptions (instrumental rationality) and empirical data. The nature of the mixture varies over time in his work, with *verstehen* becoming more prominent recently. This is probably a consequence of his recent focus on the twentieth century, since micro-level data are easier to obtain.

Mann is much more clear, explicit and detailed about his microfoundations than most other comparative-historical sociologists. His preliminary attempt to specify the conditions under which non-instrumental microfoundations will be important is a significant contribution to the literature. Although these are important advances, his work could be even stronger if he elaborated these ideas further. As noted above, Mann does not always specify the goals of actors, so rational choice theorists will see his microfoundations as incomplete, and thus find arguments based on them difficult to evaluate. In these cases, unless they know the history well, readers have to trust the author's historical knowledge and theoretical sense. Michael Mann has earned that trust.

Notes

1 I would like to thank all participants in the 'Anatomy of Power' conference, 23–24 February 2002, at UCLA, for very helpful comments.
2 Weber (1978: 13) claims that: 'Action in the sense of subjectively understandable orientation of behavior exists only as the behavior of one or more individual human beings. For other cognitive purposes it may be useful or necessary to consider the individual, for instance, as a collection of cells, as a complex of biochemical reactions, or to conceive his psychic life as made up of a variety of different elements, however these may be defined ... For the subjective interpretation of action in sociological work these collectivities must be treated as solely the resultants and modes of organization of the particular acts of individual persons, since these alone can be treated as agents in a course of subjectively understandable action.'
3 Although Collins (1986) was influential in developing a more materialist interpretation of Weber, he is not easily classified as a structural Weberian since microfoundations play an important role in much of his work.
4 Swedberg (1998: 4) argues that Weber's economic sociology is closer to the rational choice work of James Coleman than to 'much of what goes under the heading of *verstehen* in contemporary sociology'.
5 However, Mann sees micro- and macro-levels as fairly loosely coupled, arguing that the link between the two is 'too complex to be theorized' (1986: 29). Although rational choice theorists do attempt to move from micro-level assumptions to collective or institutional outcomes, they realize the difficulty of the process. Coleman (1986) noted that the aggregation of individual actions into macro-level outcomes takes place through many different causal mechanisms, and is often complex and difficult to model.
6 The focus of the book is on debates between economic determinist and militarist theories, both of which rely on instrumental microfoundations. For example, his discussion of the causes of the decline of Britain (1988: 212–27) explicitly rejects cultural arguments in favour of material causes.
7 Mann generally follows Weber in stressing the importance of multiple causal factors. Although the primacy of different power relations varies across substantive settings, all four generally play some role in every case. The same is true of microfoundations for Mann, especially in his later work (see 2005: 25–6).
8 One of the most appealing aspects of Mann's writing is his ability to outline what we do not know. His (1986: 426) discussion of whether or not people understood inflation or the effect of debasement on inflation in the Roman empire is one of many examples.
9 Brustein's (1996) *Logic of Evil* provides an interesting contrast to Mann's *verstehen*-based approach. Brustein argues that the main reason people joined the Nazi Party was that it served their basic material interests. Instead of using *verstehen*, he compares party platforms to structurally derived interests (and finds strong support for his argument). Mann (2004: 79) rejects this view, stressing the basic values of fascists, who 'situated interest-based economics or politics amid a *Weltanschauung* (a general orientation to the world)'.

References

Adams, J. 1996. Principals and Agents, Colonialists and Company Men: The Decay of Colonial Control in the Dutch East Indies. *American Sociological Review*, 61.

Bendix, R. 1977. *Nation-Building and Citizenship*. Berkeley: University of California Press.

Brustein, W. 1996. *The Logic of Evil*. New Haven, CT: Yale University Press.

Coleman, J. 1986. Social Theory, Social Research, and a Theory of Action. *American Journal of Sociology*, 91.

1990. *Foundations of Social Theory*. Harvard, MA: Belknap Press.

Collins, R. 1986. *Weberian Sociological Theory*. Cambridge: Cambridge University Press.

Elster, J. 1985. *Making Sense of Marx*. Cambridge: Cambridge University Press.

Ertman, T. 1997. *Birth of the Leviathan: Building States and Regimes in Medieval and Early Modern Europe*. Cambridge, New York: Cambridge University Press.

Gerth, H. H., and C. W. Mills. 1946. *From Max Weber*. New York: Oxford University Press.

Gorski, P. 1993. The Protestant Ethic Revisited: Disciplinary Revolution and State Formation in Holland and Prussia. *American Journal of Sociology*, 99(2).

Hamilton, G., and N. Woolsey Biggart. 1980. Making the Dilettante an Expert: Personal Staffs in Public Bureaucracies. *Journal of Applied Behavioral Science*, 16.

1984. *Governor Reagan, Governor Brown*. New York: Columbia University Press.

Hechter, M. (ed.). 1983. *The Microfoundations of Macrosociology*. Philadelphia: Temple University Press.

Hintze, O. [1902] 1975. *The Historical Essays of Otto Hintze*. Ed. F. Gilbert. New York: Oxford University Press.

Kiser, E., and M. Hechter. 1998. The Debate on Historical Sociology: Rational Choice Theory and Its Critics. *American Journal of Sociology*, 104(3).

Kiser, E., and J. Baer. Forthcoming. The Causes of Bureaucratization: Toward an Analytical Weberianism. In J. Adams, E. Clemens and A. Orloff (eds.), *The Remaking of Modernity*. Durham, NC: Duke University Press.

McDonald, T. (ed.). 1996. *The Historic Turn in the Human Sciences*. Ann Arbor: University of Michigan Press.

Mann, M. 1986. *The Sources of Social Power, Volume I: A History from the Beginning to 1760 AD*. Cambridge and New York: Cambridge University Press.

1988. *States, War, and Capitalism*. Oxford: Blackwells.

1993. *The Sources of Social Power, Volume II: The Rise of Classes and Nation-States*. Cambridge: Cambridge University Press.

2000. 'Modernity and Globalization'. Unpublished, given as the Wiles Lectures at Queen's University, Belfast.

2004. *Fascists*. Cambridge: Cambridge University Press.

2005. *The Dark Side of Democracy: Explaining Murderous Ethnic Cleansing*. Cambridge: Cambridge University Press.

Norkus, Z. 2001. *Max Weber und Rational Choice*. Marburg: Metropolis-Verlag.

North, D. 1991. *Institutions, Institutional Change, and Economic Performance.* Cambridge: Cambridge University Press.

Parsons, T. 1937. *The Structure of Social Action.* New York: McGraw-Hill.

Roemer, J. 1986. *Analytical Marxism.* Cambridge and New York: Cambridge University Press.

Skocpol, T. 1979. *States and Social Revolutions: A Comparative Analysis of France, Russia, and China.* Cambridge: Cambridge University Press.

Swedberg, R. 1998. *Max Weber and the Idea of Economic Sociology.* Princeton, NJ: Princeton University Press.

Weber, M. 1930 [1904–05]. *The Protestant Ethic and the Spirit of Capitalism.* New York: Scribners.

　　1975 [1903–06]. *Roscher and Knies: The Logical Problems of Historical Economics.* New York: Free Press.

　　1978 [1922]. *Economy and Society.* Berkeley: University of California Press.

5   Grand, yet grounded: ontology, theory, and method in Michael Mann's historical sociology

Joseph Bryant

The transdisciplinary project of historical sociology is founded upon the premise that neither historiography nor social science can proceed, independently, to a full or sound explication of any collective human action. The mutual engagement of history and sociology is an analytical prerequisite for keeping in focus the simultaneity that determines the *social constitution* of historical events and processes, and the *historical transformation* of the agents, institutions and cultures that constitute the fluxional realities within which 'history/social life' is made. The epistemological challenges entailed in this joint venture are manifold: questions of evidence, concept-formation and theory must all be rethought so as to permit an integrative comprehension of the historical and the social, the diachronic and the synchronic.

Few scholars have contributed more to this enterprise than Michael Mann, who is producing a body of research celebrated both for the scope of its historical coverage and the nuanced deploy of its categories of interpretation. Attempting nothing less than a grand historical sociology of 'world time', Mann's immense yet still unfolding 'canvas' features a mixture of styles, ranging from the broader brush strokes of generalizing macro-narratives to more finely detailed renderings of selective sociohistorical processes. Mann's many-sided efforts to lay bare the 'infrastructures of power' that have shaped the epochal trajectories of change in world history thus provide an exemplary base from which to assess the research practices of historical social science. Here I will review a select number of criticisms that have been levelled against the project of historical sociology (data deficiencies, selection-bias problems, arbitrary emplotment, *ad hoc* theorizing), and explore how these concerns are addressed in Mann's work. To illustrate the challenges commonly entailed in any 'mutual disciplining' of history and sociology, we will conclude with an examination of Mann's account of the rise of Christianity in the ancient Roman world.

Foundations: Mann's 'organizational materialist' ontology

In the opening chapter of *Sources*, Volume I, Mann lays out a conspectus of the social ontology that informs his forays in general and substantive theorizing, as well as his methodological practice. '*Societies*', we are told, '*are constituted of multiple overlapping and intersecting sociospatial networks of power.*' He continues: 'Societies are not unitary. They are not social systems (closed or open); they are not totalities ... Because there is no system, no totality, there cannot be "subsystems," "dimensions," or "levels" of such a totality. Because there is no whole, social relations cannot be reduced "ultimately," "in the last instance" to some systematic property of it' (1986: 1). The heuristic significance of this 'no system, no totality' declaration can scarcely be overstated, as it dispels at once the confusing mists of all the many 'extraneous' ontological metaphors – architectural, organismic, mechanical – that have long misinformed enquiry into the distinctive realities of social life.

While seeking to liberate us from reified models of systemic wholes, Mann concedes that societies are integrated; their institutional coherence, however, is always a matter of degree, variable over time and across cultures. The manner and extent of societal integration that obtains is in each case largely structured by a recurring tetrad of associational networks that overlap and intersect to establish *relations of social power: ideological, economic, military, and political* (IEMP). Because each of these basic arrangements addresses distinct though interrelated human concerns – what to believe and value, how to produce and distribute, how to defend or conquer, and issues of governance – it follows that the organized means of attaining these diverse ends will never fully coincide or cohere. As the permutations of concord and competition between the wielders of different forms of power are temporally and locally contingent, variation and complexity – not symmetry and integration – is the hallmark of the 'internal patterning' that is constitutive of societies. Being less unitary than affiliative, societies operate not as 'systems' but as 'loose confederations of stratified allies', with an attending multiplicity of competing interests and agendas among the actors involved (1986: 14). Nor does it transpire that social structures consistently pivot on any one particular modality of power: a differential dynamism in the sources of social power imparts an 'episodic' perturbation to historical change, as now one new or revamped power-source, now another, rises to a position of 'relative predominance', occasioning transformations in the other networks within which it is entwined.

Mann's reflections on the nature of agency are given in briefer compass:

Human beings are restless, purposive, and rational, striving to increase their enjoyment of the good things of life and capable of choosing and pursuing appropriate means for doing so. Or, at least, enough of them do this to provide the dynamism that is characteristic of human life and gives it a history lacking for other species. (1986: 4)

In pursuit of their goals, humans form relationships so as to obtain the necessities of life and to secure advantages over others in that competitive process: hence the ubiquity and centrality of questions of power. The pursuit of these diverse interests results in our participation in multiple overlapping associations, with concomitant tensions in our commitments and available courses of action. As participants in many different 'lifeworlds', human beings must exercise 'an active agency', creatively balancing their multiple involvements, their divergent interests. We strive rationally to match means to goals, but as the complexity of social life exceeds 'the understanding of contemporaries', our actions commonly issue in 'mistakes, apparent accidents, and unintended consequences'; we 'scheme' deliberatively to accomplish certain ends, but also 'drift' half-consciously in our acculturated practices and routines (1993: 3, 18–19).

This rudimentary ontology – of 'confederal' societies with fluid and overlapping boundaries, as precariously achieved and transformed over time by pragmatic agents buffeted by variegated and at times conflicting objectives and affiliations – how might this be characterized? Mann has employed the phrase 'structural symbolic interactionism', though he now appears to favour 'organizational materialism' as the distinguishing designation for his overall approach. Whatever terminology is used, it is a *minimalist, indigenous ontology* that braces Mann's historical sociology. Not only are his orienting assumptions uncomplicated and few, they are consistent with what historical and ethnographic empiricism has consistently conveyed about the contours and rhythms of social life – in marked contrast to the 'plausibility strains' that attend the metaphorical theorizing that informs both sociocultural evolutionist and rational-choice interpretations of history. Mann's conception of social structure is dynamically flexible and multifaceted, yet suitably fortified by an astute appreciation of the compulsions of organized power; while the agency of his actors introduces no tendencies or capacities that are not amply attested in the varied chronicles of the human adventure presently available.

The interpretive underpinnings of Mann's grand historical sociology are thus empirically educed and theoretically balanced. His ontology avoids the excesses of hyper-structuralist and voluntarist models of social life, and his orienting assumptions carry insights that are robust in their implications:

(i)   we are sensitized to the primacy of social power, and to the variable permutations it manifests within the organized networks that competitively and cooperatively shape and transform the worlds we inhabit;

(ii) we are alerted to the dangers of overly holistic, totalized models of the social, and duly instructed to track the shifting configurations of alignment and opposition that arise amongst the groups and organizations that confederally comprise most societies; and

(iii) idealist and teleological tendencies are held in check by a realistic appraisal of the limited rationality of acculturated human agents, who are generally incapable of harmonizing their multiple commitments and objectives, or of fully comprehending the complexity of the changing worlds they live in.

Analytics: a theory of social power

What, then, of Mann's general theory of power, his 'organizational materialist' conception of history? Power, viewed abstractly, can be defined as a 'generalized means' for the attainment of goals; more concretely, it usually manifests as a capacity 'to organize and control people, materials, and territories' (1986: 2–3). In any given situation, the exercise of power will feature the deploy of various media – resources, skills, capabilities – that activate or mobilize relations and instrumentalities requisite for the achievement of chosen objectives. It is this focus on the *infrastructures of power*, i.e. logistics, communications, organization, tools and technologies, that is the hallmark of Mann's approach. More so than in any previous historical sociology, the actual 'mechanics' of power are featured at the core of the analysis. The marching ranges and fighting capacities of armies are astutely calculated; the productive advantages of the heavy plough are enumerated; transport and communication linkages are scaled and assessed; the consequences of literacy are traced through their varied social ramifications; new accounting techniques, cartographic advances and time-keeping devices are appraised; the coordinating capabilities of bureaucratized states are specified in reference to their fiscal resources; and so on, all quite meticulously, down through the temporally and spatially uneven development of the 'leading edges' of power in both local and world history.

While Mann's preoccupation with the infrastructures of power has not been challenged as an unsound focus, two kinds of analytical criticisms have been raised: one, positivist in inspiration, is directed against the

scope of Mann's historically grounded theorizing; the second, typically
Marxist, addresses the substantive logic of the IEMP model.

As regards Mann's deploy of ideal-type categories, and his mutual
'tacking' between the empirical and the conceptual, proponents of
nomological-deductive theorizing have objected that this style of research
fails to sustain either the building of theories or the testing of hypotheses.
It is alleged that a faddish fascination with historical 'uniqueness' and
'contingency' has deflected social science from its mission to identify
omnitemporal laws and causal universals. An 'idiographic inhibition' is
purportedly taking hold, as historical sociologists produce involuted narratives that artfully 'patch' and 'amend' their 'loose conceptual frameworks' whenever the particularities of a case so warrant – all the while
congratulating themselves on their 'sensitivity to context'! (Goldthorpe
1997: 14–15.) The proposed alternative? Bypass the unwanted 'complexity'
through the standardizing procedures of *abstraction* and *reduction*. To permit
a mass processing of cases one need only identify the set-commonalities
that are ranged among the host of variable peculiarities that make for
different times and other places, thereby easing the way for their eventual
explication by way of an encompassing reductive postulate. Or, as Kiser
and Hechter put it: 'Historical scope conditions can always be translated
into abstract ones by redefining particular features of historical cases as
values on a set of parameters' (1998: 797).

But how sound is this proposed exchange, to sacrifice or subordinate
in-depth knowledge of the contexts within which social life is enacted for
the pursuit of formal abstractions that lack a secure grounding in empirical reference? Are the case-entries within a postulated set truly comparable if their alleged commonalities have been forged by way of strained
'homogeneity assumptions'? And if the outcomes of macro-social processes are determined by shifting conjunctions of causes, what is the merit
of deploying general theories that presuppose 'same cause, same effect'
scenarios? However one is inclined to answer these kinds of questions, it is
indisputable that the promised breakthrough to nomological consolidation
is yet to arrive, and that past efforts at deductive rigour have consistently
issued in a wreckage of abandoned axioms, reified abstractions and
pseudo-universals. At some inescapable point, a flight from the concrete
to the general will enter a descending arc into triviality, or tautology. So
if the purpose of our theories is the explanatory comprehension of real-life
processes, it follows that actual history must provide not merely the
content, but also the limits to our generalizations. Mann's theorizing
is, by reasoned design, resolutely historical, and sustained by a close
sociological analysis of the contexts within which social life is transacted
and transformed. Given the diligence of his engagement with the histories

he has investigated, is it plausible that he would fail to detect the operation of any grander connections, had these existed in reality, and not only as the pretences of a universalizing theory?[1]

The Marxist critique of Mann's theoretical project takes up a different issue: the relative autonomy of the four principal forms of power. Likewise concerned with relations of coercion and command, with ideologies and the economic foundations of social existence, Marxism offers a parallel, but competing historical sociology to that being developed by Mann. The key point of difference, from a Marxist perspective, is that Mann's 'organizational materialism' is *not materialist enough*, as the economic forces and relations of production are held to exercise a preponderant influence on shaping social life more generally, and in generating and sustaining corresponding forms of political, military and ideological power more specifically.

Mann objects to all theories that posit a causal or constitutive primacy. While recognizing that his four sources of power are interjoined and overlapping, Mann insists that each exerts a distinctive form of control. A patterned distinctiveness in the ways in which power is manifested is sociologically consequential, notwithstanding that the functioning of each form is conditioned by or dependent upon the others. Moreover, Mann maintains that as each power-source generates and follows its own immanent logic of development and organization, this imparts a fluctuating 'determinism' to the dynamics of social change, as major enhancements in the performance capabilities of one form of power can, on occasion, lead to a general restructuring of the other networks within which it is entwined. In these 'world-historical moments' of transformation, Mann – like Weber before him – finds no singular pattern of uniform causality, but rather a shifting matrix wherein the protean forms of power ebb and flow, coalesce and collide.

While recognizing that institutionalized power operates through a plurality of organized arrangements, Marxists generally seek to establish a fundamental dependency upon economic foundations. Perry Anderson has accordingly challenged Mann on the purported autonomy of political power on the grounds that polities cannot function without the deploy of ideological and military/policing powers, which in turn presupposes a capacity to materially fund or provision these instrumentalities. In Anderson's words, 'political regulation is scarcely conceivable without the resources of armed coercion, fiscal revenue and ideal legitimation' (1990: 61). Moreover, having afforded property relations only an occasional and sparse coverage, Anderson (1992) suggests that Mann has missed an opportunity to track more closely the integrative connections that these have commonly called forth among his quaternary forms of power.

The historian Chris Wickham, a specialist in the late antique, early medieval West, has expressed similar concerns, arguing that in Mann's analysis of classical antiquity 'the state has not been theorized sufficiently as an *economic form*, in particular in its relationships with the landowning class' (1988: 67). Wickham likewise suggests that in his account of the Roman Empire, Mann is insufficiently attentive to 'the greatest development hitherto known of slavery as a mode of production', and its centrality in the dialectical progression of Rome's political and military powers. For Wickham, 'social formations (whether bounded or unbounded) are more tightly articulated' than Mann generally allows, and it is their grounding in the material forces and relations of production that provides for that underpinning coherence (1988: 77).

Do we have an irreconcilable theoretical dispute? I think not, for when Marxists allege that Mann exaggerates the autonomy of the political or ideological, he can reply that they are neglecting his repeated insistence that the principal forms of power operate in a highly interdependent, though fluxional, manner. And he would certainly not disagree with Anderson's observation that the exercise of state power is dependent upon a triadic complex involving military force, economic resources and normative legitimacy – the verbs 'entwine' and 'intertwine', after all, are among the most frequent locutions Mann employs! But where Marxists are disposed to specifying the economic *preconditions or bases* of other forms of institutionalization, Mann is more concerned with tracking the *emergent properties* that arise from the particular developmental logics of each of the four forms of power, and the 'interstitial surprises' that periodically spring from their incomplete integration. Although his treatment of this point is not systematically articulated, *the causal 'autonomy' that Mann insists upon is emergent, not foundational*, as is made clear in two important passages. The first takes up the classic idealism–materialism polarity:

[I]deologies are not 'free floating' but the product of real social circumstances ... Unless ideology stems from divine intervention in social life, then it must explain and reflect real-life experience. But – and *in this lies its autonomy* – it explains and reflects aspects of social life that existing dominant institutions (modes of economic production, states, armed forces, and other ideologies) do not explain or organize effectively. An ideology will *emerge* as a powerful, autonomous movement when it can put together in a single explanation and organization a number of aspects of existence that have hitherto been marginal, interstitial to the dominant institutions of power. (1986: 21, italics added)

The second concerns de Ste Croix's celebrated Marxist analysis of class struggles in ancient Greece and Rome (1981), thought by Mann to overemphasize the significance of economic considerations at the expense of military and political developments[2]:

> It is not my intention, to paraphrase Weber, to replace a one-sided materialism with an equally one-sided military/political theory. *Obviously, military/political forms have economic preconditions.* But if militarism and states can be productive, *their resulting forms may themselves causally determine further economic development, and so economic forms will also have military and political preconditions.* (1986: 223, italics added)

So, just as Marxism does not maintain that 'the economic' is continuously determinant, monotonically exerting its push and pull throughout the social order, so Mann's 'relative autonomy' thesis does not dispute that political, military and ideological forms of power are entwined with and presuppose sustaining economic foundations. And just as Marx's base–superstructure metaphor does not imply that the former 'causally disables' or 'neutralizes' the latter, but only tendentially restricts its forms and modes of operation to practices that comport with established or, in times of social transition, newly emerging economic conditions, so Mann's IEMP model does not sectorally detach or isolate the organized networks of power from their confederal forms of association and reinforcement.

In recognizing that sociological theories cannot serve as deductive 'levers of construction', but only as interpretive aids in the study of actual history, Mann and his Marxist interlocutors share a common analytical orientation. That they ultimately differ on the question of 'ultimate determinacy' is, I think, less significant than their kindred interest in delving into the concrete struggles and compacts between human groups, as these find expression in the organized forms of power that impart directionality and a measure of contingent order to history's transforming processes.

Practice: Mann's historical-sociological method

In a 1989 interview, Mann provided the following characterization of his research style: 'I am an empiricist and I work to results through historical examples.' Sociology, he continued, needs to be based on a 'wide-ranging and fully critical macro-history', which in turn must be informed by historically grounded 'sociological theorising' (1989: 70). As 'theory and data perennially enmesh and correct one another', this will enable us to develop more cogent and nuanced categories of interpretation as well as sounder explications of key historical patterns and processes (1994: 42).

To illustrate Mann's method of 'zigzagging' between theoretical conceptualization and empirical engagement, let us turn to one of the major concerns of his IEMP model, the analysis of political power. Here a concept like the 'state' will figure prominently, but in applying this to different places and periods, it becomes apparent that a chained series of specifications will be required to do justice to the diverse and dynamic phenomena under investigation. Mann accordingly develops a number of historically freighted categories – e.g. chiefdoms, temple-based redistribution polities, city-states, empires of domination, feudal-conquest empires, empires of compulsory cooperation, the patrimonial state, constitutional and absolutist regimes, the national state, the liberal-capitalist state, and so on – that *allow him to bring into relief the salient differences between 'states' ancient, medieval, and modern*, and the important sub-varieties contained within each. Moreover, as these diverse forms of state organization make their entries and exits on the stages of history, Mann is able to specify the infrastructures of power that determined their actual capacities for 'extensive' and 'intensive' control, their varied dependence upon 'authoritative' and 'diffused' mechanisms of integration and coordination, and their particular mix of achieved benefits, 'collective' and 'distributive'. Far from functioning in any uniform causal manner, Mann shows that states throughout history have not only 'crystallized' variably with other power organizations and institutions over time, they have changed dramatically in their own capacities and influence, differing significantly in terms of operational size, the nature and scope of their functions, the extent of bureaucratization and their social representativeness. Does this 'tacking' procedure simply 'recapitulate observations', as critics such as Goldthorpe contend (1997: 15), or is analytical induction an appropriate methodology for a discipline that attends to the reflexive agency of acculturated actors, whose practices and identities are socially situated, and thus internal to the shifting constellations of organized power that give determinant shape to the processes of history?

Adding discipline to the mutual interrogations of theory and evidence is *the logic of comparison*, a method that 'teases out' causal variations and uniformities through a systematic alignment of cases that exhibit constitutive similarities or parallels. Mann utilizes this method, but with caution. Given his ontological criticisms of 'overly bounded, overly integrated' models of social totalities, it is not surprising that he objects to 'comparing societies as units, across different times and places' (Mann 1986: 503), or protests that in many instances, genuine comparison is precluded by an absence of truly 'autonomous, analogical cases' (Mullan 1987: 186).[3] Mann argues that comparative sociology 'must be restrained by an appreciation of world-historical time', to such extent that 'comparative analysis should also be historical', and so attentive to the often vast differences in the power organizations and resources at play in any given period (1986: 173–4).

Mann is far more comfortable with the 'before/after', 'then and now' analytics of strict *historical comparison*, where specific cases and conjunctures are located along their developmental trajectories, which allows for a temporally discriminating appraisal of the precise causal powers at work. Thus ancient and medieval 'proto-nationalisms', for example, are shown to be quite distinct from the modern forms of nationalism that have crystallized with the rise of territorially centralized states, democratization, diffused literacy and mass communications. The Assyrians, Romans, Huns, Mongols and Aztecs were hardly slackers in the terroristic slaughter of their enemies, but again, Mann convincingly demonstrates that genocides and 'murderous ethnic cleansings' are not 'primordial' or 'perennial' forms of action, but decidedly modern phenomena, contingent upon the formation of centralized nation-states, the ideological conflation of democracy and nationalism, and the cultural intensification – via religion, language and literacy – of 'macro-ethnic' identities. In principled contrast to those comparativists who 'combine promiscuously material gathered from different phases in the development of social-power sources' (1986: 173), Mann subjects his sociology to the requisite rigours of temporal specificity and periodization.

Having subsumed comparative analysis within the arching logic of historical sociology, it should come as no surprise that Mann's preferred mode and medium of explication is *narrational* in form. Although the manner in which historical-sociological narratives are composed will vary in accordance with the issues investigated, all will feature a sequentially ordered placement of human agency within the dynamic institutional and cultural contexts that give it purpose and directionality. Mann has described this interpretive effort as an attempt 'to establish "what happened next" to see if it has the "feel" of a pattern, a process, or a series of accidents and contingencies' (1986: 503). In as much as each case develops temporally, 'this dynamic must itself be part of our explanation of its structure' (1986: 174). Given that the arrangements of any momentary 'present' – as consolidated in the form of roles, institutions and cultural traditions – are the legacies of 'past' agency, it follows that our analytical narratives must encompass sufficient temporal depth so as to identify origins and turning-points. Mann has used the geological metaphor of *sedimentation* to refer to this process whereby the past gives shape to the present, selectively and cumulatively, as 'layers dating from varied previous eras become buried as enduring institutions which live on and entwine with brand-new processes and institutions' (2000: 5).

To critics who object that the norms of history are – in this 'narrative turn' – displacing scientific standards of explanation, we must reply that *the project of historical sociology is mutually transforming or synthesizing,* i.e. the social sciences are to become fully historical, just as historiography must utilize sociological insight and conceptualization in its interpretive and configuring operations. In Mann's own wide-ranging research, his narratives are simultaneously 'historical', successively charting the temporal flows of interaction and change, and also 'sociological', in that roles, institutions and social structures are specified and invoked to render intelligible the courses of action that clash and coalesce to propel each moment of the social-historical process. Those who would uphold the old idiographic–nomothetic antinomy must do more than simply complain that historical-sociological explanations are insufficiently 'theoretical' or 'deductive'; they must explain how any purported 'historical fact' can be understood without the identifying and coordinating insights of sociological knowledge, or how any proposed 'sociological theory' could lay claim to plausibility if it has not been derived and vetted through a detailed comprehension of historical cases. *Particularizing and generalizing analytical operations are not separate or independent stages: the accuracy and cogency of each ultimately presupposes the soundness of the other.* The historicist recognition that social realities are immanently dynamic, transformational, must be coupled with a sociological awareness that the events and processes that comprise history are situated within determinant cultural and structural constellations.

To clarify the preceding, let us turn to Mann's use of empirical sources. Given the immense ranges of world-time that Mann seeks to incorporate, it follows that the labours of historians will provide much of the factual basis for the narratives he constructs. A reliance upon 'secondary sources' is characteristic of most ventures in comparative macro-sociology, and this dependence has attracted the attention of critics. Two concerns have been repeatedly raised. First, just how reliable are the 'facts' of history, as initially rendered by historians and as subsequently utilized by social scientists? Secondly, in situations where historians have produced incompatible interpretations of the same case or phenomena, how are historical sociologists to arbitrate and choose?

Scepticism regarding the ability of historians to reconstruct aspects of the past takes a variety of forms, from postmodernist assertions that 'historical facts' are rhetorically or ideologically concocted rather than detected in the available sources, to positivist anxieties that such sources are generally too few and fragmentary to serve as reliable databases. Both positions are unbalanced. The 'primacy of rhetoric' perspective, which came to prominence in the work of scholars such as Barthes, Hayden White and Michel de Certeau, is fatally compromised by its complete inattention to historical method, i.e. the actual research procedures whereby historians establish their facts through a source-critical probing of the evidentiary remains and the placement of each provisional finding within a larger nexus of implicated discoveries. Salutary in alerting us to the temptations of 'reading too much' (or 'too little') into the evidence, these critics have failed to attend to the ways in which *historical sources impose limits and obligations on the configuring and emplotment designs of any narrative*, which must both 'cover and connect' the materials that bear on the topic being investigated. As for the 'poverty of historical data' line – a polemic advanced by the quantitatively oriented crowd of 'cliometric' historians – this too fails to comport with the working conditions that normally confront those who would explicate the human past. For not only is it the case that most historians will never be able to process all the available source-materials that pertain to their specialized subjects, but, more telling, the concreteness and 'social density' of most forms of historical data bestow upon historians certain interpretive advantages. Funerary deposits, diaries, pottery sherds, skeletal remains, videos, public and domestic architecture, language, implements of agriculture and war, articles of adornment, judicial transcripts: all such materials derive from real, not simulated, human use and performance; being *authentic elements from past social worlds*, they bring us into immediate contact with our subjects, their technical accomplishments, their expressed thoughts and beliefs, their practices and institutions, and the ecologies within which they lived. Each singular relic is – as an 'objectification' of a past social act – implicated in a wider plexus of circumstances and conditions that were involved with its particular creation or utility. Carrying a high level of indexicality, historical source-materials typically permit the inferential derivation of a variety of contextual features, thus allowing for integrative, and at times even 'thick descriptive', reconstructions of the living milieux of distant times. The study of history confronts daunting challenges; but principled objections to its capacity to recover aspects of the past need not be credited, for these claims do not accurately characterize either the research procedures or the resources that ground historical enquiry.

But in granting historians a capacity to establish reliable 'historical facts', does this legitimize the appropriation of such facts by social scientists? At least one critic, John Goldthorpe, has expressed doubts. In his view, the grand synthesizing ventures of historical-comparative sociology rest upon quite speculative 'interpretations of interpretations', wherein contact with the primary evidence is 'both *tenuous* and *arbitrary* to a quite unacceptable degree' (1991: 222). According to Goldthorpe, it is a 'pick-and-mix' subjectivism – driven by *a priori* theoretical or ideological commitments – that governs which 'facts' are selected for incorporation, and also determines their strategic placement within the inventive narratives composed. In deploying 'loose conceptual schemes' to explicate complex bodies of evidence for which no direct processing has been attempted, historical sociology would appear to be a hybrid discipline lacking both theoretical and empirical warrant.

These charges merit, and have received, serious consideration; and it must be conceded that historical-comparative enquiry is not braced by an infallible methodology. But Goldthorpe's critique is more categorical than substantive, and is itself based on serious mis-characterizations of both historiography and the project of historical social science.

Macro-comparative research *is* commonly reliant upon secondary sources, but does this dependence 'screen' researchers from the primary source-materials, as Goldthorpe implies? That is a dubitable inference, given that the narratives offered by historians normally carry a high level of descriptive *reportage* on the specific features of the evidence utilized. As these specialists typically seek to advance their own accounts by pointing to perceived 'weak links' in rival offerings, discussions on how the available evidence has been used or misused are usually quite explicit – a convention that minimizes the risks that non-specialists will blindly draw their mediated data from the more contested ends of the interpretive spectrum. Note, too, that source-anthologies are abundantly available, presenting reproductions of images and texts that enable non-specialists to 'turn to the sources' themselves. So not only will historical-comparative scholars repeatedly encounter primary evidence in the reportage contained in the specialist literature, they have the option of examining large bodies of collected source-materials directly. This manner of research is labour-intensive and time-consuming; and a failure to consult widely and deeply enough in the secondary scholarship – with attending forays in the primary sources as well – will result in partial or unbalanced explanatory efforts. But this, surely, only confirms that the project of historical sociology is an inherently demanding, rigorous enterprise, and hardly supportive of 'loose and tenuous' speculations.

Goldthorpe's accompanying criticism, that grand historical sociology is 'arbitrary' in its engagement with the empirical, likewise seems to presume that shortcomings in performance testify to a limitation in principle. As he describes the situation, practitioners in this field are inordinately dependent on research that is produced by specialists, yet they are undisciplined in their synthesizing utilization of the information appropriated. In treating 'historical facts' as if they were 'discrete and stable entities that can be "excerpted" and then brought together in order that some larger design may be realised', grand historical sociologists are engaged in an illicit 'scissors and paste' operation (1991: 221). A serious charge, but is the alleged 'inconsistency' real or largely rhetorical? The only social scientists who might be prone to treating historical sources in the atomistic fashion described would be those who believe that general laws and causal uniformities have been discovered, or are pending. Since most historical sociologists are convinced that 'time and place do matter', they accordingly seek to identify the ways in which social processes unfold differently as a consequence of their varied contextual placement.

Goldthorpe's characterization of the 'dependency' relation is also misleading, seeing that historical sociologists have never been mere 'passive recipients' of the interpretive labours of specialist researchers. As Mann points out, not only do historical sociologists critically 'rethink' the arguments and the evidence provided by historians, in the light of 'theories based on broader knowledge about how societies operate', they have also been known to take the step of analysing primary historical data directly (1994: 41). Consider the following exercise in 'sociological rethinking'. Having read extensively in the secondary literature on the ancient military empires – Sargon's Sumer, Assyria, the Persians, the Greeks and Alexander, Rome's conquering legions – Mann subjected contemporary as well as modern claims regarding the size and fighting capabilities of ancient armies to theoretical and comparative scrutiny. Given the rudimentary infrastructural conditions then obtaining, and the likely constraints of demography, Mann concluded that most standard accounts of the military campaigns of antiquity not only grossly overstate the numbers of combatants and victims involved, they also seriously misconstrue the nature of militarized forms of imperial domination. In societies resting upon slender agrarian foundations, professional armies would have been modest in proportion, and any fuller civilian mobilization for purposes of war exceedingly difficult to sustain. An effective marching radius of roughly 90 kilometres – the distance that could be traversed over the three days for which carried provisions would normally last – placed severe restrictions on the controlling 'reach' of would-be despots. Despite the bombastic claims recorded in the royal archives and inscribed upon the lithic monuments of self-glorification, most ancient dynasts and god-kings were constrained to rule in decentralized arrangements, owing to the undeveloped state of their communicative and administrative infrastructures, and the limited striking powers of their armed forces. While building on the insights of specialist historians, Mann has here used an integrative sociological theory to correct the 'historical facts' as presented, thereby turning what was deceptively propagandistic into a window onto the bluffs of those who laid claim to autocracies more pretended than realizable.

As for the direct examination of primary sources, Mann has again set an exemplary standard. In the opening volume of *Sources*, he offers a sociological reappraisal of state financial records, beginning with an innovative analysis of the Exchequer Rolls that provide information on the revenues and expenditures of the Tudor monarchy. He followed this up with incisive recalculations of the budgetary statistics from the five major modernizing powers – Britain, France, Prussia/Germany, Austria, and the United States – over the period (c. 1760–1910) in which their state structures and functions underwent revolutionizing transformations: in fiscal extractive capacity, size of personnel (civil and military), and in the bureaucratized coordination of social life (1993: chs. 11–14). Another noteworthy example is Mann's multifaceted analysis of German fascism (2004), which draws upon voting records, party propaganda, membership files, journalism and other contemporary sources, and also features an assembled data-set of some 1,500 biographies of Nazi war-criminals, which he compiled on the basis of published court transcripts, newspaper accounts, autobiographies, and scholarly studies of known perpetrators of atrocities. Comparative-historical research must continue to anchor itself in the professional competencies of the specialists who provide us with carefully decoded and sifted evidentiary foundations and with narrational accounts that both inform and orient. But precisely because 'theory leads us to ask questions of the data which historians have not asked', historical-comparative sociologists can at times produce nuanced revisions or entirely novel insights, 'finding patterns in the data to which historians had not been sensitive, and finding inconsistencies or implausibilities in their accounts' (1994: 43).

Consider now the charge of selection-bias, which usually registers in two keys: (1) an allegation that historical-comparative analysts are prone to selecting from the secondary literature only those 'facts' and 'story lines' that comport with their own theoretical or ideological agendas; and (2) a principled claim that whenever situations of narrational discordance arise amongst specialists, historical sociologists are incapable of objectively arbitrating between the rival interpretations (Goldthorpe 1991; Lustick 1996). Little time need be spent on the first charge, for any such partisan practice would – if it existed – simply point to a need for greater rigour in the research process. Narrational discordance is a more serious issue, but one that hardly results in a 'subjectivist impasse' or 'paralysis'. To begin with, historians themselves are not content to allow a cacophony of controversy to persist, but subject the issues in dispute to repeated scrutiny, typically by drawing in newly discovered evidentiary materials or by making connections with data hitherto neglected or marginal. More inclusive analytical frameworks are commonly pursued, and earlier theses that lacked empirical warrant are discarded. Historiography, in short, is very much a critical enterprise, and the ongoing cycle of revisionism and the qualifying resistance it calls forth functions as a progressive sifting process, such that, in most cases, 'we not only know more now, we understand better' (Martin 1998: 15). By attending to the source-critical procedures that enable historians to render discriminating empirical appraisals, synthesizing scholars should be able to make informed assessments about which interpretations carry greater factual support and which are sustained by *parti pris* commitments. As to detecting the latter, whether these be theoretical or ideological in inspiration, we can turn to the sociology of knowledge, an instrument for enhanced objectivity that scans for perspectival bias in the cognitive-evaluative frames and resources that are used in the production of knowledge-claims. By raising to reflexive awareness the paradigm affiliations of historians and area-specialists, as well as their reliance upon culturally specific normative interests and categories of understanding, the configurational tendencies that inform rival interpretive accounts can be identified, thus opening yet another vista onto the ways in which the evidentiary materials might have been abridged or repackaged owing to observational and cognitive partiality. Selection-bias is an ever-present danger, but through source-critical techniques of empirical processing and the analytical reflexivity that attends the sociology of knowledge, historical-comparative sociology need not despair of its capacity to move forward with the task of synthesizing the bodies of specialist scholarship that must be integrated if genuinely scientific insights are to be found and tested.

Performance: on the hazards of analytical 'tacking'

Mann subscribes to a 'recursively progressivist' view of science. As a self-avowed 'zigzagger' who works back and forth between historical particularities and sociological categories, Mann places the mutual interrogations of theory and evidence at the heart of his enterprise. What, then, are the hazards that he and other historical sociologists must negotiate? Two forms of capsizal are commonplace. In inclining towards or 'tacking' by the empirical – usually the safer course – it is always possible that the accumulated 'facts' can simply overwhelm any attempt at theoretical ordering. An exhausting litany of detailed qualifications, a jumbled inclusion of every available evidentiary source, narratives so involuted as to lack an appreciable direction: these are a few of the empiricist tendencies that can unbalance the interpretive process. But 'tacking' by the theoretical holds still greater hazards. Here one not only runs the risk of imposing one's theory upon recalcitrant data, deforming the evidence in a bid to preserve the formal coherence of our applied models; we can also simply fail to make contact with solid empirical ground, as the conceptual maps we navigate by might be so inaccurately or notionally drawn as to exclude from view precisely those moorings that are factually decisive or significant.

Remaining on even keel throughout the course of interpretive tacking is never an easy trial, and even the most accomplished of historical-comparative scholars will occasionally careen or veer off course. Notwithstanding the criticisms raised elsewhere in this volume, I have found Mann's navigational performances to be both exemplary and highly instructive. There is one component in his IEMP model, however, that requires theoretical broadening. I refer to ideology, one of the most elusive of concerns in the social sciences generally, and one that poses distinctive interpretive problems for any theory that seeks to explicate macro-historical processes in terms of enhancements in social power. For determining the performance capabilities and functional utility of, say, the Maxim gun, Watt's steam-engine, or a literately trained bureaucratic officialdom, is a relatively straightforward procedure; and comparisons with earlier or functionally competing instrumentalities are usually so direct that gauging their respective advantages yields quite clear inferences regarding their consequences for social power. But can the 'force of ideas' be assessed in a similar manner? In what way is monotheism a more powerful ideology than polytheism? Is nationalism or liberalism the more effective political programme? Can the threat of eternal damnation be weighed against the doctrine of *samsara*, the endless cycle of rebirth? Which of the two, 'holy war' or 'just war', produces the more committed and efficient cadres for battle? The basic difficulty to rendering precise determinations of power here is that ideologies are symbol systems, and though they undoubtedly carry differential practical implications and possibilities, they require credence and compliance for their efficacy and realization. Thus, while ideologies are *conveyed objectively*, in discursive and material forms of auditory and visual communication, they are and must be *appraised subjectively*, in cultural praxis. This latter aspect does not so easily fit within Mann's framing optic of 'organizational materialism', which is preoccupied with logistics and infrastructures, i.e. the media and mechanisms through which power is implemented and realized.

Mann's historical sociology of ideological forms of power thus displays an occasional imbalance, as an interest in explaining *how* certain beliefs and ideals gained currency skews or suppresses a concern with *why* they resonated. This asymmetry is most pronounced in his treatment of religion, and in his discussions of the Axial Age 'salvation religions' more specifically. Mann's attentiveness to the infrastructural and organizational features that enabled various religious movements to rise to entrenched positions of coordinating normative control is consistently informative; his effort to account for their initial ideological appeal, however, is too cursory on content, and so less successful. Let us clarify a few of the difficulties by reconsidering Mann's explanation of the triumph of Christianity in the ancient Mediterranean world.

For Mann, Christianity was a religion that advanced by articulating an ideology of *sociospatial transcendence*, diffusing through and across the existing boundaries of class, gender and ethnicity, and subordinating political, military and economic organizations to its higher claims of sacred authority. As a 'salvation religion', Christianity promised its devotees 'relief from earthly sufferings', on the basis of a claimed 'monopoly of, and divine authority for, knowledge of the ultimate "meaning" and "purpose" of life'. Explicating the rise of the new movement will accordingly turn on identifying 'the fit between the Christian message and the motivations and needs of the converted' (1986: 301–2). Owing to the fact that the emerging religion was heavily text-based, specifying the doctrinal content is simply a matter of exegesis; gaining insight into the sensibilities of the converts, Mann concedes, is a more difficult challenge. And it is here that he makes the first of a series of questionable assumptions. Given what he takes to be the rapidity and wide geographic and social sweep of the movement's spread, Mann infers that Christianity carried a 'universal appeal' within the Roman Empire (he titles a subsection accordingly). There are difficulties with this:

(i) Christianity's actual growth-pattern was highly uneven, and the sociologically decisive augmentations of membership occurred quite late in its historical trajectory;

(ii) given its protracted and asymmetrical course of advance, it is clear that Christian doctrines were anything but 'universal' in appeal, and could claim resonance with only specific and quite limited audiences, at key phases in its early development.

Mann argues that the 'universal appeal' of the new faith can be inferred from three evidentiary clues. First, there were clear 'monotheistic, salvationist, and syncretic currents' in Middle Eastern thought that preceded the Christian variant by centuries. Mann alludes to both Zoroastrianism and Jewish monotheism, as well as to sundry Hellenistic mystery-cults, and to Neoplatonist and other religious strands within Greek philosophy. Second, Mann infers that a concern for personal salvation was gaining momentum at this time, as he believes is indicated by the proliferation of Gnostic sects that early on split off from Christianity, each offering their own customized modality for those in quest of earthly transcendence. Third, and perhaps most importantly, Mann contends that Jesus's own salvific message was ethical, simple and rational, and hence of inclusive appeal. How secure are these interpretations? As regards the first two – the trend towards monotheism, a heightened preoccupation with personal salvation – Mann invokes a consensus that was fashioned several decades back. A principal difficulty noted by more recent scholarship, however, is that monotheistic beliefs had been in currency for some seven or eight centuries, and likewise with the promise of afterlife benefits on offer in traditional religions such as the Egyptian and in a few of the oldest of the mystery-cults (Eleusis, Orphism). Documenting an increased attraction for these beliefs in the time of Jesus remains elusive, as the evidence is too porous and counterbalanced to permit a chronologically firm specification of trends. As to the 'universal rationality' of Jesus's simple message, it would appear that Mann has here succumbed to the theological bias of modern Christian scholarship (especially liberal Protestant). Mann writes: 'by rejecting mysteries, ritual, and magic, Christ (or his gospel writers) was appealing to rational forms of faith' (1986: 305). This is an interpretation that runs counter to the evidence, seeing that the *New Testament* is literally drenched in mysteries and magic, beginning with the tales of Jesus's supernatural birth, continuing on with his ministry of miracles and exorcisms, the cosmically transforming event of his crucifixion, his postmortem elevation and pending return as judge, destroyer and redeemer, the stories that tell of the inherited charismata of his wonder-working disciples, the institutionalization of the sacramental rituals of baptism and the eucharist, the repeated insistence that faith – and not 'the foolish wisdom of world' – will bring about a rapture of deliverance for 'whosoever believeth in Him', and of course the closing text, Revelation, with its arching demonology and arcane prophesies of divine vengeance and redemption for the few. If our scan is widened to include the vast corpus of ancillary Christian texts, apocryphal and apocalyptic, the extra-canonical gospels and the apostolic pseudepigrapha, the picture that emerges is even more radically inconsistent with the 'Jesus-as-pious-ethicist' portrait that comports with modern Christian sensibilities. Similarly unfounded is Mann's accompanying premise, that 'if Christ's reported teachings were brought into contact with most groups of people of his time, they would encounter a degree of sympathetic response within the empire' (1986: 305–6). Here again the primary sources tell a different story, for not only did most of his fellow Jews reject the man-god's ministry and persecute his followers as blasphemers, but written accounts of the early Christian mission to the Gentiles are replete with beatings and arrests, scornful ridicule and riotous mobs defending their traditions in response to Christian 'atheism' and 'abominations'. Indeed, as Mann himself correctly notes later in his chapter, for some three centuries the Church would labour under a very negative public image, based partly upon popular misunderstandings of Christian ritual (the eucharist as cannibalism, the agape as a licence for incest), but also on the very real resentments that this was a *superstitio* that dishonoured the ancestral ways, alienated the goodwill of the gods, and traitorously advocated a repudiation of collective responsibilities and fellowship, ranging from military service to attendance at the games and festivals that punctuated the civic calendar. Mann's 'simple, ethical, rational' Christianity is a 'theologized' mirage, so selective in its representation that it all but derails the effort to ground the faith's difficult but eventual ascendancy in the actual confluence of circumstances that enabled it to ride out the storms of persecution and internal schism, and progressively attune its salvific programme to incorporate ever larger numbers of converts in Rome's changing and increasingly challenged empire.

Having posited an inherent appeal to the Christian *kerygma*, Mann turns to a series of 'deficiencies' within the Hellenistic–Roman world that would provide an opening for the interstitial emergence of a new form of ideological power. Mann argues that like the other great empires of the era (Persia, Han China, the kingdoms of India), Rome's very successes, its social and economic development, created a number of 'tensions' within the extended social fabric. These *contradictions of empire* turned on five paired antinomies: universalism–particularism; equality–hierarchy; decentralization–centralization; cosmopolitanism–uniformity; and civilization–militarism. The world's salvation religions are to be understood as reformist responses to the existential problems that were created by those contradictions, and this is how Mann explicates the Christian triumph. By creating and offering a 'universalistic, egalitarian, decentralized, civilizing community – an *ecumene*', Christianity 'provided a solution to these contradictions' (1986: 307). This argument is somewhat abstract, but there is a more significant concern: did not the Church itself, from its very inception, feature a series of polarizing 'contradictions' that must severely qualify any claim that it was 'universalistic, egalitarian, decentralized, and civilizing'? I refer to such matters as the early dispute over whether the message was intended for non-Jews; the ambiguous and contested relations between rich and poor brethren among the faithful (cf. Clement of Alexandria's casuistical sermon, *Who is the Rich Man That Will Be Saved?*); the recurrent conflicts over persisting patriarchical norms (as exemplified in the Montanist crisis and the challenges of Gnosticism); the contested rise of a monarchical episcopate; the pronounced anti-intellectualism and hostility to Greek culture that, in turn, was resisted by compromising Hellenizers (a tension well captured in Tertullian's defiant sneer, 'what has Athens to do with Jerusalem?'); and, not least, the long, protracted and divisive struggle over membership criteria, as disciplinary hardliners repeatedly called for the explusion of the wayward, while laxists sought their pastoral restoration and forgiveness. Mann is sound in his general claim, that Christianity constituted an alternative subcommunity that offered the possibility of salvation to all and sundry, irrespective of ethnic, gender and class identities. But given that many of the movement's own internal divisions and tensions – between competing 'orthodox' and 'heretical' factions, between 'flesh' and 'spirit', the saved and damned, this fleeting world and an eternal one to come – were simply overlaid upon existing conventions, such as male primacy, the rights of slaveowners, and the legitimacy not only of war but juridical and penal torture as well, it is exceedingly difficult to see how this banned and marginal religion – prior to its imperial adoption by Constantine – could have functioned as an egalitarian or 'civilizing' vehicle within the vast empire.

While maintaining that Christianity arose in response to 'sufferings' in the Hellenistic–Roman world, Mann is insistent that this should not be understood in materialistic terms. He takes issue with both the Marxist position, as exemplified by Kautsky, where Christianity is viewed as a proletarian movement of the disinherited and oppressed; and also the idealist spin on this proposed by Troeltsch, who held that the poor of the ancient world streamed into the new faith as part of a cultural shift 'away from materialism', in spiritual yearning for the 'purely mystical and religious values of life' (1986: 308). Mann's rejection of these positions is not compelling, as he relies on an untenable revisionism regarding the social composition of the early converts, and focuses too narrowly on what he calls 'economic-crisis theory'. The standard Marxist interpretation, he reasons, is easy to refute, for if 'economic crises and consequent political repression had played a major part in the rise of Christianity, it would have spread largely after A.D. 200 ... [whereas] the evidence points to a continuous spread of Christianity from soon after the crucifixion itself' (1986: 308). Mann does not cite any supportive evidence here, and as a matter of fact, most of the sources utilized by historians to estimate the Christian growth-pattern attest to *a late, two-phased expansion*: the first, modest but significant, arising in the aftermath of the failed Decian Persecution (*c.*250); and then a major transformation in the fortunes of the faith, upon Constantine's conversion in 312, whose imperial patronage and largesse triggered a massive influx of new and higher-status converts.[4] Indeed, on the eve of that momentous event, it has been estimated that Christians comprised, at best, roughly 10 per cent of the 50 to 60 million people who inhabited the Empire, and more plausibly only 3 to 5 per cent, of which the Greek-speaking East claimed a disproportionate concentration (cf. MacMullen 1984; Hopkins 1998). Mann's foundational premise, that Christianity grew rapidly and continuously from the outset, cannot be credited. His account is further weakened by the fact that such an 'onward and upward' momentum lacks sociological plausibility: not only is the 'convert pool' for a proselytizing religion usually diverse and changing over time, the 'context for conversion' is also in continuous flux, both on an internal level, as the new faith remakes itself through missionary advances and institutionalization, and also externally, as wider structural transformations impinge upon the social standing of the movement.[5]

In place of a 'materialist' explanation, Mann substitutes a Durkheimian reading, with religion furnishing the ideological and ritual grounds for communal identity and normative integration. As Mann expresses it, 'Christianity was not a response to a material crisis, nor was it a spiritual alternative to the material world. The crisis was one of social identity: What society do I belong to?' (1986: 309). Again, 'the early Christians were relatively happy and prosperous people, conscious of newfound wealth, powers, and vitality, seeking to articulate their emergent, interstitial social and personal identity in philosophy, ethics, and ritual. Their "suffering" was confined to the normative sphere, or deciding what *community* they belonged to' (1986: 309). In this rendering, Mann all but completely bypasses the pronounced 'world-negating' orientation of early Christianity, which ranged from a dismissive indifference to an openly bitter hostility towards the *saeculum* and the demonic forces that there held sway. 1 John 5.19: 'the whole world lies in wickedness'; 2 Peter 1.4: 'become partakers of the divine nature, escaping from the corruption that is in the world through lust'; 2 Clement 6.3: 'hate the things that are here'; James 2.5: 'has God not chosen the poor in the world to be rich in faith and heirs of the Kingdom that is promised'. Such passages could be culled almost at random from the texts of the first three centuries, and the 'Two Worlds' topos – here Satan and his minions, there the Heavenly Kingdom and His elect – was everywhere a staple of early Christian discourse. Believers prayed daily for a miraculous eschatological deliverance: 'Lord, Come!' was their fervent cry, in expectant hope that their divine redeemer would terminate this wicked aeon in a culminating act of cosmic violence and selective redemption. The early Christians undoubtedly sought 'community', but the one they thought they belonged to was only in transit, a 'sojourning' body of God's faithful, who had enrolled in the *militia Christi* to wage unrelenting war against the forces of darkness, until such time as their Saviour's return. Communalism in the early Church was ideologically tied to this millenarian, apocalyptic vision, which helps account for both the remarkable martyrdom complex that provided such a potent emotional and ritual centre for Christian expression, and also the equally daunting ascetic drive, which celebrated, among other things, encratic marriages, lifelong celibacy, and a principled turn against a host of worldly pleasures, all now transvalued as sinful pursuits that would bring eternal hell-fire in their wake.

It is perhaps a direct consequence of Mann's inattention to the defining features of the early Christian message – its apocalyptic worldview, its demonology, the primacy of faith over reason, the celebration of martyrs and virgins, its principled identification with the humble, the poor and the outcast – that he fails, ultimately, to provide a consistent account of Christianity's eventual ascendancy.[6] The interpretive synthesis he offers in the end is disjointed and chronologically confused. Christianity spread rapidly and widely, we were told, because it was ideologically organized to permit extensive recruitment and to sustain high levels of intensive commitment. Being 'universal, egalitarian, decentralized, and civilizing', the new faith was said to offer a solution to the contradictions of empire. However, in the latter third of his chapter, Mann shifts course, and argues that for the new faith to triumph, it was constrained to make a number of 'worldly compromises'. Hence the marked decline in the status of women within the Church ('Christianity intensified patriarchy'), the affirmation of the institution of slavery, and the hardening of a clerical order freed from lay controls. Mann observes: 'These revisions were part of a general move toward hierarchy, authority and orthodoxy that produced a recognizable "Catholic" church by about A.D. 250' (1986: 327). Now, since it was precisely this version of Christianity that would win Constantine's favour some half a century later, one must question Mann's original interpretation regarding the 'contradictions of empire' and Christianity's 'universal appeal', seeing as he is now allowing that those very contradictions and tensions had been taken on board long before the faith would garner imperial support. Mann correctly notes that, in the end, 'the *ecumene* was Romanized [and] Christianity was limited' (1986: 329), but in order to explicate that involved process, it is necessary to follow *in tempore* the actual internal transformations of the nascent faith, as it struggled to codify and refine its ideological principles, develop a functioning cultus, and fashion an ecclesiastical organization capable of both preserving and augmenting its beleagured membership – all in contested adaptation to ever changing circumstances within the wider world it simultaneously condemned yet sought to convert.

What analytical precept might be drawn from the foregoing? If even the best of our theories and models can bring only selected features of reality into discerning focus, it follows they will require supplementation and ongoing adjustment as we strive for greater comprehensiveness and precision in our analyses. In the case of Mann's IEMP model, it has provided original and substantive insights over vast ranges of social time and terrain, especially as regards questions of economic, political and military forms of power. An organizational materialist approach to ideology, however, is less viable, given the irreducibly subjective considerations that are involved in the creation, consolidation and competition of rival worldviews. The conveying infrastructures and media – an alphabetical script, literacy, epistles, codices, roads and shipping lanes, territorially based legal and political regulation – are capable of supporting and carrying quite diverse kinds of ideological traffic; what is sociologically and historically decisive is the quality and nature of the 'goods' communicated. *The study of ideological power thus requires a fully engaged sociology of knowledge or culture*, to explicate the cognitive and emotive content of ideas and images, as these derive salience and efficacy from the social circumstances of their derivation and functional purpose. To this necessary hermeneutic effort, a specification of the logistical conditions that facilitate the production and diffusion of cultural forms will contribute immensely; but contrary to the celebrated view of one of my university's most distinguished luminaries, the medium should never be conflated with the message.

Coda

Michael Mann's many-sided contributions to the field of historical sociology have justifiably earned the praise and critical attention of his peers. Not only do we benefit from an immensely rich and diverse body of substantive research – the temporal range of which extends from our initial passage into 'social caging' with the pristine state-based civilizations that arose along the banks of the Tigris and Euphrates some five thousand years ago, and presently continues with explorations into the driving forces of Globalization, as these restructure the institutions and conventions of contemporary societies. Along the way we have learned about the conquests of charioteering aristocracies, the Greek phalanx and the dawn of critical rationalism, Marius's Pole and the accomplishments of the Roman legion, the consequences of socially diffused literacy, the fiscal sinews of states (ancient, medieval and modern), the growth of nationalism and bureaucracy, industrial capitalism and class struggles, fascists and murderous ethnic cleansings. But Mann's achievements are also methodological and theoretical. He has reaffirmed the cogency of Weber's oft-ignored counsel that the 'construction of abstract ideal-types recommends itself not as an end but as a *means*', the aim of which is to reveal 'concrete cultural phenomena in their interdependence, their causal conditions and their *significance*' ([1904] 1949: 92). As he tacks back and forth between the conceptual and the empirical, Mann's IEMP model functions as just such a heuristic, capturing the entwined relations among the networks of power that dynamically constitute and transform the confederal and conflictive associations of social life. This is a deep historical sociology, as Mann repeatedly demonstrates that present social arrangements are the legacies of preceding collective actions, often dating from pasts long distant. Theory here does not efface or elide history; it explicates it, doing full justice to the contingencies and confluences that impart directionality to the temporally unfolding courses of agency and institutionalization that comprise our subject of interest.

The work is grounded, exemplary; given the grandeur of its scale (still unfinished!) and the skill of its execution, one might reasonably question whether it is in any way imitable.

Notes

1 Mann instructively testifies that most of the labels he utilized to classify the many social formations analysed in Volume I 'have been applicable *only* to specific eras in world-historical time. This was not my original theoretical stance. Rather, it has empirically turned out to be the case' (1986: 526).

2 Mann's counter to de Ste Croix is selective and fails to engage the immense body of evidence the historian packs into his very big book. Mann's own claim that 'military and political power organizations unconnected to conquest' were central in the Greek historical drama is uncharacteristically unnuanced (1986: 222), while the specific account he offers of the decline of *polis* (1986: 227–8) is a condensed and chronologically jumbled linkage of developments – the 'mercenary explosion', tactical innovations in warfare, the 'new tyranny', heightened civic factionalism, the rise of the Macedonian military monarchy – that need tighter specification of their complex interplay. In the 146 pages that comprise chapter 5 of my *Moral Codes and Social Structure in Ancient Greece* (1996), I take a stab at it.

3 Mann has been criticized on this score, by Anderson and Runciman most notably, who question several of Mann's arguments by alluding to comparable cases where the causal configurations failed to issue in similar results. A number of Mann's claims regarding the role of Christianity in facilitating the 'rise of the West', for example, have been challenged on the grounds that the Greek Orthodox variant provided no similar fillip for the Byzantines. Mann's thesis on the consequences of an early tenth- to eleventh-century breakthrough to highly intensive modes of agriculture in northwestern Europe is likewise challenged, as critics point to even more advanced productive techniques and commercial relations in Sung China. These are complex issues; their possible resolution must await the specialized research that will follow.

4 Even this 'bandwagon effect' should not be overestimated, as it would take another full century or more for Christianity to enroll within its ranks the vast rural majority of the population; Mann's statement that 'the final phase of the spread, from the town to the countryside' took place after *c*.250 is far too early and optimistic.
5 On these concerns, see Bryant (1998).
6 Mann's discussions of the other 'salvation religions' tend to be similarly under-weighted as regards the content of the belief-systems involved. The analysis of Hinduism is almost entirely focused on caste, and while undoubtedly central, this can hardly be understood without an accompanying exploration of the transmi-gration doctrine, and the specificities of the *karma-samsara-moksha* logic of both progressive and immediate salvation. Jainism and Buddhism are both situated by Mann as urban phenomena, with strong ethical appeals to artisanal and trading groups and of potential utility to Kshatriyas seeking to curtail the powers of the Brahminical priesthood. But here again, he says next to nothing about their respective doctrines (*ahimsa*, panpsychism, the Four Noble Truths, the Eight-fold Path, *nirvana*) or their organizational forms, which makes it difficult to understand why these religions were eventually marginalized by a revamped Hinduism, following the death of Ashoka, the 'Buddhist Constantine' (1986: 354–6). Nor does Mann look to the immensely significant salvation path of *bhakti*, passionate and sectarian devotion to a personal saviour god, which was culturally influential in India from at least the time of the *Bhagavad Gita* (*c*.300 BCE). Taoism, mentioned but briefly, is curiously styled a 'quietist, private cult', when in fact religious Taoism introduced a 'cyclical apocalyptic' theme that periodically provided the legitimacy for major social protests (e.g. the Yellow Turban Rebellion, 184–215), as well as a social reformist current, beginning with the Celestial Masters sect that actually established an autonomous regional 'theo-cracy' in southeastern China (*c*.142–215) in the later Han period. Zoroastrianism is properly identified as the first of the universal salvation religions, but the transcendent promise of this revelation, Mann speculates, was somehow usurped to furnish an 'immanent' ethnic and ruling-class ideology for the Persian imperial autocracy. The interpretation is a plausible one, but without a clearer specifi-cation of the particular mix of 'transcendent' and 'immanent' doctrinal compo-nents, Zoroastrianism's failure to rise to 'world-historic' status remains a puzzle.
  Only in the cases of Confucianism and early Islam does Mann provide a historical sociology that is sufficiently attentive to their respective ideas and beliefs, and this closer engagement seems to be related to the high social content and minimalist metaphysics of these two ideologies: the one politically oriented and kinship-based, while the other combines political, juridical and militarily preoccupations. Presumably for much the same reason, Mann's analyses of various secular ideologies – nationalism, socialism, fascism – likewise display a more secure and comfortable grasp.

References

Anderson, P. 1990. A Culture in Contraflow – I. *New Left Review* 180.
    [1986] 1992. Michael Mann's Sociology of Power. Chapter 4 in *A Zone of Engagement*. London: Verso.

Bryant, J. M. 1996. *Moral Codes and Social Structure in Ancient Greece: A Sociology of Greek Ethics from Homer to the Epicureans and Stoics.* New York: SUNY Press.

1998. Wavering Saints, Mass Religiosity, and the Crisis of Post-Baptismal Sin in Early Christianity. *Archives européennes de sociologie,* 39(1).

Goldthorpe, J. 1991. The Uses of History in Sociology. *British Journal of Sociology,* 42(2).

1997. Current Issues in Comparative Macrosociology: A Debate on Methodological Issues. *Comparative Social Research,* 16.

Hopkins, K. 1998. Christian Number and its Implications. *Journal of Early Christian Studies,* 6(2).

Kiser, E., and M. Hechter. 1998. The Debate on Historical Sociology: Rational Choice Theory and its Critics. *American Journal of Sociology,* 104(3).

Lustick, I. 1996. History, Historiography, and Political Science. *American Political Science Review,* 90(3).

MacMullen, R. 1984. *Christianizing the Roman Empire.* New Haven, CT: Yale University Press.

Mann, M. 1986. *The Sources of Social Power, Volume I: A History from the Beginning to 1760 AD.* Cambridge: Cambridge University Press.

1989. Macro-History and the Reform of Sociological Theory: An Interview with Michael Mann. Conducted by Wayne Hudson.

1993. *The Sources of Social Power, Volume II: The Rise of Classes and Nation-States.* Cambridge: Cambridge University Press.

1994. In Praise of Macro-sociology: A Reply to Goldthorpe. *British Journal of Sociology,* 45(1).

2000. Modernity and Globalization. Unpublished, given as the Wiles Lectures at Queen's University Belfast.

2004. *Fascists.* Cambridge: Cambridge University Press.

Martin, R. 1998. Progress in Historical Studies. *History and Theory,* 37(1).

Mullan, B. 1987. Michael Mann: An Interview. Chapter 7 in B. Mullan (ed.), *Sociologists on Sociology.* London: Croom Helm.

De Ste Croix, G. E. M. 1981. *The Class Struggle in the Ancient Greek World.* Ithaca: Cornell University Press.

Weber, M. 1949 [1904]. *The Methodology of the Social Sciences.* New York: Free Press.

Wickham, C. 1988. Historical Material, Historical Sociology. *New Left Review,* 171.

Part II

Types of power

Mann's theory of ideological power: sources,
     applications and elaborations

Philip S. Gorski

Even in its current, unfinished state, *The Sources of Social Power* is probably the single most ambitious work of historical sociology to appear during the last thirty years – years in which historical sociology has enjoyed a remarkable renaissance throughout the English-speaking world. The aims of *The Sources of Social Power* are grand in scope and three in number: (1) to challenge reified conceptions of society and determinist theories of history; (2) to reconceive sociology as the study of social power; and (3) to re-write Western history as a history of the growth and transformation of social power. No mean task!

This chapter does not attempt to recount or evaluate the arguments of *The Sources of Social Power* in their entirety; that is more than one chapter – and this author – can do. Rather, it focuses on one type of social power, what Mann refers to as 'ideological power'. It asks three questions: (1) What are the theoretical sources (and silences) of Mann's concept of ideological power? (2) What role does ideological power play (and not play) in Mann's interpretation of Western history? (3) How might we elaborate and improve on Mann's theory of ideological power? Its aims, in other words, are exegetical, evaluative and (re-)constructive.

My answers to these questions will become clearer below, but it may be useful to anticipate them here. Briefly, I will argue: (1) that Mann's concept of ideological power has two main sources: classical sociology of religion and the Marxism of the Second International; (2) that Mann's analysis of ideological power in Western history focuses mainly on two forms of ideological power: 'extensive' and 'authoritative' ideological power; and (3) that his conceptual framework and his historical narratives would be deepened and enriched by greater theoretical and empirical attention to two other forms of ideological power: 'intensive' and 'diffuse' ideological power.

Ideological power: sources and silences

The first volume of *The Sources of Social Power* opens with an amusing – and devastating – critique of a certain kind of vulgar sociology, which treats societies as things, and seeks law-like generalizations about social change. 'Societies' in the sense of bounded and unitary totalities, counters Mann, do not exist and never have. Society, he quips, is a 'mess'. And while it is possible to discover some order in this mess, its behaviour cannot be reduced to any general laws. But if societies don't really exist, and laws cannot be found, then what is the point of sociology? What are its proper objects and aims? These are big questions, and Mann gives bold answers. The object of sociology, he says, should be social power, and its aim to chart the growth and transformation of power through time and space.

In order to pursue this aim, one first needs a general theory of social power, and that is what Mann offers in the introduction to *The Sources of Social Power*. Social power, he argues, derives from four, main sources: meaning systems, material resources, physical violence and administrative infrastructure. Hence, we can distinguish between four basic types of social power: ideological, economic, military and political. Mann emphasizes that these four types are ideal-types *à la* Weber, and that real 'power networks' – the networks of interaction in which power is embedded and through which it is exercised – tend to draw on multiple power sources. They are 'impure' alloys in which one type of power is strengthened through the addition of others.

Of course, real existing power networks vary, not only in terms of their sources and composition, but along other dimensions as well, such as their scope and efficacy. Thus, Mann also distinguishes between 'extensive' power, which is high in (spatial) scope but low in (social) efficacy, and 'intensive' power, which is high in (social) efficacy but (often) low in (spatial) scope. In other words, extensive power networks combine a low degree of mobilization with control over a large swath of territory; while intensive power networks combine a high degree of mobilization with control over a smaller area. Mann also distinguishes between 'authoritative' and 'diffuse' forms of power.[1] Authoritative power is typically exercised through explicit commands, while diffuse power tends to operate through similarities in habits or practices. Mann is less clear about the conceptual underpinnings of this typology, but the key differences would seem to be in the degree of hierarchy and centralization, on the one hand, and on the other, in the degree to which the social actors themselves are aware of the power relationship. I will discuss this more below.

The word 'power' can be used in two rather different ways. Unlike many social scientists, Mann is very careful to keep them separate. The first is power in the zero-sum sense of 'power over'. It typically involves relations of exploitation, domination or coercion (e.g., the power of the bourgeoisie over the proletariat, the power of a monarch over her subjects, the power of an occupying army over the conquered population). Mann refers to this type of power as 'distributive' power, since it normally implies the (unequal) distribution of various life-goods (e.g. honour, wealth, territory, authority). The other kind of power is power in the non-zero-sum sense of a positive capacity or 'power to'. It typically involves systemic or organizational capacities (e.g. the productive capacities of capitalism, the administrative capacities of patrimonial states, the logistical range of a fighting force). Mann refers to this type of power as 'collective' power, because it denotes the capacity of a particular collectivity to change or control its socio-spatial environment. These two types of power are not necessarily exclusive of one another; on the contrary, most power networks embody both.

The analytic and descriptive potentials of Mann's theory of social power are enormous. By combining his distinctions between the various sources and forms of power, one can generate dozens of different types and sub-types of social power (e.g. extensive, military power or extensive, authoritative, military power). And one can use these types to characterize a wide range of highly diverse power networks – everything from the absolutist states of early modern Europe (extensive, authoritative, political) to the loose-knit, self-help circles of contemporary America (intensive, diffuse, ideological). Mann's theory also allows one to pose normatively salient questions regarding the interrelationships and tradeoffs between distributive and collective power in any given power network. The question, of course, is whether Mann fully taps these potentials in his analyses of social power. The answer, in my view, is that he does not.

Having reviewed Mann's general theory of power, I now turn to a more detailed examination of his approach to ideological power – its meaning and sources. The closest thing to a full definition may be found in volume two of *The Sources of Social Power*, where Mann states that: '*Ideological power* derives from the human need to find ultimate meaning in life, to share norms and values, and to participate in aesthetic and ritual practices' (1993: 7). In other words, ideological power flows from a deep-seated human desire to understand the nature of 'the world' and how one should act in it, and to belong to a community which shares and enacts these understandings.

Mann distinguishes between two different types of ideological power: 'transcendent' and 'immanent'. It should be noted that Mann uses the word 'transcendent' in a socio-spatial sense, rather than an ontological or phenomenological one. For him, ideological power is transcendent insofar as it encompasses and/or cross-cuts other power networks. Thus, the 'world religions' were 'transcendent', not in the sense that they divided the cosmos into mundane and otherworldly spheres, but rather insofar as their power networks encompassed and cross-cut political and economic ones, such as empires or classes.[2] Immanence is also used in a strictly sociological sense. Immanent ideological power refers to the solidarity or morale of a specific social group. An example would be the sense of identity and purpose which members of the working class have derived from socialist ideology.[3]

What are the theoretical sources of Mann's concept of 'ideological power'? Two seem key: the sociology of religion and Marxism. About the first, Mann is quite explicit. In volume one of *The Sources of Social Power*, he presents his theory of ideological power as an elaboration and synthesis of Weber's and Durkheim's work on religion.[4] For example, his claim that ideologies address questions of 'ultimate meaning' strongly echoes Weber's discussions of the world religions, and his claims that ideological power 'can be wielded by those who monopolize a claim to meaning' (1993: 22) is reminiscent of Weber's (1978: 1158–1211) analysis of 'hierocratic authority'. Similarly, the view that ideologies generate and reinforce a set of 'shared understandings of how people should act morally in their relations with each other [that] are necessary for sustained social cooperation' [*ibid.*] is clearly an adaptation of Durkheim's claim that religions instil and sustain a sense of 'moral similarity' and 'mechanical solidarity', which serves, in turn, as the normative foundation for relations of cooperation and exchange (Durkheim 1964: 70–110). Likewise, his invocation of 'ritual and aesthetic practices' recalls Durkheim's discussions of 'collective effervescence' and the Durkheimian approach to religion more generally.

While there is no mention of Marxism in Mann's discussions of ideological power, there are good reasons for suspecting its influence. The first is Mann's choice of the word 'ideology' – a word with strongly Marxist undertones – over a more neutral alternative, such as 'culture' – a word which is more in vogue at the moment.[5] But the Marxist influence on Mann probably goes deeper than simple word choice. For there are obvious affinities between Mann's notion of 'immanent ideological power' and the revisionist theories of ideology advanced during the early twentieth century by leading Marxists like Gramsci, Lukács and Lenin (for an overview, see Eagleton 1991). Different as their views were in other regards, all three believed that 'socialist ideology' was a necessary precondition of working-class solidarity and thus of socialist revolution. Mann's innovation lies in broadening this analysis beyond the proletariat and identifying ideology as a key ingredient in the solidarity of other social groups.[6] Mann's treatment of ideology also has deep affinities with another, later strand of Marxist thinking: Althusserian structuralism. For Althusser, of course, ideology was not only, or even primarily, a set of ideas; it was first and foremost a set of organizational networks or 'ideological state apparatuses', which included, *inter alia*, the church, the school and the bourgeois media (Althusser 1972). Like Althusser, Mann is at least as interested in the organizational base of a particular ideology as he is in its symbolic content, and perhaps even more so. In fact, at one point, Mann refers to his own theoretical perspective as 'organizational materialism'. Thus, while Marxism may not appear in the opening credits of *The Sources of Social Power*, it does seem to have figured quite heavily behind the scenes.

After looking at the theoretical sources of 'ideological power', it may be useful to ponder the theoretical silences as well. By 'theoretical silences', I mean the various strands of thought, either in Marxism or the sociology of religion, which are absent from Mann's theorizing. On the religion side, the most notable absence is the phenomenological school, which defines and analyses religion, not as a system of beliefs or rituals, but as a type of experience, namely, the experience of (self-)transcendence (i.e. a rupture in 'everyday' or 'wide-awake' consciousness). This school has a distinguished lineage stretching back from Berger and Luckmann through James and Simmel to Hegel. On the Marxist side, the most striking absence is the psychoanalytically informed version of Marxism championed, not only by the Frankfurt school (Horkheimer, Adorno, Marcuse, Fromm, etc.), but also the French school of structural Marxism (e.g. Althusser and Poulantzas), a school, interestingly, from which Mann draws other important ideas. Notable, too, is the inattention to, and even dismissal of, post-modern and post-structural brands of social theory as represented, for example, by Barthes and Foucault.

There are also certain analytical silences in Mann's discussion. By 'analytical silences', I mean a lack of attention – theoretical or empirical – to certain forms of ideological power which are contained in, or implied by, Mann's overall theory. Looking more closely at Mann's analysis of ideological power, we see that it is premised on two key oppositions: distributive *vs.* collective, and intensive *vs.* extensive. Drawing on these categories, Mann distinguishes between two types of ideological power – transcendent ideological power, which is collective and extensive, and immanent ideological power, which is distributive and intensive. But there are two other permutations of ideological power which can be derived from these oppositions: intensive and collective and diffuse and distributive. Strangely, they remain unexplored and nameless in Mann's work.

Of course, we should not place too much weight on theoretical or analytical completeness. Mann intends his theory of power as a heuristic device, rather than a 'general theory', so the fact that Mann ignores or downplays certain traditions of thought or dimensions of ideology is problematic only if, and to the degree that, it generates interpretive blind-spots or explanatory problems in analyses of historical change. Thus, it is to those analyses that I now turn.

The Protestant ethic revised: ideological power and the rise of the West

What explains the 'rise of the West'? Why did the Christian civilization of Western Europe and North America become the 'dominant power actor' of the modern world? This is one of the great puzzles of modern social science, of course, and it is also a central focus of Mann's work. Mann's solution can be found in the concluding chapters of *The Sources of Social Power*, Volume 1. What allowed the West to jump ahead of the rest, he says, was capitalism and 'organic states'. But what explains the genesis of capitalism, and the formation of 'organic states'? And when did it occur? These are the key questions.

Where capitalism is concerned, Mann's answer is as clear as it is unorthodox. Like Weber, Mann believes that the birth of capitalism was due, in no small part, to the peculiarities of Western Christianity. Unlike Weber, however, he locates the origins of Western capitalism a good deal earlier, in the medieval period, rather than the early modern era; and he identifies Catholicism and the nobility, rather than Protestantism and the bourgeoisie, as the key actors. They were key, he says, because they possessed ideological power which could be translated into 'normative pacification'. The ideological power of Catholicism was transcendent in form. With its vast network of churches, cloisters, courts and colleges, the Western Church was far more extensive than any other power organization in the West; indeed, it was the only organization which encompassed Europe as a whole. And with its systems of theology and ethics and its rich liturgies and symbols, the Medieval Church could provide a relatively coherent account of 'ultimate meaning' and the 'ritual and aesthetic practices' which individuals craved. The ideological power of the landed nobility took the form of immanent morale. To the degree that this morale was premised on the privileged place of the nobility within the institutions and teachings of the Western Church, transcendence and immanence were intertwined. Together, says Mann, these two networks of ideological power created fertile soil for the development of capitalism because they 'helped ensure a basic level of normative pacification', in which property relations could be stabilized and commerce could grow.

The actual seeds of capitalism, however, were economic, rather than ideological. They were first planted within the agricultural sector, where 'intensive' forms of cultivation laid the foundations of future prosperity. Here, too, Mann's account is both similar to, and different from, Weber's. It is similar in adopting a multi-causal model of capitalist development which emphasizes both ideological and economic factors. But it is different in focusing on agriculture and the countryside; for Weber, of course, it was the commercial elites of the Medieval cities who served as the early 'carriers' of the 'capitalist spirit' (Weber 1988: 312–443; Weber 1978: 1332–3). Put in the barest possible terms, then, Mann's argument is that transcendent power plus immanent morale equals normative pacification, and (extensive) normative pacification plus (intensive) agricultural technique equals capitalism.

Mann's argument regarding the formation of 'organic states' is a bit more orthodox but also a bit less clear. It is more orthodox in the sense that it highlights the impact of war and geopolitics, as has most recent work on state formation in early modern Europe (for an overview, see Gorski 2001a). The basic argument, which Mann accepts, at least as a starting point, is essentially as follows. During the sixteenth century, the costs of warfare were greatly increased by a number of interrelated technological and tactical innovations, such as the diffusion of gunpowder and firearms and the increasing use of massed infantry. Following Michael Howard, these developments are commonly referred to as 'the military revolution'.[7] The increased costs of war led to increased political conflict. To survive, rulers had to raise more and more taxes, and maintain larger and larger armies, and to do that, they needed to expand their administrative staffs, none of which was to the liking of their subjects, great or small. This expansion and centralization of state administrations often went together with a weakening of traditional 'liberties and privileges' and the marginalization of representative assemblies – in a word: 'absolutism'.[8] Thus, geopolitical competition and state formation went hand-in-hand. In Charles Tilly's well-known phrase: 'states made wars, and wars made states' (Tilly 1985). Because of its emphasis on war, I have referred to this perspective as the 'bellicist approach'. Mann affirms the basic tenets of this approach when he concludes that 'states and the multi-state civilization [of Europe] developed primarily in response to pressures emanating from the geopolitical and military spheres' (1986: 511). But he also qualifies them by inserting the word 'primarily'. For Mann, the dynamics of early modern state formation are not entirely captured by the phrases 'absolutism', 'administrative centralization' and 'military revolution'. State power was also developing in other ways and for other reasons which are not part of the orthodox account. In that account, state formation is usually conceptualized, if only implicitly, as the concentration of power in the hands of the sovereign. Mann does not deny the

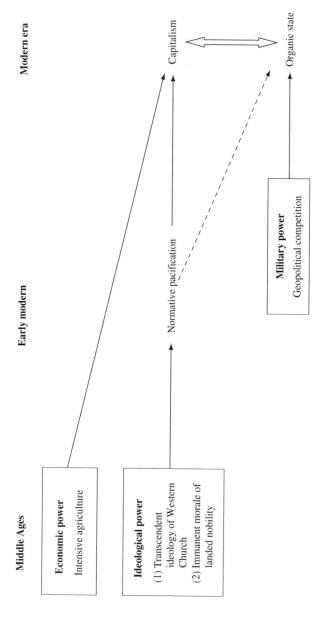

Figure 6.1. The rise of the West: Mann's model

importance of this sort of power – what he terms 'despotic power' – particularly for absolutist regimes. But he does insist on the significance of another type of power, what he refers to as 'infrastructural power', or 'the power to coordinate civil society'. And he argues that this type of power was especially important in 'constitutionalist' regimes, where the powers of representative assemblies remained more or less intact (1986: 477). In fact, he implies that 'infrastructural power' may have actually been more effective than despotic power. For how else are we to explain the hegemonic status attained by England and other constitutional regimes at various points in modern history? But provocative as this point is, it raises still further questions. Where, one might ask, does infrastructural power come from, and in what does it consist? What networks is it embodied in, and how did they come into being? Strangely enough, Mann does not give us any clear answers to these questions.

Let us put this problem to the side for one moment and focus on the argument as a whole. Combining these two lines of thought – about capitalism and about states – we see that Mann has used the four sources of social power to develop a general account of the 'rise of the West'. The model consists of two parts: a (broadly) neo-Weberian explanation of Western capitalism, which focuses on the role of ideological power in the growth and transformation of economic power; and a (mainly) neo-Hintzian explanation of early modern state formation that focuses on the role of military power in the growth and transformation of political power. While Mann treats these two processes as analytically separable, he does not regard them as historically unconnected. On the contrary! He argues that the economic surpluses generated by Western capitalism were crucial to the growth of European states. And he suggests that the competitive and multipolar character of the European state system provided fertile ground for the expansion of Western capitalism. In his view, state formation and capitalist growth were entwined with one another, and reinforced one another. Capitalist growth generated economic resources for states, and produced more organic societies, while organic states provided a favourable context for capitalist expansion. The overall argument is presented graphically in Figure 6.1. The solid arrows represent clearly specified causal relations. The dotted arrow represents less clearly specified causal relations. And the double-pointed arrow represents interaction effects – 'entwinings', in Mann's language. The graphic also contains a temporal dimension. Ideological power is placed to the left of military power because 'normative pacification' antedated the military revolution historically. Having laid out Mann's argument, let us now examine it more closely.

Logically speaking, Mann's model could be criticized on a number of different levels. First, one could argue that the temporal parameters are incorrectly specified. (Did normative pacification begin in the Middle Ages? Or did it really occur later?) Second, one could argue, as I have already done, that certain concepts are inadequately specified or explained. (What is 'infrastructural power'? Where does it come from?) Third, one could argue that key links are missing from the model. (Was there an important connection between ideological power and political or military power?) Finally, one could argue that the model as a whole is logically insufficient, because it fails to identify key differences between the West and the rest. (Didn't 'Medieval' China exhibit high levels of normative pacification?)

The criticisms I have to make fall into the first three categories.[9] Broadly speaking, they concern the when (periodization), the what (conceptualization) and the why (explanation) of Mann's argument. Let me begin with the issue of periodization, specifically, Mann's periodization of 'normative pacification'. Mann's notion of 'normative pacification' is strikingly similar to the concept of 'social disciplining' used by many European historians. The study of social disciplining has been something of a growth industry in recent years and much of this work has focused on the role of religion. Numerous articles and books have been written about the efforts of the Church to regulate social life and suppress sinful behaviour (see Hsia 1989; Gorski 2000b). But most of this work has focused, not on the Middle Ages, but on the early modern period (c. 1500–1750). There is a reason for this focus. The three major 'confessions' of the post-Reformation era – Catholicism, Lutheranism and Calvinism – were all concerned – one might even say obsessed – with 'discipline', meaning the outward conformity of the religious community to Christian morality. And they all (re)established special courts and other church bodies to enforce it. The Calvinist consistories, Lutheran marriage courts, and the various Inquisitions are the best known and most important examples. Nor was this campaign restricted to the religious realm. It also spilled over into the realm of social provision, where religious and political reformers joined together in an effort to transform 'vagrants' and other ne'er-do-wells into obedient and productive subjects through the introduction of more rational – and often more punitive – systems of poor relief. Similar developments can be observed in the military realm as well, where new regimes of discipline and drill were implemented. Indeed, it is hard to find an arena of early modern social life which was *not* affected by these new disciplinary practices, which is why I have spoken in other contexts of an early modern 'disciplinary revolution' (Gorski 1993; 2003). Of course, this was not the first attempt to forge more disciplined selves and societies. The monastic reform movements of the Middle Ages and the civic 'police ordinances' of the Renaissance are evidence enough of that. But it was the first to succeed on a broad scale (in the West, anyway). From this period on, crime, illegitimacy and other indicators of social 'disorder' commenced a steady decline which continued until the late eighteenth century (Gorski 2003). It should be noted that the disciplinary revolution was most intensive – and evidently also most successful – in those areas of Europe which came under the sway of Calvinism (e.g. the Netherlands and England) – the very areas which would dominate the global economy until they were overtaken by another society with even deeper Calvinist roots – the United States. Thus, it could be that Mann and Weber are both (half) right about the connection between religion and capitalism – Mann about the key mechanism (pacification), and Weber about the key period (early modern).

This brings me to my second set of criticisms. They concern Mann's discussion of early modern state formation. As we have seen, Mann accepts the basic premises of the bellicist approach. But he also seeks to go beyond it – with his concept of 'infrastructural power', for example. The theoretical thrust of this concept is clear enough: a highly centralized state may be good at neutralizing rival power networks but poor at building up its own. In Mann's language, it may be high in distributive power, but low in collective power. One thinks, in this context, of despotic states, both new and old. Perhaps this is why Mann contrasts 'infrastructural power' with 'despotic power'. Be that as it may, the key point is that administrative and political centralization are not the sole determinants of state strength. Strength is also a function of 'infrastructure' – of the organizational networks through which states 'coordinate civil society'. But while the theoretical thrust of Mann's concept is clear, the empirical reference remains vague. It is not clear which 'organizational networks' he is talking about. One possible answer is church networks. The Western Church played a significant role in the governance of European society throughout the Middle Ages. It disseminated political decrees, interpreted and enforced the law, and provided poor relief and health care. The early modern era witnessed a major expansion in this role. Churches began to maintain public records (e.g. of births, deaths and marriages), provide popular education, police popular behaviour and monitor cultural life, amongst other things. The early modern era also witnessed a major expansion – and tightening – of the networks themselves. The quantity and quality of parish clergy and church buildings increased dramatically. So did the number – and power – of lay offices and institutions. In the language of the specialist, church networks were 'filling in'. And not only that. They were also becoming more tightly entwined with political and social networks. Rulers now exercised greater control over ecclesiastical officials and institutions, and churches often enlisted the aid of the state in the enforcement of discipline and the suppression of dissent. So if Mann is correct in arguing that the infra-structural power of European states increased during the early modern period – and there is good reason to think that it did – then one reason may be the expansion of church networks and their 'entwining' with political ones.

It is worth noting, at least in passing, that this focus on church networks also sheds light on another puzzle raised by Mann: the apparent affinity between constitutional regimes and infrastructural power. Why did constitutional regimes, such as Britain or the Netherlands, have more powerful infrastructures than absolutist ones like France or Spain? Part of the answer, no doubt, is that absolutizing princes often dismantled or undercut potential sources of infrastructural power, such as civic com-munes or regional parliaments, in their quest for despotic power. But this cannot be the whole answer, because there were also other states, such as the Polish Republic or the Kingdom of Hungary which had strong constitutions and weak infrastructures. Another part of the answer, I would suggest, was Calvinism. Calvinism played a crucial role in the defence of constitutional government. It provided the political muscle and the ideological backbone for anti-absolutist uprisings throughout Western and Central Europe, not only in Britain and the Netherlands, but also in Hungary and Poland and, less successfully, in France (Gorski 2001b; Te Brake 1998; Evans and Thomas 1991). Calvinism also generated immense amounts of infrastructural power, at least in those countries where it took root, such as Switzerland, Britain and the Netherlands. This is because Calvinists were more concerned with reli-gious discipline and social order than Catholics and Lutherans were, and because they developed more effective systems for maintaining it. Thus, the apparent correlation between constitutional regimes and infrastruc-tural power is at least partly spurious, insofar as both of these outcomes are the product of a third factor which was not included in Mann's model: Calvinism.

There is at least one more problem with Mann's analysis of early modern state formation, a type three problem involving a missing causal link, in this case between ideological power on the one hand and political power on the other. As we have seen, Mann is openly critical of the bellicists for ignoring the significance of infrastructural power. However, he tacitly accepts their claim that the growth of despotic power was primarily due to geopolitical and military factors. I am less prepared to do so. This does not mean that I regard the bellicist perspective as false. Bellicist scholars have identified a number of the key mechanisms which drove early modern state formation. But they have not been able to produce a general model of early modern state formation which fully explains the structural and political variations in which they are interested. Even the most nuanced and complex discussions of the relationship between geopolitics and state-building have generated perplexing anomalies and theoretical inconsistencies.[10] One reason for this, perhaps even the main reason, is that they have systematically ignored religion. This is unfortunate, because 'bringing religion back in' greatly enhances our understanding of early modern states and regimes. While disputes over war finance were often an ingredient in fights between advocates of absolutism and defenders of constitutionalism, they were rarely the only one. Confessional conflict – usually between Calvinists and Catholics – was often a factor as well, and it played a catalytic role in many of the most violent and consequential conflicts of the sixteenth and seventeenth centuries, from the French Wars of Religion and the Dutch Revolt through the Bohemian Uprising to the English Civil War. Where the militant Calvinists and their republican allies won, as in the (Northern) Netherlands and England, the powers of representative assemblies were preserved and expanded; where they lost, as in France and Bohemia, they were effectively abolished, and the road was paved for extreme forms of princely absolutism. There was also an Imperial-German variant of confessional conflict, which pitted Lutheran 'estates' against a Calvinist monarch, as in Prussia and (some parts of) Hessia. In these cases, a Calvinist victory culminated in royal absolutism. Thus, while there is no law-like relationship between religion and regime, it is evident that confessional conflict, like geopolitics, was a key mechanism in the development of early modern states.

Greater attention to religion also helps to explain a second, key aspect of state formation: the degree of bureaucratization. The degree of bureaucratization among early modern states was highly variable. It was once assumed that bureaucracy went together with absolutism – and patrimonialism with constitutionalism. If this were the case, then there would be no need to analyse administration separately from regime. But revisionist work has shown this claim to be insupportable. Some states, such as Spain and France, had absolutist regimes and venal administrations; others, such as Britain and Sweden (in its 'Age of Liberty'), had constitutional regimes and bureaucratic administrations. As Thomas Ertman has recently noted, the more bureaucratic states form an arc stretching from the British Isles through Scandinavia and down into the German-speaking lands, while venal states also run from the northwest to the southeast, from Spain through France and into Italy (Ertman 1997). Interestingly, the divide between bureaucratic and venal states lines up closely with the border between Protestant and Catholic Europe. The correlation is not perfect. There were some Protestant countries which were not particularly bureaucratic, such as the Dutch Republic; and there were some Catholic countries, like Bavaria, which were. But the most bureaucratic states (England, Sweden and Prussia) were all Protestant, while the most venal ones (Spain, France, Naples) were all Catholic. I have argued elsewhere that this pattern was the result of two processes (Gorski, 2005). The first was the invention of venality during the Papal Schism, and its subsequent diffusion from the Papal Curia to the monarchies of the Mediterranean (i.e. France and the Iberian and Italian Peninsulas). The second was the invention of a non-proprietary system of clerical office-holding during the Reformation, and their subsequent diffusion to the state administrations of most Northern European polities. It is the interaction of these processes, I conclude, which goes furthest towards explaining the geographical distribution of bureaucratic and venal systems of office-holding in early modern Europe.

Of course, one could take this critique of the bellicist perspective even further, by emphasizing the various ways in which religion and the Reformation fed into geopolitical competition and the military revolution. In their discussions of early modern state formation, bellicists often point to the marked increase in the scope and intensity of warfare during the sixteenth and seventeenth centuries.[11] And they usually attribute this increase to 'the military revolution' and, more particularly, to the use of gunpowder, which made existing stone fortifications obsolete, and to the use of lightly armed mercenary soldiers, who could be trained and equipped more easily and more quickly than armed knights. I do not doubt that this is part of the explanation for the increased scope and intensity of early modern warfare. But I do question whether it is the whole explanation. After all, most of the major wars of this period, whether civil or multinational, were at least nominally about religion. Of course, religion was rarely the only ingredient in these conflicts. But by introducing new confessional and sectarian cleavages into old political and dynastic conflicts, the Reformation destabilized the *status quo ante* and created new opportunities for political consolidation and expansion – and new occasions for political conflict and resistance. Over time, conflicts about religion and conflicts about politics tended to become entwined with one another. Unlike most proponents of the bellicist position, Mann gives these dynamics their proper due.

Up to the seventeenth century grievances expressed in religious terms were paramount in social struggles; yet they took on an increasingly state-bounded form. The breakup of Europe's religious unity in the sixteenth century was predominantly into politically demarcated units. Religious wars came to be fought either by rival states or by factions who struggled over the constitutions of the single, monopolistic state in which they were located. (1986: 435)

But there is another connection between ideological and military power which Mann does *not* recognize, and that is the connection between religious and military discipline. In some cases, this connection was quite obvious and direct. Here, one thinks especially of the New Model Army, whose discipline and morale were grounded in Puritan morality and the elan of the 'elect' (Gentles 1992). In other cases, the connection was probably more subtle and indirect. Here, one thinks more of the (re-)discovery of drill by Maurice of Orange and Simon Stevin – one of the key elements of the military revolution (Hahlweg 1987). While the models on which they drew were Roman in origin, one cannot help but wonder whether their receptiveness was not heightened by their convictions, which were strongly (if not orthodoxly) Calvinist. Nor are these the only examples one could cite. On the contrary, most of the great innovations in early modern training and tactics seem to have been pioneered by ascetic Protestants – Oliver Cromwell, Gustavus Adolpus, Frederick William I. Thus, there are good grounds for supposing an 'elective affinity' between ascetic Protestantism and military 'rationalism' – and for adding an arrow to Mann's model, an arrow from 'ideological power' to 'military power'.

Thus far, I have criticized Mann on three counts. First, I have argued that his periodization of 'normative pacification' is problematic. While one might, perhaps, speak of an extensive phase of pacification during the Middle Ages, it seems clear that the more intensive – and probably more decisive – phase came later, following the Reformation. I have also argued – and this is the second point – that Mann's discussion of 'infrastructural power' is more theoretical gesture than historical analysis. More concretely, I have argued that the sources of infrastructural power were largely ideological, and that church networks were the heart of state infrastructure during this period. Finally, I have argued that Mann's model misses the key connections between ideological power, on the one hand, and political and military power on the other. Specifically, I have suggested that confessional conflict and ascetic Protestantism played a crucial role in shaping early modern political regimes and administrative structures, and thus contributed to the development, not only of infrastructural power, but of despotic power as well. In addition, I have suggested that religious discipline may also have exercised a subtle influence on military discipline. These various lines of criticism are summarized graphically in the revised version of Mann's model presented in Figure 6.2.

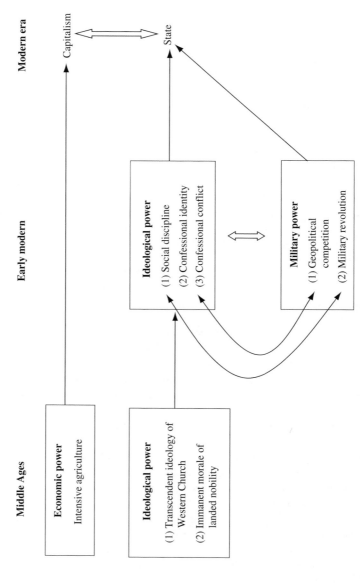

Middle Ages　　　　　　　**Early modern**　　　　　　　**Modern era**

Economic power
Intensive agriculture

Capitalism

State

Ideological power

(1) Transcendent ideology of Western Church

(2) Immanent morale of landed nobility

Ideological power

(1) Social discipline

(2) Confessional identity

(3) Confessional conflict

Military power

(1) Geopolitical competition

(2) Military revolution

Figure 6.2. Ideological power and the rise of the West: Mann's model revised

Their positive content is three-fold: (1) greater interpretive stress on the early modern period as the key turning point in Western history – the period when the West surged ahead of the rest; (2) greater explanatory stress on the role of 'ideological power' (the Protestant and Catholic Reformations) in the transformation, not only of economic power (capitalism), but also of political and military power ('organic states' and 'the military revolution'); and (3) greater theoretical stress on intensive and collective forms of ideological power – on the ways in which post-Reformation religiosity mobilized human energies and directed them towards social transformation. The third point may well be the key one, at least from a theoretical point of view. As I indicated in the first section of this chapter, the concept of intensive ideological power is implicit in Mann's general theory of social power but absent from his specific typologies of ideological power, which focus on extensive (transcendent) and distributive (immanent) forms of ideology. It is now clear that this analytical silence has heuristic consequences – negative ones. In the following section, I will suggest that the (relative) absence of diffuse forms of ideological power from Mann's analysis may also be a source of interpretive and explanatory problems as well.

The end of ideology? Ideological power and 'causal primacy'

In the opening pages of *The Sources of Social Power*, Volume II, Mann takes up the question of causal 'primacy'. He begins by criticizing 'pure or monocausal theories' such as orthodox Marxism, and rejecting all claims of 'ultimate primacy' – claims that a particular level or dimension of social reality (e.g. production, the material) is always and everywhere the decisive one. But he does not eschew the search for primacy as such. Rather, he argues for a more restrictive notion of primacy, a historically delimited type which obtains only in particular times and places. He then presents his own conclusions about primacy. They are as follows. 'Medieval Europe', he says, 'had been decisively structured by Christendom' (1993: 1). But 'Christianity lost much of its force from the sixteenth to the eighteenth century, broken by mutually reinforcing developments, in economic, military and political power'. After that, says Mann, it became sufficiently unimportant, that it can be safely omitted from subsequent discussion (1986: 472). 'During the eighteenth century', he adds later, 'two sources of social power, the economic and the military, preponderated'. In the nineteenth century, however, 'economic and political power sources began to dominate' (1993: 1). Ideological power had not disappeared, of course. But its key sources were now classes and nations, rather than clergies and churches; socialism and nationalism, however, could not fully or permanently fill the void left by socialism and nationalism. Broadly speaking, then, Mann argues that ideological power has declined since the Reformation, at least relative to other power sources.

This is a somewhat different kind of argument than the one we examined in the preceding section. It concerns causal weighting rather than causal connections. Accordingly, the kinds of objections to which it is susceptible are slightly different, though they, too, are of three basic types. First, one could argue that the evidence Mann considers has not been weighed properly. Secondly, one could argue that important evidence has not been weighed at all, either because it has been accidentally overlooked or because it has been systematically excluded, due to biases within the conceptual framework. Finally, one could argue that the weighing procedure itself is problematic, either because the metric is unclear or because it has been applied inconsistently. My comments will be mainly, if not exclusively, of the first two sorts.

Mann's conclusions about the declining significance of ideological power is premised on two basic claims. The first is that the splintering of Western Christendom decreased the 'extensive' power of the Church, and hence 'its capacity for social organization' (1986: 471). The second is that the rise of Protestantism decreased the overall power of religion (1986: 470).

Now, the major premise of the first argument is clearly correct, at least in the following sense: where there had been one, unified religious network, which encompassed and shaped all of Europe, at least to some degree, there were now many. To be precise, there were now three major networks (Roman Catholic, Lutheran, and Reformed or Calvinist) as well as several minor ones (e.g. Baptists, Unitarians, and so on). Thus, Europe's church networks became (relatively) more fragmented and less centralized. But the conclusion which Mann draws from this premise does not necessarily follow. There is no *prima facie* reason to assume that a (relative) decline in extensive (and perhaps authoritative) power results in an overall decline in the 'capacity for social for organization', since the decline in extensive (and authoritative) power could have been counterbalanced by gains in intensive (or diffuse) power. And, in fact, there is considerable evidence to suggest that this is precisely what happened. As we saw in the preceding section, the Reformation era was a period, not only of state-building, but of church-building as well, a period in which the numbers of church officials, church buildings, church organizations and church rituals were all dramatically on the upswing. As a result, most churches were probably much better able to mobilize and control their followers than they had been before. Thus, while church networks did lose their capacity to organize and unify Europe as a whole, they did not lose their 'capacity for social organization' *per se*. On the contrary, one could argue that the churches' capacity for social organization actually increased during the Reformation era, insofar as they were better able to shape individual conduct and penetrate into everyday life.

Mann's arguments about Protestantism are subject to the same objection. Insofar as it failed to bring all of Europe under its sway, Protestantism was not a 'transcendent, society-creating force', at least not on a Continental scale. But this loss of extensive or 'transcendent' power could have been – and in my view was – counter-balanced by gains in intensive, 'society-creating' power. For while Protestant Churches failed to recreate Western Christendom, they were quite successful in forging territorial societies. By diffusing the literate biblical culture of the elites to the middling and even lower strata, and imposing greater doctrinal and liturgical consistency and religious and social discipline, the Protestant Churches of the Reformation era actually decreased the level of cultural stratification and regional segmentation within the territories under their control and were, in this sense, 'society-creating' and even 'transcendent' (Gorski 2000a).

In sum, I am not sure that Mann has weighed the early modern evidence properly. The root of the problem would seem to be the unstated minor premise which underlies his conclusions, namely, that the 'capacity for social organization' is solely (or at least mainly) a function of extensive (or perhaps authoritative) power. But as Mann himself has emphasized, the capacity for social organization can be measured in different ways. One can look at the number of people or the amount of territory (extensive) organized, or one can look at the level of mobilization or the degree of control (intensive). While the Reformation may have brought a decline in the former capacity, it also brought an increase in the latter. Thus, it is not so obvious that 'ideological power' declined during the early modern era; in fact, depending upon how one weights the relative losses and gains in extensive and intensive power, one could well conclude (as I would) that it actually increased, at least in absolute terms.

What about the modern evidence? Here, Mann would appear to be on safer ground. After all, church networks in the West have now lost much of their intensive power as well, especially in Europe. The sinking levels of 'religious participation' (e.g. church attendance, church marriages, etc.) and 'religious authority' (judicial, political, cultural, etc.) documented by several generations of sociologists is certainly ample evidence of that. But this decline is probably more recent, and less complete, than Mann, and most social scientists, appear to realize (for an excellent overview, see

Höllinger 1996). To be sure, one can find harbingers of 'secularization' quite early – in the relaxation of church discipline during the late seventeenth century, or the growth of religious scepticism among intellectuals during the eighteenth. But the real turning point seems to have come a good deal later; it was not until the early twentieth century that religious disaffection and disaffiliation became mass phenomena, and church control of schools and social provision was seriously weakened or abolished. Until this time, Western church networks retained a great deal of mobilizing power, and remained a key element of state infrastructures. So even if Mann is correct about the ultimate outcome, the decline of ideological power – and he may not be, for reasons discussed below – he is most likely wrong about the timing, because the real decline in church power occurred a good deal later than he suggests – almost four centuries after the Reformation.

Despite these problems of periodization, it should be emphasized that Mann's explanation for the decline of church networks is still superior to the conventional accounts of 'secularization'. The weakening of church networks was due, not to generic processes of 'modernization' or 'social differentiation', as the classical theories of 'secularization' imply (Tschannen 1992). Rather, it was due to the emergence of rival networks (states, nations, classes) and rival ideologies (liberalism, nationalism, socialism) which provided competing forms of ritual participation and alternative sources of 'ultimate meaning'.

What Mann's account misses, however, is the persistence of religious networks and ideologies into the modern era, their 'entwining' with secular networks and ideologies, and the effects which this had on the latter. Consider nationalism. Mann is right in emphasizing the relationship between religion and 'proto-national consciousness' in the early modern era (Gorski 2000b; Hastings 1996; Marx 2003). And he is also right in emphasizing the growth of a secular strand of nationalist discourse following the French Revolution. But it is wrong to imply that secular nationalism *replaced* religious nationalism. The religious strand of nationalist discourse remained strong among segments of the European population until well into the twentieth century, and survives even today in places like Ireland, Poland and, to a certain degree, the United States (O'Brien 1988; Hutchison and Lehmann 1994; Zubrzycki 2000). Class formation was also affected by church networks. The story of class formation is not just a story of class struggle between labour and capital; it is also the story of a struggle between socialist and confessional movements and parties for the hearts and minds of workers (Rueschemeyer, Stephens and Stephens 1992; Luebbert 1991; Nipperdey 1988; McLeod 1995; Hölscher 1989). And the outcome of this latter struggle was important, not only for the salience of class cleavages, but also for the direction of social reform – liberal, social-democratic, or Christian democratic.[12] And in this sense, church networks also influenced the second wave of European state formation: the emergence of 'welfare states'.

This is not to say that church networks retained the 'ultimate primacy' which Mann claims they had in the Middle Ages. Nor is it to dispute the growing importance, and perhaps even dominance, of other networks in the modern era. Rather, it is to suggest that Mann's claims about the timing and extent of their decline are misleading and somewhat overstated. Church networks did not lose 'much of their force from the sixteenth to the eighteenth centuries'; in some ways, their force actually increased, at least for ordinary people. Nor is it 'safe' to omit them from the next century either, when they continued to exert considerable force, not only in the private lives of individuals, but on the shapes of other networks, as well. Indeed, one could argue – and some historians have argued – that Western Christianity reached its apogee, not in the Middle Ages, but in the nineteenth century. For all these reasons, I would argue, church networks weighed a good deal more heavily; and quite a bit longer than Mann allows.

Thus far, I have argued that Mann's account of ideological decline is marred by a mis-weighing of the evidence on church networks – the first of the three types of potential problems I identified above. In focusing on the decline of Christianity's extensive power, I contended, Mann overlooked its growing intensive power. And this led him to locate its (relative) decline a full four centuries too early. In this section, I ask whether there might also be other evidence that is missing from Mann's account, evidence that might alter his conclusions regarding causal primacy – a criticism of the second type. Specifically, I ask: (a) whether there are additional types of ideological power networks which are absent from Mann's analysis; and, if so, (b) whether taking these networks into account could undermine Mann's claims about the (relative) decline of ideological power. My answers to these two questions, to anticipate, are (a) 'yes' and (b) 'maybe'.

As we have just seen, Mann's analysis of ideology in medieval and early modern Europe focuses mainly on the growth and transformation of 'transcendent' and authoritative power, specifically the hierocratic power of the Christian churches. 'Intensive' and diffuse forms of ideological power enter into this analysis only peripherally, in the 'immanent morale' of the landed nobility; they do not figure in Mann's discussion of church networks.

If we look closely at Mann's analysis of ideology in modern Europe, we find different networks but a similar emphasis. Here, the focus tends to be on nation-states and political religions, especially socialism and fascism. These networks are somewhat less (socially) transcendent than their Christian predecessors, since they organize particular classes, nations or 'races'. But they are arguably also somewhat more authoritative – more likely to employ commands and coercion. Once again, intensive and diffuse forms of ideological power enter into the picture only at the margins, usually as precursors to more authoritative ones.

If we focus on these particular networks, then Mann's conclusions about the decline of ideological power seem quite plausible. The extensive power of the Christian churches did decline somewhat after the Reformation, and their intensive and authoritative powers have now declined as well (if not as early or as quickly as Mann and others presumed). Of course, the institutional and numerical contraction of Christianity during the late nineteenth and early twentieth centuries was also accompanied (and to some degree caused) by the expansion of the great 'political religions' of the modern era. And for a time, these secular faiths generated networks which were even more extensive (socialism) or more intensive (fascism and nationalism) than those of their religious rivals. But the great world wars of the twentieth century – two hot and one cold – sapped these networks of their strength, perhaps irreversibly. They live on in the routines of politics and platforms of socialist and nationalist parties, but in a severely weakened form.

But what if we expanded our focus, to include more diffuse networks of ideological power? Would we still arrive at the same conclusions? Before we can answer these questions, we must first be clear about their terms, especially the term 'diffuse ideological power'. To my knowledge, Mann does not define, or even discuss, this particular permutation of power. But by building on his definitions of diffuse power and ideological power, and examining the contrasts he draws between authoritative and diffuse power at various points, we can piece together a definition of diffuse ideological power which is very much in the spirit of Mann's theory. I present it in summary fashion. Diffuse ideological power differs from authoritative ideological power in at least four ways: (1) *Organizational and spatial structure*: While authoritative networks (e.g. churches and political parties) tend to be organizationally unified, geographically centralized and internally hierarchical, diffuse networks tend to be fragmented, de-centralized and flat. (2) *Means and methods*: Unlike some authoritative networks (e.g. nation-states and hierocracies), which rely on the exercise or threat of physical or psychological coercion, diffuse networks employ peaceful and persuasive tactics to diffuse their ideologies. (3) *Onto-logic*: Authoritative ideologies (e.g. world religions and political religions) provide relatively complete worldviews, which purport to explain how the world works, and how we should act in it; they are explicit, formal and systematic, and possess a relatively high degree of internal, logical consistency. Diffuse ideologies provide partial or incomplete worldviews. They focus on particular realms of life, and provide scripts for acting within them. They do not necessarily provide a coherent picture of the world, a complete system of life-conduct, or an explicit set of values. (4) *Ideology and action*. Authoritative ideologies can be consciously and intentionally taught, learned and applied. This is not always the case with diffuse ideologies, which are often absorbed and deployed without the conscious will or knowledge of the actor. (The usual caveats about typologies apply: authoritative and diffuse ideological power, as defined here, will rarely be encountered in 'pure form'; mixed and intermediate types are both possible and likely. Thus, the two types are best seen as the end-points of a spectrum, their four characteristics as a means of locating a particular network on that spectrum.) Thus, we can imagine a network which has a very diffuse organizational and spatial structure, but authoritative methods and ideas (e.g. a network of terrorist cells). Or conversely, a network with an authoritative organization, but diffuse methods and ideas (e.g. a certain type of business corporation).

What does a diffuse ideological network look like? And where might we find one? Classical and contemporary theory provides some useful signposts and examples.

Consider Weber's discussion of the various types of religious leaders and the sorts of communities which form around them (Weber 1978: 438–50). For Weber, the main purpose of this discussion is to delineate the unique features of a particular kind of leader that (Weber believes) played an especially consequential role in the 'rationalization' of Western religion: the 'ethical prophet'. What is of interest to us in this discussion, however, is not Weber's typology of the prophet and his antagonist and arch-rival, the 'priest', so much as the other types of leaders which he uses as analytical foils for them, especially 'magicians', 'mystagogues' and 'exemplary prophets'. For they form the nodes of more diffuse networks of ideological power, the power of the magician being the most diffuse, and that of the exemplary prophet the least. Magicians, as Weber understands them, do not issue commands; they provide services. Consequently, their 'communities' consist of 'clients' rather than 'followers'. And because their clients are more concerned with the efficacy of their services, than the coherence of their worldviews, they need not provide an authoritative onto-logic. Mystagogues also provide services, though of a somewhat different kind. They dispense 'boons of salvation' rather than worldly goods. But they do not claim a monopoly over these boons, just a reliable supply. Further, since the source of salvation is magical (or charismatic), there is little pressure to articulate a clear and explicit doctrine. Exemplary prophets also promise salvation, but not by magical means. It is not difficult to find modern, Western analogues of these different, historical figures – psychic healers, 'cult' leaders, travelling gurus, and so on. And if we look beyond the religious sphere, broadly construed, the list swells further, with 'self-help' authors, 'twelve-step' programmers, and 'inspirational speakers', and other ideological entrepreneurs who cater to the 'human need' for 'concepts and categories of meaning', 'understandings of how people should act morally', and 'aesthetic/ritual practices' (1986: 22). All of which leads one to wonder whether dis-enchantment has given way to re-enchantment. Has the contraction of traditional religion opened space for the expansion of post-modern magic? The answers to those questions will depend in large part upon how one defines religion and magic – a tricky and controversial issue. This much is clear, however: the (relative) decline of the 'great traditions', sacred and secular, has been followed by an (equivalent?) increase of 'little traditions'. What distinguishes the big and the little traditions, then, is not the 'human need' they address, but rather their comparatively diffuse organizational and onto-logical structures. As intellectuals, we may find such ideologies to be 'trivial' or even distasteful, but we should not assume that they are socially insignificant.

A strikingly similar argument with a slightly different emphasis can be found in the work of Thomas Luckmann, a sociologist of religion in the phenomenological tradition. For Luckmann (1990), the contrast is not between great and small traditions, but between great and small 'transcendences'. 'Transcendence', in Luckmann's usage, is a quality of individual experience, not a property of social networks. Transcendent experiences, as he defines them, are ones that point beyond the physical boundaries of our existence or the temporal boundaries of immediate experience, and make us aware of, or feel a part of, some larger process or entity. Luckmann distinguishes three different levels or degrees of transcendence. 'Little' transcendences involve consciousness of things which are not immediately given, but could be, or have been, directly experienced – day-dreams and memories, for example – and which thereby create a rupture or break in the flow of sensory experience. 'Intermediate' transcendences involve a feeling of union or sameness with someone or something which is other than ourselves, but which are understood as part of our experiential reality, such as 'nature' or another person. Great transcendences, finally, pertain to entities or processes that cannot be experienced directly, and that are not a part of ordinary or sensory reality.

This is the level at which the great world religions are situated. However, all three levels are susceptible of religious interpretations, and most religious traditions have offered – or imposed – certain ways of ordering them (e.g. through sacralized understandings of personhood and experience or ritualized forms of interaction). While transcendent experiences of one sort or another are a human universal – an inherent feature of our consciousness – their phenomenological and sociological structures are highly variable – and strongly correlated. Which brings us to the part of Luckmann's argument which is relevant to our concerns – the structure of transcendence in 'modern, functionally differentiated societies'; it differs sharply from that found in traditional and undifferentiated ones. According to Luckmann, it is flatter, more fragmented, freer and more personalistic. It is flatter in the sense that little and intermediate transcendences predominate, because the overarching world pictures which are the *sine qua non* of great transcendences are no longer accepted by large numbers of people. It is more fragmented in the sense that such experiences of transcendence which people do have, whether great or small, are highly diverse in character: physical elation, sexual union, aesthetic contemplation, and so on. It is freer in the sense that priestly elites have lost their ability to monopolize and control the interpretation of transcendent experiences; they now face competition from other specialists, both religious and secular (mystagogues and moralists, psychics and psychoanalysts), whose interpretations lack juridicial force. Finally, it is more personalistic insofar as individuals can – and often do – assemble their worldviews *à la carte* from the ideological smorgasbord of modern culture. Thus, where Weber's analysis of religious leadership focuses our attention on the changing structure of ideological networks, Luckmann's analysis highlights the changing nature of ideology itself. Whether the great transcendences will be restored in some form in some future society, we cannot know. That the small and intermediate transcendences are of greater importance to many members of contemporary society, no one will doubt.

The works of Weber and Luckmann suggest how we might think about the structural and onto-logical characteristics of diffuse power. For insights into its means and methods and its relation to action, the Durkheimian tradition is of more use. Of course, Mann invokes this tradition himself when he identifies 'aesthetic/ritual practices' as one aspect of ideological power. In practice, Mann tends to view ideological power through a Weberian lens: he focuses his attention on the organizational structure and intellectual content of ideological networks. 'Aesthetic and ritual practices' are generally absent from the picture. This is unfortunate, because ritual is arguably the chief means through which beliefs and values – which is what Mann means by 'ideology' – are reproduced and rendered plausible. The *locus classicus* on the relationship of ritual, belief and ideology is of course Durkheim's *Elementary Forms*, his *magnum opus* on the social origins of religion (and the religious origins of social categories) (Durkheim 1995; see also Marshall 2002). Durkheim's analysis will be familiar to most readers, but it is worth recalling its basic outlines. It begins with the argument that the one thing that all religions have in common is a distinction between the sacred and the profane. The central question, then, is how this distinction arises, and why it seems plausible. The answer, he argues, is to be found in the experience of 'collective effervescence', the feeling of energy and unity which is generated by mass rituals. It is the contrast between these moments of collective elation, and the routines of everyday life, which gives rise to the distinction between sacred and profane, and to notions of a larger force or external power which governs our lives. Now in reality, says Durkheim, this force or power is society, itself. But it is not recognized as such, at least not in pre-modern, pre-scientific and pre-sociological (!) societies. Rather, it is interpreted as a supernatural power or divine being. Religious beliefs are thus true to the extent that they are grounded in actual experience (collective effervescence) and refer to something real (society), but false insofar as they mis-interpret the experiences and mis-recognize their actual source. The importance of this analysis for our purposes is that it specifies a diffuse means – meaning a non-coercive, non-violent means – for the production and diffusion of ideological power, namely, ritual. Of course, the religious networks which are the subjects of Durkheim's study are diffuse mainly in their means; they can be (relatively) authoritative in structure and onto-logic. But Durkheim's analysis could easily be extended to structurally and onto-logically diffuse networks as well, and already have been by various neo-Durkheimians (see, e.g., Bellah and Hammond 1980; Warner 1959).

Mann also tends to adopt a Weberian point of view in his analyses of ideology and action: ideology is conceptualized as an explicit system of values that individuals use to guide or orient their actions. Here, too, Durkheim's work suggests a very different perspective, one which focuses on the embodiment and naturalization of ideology, rather than on its codification and application. This line of analysis has been pursued by many social theorists, but its most famous advocate, at least in sociology, is undoubtedly Pierre Bourdieu. For Bourdieu, of course, the key issue is not the origin of beliefs and values, so much as the legitimation of inequality and domination.[13] This is a Weberian question, but Bourdieu's answer draws heavily on Durkheim. As in Durkheim's analysis of ritual, however, Bourdieu's work on legitimation focuses on a process of mis-interpretation and mis-recognition. What is mis-interpreted and mis-recognized in this case, however, is the nature and source of class 'distinctions', the subtle differences in taste and manners which serve as 'principles of vision and di-vision' – as signs and markers of social status. The origins of these differences are social: they are to be found in an individual's upbringing and education. But they are (mis)interpreted as natural differences in individual endowments – a mis-interpretation whose plausibility and persistence derives from the fact that such differences in '*habitus*' are inscribed in the individual body. The result is that class differences are seen as natural differences, not only by dominant groups, but also, even especially, by the subordinate strata. Bourdieu's work of 'distinction' shows us what a diffuse relationship between ideology and action might look like, that is how an ideology might be 'absorbed and deployed without the conscious knowledge or will of the actor'.

Based on these brief discussions of Weber, Luckmann, Durkheim and Bourdieu, I think it is fair to conclude that there are indeed forms of ideological power which are present in Mann's conceptual framework, but absent from his historical analyses, diffuse ideological power being one of them. This brings us to the second and more important question, namely, whether the existence of these networks challenges Mann's conclusions about ideological power and causal primacy in the contemporary world. To answer this question properly, one would need to assess the pervasiveness of these networks and the power of their effects in the modern West. I cannot hope – and will not pretend – to provide any sort of definitive answer in the closing pages of this chapter. What I would like to do instead is offer a few hypotheses, which could serve as a starting point for further reflection.

My first hypothesis is that networks of diffuse ideological power have grown in number and size, and that they are considerably more important now than they were, say, two centuries ago, at least within the West. In fact, I would go so far as to argue that the growth of diffuse ideological power is one of the hallmarks of 'modernity'. I am by no means the first to remark on this development. It has been described by many social theorists, albeit in different language. Weber conceptualized it as the differentiation of autonomous and competing 'value spheres', while Durkheim treated it as one aspect of the 'division of labor'.

My second hypothesis is that the growth of diffuse ideological power is both the cause and the consequence of 'secularization', understood here as a decrease in the size and influence of authoritative church networks. Many sociologists have noted this process, of course. But their descriptions of it are usually incomplete, both empirically and theoretically: empirically incomplete, insofar as they focus only on the negative side of the process – on the declining power of church networks; and

theoretically incomplete, insofar as they trace it to abstract and imperso-
nal forces operating 'behind the backs' of social actors. This description misses the positive side of secularization – the growth of non-
ecclesiastical and/or non-religious networks in the interstices of the
old church networks. Metaphysics, cosmology, pastoral care, marital
counselling, social welfare, moral and practical education – these and
other 'functions' have been usurped or assumed by non-clerical elites
with ideologies of their own. The other problem with these theories is that
they take the action out of the process. It is important to remember that
'secularization' was a category of practice long before it was a category of
analysis – that it was a political programme before it became a heuristic
device. As we have seen, Mann does not make this (theoretical) mistake.
But he does miss the 'positive' side of the secularization process.

If these two hypotheses are correct, then one could reason that the
growth of diffuse ideological power in the modern West has in some sense
counter-balanced the decline of authoritative, church networks. The
question, of course, is in *what* sense, and to what degree. One answer –
the answer usually given by liberals, modernists and other defenders of
the Enlightenment – is that the decline of authoritative ideological power,
in both its religious and political forms, results in a decline of ideological
power *per se*. In this perspective, the fragmentation and de-legitimation of
extensive and centralized networks of ideological power creates a space
free of violence and coercion in which individual choice and rational
discourse can unfold. This is the position which is implicit within
Mann's work. Another answer, more consistent with a post-modernist
perspective, is that the growth of diffuse ideological power, especially
within civil society and the private sphere, results in a strengthening of
ideological power *tout court*. The reasoning here is that diffuse ideological
power is actually more insidious, precisely because it is more fragmented,
less articulate, more unconscious, and so on. Indeed, post-modern
cultural criticism could be seen, in part, as an attempt to make diffuse
ideological power more visible, to reveal the underlying homologies and
connections between seemingly disparate discourses and practices. The
position one takes on this issue will determine how one responds to
Mann's claims about causal primacy. Whatever position one takes, however, it is clear that the tasks of *Ideologiekritik* are quite a bit different
today, than they were in Voltaire's age.

Summary and conclusion

In *The Sources of Social Power*, Michael Mann makes two broad sets of
claims regarding the significance of ideological power in Western history.

The first has to do with its role in the rise of the West. Mann argues that the extensive power of the Western Church and immanent morale of the landed nobility helped to pacify Western society during the Middle Ages, thereby creating a key precondition for the emergence of modern capitalism: social order and stability. The second has to do with the role of ideological power in the modern era. Mann contends that the influence of church networks has decreased since the early modern era, and the importance of ideological power along with it.

In this chapter, I have raised a number of concerns about these claims. First, I have argued that the impact of ideological power and Western development was both later and more complex than Mann suggests. Specifically, I have argued that the key period of normative pacification was the early modern era, rather than the Middle Ages, and that the impact of religious ideology was not just economic but political and perhaps even military. Thus, ideological power 'intertwined' with and 'changed the shape of', the three other 'power sources' during the Western take-off. Second, I have raised questions about the timing and extent of the decline in ideological power. In particular, I have argued that the decline of church networks occurred much later than Mann (and others) have (routinely) claimed; and that the decline of church networks and other more authoritative forms of ideological power since the nineteenth century may have been offset by the emergence of more diffuse types of ideological power, thereby complicating any assessments of 'causal primacy'. In developing these criticisms, it should be noted, I have drawn heavily on Mann's own concepts. Thus, this chapter can be read, both as a criticism of some of Mann's historical interpretations *and* as a testimony to the power of his conceptualizations.

Unlike history, which values the study of the past largely (if not wholly) for its own sake, sociology is rooted, first and foremost, in a concern for the present. Thus, it is not unfair to ask what light, if any, the foregoing discussion might shed on the contemporary situation. One conclusion which one might draw is that the tasks of *Ideologiekritik* are quite different than they were during the classical era of sociology, at least in contemporary Western societies. For the classical theorists – Marx, Weber and Durkheim – the critique of ideology generally took the form of a sociology of knowledge, in which a particular set of ideas (whether conceived as ideology, values or norms) was linked to a particular social group (via material interests, ideal interests or collective rituals). In this way, it was hoped, the universalistic pretensions of a particular set of ideas were torn away to reveal the particularistic context in which they were rooted, thereby clearing the ground for a truly universalistic perspective. Today, one could argue, the task of ideological critique has been turned on its head. Confronted with diffuse forms of ideological power, the task of the social critic is to reveal the universalistic pretensions which lurk beneath apparently particularistic sets of ideas, so as to render them subject to explicit discussion and rational reflection. It is not an easy task. Diffuse ideological networks are more difficult to identify than authoritative ones. They usually do not have a central headquarters, resort to explicit threats or physical violence, publish comprehensive platforms or doctrinal statements, or preach the message which they practise. Finding them may therefore require procedures and concepts quite different from the ones bequeathed to us by classical sociology. I would suggest four methodological rules for the study of diffuse ideological power:

1. Spatial and organizational structure: look for informal linkages and organizational homologies, rather than formal ties and organizational hierarchies.
2. Mechanisms and modalities: look for tactics of seduction and a politics of pleasure, rather than brute commands or naked interests.
3. Ideology and action: search for rules-of-thumb and recipes for success and the practical strategies and cultural scripts embedded within them, rather than internally consistent worldviews or comprehensive systems of life-conduct.
4. Embodied ideology: be on the lookout, not just for what is said, but what is done, that is for the mute practices and rituals through which ideology acts on the body, and not just for the noisy words and phrases through which it announces itself.

If these methodological rules have a post-modern ring, that is no accident, because it is post-modern theorists who have developed the sharpest ears for diffuse ideologies, with their focus on practices, pleasures, discourses and the body. Sociologists need not accept the epistemological premises and political conclusions advanced by the post-modernists, or the opaque style and polemical rhetoric which often go along with them. But they should probably be more open to the themes and concepts developed by post-modern theorists.

This is not to say that authoritative ideologies can now be safely ignored. The 'old' religious and political ideologies of the West may have weakened during the past half century, but they are by no means extinct. The political power of Christian fundamentalism in the United States and of ethno-cultural nationalism in post-Soviet Europe, both East and West, are certainly evidence enough of that. To ignore authoritative forms of ideological power would be as grave an error as ignoring its more diffuse forms. Where the West is concerned, the most important task may be to trace out the relation between diffuse and authoritative networks – to understand the links between consumerism and liberalism, say, or between patriotism and nationalism, or self-help and evangelicalism.

Neither should we assume that the decline in authoritative ideologies is irreversible. For new ideological networks are now emerging outside the West, and in opposition to it. Viewed from Los Angeles, London, or Berlin, these networks may appear anachronistic and irrational, as the last cry of a moribund traditionalism. But that is probably how Protestantism looked to the elites of Madrid, Paris and Rome during the early sixteenth century. And how wrong they were! Historically, authoritative ideologies have usually incubated in the peripheral regions of the world. There is no reason to assume that the future will be any different.

Notes

1 As the reader may have noticed, the analytical categories underlying the distinction between authoritative and diffuse power are not as clear as they are for the distinction between intensive and extensive power. I will discuss this problem, and some possible solutions, in the third section of the chapter.

2 This is quite different from the way that students of religion have used this term, namely, to describe religious worldviews which postulate a 'transcendent' or supra-mundane reality or to describe experiences which interrupt or 'transcend' the phenomenal flow of sensory experience and seem to point to another realm or dimension of consciousness.

3 Unlike some of the other types of power which Mann identifies, these two do not seem to stand in a zero-sum relationship to one another; a particular power network can possess high levels of transcendent and immanent ideological power. Take Hinduism: it transcended and encompassed political and social divisions between kingdom and caste, even as it undergirded the morale of a particular group – the Brahmins.

4 This is by no means the first attempt at such a synthesis. A particularly well-known example, which resonates with Mann's in various ways, is Geertz (1973).

5 This choice is not entirely surprising, given Mann's own background, his working-class roots, Labourite leanings, and early engagements with French Marxism.

6 Marx himself used the term 'ideology' in at least two distinct ways: (1) to deride 'idealistic' or 'utopian' forms of theorizing (as in his early polemics against the young Hegelians and Proudhonian anarchism); and (2) to criticize the rhetorical trickery through which dominant groups conceal their material interests from the dominated (as in his vitriolic attacks on liberalism and rights as a mask for capitalism and exploitation). Nowhere, however, does Marx use the term 'ideology' in conjunction with the terms 'socialism' or 'communism'; for he regarded socialism as scientific, and ideology as its opposite – as un-truth. Of course, there is one place where Marx discusses the role of ideas in sustaining morale, and that is 'The Eighteenth Brumaire', where he points out how

revolutionary leaders have drawn on 'the languages of the past' to fashion the societies of the future. And it is this analysis which Gramsci and other *fin-de-siècle* Marxists used to construct a positive view of ideology *qua* immanent morale, that allowed them to speak of 'socialist' or 'proletarian ideology' without apparent contradiction. I would suggest that Mann's concept of 'immanent' ideology is inspired by this strand of Marxist thought, at least implicitly.

 7 See Howard (1976). For a more thorough treatment of the military revolution *per se*, see especially Parker (1988).

 8 On the connection between the military revolution and state formation, see especially Downing (1992).

 9 I leave the fourth type of criticism to one side, not because I think it is less important, but because I lack the qualifications to take it up.

10 This is not the place to review the various versions of the bellicist model, and the empirical anomalies and theoretical conundrums confronting each of them. More detailed discussions of these issues can be found in Gorski (2003, ch. 1) and Gorski (2005).

11 For an overview and empirical test of this literature, see Kiser and Linton (2001).

12 This connection is implicit in Esping-Andersen (1990) and is more explicitly developed in Kersbergen (1995).

13 This idea runs like a red-thread through most of Bourdieu's *oeuvre*. The most concrete and detailed treatment is to be found in Bourdieu (1984).

References

Althusser, L. 1972. Ideology and Ideological State Apparatuses (Notes towards an Investigation). In Althusser, *Lenin and Philosophy and Other Essays*, pp. 127–85. Trans. B. Brewster. New York: Monthly Review Press.

Bellah, R., and P. E. Hammond. 1980. *Varieties of Civil Religion*. San Francisco: Harper & Row.

Bourdieu, P. 1984. *Distinction: A Social Critique of the Judgement of Taste*. Trans. R. Nice. Cambridge, MA: Harvard University Press.

Downing, B. 1992. *The Military Revolution and Political Change: Origins of Democracy and Autocracy in Early Modern Europe*. Princeton: Princeton University Press.

Durkheim, E. 1995. *The Elementary Forms of the Religious Life*. Trans. K. Fields. New York: The Free Press.

1964. *The Division of Labor in Society*. Trans. G. Simpson. New York: The Free Press.

Eagleton, T. 1991. *Ideology: An Introduction*. London: Verso.

Ertman, T. 1997. *Birth of the Leviathan: Building States and Regimes in Medieval and Early Modern Europe*. Cambridge: Cambridge University Press.

Esping-Andersen, G. 1990. *The Three Worlds of Welfare Capitalism*. Princeton: Princeton University Press.

Evans, R. J. W., and T. V. Thomas (eds.). 1991. *Crown, Church, and Estates: Central European Politics in the Sixteenth and Seventeenth Centuries*. Basingstoke: Macmillan.

Geertz, C. 1973. Religion as a Cultural System. In Geertz, *The Interpretation of Cultures* pp. 87–125. New York: Basic Books.

Gentles, I. J. 1992. *The New Model Army in England, Ireland and Scotland, 1645–1653.* Oxford: Blackwell, 1992.

Gorski, P. S. 2005. The Protestant Ethic and the Spirit of Bureaucracy. In C. S. Camic, P. S. Gorski and D. Trubek (eds.), *Max Weber at the Millennium, Economy and Society for the Twenty-First Century.* Stanford: Stanford University Press.

2003. *The Disciplinary Revolution: Calvinism, Confessionalism and State Formation in Early Modern Europe, 1500–1750.* Chicago: University of Chicago Press.

2001a. Beyond Marx and Hintze? Third Wave Theories of Early Modern State Formation. *Contemporary Studies in Society and History*, 43 (4).

2001b. Calvinism and Revolution: The Walzer Thesis Re-Considered. In R. Madsen, A. Swidler and S. Tipton (eds.), *Meaning and Modernity: Religion, Polity and Self.* Berkeley and Los Angeles: University of California Press.

2000a. Historicizing the Secularization Debate: Church, State, and Society in Late Medieval and Early Modern Europe. *American Sociological Review*, 65 (1).

2000b. The Mosaic Moment: An Early Modernist Critique of Modernist Theories of Nationalism. *American Journal of Sociology*, 105(5).

1993. The Protestant Ethic Revisited: Disciplinary Revolution and State Formation in Holland and Prussia. *American Journal of Sociology*, 99 (2).

Hahlweg, W. 1987 [1941]. *Die Heeresreform der Oranier und die Antike.* Osnabrück: Biblio Verlag.

Hastings, A. 1996. *The Construction of Nationhood: Ethnicity, Religion and Nationalism.* Cambridge: Cambridge University Press.

Höllinger, F. 1996. *Volksreligion und Herrschaftskirche: die Wurzeln religiösen Verhaltens in westlichen Gesellschaften.* Opladen: Leske and Budrich, 1996.

Hölscher, L. 1989. *Weltgericht oder Revolution.* Stuttgart: Klett-Cotta.

Howard, M. 1976. *War in European History.* New York: Oxford University Press.

Hsia, R. Po-Chia. 1989. *Social Discipline in the Reformation: Central Europe, 1550–1750.* London: Routledge.

Hutchison, W. R., and H. Lehmann (eds). 1994. *Many are Chosen: Divine Election and Western Nationalisms.* Minneapolis: Fortress Press.

Kersbergen, K. 1995. *Social Capitalism: A Study of Christian Democracy and the Welfare State.* London: Routledge.

Kiser, E., and A. Linton. 2001. Determinants of the Growth of the State: War and Taxation in Early Modern France and England. *Social Forces*, 80 (2).

Luckmann, T. 1990. Shrinking Transcendence, Expanding Religion? *Sociological Analysis*, 51 (2).

Luebbert, G. M. 1991. *Liberalism, Fascism, or Social Democracy: Social Classes and the Political Origins of Regimes in Interwar Europe.* New York: Oxford University Press.

McLeod, H. (ed.). 1995. *European Religion in the Age of Great Cities, 1830–1930.* London: Routledge.

Mann, M. 1986. *The Sources of Social Power, Volume I: A History from the Beginning to 1760 AD.* Cambridge: Cambridge University Press.

1993. *The Sources of Social Power, Volume II: The Rise of Classes and Nation-States.* Cambridge: Cambridge University Press.

Marshall, D. A. 2002. Behavior, Belonging and Belief: A Theory of Ritual Practice. *Sociological Theory*, 20 (3).

Marx, A. 2003. *Faith in Nation: Exclusionary Origins of Nationalism.* New York: Oxford University Press.

Nipperdey, T. 1988. *Religion im Umbruch, Deutschland 1870–1918.* Munich: Beck.

O'Brien, C. C. 1988. *GodLand: Reflections on Religion and Nationalism.* Cambridge, MA: Harvard University Press.

Parker, G. 1988. *The Military Revolution.* Cambridge: Cambridge University Press.

Rueschemeyer, D., E. H. Stephens and J. D. Stephens. 1992. *Capitalist Development and Democracy.* Chicago: University of Chicago Press.

Te Brake, W. T. Th. 1998. *Shaping History: Ordinary People in European Politics 1500–1700.* Berkeley: University of California Press.

Tilly, C. 1985. War Making and State Making as Organized Crime. In P. B. Evans, D. Rueschemeyer and T. Skocpol (eds.), *Bringing the State Back In.* Cambridge: Cambridge University Press.

Tschannen, O. 1992. *Les théories de la sécularisation.* Geneva: Droz.

Warner, W. L. 1959. *The Living and the Dead: A Study of the Symbolic of Americans.* New Haven: Yale University Press.

Weber, M. 1988. *Gesammelte Aufsätze zur Sozial- und Wirtschaftsgeschichte.* Ed. M. Weber. Tübingen: J. C. B. Mohr.

1978. *Economy and Society.* Ed. G. Roth and C. Wittich. Berkeley: University of California Press.

Zubrzycki, G. 2000. 'We, the Polish Nation': Ethnic and Civic Visions of Nationhood in Post-Communist Constitutional Debates. *Theory and Society*, 30 (5).

7   Political power un-manned: a defence of the Holy Trinity from Mann's military attack

Gianfranco Poggi

This brief contribution addresses only one of the problems raised by Michael Mann's imaginative and substantial discussion of the military phenomenon in his *magnum opus* (Mann 1986; 1993). The problem concerns the conceptual status Mann confers upon that phenomenon by considering it as the locus of a distinctive, relatively self-standing source of social power, on which it falls occasionally to play an autonomous role in the making and unmaking of societies, and which in any case interacts with the other sources as the custodian of a resource – organized coercion – which *they* don't control while *it* does.

Put otherwise, I question, below, Mann's decision to stage his show with four protagonists – IEMP – rather than with the usual trinity of political, economic and ideological power. In doing so, he expressly and, one might say, gleefully sets himself against the trinitarian orthodoxy. I contend that, on purely conceptual grounds, this a doubtful decision, though I concede that it has occasionally some justification in specific empirical circumstances.

In making that decision, I believe, Mann was carried away by the intensity of his reaction against the social theorizing prevalent at the time he conceived and planned *Sources of Social Power*, for there the military phenomenon was sometimes ignored, more frequently treated diffidently and without an adequate sense of its nature and significance. By adding military power to the orthodox trinity, Mann placed it on the high ground, and made it axiomatic that a valid, theoretically inspired account of the story of human civilization required, among other things, a sensitivity to the nature and dynamics of organized violence – not *just* those of the material metabolism between human beings and nature, of the construction and maintenance of collective entities via relations of command and obedience, or of the elaboration of authoritative understandings of what is true, proper, or beautiful.

While recognizing the significance of this theoretical concern, and the relevance of the insights it has produced in the writings of Mann himself

135

and of other scholars, I suggest that at the conceptual level none of this justifies abandoning the conventional trinity of political, economic and ideological power.

One must admire Mann's courage in refusing to abide by that trinity, for a multitude of diverse sources affirm it, imply it, or assume it. I, for one, find it all over the place. Recently, Runciman has forcefully restated it in his treatise (Runciman 1983). Weber's opening sentence in 'Class, status group, and party' asserts it almost explicitly. Etzioni's typology of compliance structures in complex organizations uses it (Etzioni 1975). One of Gellner's best book titles, *Plough, Sword and Book*, echoes it (1988). Statements about the nature of economics suggest that the discipline deals with only the first of three modes of allocation – contract, custom, command. Books and essays I come across often pattern on the Marxian notion of 'means of production' those of 'means of coercion' and 'means of interpretation'. Kant has a parallel trinity of three evil dispositions, 'hankering after lordship', 'hankering after possessions', and 'envy', which last one with a little massaging can be rephrased as 'hankering after recognition'.

I am sure Mann can easily add other entries to this haphazard list of trinitarian views on power, but no matter – to him, they are all out of step. Military power deserves equal time with the members of the established trio, as his own Grand Narrative intends to prove, at any rate to his own satisfaction; not entirely to mine, though, for two main reasons.

First – apart from my own stubborn preference for conceptual trinities, at any rate over against quartets if not always over against pairs: for, let us face it, *omne trinum est perfectum* – I sense that, if he read Mann, Occam would reach for his razor; for, although the phenomenon of organized, technically assisted capacity for sustained coercion performs a significant amount of analytical and empirical labour for Mann, such labour does not justify promoting that phenomenon to the rank of a fourth source of social power.

A further reason against that promotion is the fate it inflicts on a particular member of the established trio – political power. The latter is, as it were, un-manned by being denied its conventional grounding in organized violence, and rendered sterile. Mann's operation of placing the discourse on power no longer on a tripod but on a four-legged table is deceptive, for one of the other three legs is rendered lame by the operation itself, which deprives political power of the conceptual identity bestowed upon it by centuries of theoretical reflection.

This is no place to review the intellectual itinerary which grounded that conceptual identity in coercion. I will just mention that it began, of course, in Greece; but on the face of it the Greeks, by inventing and naming politics, did not subscribe to my own bloody-minded identification of politics with violence. Indeed the Greeks had a fancy notion that politics was based on the human's capacity for talk, which allowed them, under appropriate conditions – those characteristic of the *polis*, which they proudly saw as an exclusive privilege of their own kind – to collectively envision conceptions of virtue of the *polis*'s own making and to design institutions oriented to those.

Where is the violence in all this? Well, ask the (relatively) old man who in *Crito* rattles on to his horrified friends and disciples (who have arranged to save his life by spiriting him out of Athens) about the only way he can show his own true devotion to the city's Laws – drinking the hemlock. The point is that even discursively generated laws, the product of politics understood in that fancy Greek manner, have to be sanctioned by collective coercion.

Coming straight to our own times, again we find notions of politics which on the face of it do not ground it in violence. Bertrand de Jouvenel (1963) and Jean-Yves Calvez (1967), for instance, claim that politics arises, instead, from the confrontation with Other-dom – *l'autruité*. But there are ways of dealing with The Other which are not political – we can be curious about The Other, we can traffick with It, we can ignore It. The ways that are political turn out to revolve on the decision to fight It, or to submit to It, or to incorporate It, that is to subsume It under a community bounded, again, by the validity of certain enforceable norms.

Field and Higley (1981) understand politics as the settling of conflicts which the parties do not allow themselves to negotiate – but for this very reason the settlement must be coercively impos*able* if not always coercively impos*ed*, otherwise it would not settle matters. The frequent reference in other American literature to the 'binding' nature of political decisions coyly points in the same direction. Witness Mann's own, four-point definition of the state, 'much influenced by Weber', where the last feature is '4. some degree of authoritative, binding rule making, backed up by some organized physical force' (1993: 55).

When it comes to the state, the central political institution of modernity, Weber's definition, with its 'monopoly of the legitimate use of force', seems absolutely *de rigueur* these days, and we know from Anter's work (1996) that it was widely shared in Weber's own time. Parts of Weber's own *Politik als Beruf* become mystifying without that definition – particularly its discussion of the Machiavellian problem, of the moral dangerousness of political leadership. Many successive theorists, from Elias to Tilly, have discussed it at length. But that monopoly is an elaboration (quantitatively and qualitatively *variable*) of a conceptually (and historically) prior relationship, once more, between political power in a generic sense, and not-yet-monopolized physical force. In sum, politics is a recurrent, constitutive aspect of social life among humans *because*, as Popitz states, 'there is no social order based on the premise that violence does not exist' (1992: 23).

While 'loosening', as he says, the ties between military and political power, Mann repeatedly and emphatically stressed instead the relationship between political power on the one hand and territoriality, centrality and administration on the other. About none of these three features, however, one could say, as Popitz suggests about violence, that no social order is thinkable without it. This means, to me, that political power as Mann construes it is without anthropological grounding.

As against this, the construction of the 'classical trinity' offered by Popitz (I like to refer to this author, who died recently, because in my judgement he has received within anglophone sociological circles nothing like the recognition he deserved) anchors each of its components in a distinctive kind of inescapable human vulnerability – respectively, vulnerability to death and suffering (political power), to hunger and deprivation (economic power), to a sense of personal insignificance and cosmic meaninglessness (ideological power). I wonder what human vulnerability is addressed, presupposed, managed by a power characterized by centrality, territoriality and administration.

Or, seeing that Mann himself derives ideological power from a distinctive set of human needs, and economic power from another set, I wonder from what set of human needs he would derive political power as *he* understands it. In fact, in the text I have in mind (1986: ch. 1), he does not mention human needs, but derives political power from 'the usefulness of territorial and centralized administration'. Usefulness to whom, one wonders, given that in the course of both prehistory and history hundreds of populations lived cheerfully enough without the benefits of administration, let alone its centralized and territorial forms. And as concerns many of the populations which did experience administration, its benefits, one suspects, had to be imposed upon them, at any rate early on. *Guess how?* By the application of physical force, expressly and compellingly addressing the first of Popitz's vulnerabilities.

Another standard way of conceptualizing different power sources is by grounding each not (at the negative end) on distinctive needs or vulnerabilities, but (at the positive end) on distinctive resources. For instance, my former colleague at the University of Virginia, Murray Milner, Jr, has developed in his *Status and Sacredness* a sophisticated 'resource-based' theory of status which juxtaposes it to power and privilege (1994). Again, Mann's understanding of political power must part company with this approach, for administration, centralized and territorial or otherwise, is not a resource, but a task.

In dealing with these matters, Mann knows he stands in a (to say the least) uneasy relationship to Weber's theoretical legacy, given that the latter is trinitarian as concerns power. He seems less aware of the extent to which he differs from Weber on a related question: the conceptual relation between political power and the state. To him, 'political power means *state* power' (1993: 9). To Weber it doesn't. Underlying this difference there is another one: in most texts of Weber's, and probably in all the more significant ones, the adjective 'modern' in the expression '*modern* state' is pleonastic. The state as he characterizes it (particularly in other definitions than the one quoted above, which do not limit themselves to the above 'monopoly of the legitimate use of physical force') is another of those distinctive Western products Weber writes about in the 'Author's Introduction' to *The Protestant Ethic*, and indeed belongs, among those, in the subset of specifically modern ones. This does *not* hold for the way Mann understands 'the state'; though he does devote special attention to the *modern* state, he's willing to call 'states' all manner of other polities.

This is of course a perfectly legitimate preference, and one which Mann shares with a number of other authors, though my impression is that these are outweighed if not outnumbered by those who stand with Weber on this question. Yet that preference leads to some awkwardnesses when Mann tries to square it with Weber's own. On page 55 of the second volume of *Sources of Social Power* (1993), for instance, after quoting the standard Weberian definition, focused again on the monopoly of the legitimate use of physical force, Mann claims to differ from it 'on one point. Many historic states did not "monopolize" the means of physical violence.'

Now, I find this confusing, for three reasons. First, the category of 'historic' states, so far as I remember, is not used by Weber, which makes it difficult to see against what background of understandings shared with Weber Mann posits his one difference from him. Second, Mann shifts from Weber's *use* of physical violence to the *means* of it – not an insignificant shift, since the crucial notion of legitimacy can be applied only to the *uses* of violence, not to its *means*. Finally, given that Weber never imputed *his* monopoly to other than the (modern) state, what's the use of reminding him (so to speak) that it does not hold for other polities?

Mann's last quoted passage goes on to say that 'even in the modern state the means of physical force have been substantially autonomous from (the rest of) the state'. This clause is again conceptually untidy, for 'means' as such cannot be autonomous or otherwise – the subjects who wield them can. It also surprises one by conceding a lot to the argument Mann is opposing, for it implies that at any rate in the modern state those means are a however wayward *part* of the state itself – *quod NON erat demonstrandum*. Against these petty objections to the clause in question must be set the fact that it opens Mann's way to a number of significant, empirically grounded arguments, as I shall soon argue.

A final difficulty with Mann's treatment of both the political and the military components of his quartet lies in his insufficiently elaborate and differentiated discussion of physical force, coercion or what you will. What drives Mann to give 'separate and equal' status to military power is essentially his intent to give full conceptual recognition to the difference which *armies* have repeatedly made at a number of significant points in history, to the contribution which periodically 'men on horseback' have made to the course of Western history in particular. Here again he both agrees with Weber and differs from him.

The difference lies chiefly in the fact that, although Weber was fully aware of the historical significance of the military factor and of related institutions (especially fiscal ones), when he emphasizes the significance of physical force for his concept of politics and the (modern) state, he seems to have primarily in mind its employment by domestic agents of the executive and the judiciary: bailiffs, policemen, excisemen, customs officers, prison guards, truant officers, executioners – *and* soldiers when they play a direct role in repressing aggressive expressions of popular discontent and in re-establishing the public order at the behest of the authorities.

This is in keeping with Weber's keen sense that the state, like other polities, is in the first place a set of institutional and material arrangements for the domination of one part of society by another, and it is this domination which the employment or the threat of employment of organized physical violence primarily grounds, expresses and sanctions.

This emphasis is reflected also in the place held by the notion of legitimacy in his political thinking. There is no place for such a notion within 'politics between nations', at any rate in the Westphalian/ Hobbesian/anarchical understanding of such politics which presumably Weber shared. For him legitimacy is a (contingent) quality of the 'vertical' relationship between the dominant and the dominated part of society, a (contingent) aspect of the command/obedience relation – and there is no such thing as command/obedience in the 'horizontal' relationship between sovereign nation states.

At this point I would like to digress briefly on whether and how, in his understanding and appreciation of politics, Weber squared the emphasis on domestic aspects I just attributed to him with his passionate commitment to the might of the German nation and thus to the 'primacy of foreign policy'. Perhaps it is not unjustified that most commentators distinguish between Weber's *political* writings and his *politological* ones, placing those focused on the 'primacy of foreign policy' among the former rather than the latter. But in Weber's own mind, of course, that distinction sometimes gets short-circuited.

It is my impression – I voice it hesitantly, for to turn it into something more than just an impression would require a revisitation of the sources I cannot undertake at this point – that this happens in particular in a most significant piece of writing: the published version of his talk *Politik als Beruf*.

This talk was given early in 1919, at which time unavoidably (whether Weber wanted and admitted this or not) his thinking about politics was chiefly preoccupied with the question, how to make sure that Germany, a recently and disastrously defeated nation, would soon resume its rank as a most significant European and world power. Weber was a revanchist. Did he not say at Versailles, to some representatives of the allies, 'we shall meet again, gentlemen, on the field of honor', or words to that effect? (Incidentally, I have long felt that this imagery, appropriate to the joust or the medieval battlefield, was almost insultingly inappropriate in the mouth of someone who well knew how men in their thousands had died, say, at Tannenbaum or at the Somme.)

That preoccupation, I sense, lays a heavy mortgage, in particular, on the conception of democracy presented in *Politik als Beruf*, giving it its peculiar plebiscitarian twist, and possibly informing also Weber's famous conception of an ethic appropriate to the political realm. As late as 1917, in texts foreshadowing changes to be introduced in the German constitution after the war – which he still hoped Germany might win – Weber had carefully discussed institutional arrangements for ensuring the *account-ability* of parties and bureaucracies. In *Politik als Beruf* this no longer matters as much, and Weber holds forth about something as rum – let us say it outright – as 'the ethic of *responsibility*' central to The Leader's sense of personal honour.

One reason for this, I suspect, is that *patriai tempore iniquo* Weber's thinking is thrown all in the direction of foreign policy and thus, when all is said and done, of war. Hence its occasionally disturbing overtones, remindful of the later Schmittian definition of 'the political' as an ambit of decision revolving around the question who's friend and who's foe, a question unavoidably 'existential', the answer to which must rest on the judgement of a single person. Or, put otherwise, in the situation of early 1919 the cry 'Bismarck, Bismarck, where art thou now?' becomes more and more compelling for Weber, and biases many aspects of his understanding of politics.

With this, we can return to the contrast between Mann's and Weber's ideas. While, as I argued, when Weber discussed the state the 'professionals of violence' on his mind were chiefly those involved in domestic affairs, Mann's second volume of *Sources of Social Power* contains a useful, brief discussion of the relationship between police forces and armies, but the latter markedly predominate in Mann's thinking. This is common among authors who make much of the relationship between politics and violence in interpreting (in particular) European history, and most particularly, of course, among those who emphasize the impact of the changing technology of warfare on political institutions. Among significant contemporary writers only Foucault, I think, has theorized the relationship between coercion and the state by emphasizing instead the domestic, repressive, law-and-order-keeping uses of the former: and in this he agrees with Weber – and disagrees with Mann.

Perhaps one reason for Mann's opposite emphasis is that in a work such as *Sources of Social Power*, with its focus on momentous changes and a narrative approach, it makes little sense, when dealing with organized violence, to emphasize those forms of it that from the material standpoint have changed *relatively* little in the course of history. For instance, the firepower deployable in operations of law enforcement and repression has certainly undergone remarkable quantitative and qualitative changes in the course of modern history, but nothing as remarkable as those undergone by firepower on the battlefield. Even when the army is called out to repress domestic disturbances, it is typically its most archaic component – mounted troops – that first makes its appearance. (Incidentally, in some countries those troops are not supposed to charge at a crowd before playing the bugle three times!)

Oddly enough, Mann's definition of politics-and-the-state, with its focus on territoriality, centrality and administration, shares the conceptual emphasis I attribute to Weber on the domestic side of the political enterprise. However, he deprives it of its coercive edge, by turning over most of the nasty stuff to a separate fourth power source, where the name of the game is not *just* repressive and punitive violence inflicted on individuals or on groupings of individuals, but, at bottom, mass killing.

The alternative would have been to stick with the conventional conceptual trinity, to confirm the intimate, constitutive relationship between political power and force, to emphasize that the actual recourse to force tends to be exceptional, being routinely replaced by material and symbolic ways of threatening that recourse and keeping it available as a last resort. It would have been possible, then, to thematize the oscillation, in the conduct of political business, between a minimum and a maximum of actual or symbolic use of force – between hegemonic, consensus-building moments and repressive moments, between carrot and stick, between welfare state and warfare state, between one and the other of the typical postures of the contemporary state towards the lower orders in particular theorized by Piven and Cloward (1971).

Such oscillations could have been correlated (the direction of causal influence might of course be difficult to determine) with the ways in which and the extent to which 'even in the modern state the means of physical force have been substantially autonomous from (the rest of) the state'. I have already quoted this passage, and although on that occasion I had typically gone out of my way to find something *conceptually* wrong with it, I had also suggested (untypically, this time) that it has a lot to recommend it at the *empirical* level. I shall develop this point by drawing on a chapter of a recent book of mine (Poggi 2001).

First, let me restate the trinitarian view I am 'pushing' here, by quoting the definition of 'politics' in Collins's *Conflict Sociology*:

What we shall deal with here is the ways in which violence has been organised in society ... In this fashion we can deal with all questions that might arise about politics ... Politics, in this approach, involves both outright warfare and coercive threats. Most of what we refer to as politics in the internal (but not external) organisation of the modern state is a remote version of the latter ... Much politics does not involve actual violence but consists of manoeuvering around the organisation that controls the violence. (Collins 1975: 157)

The expression 'the organisation that controls the violence' has some implications worth teasing out. First, 'organisation' implies a readiness, a capacity to exercise (or threaten) violence; the violence exercised or threatened is a product, a manifestation of pre-constituted, abiding arrangements. Second, 'organisation' implies that these arrangements constitute an expressly contrived, differentiated, relatively self-standing aspect of a broader social reality. Third, the notion of 'control over violence' suggests that from the standpoint of that broader reality, the phenomenon of violence has costs (including the risk of being challenged and overcome by greater violence, or the risk of being overused) which it is the task of organization to curb.

The institutionalization of political power in general and, more specifically, the development of the state, point up the complex and sometimes paradoxical relationships between these implications. The state tends to restrict the play of diffuse violence in the society and thus to pacify society, in two closely related ways. It declares illegitimate much of the violence people would otherwise indulge in – *much*, not all; as feminist critics have pointed out, the violence exercised and threatened by men in their dealings with women has mostly *not* been considered illegitimate. And it tries, more or less consistently and successfully, to reserve to itself the social and material devices that make violence more formidable – from uniforms to military and police command systems to weapons.

This last one is the critical process in the curbing of domestic violence. The political centre vests in a part of itself, specifically organized to deal with it, an overwhelmingly superior capacity for violence. Thus, individuals or groups which might otherwise attempt to engage in violence on their own behalf are persuaded to cease and desist from such attempts. What pacifies society, thus, is not the disappearance or the utter rarity of social and material devices for restraining, killing, maiming, destroying, but the fact that these are vested, in principle, only in the political system, which entrusts them in turn to a specialized part of itself. To the extent that this happens, a paradox presented by Hobbes is confirmed: as the *potential* for violence increases, its *actual* exercise (or the threat of it) diminishes. This requires that the part of the political system entrusted with the potential for violence be – again – an 'organisation': a purposefully contrived and coherently controlled set of practices, people, resources, specialized in building up and maintaining that potential. The political system must ensure that the organization in question packs enough of a punch to 'pacify' the social process at large and, when necessary, to keep outside political forces from interfering with it. It must also ensure that the potential for violence it vests in the organization does not become dispersed into the rest of society by a kind of osmosis or entropy. Finally, the organization itself should not, as a whole or in its parts, exercise or threaten to exercise violence on its own behalf, against the larger society or the political system itself.

Let us restate this argument. The larger society can be secured against internal disorder and external aggression only if, through its political system, it possesses itself of a potential for violence which is *formidable* – in the etymological sense of the expression, meaning 'such as to evoke fear'. Organization serves this aim, for it entails that violence will be primarily (indeed, as far as possible, exclusively) engaged in an effective, workmanlike fashion by trained, competent specialists. It also serves the aim of differentiating institutionally the business of violence from the remainder of the social process.

Here comes the tricky part. Exactly that institutional differentiation creates an awkward possibility: the specialists in question may use their own exclusive guardianship of a critical social resource (organized violence) to affect the definition of public interest with which are charged other parts of the political system, and the related policies. The organization they inhabit may become self-absorbed, relatively unresponsive to the requirements and expectations of the rest of society. It can foster its own autonomy of other parts, increase its claims upon the resources they produce and manage, or seek to impose on the rest of the political system a self-interested understanding of what the larger society, taken as a whole, can and should do.

These possibilities are enhanced by the fact that an organization built around violence tends to have a strongly hierarchical structure; this, on the one hand, allows it to confront promptly and effectively the contingencies requiring violence to be threatened or exercised; on the other, it allows the top levels of the structure to deploy the organization's resources in a coherent and unitary fashion. Thus the organization can present more of a challenge *also* to other parts of the political system. The guardians and practitioners of organized violence may deal with the rest of the system *as if* from the outside, disregarding or subverting their own subordination to other parts, including those instituted to stand for the whole of the political system. In this fashion, the relationship between organized violence and political power, although it is a part-to-whole relationship, may come to resemble those between ideological or economic power on the one hand, and political power on the other.

There is of course great diversity in the extent to which the top-level military personnel act as a semi-independent elite, in the nature of the claims they advance, and in the content of the arguments by which they support those claims. Some countries have occasionally experienced the outright usurpation of political power by military leaders, in others these have successfully blackmailed the political elites into undertaking policies (sometimes of no direct military significance) different from those they had intended to pursue, in yet others the military have traditionally been, at worst, a pressure group seeking to increase or maintain its share of the state's budget.

In spite of this variety, it is possible to identify, among the recurrent issues, two particularly significant ones: on the one hand, how significant is, in the context of political experience in general, the problem of war and of the preparedness for it; on the other, how necessary it is that the institution specifically committed to handling that problem be granted a large amount of autonomy. I will comment briefly on these themes.

In the context of the modern state, and particularly in the West, the first theme – the persistent significance of war – has had a complex career. On the one hand, in the nineteenth century the war phenomenon, from time immemorial the central issue and the central instrumentality in the relations between states, acquired a monumental, ominous dimension, first fully displayed in the mass carnage of the American Civil War; and in the first half of the twentieth century, two world wars enormously amplified and deepened that experience. Through most of the second half of the century, the capitalist West and the collectivist East stood in a relationship which some claimed to be akin to war, and which occasionally seemed to push them towards the brink of an unprecedented kind of warfare of total mutual annihilation. Besides, a distressing number of highly murderous wars took place outside the areas directly occupied by the blocks, and without involving them in direct military confrontation, though many of those wars were related to the blocks' policies.

On the other hand, in our own time war seems to have become something of a dirty secret, at any rate for the Western publics, which preferred to emphasize political issues related to economics. Even in the West/East contest, it was widely felt, the key issue was not the military might of the two blocks, but the productive capacities of the respective socio-economic systems, and their ability to promote industrial growth both in the countries of each block and in the so-called Third World. Only in the USA and the USSR (especially, perhaps, in the latter) were the military elites spared the suspicion that their role in the politics of the respective countries had become a recessive one.

Naturally enough, this was for military elites a threatening feeling. They often reacted to it by arguing that, for all appearances to the contrary, war unavoidably remained the overriding concern of states, and organized, armed might their bottom-line resource. In some cases, military elites acknowledged that all-out war (not just nuclear, but also conventional) had become a highly improbable option; however, they began to prospect alternative uses for their own distinctive competences, and developed a set of neologisms and euphemisms for such uses – for instance, counter-insurgency measures, low-intensity military operations, peace-keeping interventions, aid to civil authority.

The persistent centrality of the military phenomenon to political experience is not, however, the sole theme to which military elites connect their claims. Another is the necessity that, for many intents and purposes, the military institution be run according to criteria exclusive to it, and enjoy a high degree of autonomy with respect to other political and social institutions. In order to understand this requirement, we may consider the utter peculiarity of the core activity of fighting soldiers, which (when all is said and done) consists in seeking to kill people who in turn seek to kill *them*.

Soldiers are supposed to carry out this activity in a frame of mind, which is well conveyed by the meaning of the expression 'mission' in the military context. This entails that one is *sent* to accomplish a task not of one's own, but in the accomplishment of which one is to invest all one has and is. 'Mission' also suggests that the task in question is a distinct phase or aspect of a broader project, of which one may not be even aware. The responsibility for formulating and assigning the task, and of coordinating it with other phases or aspects of the same project, falls with others. The connection between one's specific activity and those of others assigned the same mission, between that mission and other missions, can only be ensured by prompt and thorough obedience to commands.

However, the execution of commands by a soldier, while (so to speak) *oriented* by obedience, must also be *motivated* by a sense of personal engagement. It would not be safe for this to be provided exclusively by the soldiers' attachment to their personal survival and bodily integrity, for all too often this might induce soldiers to flight rather than to fight. (In French, *sauve-toi*, literally 'save yourself', also means 'run away'.) An additional, and sometimes an overriding, motivational ingredient must instead be solidarity – a keen sense that one has a significant personal stake also in the survival and bodily integrity of others with whom one is closely associated. One might say that obedience provides a vertical tie between the individual soldier's conduct and that of his or her superiors; and solidarity a horizontal linkage between the individual soldier and his or her peers. A further emotional requirement is that, in the combat situation, soldiers should feel called upon to *prove themselves* in the face of an extremely testing and threatening situation.

What soldiers are to prove about themselves used to be characterized as manliness; if this notion is to be disposed of because of its sexist connotations, one should replace it with another one bearing the same complex semantic freight. This embraces the capacity, in extremely stressful situations, to give and execute commands, to demonstrate solidarity toward one's associates, to perform complex activities, to endure deprivation, suffering, the prospect of painful death; it also encompasses a willingness to engage in violent, armed aggression and to overcome others' resistance to it.

In the context of a more-or-less modernized society, such psychical dispositions tend to be rare, as well as potentially dangerous. Their inculcation, therefore, requires a specialized environment, which insulates those who impart them, as well as those in the process of acquiring them, from the rest of society, and thereby both protects the society itself and maximizes the probability of having those dispositions duly learned and experimented with. The insulation is both symbolic (for instance the wearing of uniforms, the ceremonies of induction of soldiers) and physical. (As an Italian saying goes, the reason army barracks are guarded by sentinels is – to keep common sense out.) Above all, it is institutional; that is a set of publicly acknowledged, sanctioned practices structure military life differently from all other forms of social life, for instance by valuing obedience, solidarity and various aspects of what one used to call manliness over contrasting attitudes and dispositions rewarded by the larger society.

As Mann has shown in his writings, typically a state's military component is not content with being an object of public controversies over its nature and significance, but actively intervenes in them in order to asserts its autonomy of other parts of the state, and maximize its leverage on the state's policies. This is indeed something Weber himself knew a lot about, though he preferred to discuss similar tendencies with reference to the state's bureaucratic apparatus rather than its army. (We know, however, that he resented the semi-dictatorship Ludendorff imposed upon German public life during the last phase of the Great War.)

I think Mann has rendered us all a service by reminding us of the military's drive towards autonomy. This results from its position as a relatively segregated and highly specialized institution, entrusted with formidable resources which, if it disregards or 'suspends' its constitutional position as a mere executor of political decisions made by other state organs, it can mobilize to affect their policies, or even to take over the state's commanding positions.

Mann knows and relates a great deal about the rich phenomenology generated by that drive, and emphasizes those moments and aspects of it which have made a significant difference at various salient points in modern history, sometimes through complex 'intertwinings' between what he calls military power on the one hand, economic and/or political power on the other.

The question remains, whether any of this authorizes Mann's view that military power has the same analytical status as political, economic and ideological power. As is clear from all the above, I would answer that question in the negative, though I concede that in certain contexts the relationship between military and civilian elites comes to resemble that between two self-standing powers. But my sense is that even when this happens, it happens *within and about the state*, and thus confirms the higher conceptual status of political power over against 'military power'.

Take the Pinochet episode, for instance. It was a classical military take-over of *state* power, brutally bringing organized violence to bear in order to change the *Chilean state's* constitution, regime and policies, in alliance with and in the service of domestic economic power. One *part* of the state sought to increase its sway over *other* parts and thereby over the *whole* of the state. One constitutive component of institutionalized political power prevailed upon and subordinated others – it did not try to 'go it alone'. The point of the exercise was to place the main levers which controlled the state machine in the hands of the military leaders. In this, the episode confirms, rather than negating, the intrinsic institutional identity of the military as the custodian and the specialized practitioner of that most distinctive and fearsome resource *of political power* – organized, armed violence. No less – and no more.

References

Anter, A. 1996. *Max Webers Theorie des Modernen Staates: Herkunft, Struktur und Bedeutung*. Tübingen: Mohr Siebeck.

Calvez, J.-Y. 1967. *Introduction à la vie politique*. Paris: Aubier-Montaigne.

Collins, R. 1975. *Conflict Sociology: Toward an Explanatory Science*. New York: Academic Press.

Etzioni, A. 1975. *A Comparative Analysis of Complex Organizations: On Power, Involvement, and their Correlates*. New York: Free Press.

Field, G. L., and J. Higley. 1981. *Elitism*. London: Routledge.

Gellner, E. 1988. *Plough, Sword, and Book: The Structure of Human History*. London: Collins Harvill.

Jouvenel, B. de. 1963. *The Pure Theory of Politics*. New Haven, CT: Yale University Press.

Mann, M. 1986. *The Sources of Social Power, Volume I: A History from the Beginning to 1760 AD*. Cambridge: Cambridge University Press.

  1993. *The Sources of Social Power, Volume II: The Rise of Classes and Nation-States*. Cambridge: Cambridge University Press.

Milner, M. Jr. 1994. *Status and Sacredness: A General Theory of Status Relations and an Analysis of Indian Culture*. New York: Oxford University Press.

Piven, F. F., and R. Cloward. 1971. *Regulating the Poor: The Functions of Public Welfare*. New York: Vintage Books.

Poggi, G. 2001. *Forms of Power*. Cambridge: Polity Press.

Popitz, H. 1992. *Phaenomene der Macht*. Tübingen: Mohr Siebeck.

Runciman, W. G. 1983. *A Treatise on Social Theory*. Cambridge: Cambridge University Press.

8   Mann, the state and war

John M. Hobson

Michael Mann's two-volume *magnum opus*, *The Sources of Social Power*, is, in my opinion, one of the most impressive works of scholarship produced in the last fifty years. Indeed, the striking mix of empirical sensitivity and sweeping historical narrative within a sophisticated theoretical framework is such that the informal label of Mann as the 'modern-day Max Weber' is – despite his effacious modesty – richly deserved. That said, I do see some significant problems in his work, though I will argue here that these *can* be remedied. In this chapter I reconsider and evaluate Michael Mann's broad corpus of work through the lens of International Relations theory. This makes sense because Mann's work has direct relevance for International Relations (IR), and to the extent that he invokes the importance of the 'international' when explaining social change, so he inevitably and unavoidably enters the terrain of IR theory. My central objective here is to use insight from IR theory to enter into a constructive dialogue with Mann, ultimately so as to suggest ways in which his pioneering theory can be further enhanced.

It is important to begin by noting that, unbeknown to most historical sociologists, in the last decade or so a growing number of IR scholars have begun to look towards the neo-Weberian historical sociological works of Mann and others. The reason for this is straightforward. The hitherto dominant paradigm of IR – neorealism – has increasingly been found wanting for at least four major reasons. These comprise:

   (i) an ahistorical approach that denies the importance or possibility of change;
  (ii) a pure structuralist ontology that denies agency and 'kicks the state back out';
 (iii) an excessive materialist epistemology;
 (iv) a reductionist causal model.

First and foremost, neorealism explicitly rejects historical sociological analysis insofar as it insists that the international system has been forever governed by *continuity* associated with the timeless logic of international 'anarchy' (where there is no higher authority standing above states in the international system). Elsewhere I have described this ahistoricism as 'tempocentrism'. I define *tempocentrism* as a mode of ahistoricism, which in effect takes a snapshot of the present international system and extrapolates it back through time such that *discontinuous* ruptures and *differences* between historical epochs and state systems are smoothed over and consequently obscured. In this way, history appears to be marked, or is regulated, by a regular tempo that beats according to the same, constant rhythm of the present system. This is in fact an *inverted* form of 'path dependency' (Hobson 2002: 9–10). Thus in reconstructing all historical systems so as to conform to a particular conception of the present, neorealists tarnish all systems as homologous or 'isomorphic' (i.e. as having the same properties or structure). In this way, the study of international relations takes on a 'transhistorical' quality, as all political actors behave in *uniform* ways regardless of time and place. Consequently, this abolishes the need for historical sociology (HS) altogether. Thus, by deploying tempocentrism, neorealists write off the process or study of 'change' from the mainstream IR research agenda. But with the end of the Cold War and the growing awareness of globalization, the question of international change has been fundamentally resuscitated as a subject worthy of theoretical and empirical investigation. Because neorealism is unable to offer ways to understand this, many IR scholars began to turn to historical sociologists such as Mann in order to furnish them with the means to theoretically grasp the problem of change.

Second, IR scholars became increasingly dissatisfied with the *structuralist* logic of neorealism. Not only is structuralist analysis weak in explaining or even focusing on the question of change, but it also brackets out the effects of agency. Moreover, Waltz denies the possibility of a theory of the state, leading him to effectively 'kick the state back out' (see Hobson 2000: 19–30). Above all, the social properties or identities of states, societies and transnational actors are explicitly bracketed in the formation of inter-state behaviour. Mann's highly sophisticated non-reductionist theory of state power as well as social power provided a second reason as to why some IR theorists began to look towards HS. Third, the excessive emphasis on *material* structure found in neorealism meant that social process became bracketed or ignored. This has in particular spurred on the 'sociological turn' within IR, with the meteoric rise of constructivism. Mann's focus on ideology at first sight appeared attractive in this respect. Fourth, neorealism has been found wanting for its 'reductionism' – reductionist in the sense that *domestic* social relations or state–society complexes are irrelevant for understanding inter-state behaviour, such that the international structure is ontologically privileged. Accordingly, the international is conceived of as wholly autonomous from the domestic realm and is, therefore, 'self-constituting'. Again, Mann's conception proffered on the first page of *Sources of Social Power* points to an alternative approach: that 'Societies are constituted of multiple and intersecting sociospatial networks of power' (Mann 1986: 1). Just as there is no such thing as 'society' understood as a 'pure' or self-constituting entity, so by implication there is no such thing as international society or the international system, understood as a separate and self-sufficient realm. Mann's analysis of overlapping power networks on the one hand, and his multi-causal IEMP model on the other, has also been important here as a means to redress this problem within IR.

These four major insights amount to what I call the 'promise' of historical sociology for IR. Put simply, the *promise* of historical sociology within IR is to provide a remedy for the defects that neorealism gives rise to. And for these four reasons then, Mann's name (and others) began to appear in the footnotes of IR works. But while Mann's work has undoubtedly much to offer IR, it is also the case that IR theory can contribute to enhancing Mann's macro-historical-sociological approach. For despite the fact that Mann's work provides many cues for a theoretical alternative to the hegemony of materialist neorealism within IR, the extreme irony here is that Mann himself frequently slips into a neorealist analysis of the international.

I suggest that insight from IR reveals two 'twin paradoxes' with respect to Mann's work: first, the reproduction of a neorealist conception of the international leads him to contradict many of the insights that he offers, and simultaneously leads him to reproduce the four limitations found in neorealism as mentioned above (none of which, I'm sure, Mann would remotely want to be associated with). Second, despite the fact that Mann's non-reductionist approach goes further than most historical sociologists in challenging materialism, nevertheless he does not fully escape materialist logic, and his non-materialist analysis often becomes obscured. This, like the first paradox, ironically limits his ability to provide either a satisfactory analysis of 'change' through time or to fully realize – or retain the integrity of – his multi-causal model, or even to deliver on the 'promise' of historical sociology for IR more generally. And at the extreme, his reproduction of materialistic-neorealism leads to an *ahistorical* analysis that denies the rationale for historical sociology in the first place. Accordingly and paradoxically, these two paradoxes emerge through the lens of constructivist and historical sociological insight found within the discipline of IR.

The purpose of this chapter is to reveal these limitations and suggest ways that these problems can be addressed – not so as to transcend

Mann's approach, but to enhance it. Above all, I suggest that movement towards what I call a 'thick' historical sociology can overcome the twin limitations of excessive materialism and neorealism that exist within the broad canvass of his work, both of which cause various problems for Mann's historical-sociological theoretical model. The first section of the chapter reveals his preference for a neorealist definition of the international, while the second section examines his tendency towards a 'thin' (or materialist) historical sociology.

Between neorealism and non-realism in Mann's definition of the international: negating the rationale for historical sociology and compromising the IEMP model?

Let's briefly begin by noting the fundamental claims made by IR's most well-known neorealist – Kenneth Waltz. His approach was first laid out in his famous text, *Man, the State and War* (Waltz 1959), but took its clearest and most definitive form in his *Theory of International Politics* (Waltz 1979). In this latter book, Waltz argued that the principal focus of enquiry *must* be to explain historical 'continuity'. His whole theory stemmed from his particular observation that international politics has always remained the same, by which he means that in an anarchic state system, the political units are always destined to compete and conflict as all seek to survive. This is true regardless of the *type* of political unit in existence – city-states, empires or nation-states – and regardless of the *social* properties or *identities* of the actors (e.g. capitalist, feudal; Christian or Islamic; democratic or authoritarian). To wit his well-known statement: '[t]he texture of international politics remains highly constant, patterns recur and events repeat themselves endlessly. The relations that prevail internationally seldom shift rapidly in type or quality. They are marked by a dismaying persistence' (Waltz 1979: 66). And no less importantly, it was this observation that led him to create a theoretical model that was causally *reductionist* – where international anarchy is ontologically privileged. This move was made because anarchy, unlike national societies, does not change over time. Accordingly, anarchy – and only anarchy – can explain why IR has always been governed by the timeless and universal conflict of political units.

Waltz's claim is that under the anarchic structure of the international system, states are engaged in an inevitable struggle for survival and power. Given that there is no higher authority to regulate the political actors (i.e. anarchy), they have no choice but to adopt 'self-help' in order to ensure their own survival. This requires them to *emulate* the successful powers as well as *balance* against them, so that they can minimize the 'relative power gap'. Failure to do so means that they will become vulnerable to the predatory behaviour of other powers and will be attacked at best, and swallowed up at worst (Waltz 1979: 73–4, 76–7, 88–99, 118, 127–8). The crucial point here is that in conforming to this competitive and singular logic of anarchy (emulation and balancing), states unwittingly reproduce anarchy because their behaviour prevents any one state from swallowing all the others up, and thereby closes off the possibility for a single 'hierarchy' to emerge. In this way, the anarchic multi-state system is *perpetuated over time*, thereby negating the possibility of 'change'. Thus not only does the possibility of 'change' disappear, but so too does the notion of agency. For, as I have explained elsewhere, the logical corollary of Waltz's structuralism is that he in effect 'kicks the state back out' (see Hobson 2000: 19–30; 2002: 5–20).

But perhaps the main problem with Waltz's model lies in its inherent 'tempocentrism', such that the international system takes on a *transhistorical* quality, as all actors regardless of their 'identity' or 'social systems' and regardless of time and place, behave in exactly the same way. It is *this* tempocentric manoeuvre which leads neorealists to look constantly for signs of the present in the past, and, in a type of self-fulfilling prophecy, come back and report that the past is indeed the same as the present. Thus they assume that either history is repetitive such that nothing ever changes because of the timeless presence of anarchy (Waltz 1979), or, that history takes on the form of repetitive and isomorphic 'great power/ hegemonic' cycles, each phase of which is essentially identical, with the only difference being *which* great power is rising or declining – i.e. same play, different actors (Gilpin 1981). In this way, neorealists assume that the 'superpower' contest between Athens and Sparta is equivalent to the recent Cold War between the USA and USSR; or that current US state behaviour is broadly equivalent to that of historical great powers such as sixteenth-century Spain and especially nineteenth-century Britain (Gilpin 1981; Kennedy 1988). At the most general level, neorealists tempocentrically conclude that 'the classic history of Thucydides is as meaningful a guide to the behavior of states today as when it was written in the fifth century BC' (Gilpin 1981: 7). It is this 'trick' to represent all historical actors and systems as isomorphic that leads neorealists to conclude that world politics *must* always have been governed by the timeless and constant logic of anarchy, which thereby enables them to dismiss the utility of historical-sociological enquiry (see Waltz 1979: 43–9).

Historical sociology's prime purpose *should* be to counter the tempocentric ahistoricism of neorealism and other structuralist approaches, thereby bringing the issues of change and agency back in. This is its *promise*. But while the *spirit* of Mann's enterprise undoubtedly provides such a remedy, nevertheless to the extent that Mann reproduces neorealism, so he falls into the same trap and thereby fails to deliver on the 'promise' of historical sociology. The key question then is: how and to what extent does Mann fall into this trap?

Mann's work has had a particularly strong impact within historical sociology not least because he has sought to 'bring the international back in'. As with Skocpol (1979), Collins (1986) and Tilly (1990), Mann's conception of the 'international' tends mainly to rely on a neorealist definition. Indeed, for the most part when Mann 'thinks' of the international he tends to equate, or conflate, it with 'geopolitical militarism'. Particularly revealing here is that in *every* empirical chapter of the second volume of *Sources of Social Power*, when he discusses the role of the international it is invariably under the heading of 'geopolitical militarism' (or something similar). But it makes sense to begin this analysis with Mann's 'early' discussion of militarism, outlined in chapter 4 of *States, War and Capitalism*.

Mann's basic argument is that *contra* Marxism, militarism does not derive from capitalism or social processes, but from the logic of inter-state geopolitics: '[M]ilitarism derives from geo-political aspects of our social structure which are far older than capitalism' (Mann 1988: 128). Many passages are striking for their neorealist content, to wit:

[W]arfare has been a normal way of conducting international relations throughout recorded history ... But always in conjunction with peace: war and peace succeed each other as the characteristic instruments of inter-state relations. These are carried on in relatively rational, calculative forms, with an eye to the particular advantages in any situation of either war or peace. To these historic patterns of diplomacy, capitalism cannot have contributed much, one way or another. (Mann 1988: 131)

And just as Waltz (1979: ch. 2) tempocentrically argued against Lenin's theory of imperialism – that capitalism could *not* have been responsible for the imperial struggle at the end of the nineteenth century precisely because imperialism and geopolitical rivalries have existed as long as political units have existed (to wit Athens and Sparta) – Mann does likewise. 'Politically speaking, neither the capitalism of the West, nor the state socialism of the Soviet Union, are the key enemies of those who desire peace and survival today. The enemies are rather the common geo-political pretensions of the super-powers – the *same* pretensions as Greece and Persia, Rome and Carthage, possessed' (Mann 1988: 144, my emphasis). Accordingly he concludes that, 'the main theory of the force of geo-political militarism [is] one that still endures today' (Mann 1988: 132). In this way, Mann subscribes to the standard neorealist view of (geopolitical) 'historical continuity'. But the link with neorealism does not begin and end with chapter 4, for the rest of the book reiterates the argument. Thus Mann takes liberalism to task for its theory of pacific-capitalist modernity, and argues that warfare has crucially informed the rise of citizenship and class struggles (chapters 5 and 6), as well as 'ruling-class strategies' (chapter 7), and finally the rise and decline of great powers (to which I return below).

If the deployment of neorealist-inspired arguments was only confined to *States, War and Capitalism*, then the power of my critique here would certainly be much diminished. But the argument is faithfully reproduced across the vast corpus of Mann's writings. This is especially apparent in his famous discussion of state formation, where it was geopolitical inter-state conflict that centrally informed the process of state-centralization and the growth of infrastructural power (Mann 1986: 419–99; 1988: 73–123; 1993: chs. 11–12). Furthermore, the international was important to the rise of British and German industrialization; and once more, this is exclusively understood in terms of warfare and inter-state competition (Mann 1993: chs. 4 and 9). And from the British case, the process of state *emulation* (as in Waltz and Gilpin) ensured the spread of industrialization across the European continent: 'Once it became clear across the multistate system that Britain had stumbled on enormous new power resources, it was swiftly copied' (Mann 1986: 450). Moreover, the role of warfare is important within his explanation of both domestic class relations and social revolutions (Mann 1986: chs. 12–15; 1993: chs. 5, 6, 7, 18).

Neorealist analysis is strikingly reproduced in chapter 8 of *States, War and Capitalism*, where he analyses the rise and decline of great powers (in this case using Britain as an example). Here, Mann's analysis is identical to that found in the work of Robert Gilpin (a leading neorealist scholar). Gilpin argued that under anarchy, the rise and decline of great powers was inevitable. In essence, he argued that those states which could best adapt their domestic social structures to the logic of (anarchic) inter-state competition would rise – namely by emulating the leading practices of the dominant states – while those that were maladaptive would necessarily decline (Gilpin 1981; and for a full discussion see Hobson 2000: 30–7). This idea implicitly derives from Waltz's claim that: 'Actors may perceive the structure [of anarchy] that constrains them and understand how it serves to reward some kinds of behavior and to penalize others ... those who conform to accepted and successful practices more often rise to the top' (Waltz 1979: 92, 128). Here's Mann:

In [an anarchic] multi-state civilization it is virtually inevitable that [the rise and decline of great powers] will happen. The dominant power will be caught up by several others and then be merely one among equals ... The conditions that first led to [a great power's adaptive] success are institutionalized, but then those very institutions hold the [maladaptive] power back from further developing if the environment changes. (Mann 1988: 211)

No less significant is the point that this 'adaptive' game of survival arguably permeates the *central* aspect of Mann's *Sources of Social Power* volume I, where much of his focus is on the dialectical swing between 'multi-actor-power civilisations' (more or less equivalent to 'anarchic multi-state systems') and 'empires of domination' (broadly equivalent to what Waltz calls 'hierarchies'). And though Mann does indeed pay considerable attention to the role of domestic forces (as does Gilpin), nevertheless the key point is that the rise and decline of these regional entities is at all times governed by their ability to adapt to the international military system (Mann 1986: 533–8). Accordingly, the international structure is, once again, ontologically privileged. And in turn, this means that tracing the 'leading edge' of international power can be undertaken by an analysis that mirrors that of Gilpin's theory of the 'rise and decline of great powers'.

Nevertheless, while a neorealist conception clearly predominates his understanding of the international, it is noteworthy that there are (albeit occasional) junctures where Mann points to or hints at various non-realist definitions. In a particularly sophisticated discussion of Mann's work, Steve Hobden (1998: ch. 6) correctly points out that there are a series of competing views in Mann's definition of the international (in addition to the neorealist conception). One is a constructivist conception. Thus, for example, when discussing 'foreign policy' Mann emphasizes the point that:

Statesmen had social identities, especially of class and religious community, whose norms helped define conceptions of interests and morality ... [D]iplomacy and geopolitics were rule-governed ... Even war was rule-governed, 'limited' in relation to some, righteously savage in relation to others. (Mann 1993: 69; also 70–5)

Moreover, much of this overlaps with the analysis advocated by the English School of International Relations. Indeed Mann's definition of what he calls 'multi-power-actor civilisations' is similar (though not equivalent) to the English School's definition of *international society*, to wit: 'decentralized power actors competed with one another within an *overall framework of normative regulation*' (Mann 1986: 534, my emphasis; also, Mann 1993: 270, 278–82, 293).

It is also worth noting that Mann seems to be aware of some of the problems with neorealism. As he has candidly noted:

Some IR practitioners have been examining the impact of social relations on geopolitics for well over a decade. Sociologists did not respond as helpfully as we might. It was over a decade ago that some sociologists became aware that our specialism was neglecting the impact of geopolitics on social relations. We first borrowed precisely the traditional form of realism from which many IR practitioners were then fleeing ... We passed each other in the night. (Mann 1996: 223)

It is no less important to note that there is nothing intrinsic to Weberianism that makes for a neorealist definition of the international (Hobson and Seabrooke 2001; but for the contrary position, see Schroeder 1998). Certainly Mann is less prone to neorealism than are other neo-Weberians, particularly with reference to his complex theory of the state (see Hobson 2000: 192–203; cf. Hobden 1998: chs. 4–6, 8). And at many points in *Sources of Social Power* volume II, Mann explicitly argues against neorealism (e.g. Mann 1993: 48–51, 256–8, 293, 743–57).

Despite all this, though, it seems clear that Mann's definition of the international is clearly dominated by a neorealist approach. And my major point is that this is problematic because neorealism's reductionist structuralist ontology and ahistorical predisposition undermines the integrity of his multi-causal IEMP model on the one hand, and undermines the rationale for a genuine historical sociology of IR and HS on the other. It is also significant to note – especially with respect to scholars such as Skocpol and Tilly – that their deployment of a neorealist conception of the international system unwittingly leads them to 'kick the state back out' (see especially, Hobson 2000: 174–91). Thus if Mann wishes to realize his serious commitment to a multi-causal model of historical-social change, he will need to critically rethink his conception of the international.

Should he seek to revise his views of the international, the obvious question becomes: 'How?' Ironically, sociologically inspired IR theory can help to remedy the problem here; 'ironically' that is, because Mann's import within IR is based on the fact that in part he supposedly provides a sociological model. There are more ways of envisaging the international than simply equating it with geopolitical militarism (as he implicitly recognizes). One might, for example, focus on the social and ideational forces that go to construct the international system or 'international society'. Two obvious approaches of relevance here are the English School of International Relations and constructivism. In its original English School incarnation, Hedley Bull (1977) and Martin Wight (1977), though leaning on a materialist approach, nevertheless went beyond neorealism by advocating two central insights: first, that states are not passive victims or bearers of international structure, but can reshape the international system into a relatively cooperative 'international society' (thereby returning the lost theme of agency). And second, they argued that states set up normative institutions which prescribe certain forms of behaviour, which states voluntarily conform to because they value order over insecurity. This might fit well with Mann's broader objectives, especially in his desire to produce a non-reductionist and 'agential' theory of the state. And, as noted above, there are echoes of this argument found at various points in his work. Needless to say, this clashes with his bald neorealist statements and rests uneasily with much of the implicit neorealist analysis found across his extensive writings.

Or he might seek to draw on a constructivist approach, where the international 'system' does not exist 'out there', but is a society that is embedded within particular norms and inter-subjective understandings between the agents. Mann himself hints at this at different points (as mentioned above). Of course there are many ways to develop such an approach (see Hobson 2000: ch. 5). One might look to the domestic identities of the agents and look at how domestic norms and moral purpose are internationalized to govern international political life, which then react back on states and their identities (e.g. Reus-Smit 2002). Or he might draw from a Weberian-constructivist approach, where the degree to which states can embed themselves within the legitimate prevailing norms of society enhances their ability to project financial power internationally (Seabrooke 2006). This is congruent with Mann's general desire to show how the international and domestic realms overlap in a seamless whole, while also producing an approach that successfully reveals changing international practices over time. Moreover, it complements his approach to the state in which the exercise of infrastructural power entails a strong degree of consensus between state and society. And given that Mann *is* interested in the power of ideology or norms, this *could* complement his general model. But whichever particular path Mann might choose to follow ultimately matters less than the point that *maintaining* his neorealist definition of the international, at the very least, compromises the integrity of his approach.

The question now becomes: is Mann's commitment to a multi-causal model – in which materialism and ideationalism (or 'constructivism') are adequately combined – fully realized in his overall work? The argument of the next section is that the balance he achieves between these two approaches is lop-sided in favour of materialism. Once again, I argue that on the one hand this hinders his ability to provide an adequate historical-sociological approach with respect to domestic and international, social and political change, and on the other hand it threatens the integrity of his multi-causal IEMP model.

Between *thick* and *thin* historical sociology: negating the rationale for historical sociology and compromising the IEMP model?

It is a curious irony that mainstream historical sociologists reject the importance of norms, culture and identity in their models of social change (something that I have sought to remedy in my own work; Hobson 2004). And it is all the more curious that Weberian-inspired scholars are so resistant to this focus given that Weber became famous for his 'constructivist' thesis outlined in his *The Protestant Ethic and the Spirit of Capitalism* (Weber 1976). Even if Mann had no truck with such a focus, a discussion of this issue would still be relevant. But given that ideology forms one of the four core defining aspects of his theoretical model, a discussion of this issue becomes all the more pressing. The two guiding questions for my discussion are: 'how successfully has Mann imported the issue of "ideology" into his work?'; and 'what are the consequences for his overall theory if ideology is not satisfactorily dealt with?'

Definitionally speaking, I argue that a *thin* historical sociology (HS) rests on materialist or rationalist premises, while a *thick* HS invokes a social constructivist approach. Materialist frameworks ultimately rest upon the notion of a 'universal will to power'. Actors know what their interests are *prior* to social interaction, and the game they play in society or international society is to maximize these interests. To the extent that rationalists discuss the role of ideas at all, they are viewed as merely functional to the power-maximizing interests of various agents. Constructivist frameworks, by contrast, do not presuppose actors' interests as exogenously given. Rather, they are informed through the process of social interaction. More specifically, agents' interests are informed by their identities, and their identities are shaped by the normative and social environment within which they reside. And such identities are *constructed* through what might be called 'statecraft' and 'socialcraft'. In short, while materialists are concerned with the process of *defending* agents' interests, social constructivists are concerned with *defining* agents' interests.

As in his discussion of the international, so Mann's writings oscillate or slip between various positions; in this case between a 'thick' and 'thin' HS. In a recent essay, Chris Reus-Smit claims that Mann's analysis is ultimately materialist and rejects it in favour of a constructivist approach (Reus-Smit 2002: esp. 123–6). While there is much in what he says, nevertheless he omits discussion of Mann's notion of 'transcendent ideological power'; a conception that is entirely congruent with Reus-Smit's preferred constructivist approach. Put differently, it is unfair to claim that

Mann's HS is a *purely* thin one. For, more than most theorists in HS, Mann pays explicit attention to 'ideology'.

Mann invokes two definitions of ideology. His 'thin' definition is broadly congruent with the notion of 'regulatory norms' found in ortho-dox rationalist/materialist approaches, which views ideology as some-thing that merely reinforces (or is reducible to) the interests of certain power-actors. He calls this 'immanent ideological power'. But his second definition is congruent with that of 'constitutive norms' as favoured by constructivists, where ideology takes on a 'transcendent', autonomous quality. Here such norms transcend given class and social structures and reconfigure societies along new normative lines (as discussed in Mann 1986: chs. 3, 4, 10, 11). My point is slightly different to that made by Reus-Smit: that like his theoretical ancestor, Max Weber, Mann's approach steers an inconsistent path between (genuine) constructivism and materialism, though he steers much more strongly towards the materialist pole. And to the extent that he does, he either compromises the integrity of his multi-causal IEMP model, or he jeopardizes the power of his *historical-sociological* conception of international and social change.

What then are Mann's constructivist credentials and what are their limits? Almost exactly like Max Weber who began his first volume of *Economy and Society* by arguing that the task of the historical sociologist should be to get to grips with the *meaning* of human action (Weber 1978: ch. 1), Mann begins *Sources of Social Power* volume II by making three broadly constructivist claims about ideological power:

First, we cannot understand (and so act upon) the world merely by direct sense perception. We require concepts and categories of *meaning* imposed upon sense perceptions. The social organization of ultimate knowledge and meaning is necessary to social life, as Weber argued ... Second, *norms*, shared understand-ings of how people should act morally in their relations with each other, are necessary for sustained social cooperation ... [And] to monopolize norms is ... a route to power. The third source of ideological power is *aesthetic/ritual practices*. These are not reducible to rational[ist] science. (Mann 1986: 22–3)

From there, Mann sporadically engages in genuine constructivist ana-lysis, mainly through his discussion of 'transcendent' (constitutive) norms and their impact on reshaping society. This was applied most keenly in his discussion of the Roman Empire (1986: ch. 10), where in particular he claims that, 'Christianity was not a response to material crisis [or material needs] ... The crisis was one of social identity: What society do I belong to?' (1986: 309). He also applied this analysis both to the emergence of civilization in Mesopotamia and world religions (1986: chs. 3, 4, 11). And perhaps most famously, he placed a great deal of emphasis on the norms that held feudal Europe (i.e. Christendom) in place (1986: ch. 12).

Furthermore, the constructivist emphasis on the role of *legitimacy* is a feature of Mann's theory of the state. For it is one of his central claims that states which can ground themselves within, and cooperate with, social actors through infrastructural (consensual) power generate greater amounts of governing capacity than do those states which seek to isolate themselves from society through despotic power (Mann 1993: ch. 3). In short, Mann *does* take ideology seriously, and certainly points to the importance of legitimacy in the realms of social action as well as the state. At this point of proceedings, his preferred descriptive label for his model – 'organisational materialism' – is clearly inappropriate.

But this constructivist commitment is significantly compromised at other points in his writings, where in *Sources of Social Power* Volume I, for example, he begins by asserting, in classic materialist fashion, that:

Human beings are restless, purposive, and rational, striving to increase their enjoyment of the good things of life and capable of choosing and pursuing appropriate means for doing so ... [Accordingly] we can take for granted the motivational drive of humans to seek to increase their means of subsistence. That is a constant ... Human motivation is irrelevant except that it provided the forward drive that enough humans possess to give them a dynamism wherever they dwell. (Mann 1986: 4–5)

Mann generally equates ideology with religion and his major discussions of the role of 'transcendent ideological power' refer exclusively to religious instances. Not that there is anything wrong with such an emphasis, but it becomes problematic when other sources or forms of 'thick' norms and identity are ignored or omitted.

This problem becomes most acute in his discussion of the post-1500 world, where his analysis of the role of norms or ideology is heavily, though intentionally, downgraded. In *Sources of Social Power* volume I his discussion of the rise of capitalism intentionally pays no attention to the Renaissance, the Reformation and the Scientific Revolution, since they came too late to explain the rise of Europe, which he sees as beginning around 800 CE (1986: esp. 377). Moreover, one can search only in vain for an analysis of the ways in which norms and identity inform the process of state-formation. And in *Sources of Social Power* Volume II when discussing the 1760–1914 period, he asserts that 'Ideological power relations were of declining and lesser power significance ... [I]deological power ... was more "immanent" than "transcendent"' (Mann 1993: 2). Does this mean that after 1500 'constitutive' (or 'transcendent') norms are of little importance? Presumably not, but Mann writes *almost* as if it were so. Nevertheless, it is interesting to note here that Mann himself conceded during the conference that 'the twentieth-century, probably more than any other, has been the age of ideology'.

Mann might reply to all this by saying that it is not his intention to produce a full or 'thick' theory of ideology (or constitutive norms and identity) along the lines that I am pressing for. This is because to do so it *might* ultimately lead one down the road towards ideational *reductionism* – something which he warns expressly against. In any case, as he verbally put it to me during the conference when this chapter was presented as a paper, 'Sociologists long ago went through a flirtation with social constructivism, but the moment quickly passed.' Arguably though, such a 'response' is surprisingly thin (no pun intended). And in another sense, such an answer is surprising because in *Sources of Social Power* Volume I he clearly had no problems with producing a 'thick' theory of ideology, even if it was done so sporadically. Moreover, it is important to note that I am not suggesting that this should be done at the expense of sacrificing the materialist aspect of his model. In other words the issue at stake here should not be viewed as a zero-sum contest between ideationalism and materialism.

Thus the crucial question now becomes: why is an approach that focuses more fully on the role of 'thick' norms and identity (as well as legitimacy) important? The short answer is that failure to do so jeopardizes the *rationale* for historical sociology at worst (thereby leading on to an 'ahistorical historiography'), or at best compromises Mann's multi-causal methodology and undermines the integrity of his IEMP model. How is this the case? As noted earlier, all materialist analyses tend to view societies in different times and places as governed by a 'universal will to power'; a rationality that is independent of social process or interaction. Agents know prior to social interaction what their interests are and seek to maximize them with whatever *means* or *resources* they have at their disposal. Accordingly, the only 'differences' over time that materialist historical sociologists can point to is changes in the material or resource environment. Not surprisingly, materialist theorists invest a great deal of time and energy in revealing the different 'technological forces' or different means (or modes) of production through time. But this is symptomatic of a 'thin' historical sociology in which tempocentric ahistoricism occupies centre-stage, precisely because the agents, regardless of time and place, behave in exactly the *same* ways. That is, the game that agents play, in either the domestic or international spheres – regardless of time and place – remains the same, as they seek to defend or maximize their interests.

In the context of Mann's overall theory, this ultimate marginalization of 'thick' norms and identity-formation processes is puzzling. For example,

Mann emphasizes the point that peasants under feudalism were very much constrained and informed by the religious context and that this was crucial in achieving normative pacification (Mann 1986). In the absence of this Christian identity, feudalism would presumably have imploded if we follow the logic of Mann's argument. And clearly agents under capitalism think and act differently. Ironically, this was in fact the whole point of Max Weber's famous thesis outlined in his *The Protestant Ethic and the Spirit of Capitalism* (Weber 1976). But curiously, this most Weberian of issues is left aside in Mann's analysis, as indeed it is in the works of other prominent neo-Weberians on this subject (e.g. Giddens 1985; Collins 1986; Hall 1986). The key point is that historical sociology *should* be able to reveal these ideational processes if it is to adequately reveal social change over time. For without this, we are left with a model in which actor-behaviour remains constant through time (as it is guided by an ahistorical and asociological 'universal will to power'). Put simply, the bracketing of 'thick' ideational processes means that the core rationale for historical sociology is basically lost. For if Mann's historical sociology is ahistorical and asociological, then what is historical or sociological about it?

If this conclusion might be seen by some as somewhat excessive, then it is surely less controversial to suggest that failure to theorize the role of 'thick' norms and identities compromises the integrity of his multi-causal IEMP model. For if 'ideology' is omitted then clearly all we are left with is an EMP model. To which might come the reply that the deployment of a 'thin' conception of ideology would retain the integrity of the IEMP model. But this is not the case. Mann's fundamental objective is to break with reductionist methodology. And perhaps his ultimate contribution is to reveal how all (four) sources of social power entwine and mutually constitute each other. But a 'thin' definition of ideology (as 'immanent' rather than 'transcendent' power) is unable to perform this constitutive role in shaping the other power sources. This is because 'immanent' ideological power merely supports, or is functional to, the other power sources and, therefore, has no autonomy. Accordingly, in being unable to constitute the economic, military or political sources of social power it is, therefore, unable to play the role ascribed to it by Mann's non-reductionist methodology. Put simply, without a 'thick' conception of ideology, 'there ain't no I in the IEMP model'.

Conclusion

In his important discussion of Mann's conception of the international, Steve Hobden (1998) concludes that Mann's multiple conceptions necessarily produce a contradictory approach owing to the deployment of incompatible epistemologies – naturalist and interpretivist. I believe this is too harsh not least because it *is* possible to produce a model that combines materialist and constructivist insight. In any case, as already noted, Mann has to a certain (albeit inadequate) extent achieved this. And to the extent that this has been sufficiently recognized, no one has yet seen this as problematic. My concern lies more with the point that Mann's deployment of reductionist neorealism, on the one hand, and excessive materialism, on the other, threatens to compromise the integrity of his multi-causal IEMP model at the very least, and undermines the rationale for HS at most. The problem then *is* significant, but it is nowhere near as grave as Hobden or Reus-Smit suggest and, most importantly, it *can* be remedied.

In sum, therefore, I am suggesting that Mann needs to produce a more carefully thought-out analysis of the international (which, of course, properly plays a very important role in his overall historical sociological analysis). And I also invite him to drop the preferred label of *organizational materialism* and consider renewing his original focus on the role of 'transcendent ideology', which has unfortunately become significantly downgraded in *Sources of Social Power* volume II (dealing with the post-1760 period), as well as *extending* it to incorporate the issue of 'identity'. I ask this not so as to transcend his overall model, but so as to fully realize the laudable theoretical and empirical objectives that underpin his remarkably impressive intellectual enterprise.

References

Bull, H. 1977. *The Anarchical Society*. London: Macmillan.

Collins, R. 1986. *Weberian Sociological Theory*. Cambridge: Cambridge University Press.

Giddens, A. 1985. *The Nation-State and Violence*. Cambridge: Polity.

Gilpin, R. 1981. *War and Change in World Politics*. Cambridge: Cambridge University Press.

Hall, J. A. 1986. *Powers and Liberties*. Harmondsworth: Penguin.

Hobden, S. 1998. *International Relations and Historical Sociology*. London: Routledge.

Hobden, S., and J. M. Hobson (eds.). 2002. *Historical Sociology of International Relations*. Cambridge: Cambridge University Press.

Hobson, J. M. 2000. *The State and International Relations*. Cambridge: Cambridge University Press.

2002. What's at Stake in 'Bringing Historical Sociology *Back* into International Relations'? Transcending Chronofetishism and Tempocentrism in International Relations. In S. Hobden and J. M. Hobson (eds.), *Historical Sociology of International Relations*. Cambridge: Cambridge University Press.

2004. *The Eastern Origins of Western Civilisation*. Cambridge: Cambridge University Press.

Hobson, J. M., and L. Seabrooke. 2001. Reimagining Weber: Constructing International Society and the Social Balance of Power. *European Journal of International Relations*, 7(2).

Kennedy, P. M. 1988. *The Rise and Fall of the Great Powers*. London: Unwin Hyman.

Mann, M. 1986. *The Sources of Social Power, Volume I: A History of Power from the Beginning to 1760 AD*. Cambridge: Cambridge University Press.

1988. *States, War and Capitalism*. Blackwell: Oxford.

1993. *The Sources of Social Power, Volume II: The Rise of Classes and Nation-States*. Cambridge: Cambridge University Press.

1996. Authoritarian and Liberal Militarism: A Contribution from Comparative Historical Sociology. In S. Smith, K. Booth, and M. Zalewski (eds.), *International Theory*. Cambridge: Cambridge University Press.

Reus-Smit, C. 2002. The Idea of History and History with Ideas. In S. Hobden and J. M. Hobson (eds.), *Historical Sociology of International Relations*. Cambridge: Cambridge University Press.

Schroeder, R. 1998. From Weber's Political Sociology to Contemporary Liberal Democracy. In R. Schroeder (ed.), *Max Weber, Democracy and Modernization*. Basingstoke: Macmillan.

Seabrooke, L. 2006. *The Social Sources of Financial Power*. Ithaca: Cornell University Press.

Skocpol, T. 1979. *States and Social Revolutions*. Cambridge: Cambridge University Press.

Tilly, C. 1990. *Coercion, Capital and European States, AD 990–1990*. Oxford: Blackwell.

Waltz, K. N. 1959. *Man, the State and War*. New York: Columbia University Press.

1979. *Theory of International Politics*. New York: McGraw-Hill.

Weber, M. 1976. *The Protestant Ethic and the Spirit of Capitalism*. London: Allen & Unwin.

1978. *Economy and Society, I*. Berkeley: University of California Press.

Wight, M. 1977. *Systems of States*. Leicester: Leicester University Press.

9 Infrastructural power, economic transformation, and globalization

Linda Weiss

This chapter attempts two things. One is to show how Mann's theory of state power continues to generate new insights that advance the debates on state capacity, economic transformation, and globalization. The other is to suggest how these insights are at odds with some aspects of Mann's recent work on globalization.*

Mann's theoretical and historical work on state power, as even the most cursory survey would reveal, has influenced scholars young and old across the social science disciplines. His theory of state power and the distinction between infrastructural and despotic power have offered particularly fertile soil for scholars of comparative politics and political economy. Many scholars of comparative politics have applied his concepts to explain failed or weak states in the developing world (e.g. Lucas 1998; Centeno 1997), to account for developmental blockages or break-throughs in transition economies (Stoner-Weiss 2002; Zhu 2002), to revise conventional explanations for the rise of the West (Hall 1985), and to explain why some states, whether European or Asian, have been more effective than others at economic development (Weiss and Hobson 1995). In recent years, young sociologists have also sought to extend Mann's idea of the modern state's infrastructural power (IP) to symbolic and social infrastructures (e.g. Loveman). As the range of applications attests, Mann's theoretical and conceptual innovations continue to bear fruit.

Infrastructural power and economic transformation

In general, Mann's theory of state power has been most fruitfully applied to explain broad *historical* differences in types of state and contrasts in state autonomy. But I want to emphasize that his state power concepts also offer an invaluable tool for analysing *contemporary* power differences among industrial states in an era of globalization. Indeed they have played a central role in structuring my own efforts to explain cross-national variations in the industrial state's transformative or developmental capacity. At one level, this may seem surprising. For if we accept Mann's point that all modern states presiding over capitalist economies are, by definition, infrastructurally strong states, then IP would at first glance appear to be a blunt instrument for *differentiating* contemporary varieties of state capacity associated with different state orientations, structures and state–society relations.

Nonetheless, as I have argued in earlier work (1998), it is precisely the notion of IP that allows us to make advances in understanding what I have called the transformative capacity of modern states – the ability to coordinate structural economic change in response to external pressures. The state's ability to link up with civil society groups, to negotiate support for its projects, and to coordinate public–private resources to that end make up the broad tapestry of IP. They also constitute – at the micro-level of the industrial economy – the finer fabric of interconnectedness and negotiations that can be captured by the phrase 'governed interdependence' (GI). I have deployed the concept of GI to indicate a range of state–economy relationships in which government agencies and economic actors enter into cooperative arrangements for the pursuit of jointly coordinated projects under the goal-setting auspices of the state. GI defines a network of collaborative relationships between government and business in the joint pursuit of transformative projects; in this relationship each party retains interests independent of the other, while the state remains the ultimate arbiter of the rules and goals of interaction in which information is exchanged, resources are pooled, and tasks shared. I have called GI an outgrowth of IP because, through its linkages with key economic groupings, the state can extract and exchange vital information with producers, stimulate private-sector participation in economic projects, and mobilize a greater level of industry collaboration in advancing national goals.

Like Mann's theory of IP, the GI argument rejects the notion that the state's ability to 'impose' its decisions is central to its transformative capacity. Like IP, GI refers to a *negotiated* relationship in which state and civil society actors maintain their autonomy, yet which is nonetheless governed by broader goals set and monitored by the state. Of central importance is the state's ability to use its autonomy to consult and to elicit consensus and cooperation from the private sector. *One might say that IP is the genus from which the GI species is derived.* From this perspective, then, when the task is to explain why the state's transformative capacity in the economic arena varies cross-nationally, there is a clear analytical advantage in ridding ourselves of the more coercive 'statist' notions of state strength and weakness, and adapting and extending Mann's notion of IP.

The first argument I shall try to develop is that Mann's insights concerning shifts in political power and state–society relations – generated by his analysis of the rise of the modern state – can be applied in a parallel manner to our own era. For example, in contemporary political economies, governed interdependence may be viewed as the obverse of statism (or top-down direction of the economy), much as infrastructural power – as Mann (1993) has argued in a broader historical perspective – came to be the obverse of despotic power (in the transition from pre-industrial to modern states). In both cases, state–society relations become closer and more negotiated in character as states seek to achieve their goals. However, while infrastructural power is a defining characteristic of all modern states, with their territorial reach, their penetrative and extractive capacities, governed interdependence is a more specialized version of infrastructural power, vital to the state's transformative capacity in a variety of economic arenas. (As such, GI is not developed to the same degree in all industrial states.) The main point, then, is that GI is to statism, what IP is to despotic power.

Infrastructural power and globalization

The key issue for discussion of these concepts of state power today is the impact of globalization. Many believe that globalization is modifying the state's infrastructural powers. But are the important modifications most aptly described as constraints limiting state power, or as enabling conditions for the exercise of new forms of state power such as, for example, GI? This is what I shall suggest, extending Mann's ideas of IP to make sense of current developments in state–economy relations in the globalizing developed democracies. In what follows, I will consider the implications of globalization for state power in both Mann's general logistical sense of IP and in the more particular transformative sense of GI.

In this context of rising interconnectedness, I develop a second argument. It proposes that Mann's recent writings on globalization contain two insights at odds with each other; one of these insights is developed at the expense of the other, and this leads him to take a somewhat 'conservative' position on the question of the state's utility to social life, especially in the economy – a point which I shall return to shortly. In *Modernity and Globalization*, Mann observes that globalization and the growth of the state have gone hand in hand, and that 'In the long run, we must conclude that transnational and national economic interaction have surged together, not one at the expense of the other' (2000: 44). In his 1997 piece, Mann characteristically poses the two breakthrough questions: first, how much have transnational networks grown? Second, is their growth at the expense of national networks? To my knowledge, no one before Mann had made this fundamental distinction; a great many participants in the debate had simply elided the two issues, thereby assuming that the more globalization, the less scope for the nation-state. (Reflecting this elision, many definitions of globalization thus became little more than tautologies, since one hardly needed to go beyond the fact of rising interconnectedness to conclude that state power was in decline.)

I want to show (and this is the substance of my second argument) that Mann's point that the 'transnational and the national have surged together' deserves to be taken more seriously, not least by Mann himself. Why? Because this point has quite different implications from, and is somewhat at odds with, the emphasis he then gives to measuring economic globalization, and his conclusion that 'Nation-states remain brute economic realities, in the sense of remaining discrete, bounded networks of economic interaction' (2000: 41). While I fully agree with his estimate that 'national economies bound four-fifths of the world's economy [production and investment], one-fifth being international' (40), I do not concede that 'globalization's (quantitative) limits' form the yardstick of the state's room to move or its continuing importance to social life. I propose instead that globalization and state growth have gone hand in hand precisely because economic interdependence – or the exposure of social relations to international pressures – increases, not decreases, the social utility of the state.

This notion of social utility is of course fundamental to Mann's theory of IP. Mann defines IP as 'the institutional capacity of a central state, despotic or not, to penetrate its territories and logistically implement decisions' (1993: 59), and likens its effects to a kind of 'caging' process, giving a quality of 'boundedness' to social relations. The state acquires an organizational autonomy and *usefulness* to social life that derives from its territorial centrality. In Mann's terms, political power (*qua* state power) 'derives from the usefulness of centralized, institutionalized, territorialized regulation of many aspects of social relations' (1986: 26).

Globalization however is widely viewed as a process that 'uncages' social relations, making territorial centrality less salient. So the issue examined here is whether the state's IP has reached its limits in an era of growing interdependence. Does globalization – for example by increasing exit options for capital – reduce and redefine the state's utility to social life, thus limiting IP? How, in particular, does Mann view the impact of this uncaging process on the state's IP? Since it is the uncaging of *economic* relations, implied by the growth of capital mobility, that is considered the most threatening to IP, I shall focus my comments on this aspect of interdependence. I shall argue, with the globalists, that globalization is impacting on state power, but that contrary to their expectations, it is impacting in ways unanticipated by constraints theory.

Paradoxically, I suggest, globalization increases, not diminishes, demand for the state's centralized powers of coordination. The more general point to emphasize is that openness can create strong pressures for maintaining or extending cooperative ties between government and industry, as well as for information sharing, for coordinated responses to collective action problems, and more generally for the state to act as provider of collective goods. The state's infrastructural powers thus appear to be increasingly salient for many sectors and countries. This is not to say that the 'increasing demand' is always met – but rather that there is more external impetus for the state to coordinate responses in diverse economic sectors. I discuss this impact as the tendency of globalization (*qua* heightened vulnerability via intensification of international exposure, systemic risks and competitive challenges) to elicit a 'governed interdependence' response and thus to increase the incidence of GI – a state capacity enhancing effect.

I start with a discussion of Mann's theory of state power and his assessment of globalization's impact on infrastructural strength; the second section outlines recent findings on state activities in taxation, welfare and production-enhancing programmes that are consistent with a less conservative view of the globalization–state relationship; the third section shows one way in which Mann's novel but underdeveloped points in the 1997 paper regarding the complementarity between global and national networks of interaction may be developed (in my examples, via the extension of the idea of IP [as GI] to the sphere of industrial governance).

The state's infrastructural power

Mann's theory of state power, outlined in his 1994 essay, then further developed and applied in Volume II of *Sources of Social Power* (1993), makes a theoretical breakthrough in clarifying what is distinctive about the state's power in the modern industrial era. Whereas modern states have developed 'infrastructural' powers by negotiating with and acting through civil society – thus penetrating, extracting and coordinating their resources – the powers of pre-industrial states take a more despotic form, by virtue of their ability to issue commands (but not necessarily to implement them) without such routine negotiation. The key contrast drawn between the two types of state power is that of exercising power *through* civil society, rather than *over* it. In Mann's terms, this is the difference between collective and distributive notions of power.

The real innovation, however, lies in the understanding that the state's (collective) power rests on organizational means or logistical techniques, which modern states develop by virtue of their centrality to a particular territory. Unlike other power actors, states have the organizational distinction of being bound to a particular geographical space (1993: 27). This defines their territorial centrality and gives them an 'in principle' utility for other actors within that space, whose organizational reach may differ. The fact that the state is centralized and that non-state groups are not, writes Mann, 'gives to it logistical capacities for exercising autonomous power' (1986: 521).

There does however appear to be some ambiguity in Mann's writing about whether the modern state has autonomy in any real sense. On one hand, Mann implies that it is necessary to expunge 'autonomy' from a general definition of the (modern) state's power – since this is an empirical question, to be determined on a case-by-case basis (i.e. the question of who controls whom that has long fascinated Marxists and liberal pluralists). On the other hand, if we take autonomy to mean the *room to manoeuvre* – or the capacity for social goal-setting that is independent from any particular power grouping in civil society – then Mann appears to concede this possibility by virtue of the state's unique territorial centrality to social life.

Thus the modern state acquires autonomous power *vis-à-vis* other groups by virtue of its territorially organized centrality. As Mann puts it, 'any autonomous power that the state can acquire derives from its ability to exploit its centrality', in other words, *by the performance of certain services or activities that are more effectively performed if centrally coordinated* (1986: 171). In order to provide those services on a stable basis, the state has to develop organizational means and logistical techniques that enable it to penetrate and extract resources from society. This requires routine negotiation: the capacity of the state to extract resources is closely linked to the willingness of the population to accept these burdens. Thus, IP is fundamentally negotiated power, its core features being the capacity for social penetration, resource extraction and collective coordination.

Let us now place this discussion in the context of current changes in the international political economy. In view of such changes and the standard conceptions of globalization, the question that Mann's work poses for analysis is not whether the state as a set of political institutions, or the nation-state as a political and territorial entity, is declining – *pace* radical globalists. Rather, as so-called moderate globalists (*qua* 'constraints theorists') might contend, the real issue – to use Mann's state power language – is whether the growth of economic networks that transcend the boundaries established by political power has reduced the state's room for manoeuvre and thus its salience for social life.

As the constraints theorists see it, states generally are losing their independence or autonomy for social goal-setting; their rule-making authority, decision-making powers and ability to control domestic outcomes, in short, their room to move is becoming increasingly restricted and specialized over a far narrower terrain than ever before (e.g. Held *et al.* 1999). In economic terms, this argument implies that the state has a diminishing capacity to extract revenue in order to pursue its social and economic goals, hence a declining ability to provide for social protection, and a reduced relevance and capacity to promote economic renewal.

Mann writes that the most infrastructurally powerful states are those which cage more social relations within their 'national' boundaries (1993: 61). Is this at all times correct? From the historical perspective of modern state formation and the struggle to establish territorial boundaries, this statement seems true. Yet it may have more limited relevance today. For one thing, many weak Southern states meet this criterion ('cage more social relations') simply by virtue of being largely excluded from the global economy. For another, there is evidence to suggest that the more globalized the economy, the more important the state becomes to social life, a point I shall take up shortly.

So let us pose the question from the perspective of the developed North. How is the uncaging of social relations, implied by globalization, impacting on Northern IP – on the state's penetrative, extractive and coordinating capacities? To date, Mann's main answer to this question has been to stress not only the limited nature of global economic networks, but also the *heterogeneity* and *plurality* of national outcomes, as contained in his 1997 essay on globalization. Therein he recognizes the 'global variety' of nation-states in terms of their size, power, form and geography, and proposes that this variety itself ensures that globalization's impact will vary. That piece also contains a novel argument. It says that global and national networks of interaction are not competing for space, but are intertwined. Here Mann sets out to identify the various networks that make up the global and notes that 'What adds up to the global is a very complex mix of the local, the national, the international . . . and the truly transnational' (1997: 481). The fact that multinationals concentrate so much of their ownership, assets and R&D at home is offered as an example of how 'an economy may be global, but this may be conferred by help from national and international networks of interaction' (479). The implication is that global networks are limited to some extent by their dependence on non-global networks for their operation. But Mann does not explore the mechanisms of this intertwining.

In a second related argument that, like the first, encompasses military, political, economic and ideological power relations, Mann argues quite compellingly that globalization is not creating a single, unified system of social relations across the globe, but a set of contradictory tendencies, which include uneven and divisive, as well as unifying, outcomes. 'Though globalization is occurring, it is not singular but multiple, and it disintegrates as well as it integrates' (2001: 1). The thrust of Mann's arguments, then, is that globalization does not generally hurt or hollow out the state for one or more of three reasons: either because globalization is *limited* and intertwined with national (and other) networks of inter-action; or because states themselves *differ* (and therefore external impacts vary); or because globalization itself has *multiple* consequences, some of which can only be effectively dealt with by nation-states (e.g. the environmental degradation that the spread of industrialization sets in train).

All three arguments advance the debate enormously and I do not wish to dispute any of them. In fact, in contesting the standard view of global-ization's impact on the state, my own work has taken a similar tack in stressing the institutional basis of national responses to economic inter-dependence and the corresponding variety of outcomes – albeit from a much narrower analytical perspective than Mann's. But the point worth making here is that in so far as such arguments concern the diversity or variety of globalization impacts, they qualify rather than undermine the standard view of globalization as a fundamentally *constraining* force.

I must remind the reader at this point that my comments are aimed at Mann's analysis of how global economic relations impact on state power, not at his analysis of globalization in general. In this narrower – though unquestionably important – context, Mann's response to globalizers is now sufficiently accepted, dare one say, that it may almost be seen as part of the respectable mainstream. As Mann puts it, states are not hollowing out because government regulation is still necessary: 'markets require rules and the vast bulk of these are provided by nation-states' (2000: 44). Moreover, Mann continues, states are still big spenders, and they inter-vene much more today than did nineteenth-century states. However, they are strongly constrained by financial capital and this is manifested in their relinquishment of macro-economic policy tools, in particular Keynesian techniques of demand management (41–5).

So far so good. But can Mann go a little further in offering an answer to the question raised by his own work, namely, how globalization impacts on the state's usefulness to social life? In the economic arena at least, Mann seems to define 'usefulness' chiefly in *regulatory* terms. Is there more to the role of political power in the globalizing economy? I propose that there is, and that it means taking seriously Mann's idea of a *positive* relationship between globalization and the growth of infrastructural power. For while his work has made us take more and more note of variety, unevenness and plurality of national responses, we may have become less and less inclined to notice certain features of globalization that tend to invite a range of common (though not convergent) responses, which point in a state-enhancing direction.

In what follows, I shall indicate findings from recent research to show how globalization is bringing the state back in (or keeping it there). I shall emphasize as a tendency of globalization the propensity to provoke a range of responses at the national level that have certain features in common, regardless of state size, tradition or culture, which nonetheless conflict with standard constraints/convergence theory; and I shall offer some tentative hypotheses for this development.

We shall start with the research findings in three major areas of government activity – that of taxation, social spending and industrial governance. Mann has something to say about the first two, much less about the third, since he appears to accept the 'regulatory state' hypothesis that, post-Keynesianism, there's not much for states to do in the economic arena.

The state's declining social usefulness?

The taxing and spending behaviour of nation-states offers one of the clearest indications as to the stability (and strength) of IP over time. If the extractive capacity needed to sustain social infrastructures is clearly in decline, then this must be taken as one important indicator of the state's diminishing usefulness to social life. An equally important measure in this regard is the actual welfare effort of the developed democracies. A third indicator of social usefulness must look beyond 'distribution' to matters of 'production' and the state's supportive and coordinating role in that context. Of course, declining state effort in any of these areas may not necessarily be linked to globalization, but that is a separate issue which we leave to one side.

Let us begin with the OECD data on taxation and welfare effort, which offer an important measure of infrastructural strength.

Taxation

In matters of taxation, the findings of recent studies are in important ways uncongenial to the constrained state thesis (Tanzi and Shuknecht 2000; Quinn 1997; Garrett 1998; Hobson 2003). In the developed democracies, average tax burdens have grown and expenditure has risen by 20 per cent and 23 per cent respectively over the period of rising interdependence (1965–1999). If this is unexpected, so too is the finding that the tax burden on capital has grown, with increases of 52 per cent, somewhat outpacing labour tax increases of 44 per cent. Where nominal corporate rates came down, governments found scope to protect revenues by 'broadening the base' – e.g. by reducing tax concessions. Moreover, only four out of twenty OECD countries reduced their average company tax burdens (two very marginally) in the 1995–7 period, compared with the base of 1970–4. Tellingly, all but one of the 'tax cutters' belonged to the Anglo-Saxon group of low-taxing nations (Weiss 2001: 11). It is true that states generally do not treat the corporate sector as a 'cash cow', historically extracting a relatively small share of their total revenue from corporate taxes (today ranging anywhere from *c*. 2 per cent to 15 per cent). But this structural restraint remains more or less stable and is not a product of rising interdependence. If there is a significant constraint from globalization, it is not in the direction expected. States have *increased* direct tax yields, but at the price of a partial loss of progressivity in personal income tax, by squeezing middle-income earners. Hence, as Hobson concludes, not a race to the bottom, but 'to the middle'.[1] The evidence overall leaves little room for doubting the general trend: Notwithstanding limited oscillations and country particularities over time, it is clear that the tax burden on corporations in the OECD has generally *increased* rather than declined in the period of rising economic interdependence, that governments have *not* shifted the tax burden from capital to labour and, moreover, that they have generally *increased* taxes.

It is too obvious to belabour the point that there are limits to the state's extraction capacities; less obvious is that those limits are *negotiated domestically rather than determined externally*. Thus, aggregate tax burdens continue to vary cross-nationally, quite significantly. Does this mean IP is *ideologically* (or culturally) diversified? That appears to be one part of the story. The other part has to do with the structure of political and economic *organizations*, in particular, variations in the strength of labour organization and party dominance in parliament (cf. Steinmo and Tolbert 1998 on the link between taxation patterns and organizational arrangements). If we put ideology and organization together, we might say that *domestic institutions* (as constellations of orienting norms and arrangements) *mediate extractive capacity*. Globalization may invite a stronger fiscal response by virtue of the economic and social pressures it generates in some sectors, but domestic institutions mediate the nature of that response. The point seems clear. If the state's social usefulness is in decline, it is not evident from either its propensity to tax in general, or its responsiveness to civil society in particular.

Social welfare

The findings on social welfare tell a similar tale of sustained IP and scope for political choice within domestic constraints.[2] While all developed welfare states have experienced rollbacks in benefit levels, eligibility restrictions and cost controls, including neoliberal reforms of health and social services, nonetheless total welfare effort (public social expenditure as a share of national income) has not declined in the period of high globalization. Indeed, as with taxation, welfare behaviour has varied in important ways across different groups of nations. Increases in international capital movements are associated with quite different spending outcomes linked to distinctive institutional patterns. Slight spending *declines* in some welfare states (i.e. in liberal market economies (LMEs)) have thus been offset by either the *maintenance* or moderate *expansion* of welfare commitments in others (i.e. in coordinated market economies (CMEs)). As these labels imply, the outcomes are linked to domestic institutions. In the case of welfare states, the latter include: distinctive programmatic *norms* (embedded ideas regarding the value of either universalistic or means-tested benefits) and structures of economic and political *organization* (e.g. the extent to which these aggregate and offer broad representation of interests resistant to welfare retrenchment) (cf. Swank 2003).

Thus in the developed democracies the state's fiscal behaviour over the past three decades or more of 'rising globalization' has not been consistent with the idea of a tightly constrained state, or one whose social usefulness is in decline – in short, an all-out 'race to the bottom'. This in no way contradicts the fact that income inequality has risen in *some* nations, and that it may in part be associated with globalization (cf. Quinn 1997). The key point is that while some aspects of globalization may contribute to rising income inequality, this impact varies cross-nationally, appearing stronger in LMEs (notably, the US, New Zealand and Britain), and weaker in the CMEs (notably Scandinavia) (cf. Galbraith 2001).

In noting cross-national variation in the welfare effort, Mann suggests that this highlights a 'cultural' division within the globalization of economic relations. At one level this seems true – if by culture we mean domestically institutionalized value orientations and arrangements for responding to the big questions of social life. (As noted above, the divergent responses to external pressures of the CMEs and LMEs are closely correlated with such institutional differences.) But there are grounds for considering that both cultural and institutional explanations for diversity of outcomes may be true only in a *proximate* sense. Consider the proposition: the more liberal the state tradition (or Anglo-Saxon the culture), the weaker the support for domestic protection. But if we adopt a *longer time horizon*, and add another element to the equation – the level of globalization/trade interdependence – note how the pattern changes: *the less exposed the economy* and the more liberal the state tradition, the weaker the support for domestic protection (the United States being the exemplary case). Conversely, *the more exposed the economy* and the more entrenched an ideology of social partnership, the more support for domestic compensation (the exemplary case being Sweden). This last proposition was of course famously developed by Peter Katzenstein (1985). Numerous studies have also added a robustness to this proposition, establishing firmly the link between level of economic openness (*qua* trade interdependence) and level of social expenditure.

Indeed, the relationship between level of trade interdependence and welfare effort is by now sufficiently robust to suggest something more positive about globalization's impact on the state's usefulness to social life. I will suggest what that 'something more' might be in a moment, noting that while we hear constantly about the *constraints* of globalization, we hear far less about its *enabling* logic. And while we hear much about the association between globalization and the *distribution* effort, we hear almost nothing about its association with the *production* effort, which I discuss next, under the label of 'industrial governance'.

Industrial governance

We turn now to an area marginalized in Mann's analysis. This concerns the state's role in upgrading production, or industrial governance. A recurring argument is that in a world of mobile capital and international agreements, all states, even those which may have long been involved in sponsoring economic upgrading, are compelled to minimize or withdraw from industry and trade promotion – in short, from any action aimed at protecting or promoting one's economic advantage. If this is not because of an incompatibility with WTO rules, then it is argued to be due to its sheer futility – tantamount to watering one's own garden in a world where the plants can relocate. Yet there is substantial evidence to show that the state's capacity for industrial policy is not waning with increased interdependence. States continue to foster new growth sectors, subsidize technological innovation and upgrading, invest in infrastructure, finance education and training, including active labour market policies, and regulate industry and finance in distinctive ways to buttress national competitiveness – all in stark contrast with the predictions of the 'constrained state' view.[3]

While the tools of industrial policy often undergo change as circumstances alter, states constantly adapt their instruments to the new tasks. Thus, for instance, the Koreans have abandoned directed credit, central to their post-war growth strategy; but they have not withdrawn from transformative projects. Deploying a range of instruments, old and new, the state remains essential to everything from the restructuring of the *chaebol* and financial sector to the creation of a venture capital industry and retail market for Korean software (Weiss 2003b). The Japanese, on the other hand, continue to find ways of structuring competition in order to achieve their long-held goals of increased investment and technological upgrading (Tilton 2003). Even more significant in overturning expectations, as the global race in high-technology intensifies, the German state has abandoned its relative passivity in industrial policy in favour of strategic initiatives in the high-technology sector and venture capital industry. At the same time, states have not stood by idly after signing up to the WTO's market-opening measures. Thus, neo-developmentalism continues to involve the state as a pivotal force in Taiwan's industrial latecomer strategy, constantly moving Taiwan upscale in IT in the bid to remain ahead of its mainland neighbour. In the banking industry as well, state sponsorship of mergers and acquisitions (M&As) (via regulatory and tax incentives) has become the favoured tool of both the Europeans (especially France and Germany) and the Asians (notably, Taiwan, Korea and Japan) – all seeking ways to strengthen their financial sectors as foreign competitors prepare to take advantage of the WTO's market access agreements.

While we need more systematic research for the developed democracies, the existing findings on competitive strategy and regulatory reform are significant for at least two reasons. First, they indicate that states are just as important as ever in making interdependence possible (Alamgir 2003; Zhu 2003), and in ensuring that global financial markets work rather than self-destruct (Coleman 2003). Moreover, states are just as central as ever in sponsoring new industry sectors, even – or especially – in less developed contexts, like Thailand, where these initiatives may be blocked (Doner and Ramsay 2003).

Second, such findings show that states constantly adapt their policy tools, using a mix of old and new instruments (Woo-Cummings 2003) – from tax laws and national competition prizes to venture capital funds – to achieve their policy goals. Among the old instruments, Woo-Cumings observes that administrative guidance – otherwise known as bureaucratic discretion 'to make, interpret and enforce detailed rules of economic behaviour' – has been modified to function in less despotic ways and for entirely new national goals including financial restructuring and corporate reform. (I shall return to this point in a moment.) At the newer end of the 'policy instruments' spectrum, one of the most important is the *public–private 'partnership'* which takes various forms in different settings, and develops as governments extend and deepen ties with organized economic actors to pursue transformative projects. In many cases, the competitive pressures of global markets appear to be encouraging producers to enter into such networks. Such relationships of 'governed interdependence', as I have argued elsewhere, and as a number of other studies have begun to show in distinctive ways (Coleman 2001; 2003; Doner and Ramsay 2003), are the stuff of transformative capacity in today's states. I elaborate on these below.

The cumulative evidence thus weighs against accepting a purely 'constrained state' view in which declining social usefulness compromises infrastructural strength. It suggests two conclusions. First, it shows that, however much globalization throws real constraints in the way of state activity (most notably in the macroeconomic arena), it also allows states sufficient room to move, and thus to act consonant with their social and economic objectives. Second, as mentioned earlier, the evidence indicates that there is 'something more' to globalization than a constraining logic. This is strongly suggested but not developed in Mann's analysis of globalization.

The state-enabling logic of globalization

To make sense of the counter-evidence we therefore need to add an extra dimension to the globalization dynamic. Like the proverbial sword, globalization appears double-edged: *enabling* as well as constraining. Enablement implies that in the face of relatively similar globalization pressures, there are countervailing pressures on governments and, often, political incentives to intervene. One can therefore explain the state's room for manoeuvre in terms of the dual logics of global capitalism – not simply limiting, but also offering scope for policy choice by virtue of the pressures felt by particular social constituencies, the corresponding demands they place on governments, and the political incentives for policy responses.

Competitive challenges and state capacity We can offer at least two theoretical arguments as to why globalization has enabling rather than simply constraining effects on the state's delivery of production-enhancing policies, both of which highlight the competitive pressures of interdependence and the social usefulness of IP, the second of which underscores the transmogrification of IP as transformative capacity in the form of governed interdependence (GI).

The first argument about enablement concerns the conditions of global competition, which serve to valorize business access to national innovation structures, to a constant supply of skilled labour, and to various other infrastructural resources on which firms depend. However potentially mobile the modern corporation may be, increased exposure to world markets heightens the firm's need for continuous innovation, industrial upgrading and competent workers. So instead of generalized slashing of corporate taxes and shifting the tax burden from capital to labour, governments will often have strong incentives to provide services to capital in exchange for maintaining tax revenue. As a number of scholars have observed, for all the neoclassical strictures about the harm wrought by state intervention, internationally oriented firms are still prone to welcome the benefits offered by a host of government programmes (Boix 1998; Garrett 1998). At the very least, this offers a plausible way of explaining why, in many national settings, internationally mobile firms may be willing to sustain relatively high tax (and spending) levels, contrary to the standard expectations of capital exit.

There is a second argument as to why globalization enables room for manoeuvre and in so doing creates pressures for state–business alliances (and, in particular, governed interdependence). This concerns the way in which intensified competitive pressures may threaten to destabilize key sectors of the economy – from agriculture to telecommunications and finance. The effect of such competitive challenges is to urge governments to devise new policy responses, new regulatory regimes and similar restructuring reforms. Most critically, responding to these new challenges creates incentives for governments to develop new or strengthen existing policy networks. For some purposes, this entails the expansion of *inter-governmental* cooperation in more or less permanent forums (e.g. the EU, WTO, Bank for International settlement, G8). For others, it involves the extension of links *between government and business* (involving both domestically and transnationally oriented firms), which enhance coordination of transformative projects. In each case, neither governmental nor business autonomy is thereby negated, but rather 'enmeshed' in a network of interdependencies, the rules for which are established by government – hence 'governed interdependence'. This entails a variety of public–private partnerships and alliances, policy networks, information exchange and self-regulation under the state's goal-setting auspices.

Infrastructural power as a globalization tendency? The claim is not that GI has generally supplanted statist and liberal pluralist state–society relations. Rather, the claim is that GI is a *tendency* of globalization, and that to the extent that it is emerging in different forms in different national settings and sectors, two things follow: theoretically, it implies a positive relationship between openness and state power; empirically, it implies that states are likely to gain or increase their transformative capacity.

What evidence do we have of the growth of GI? One way in which the growth of governed interdependence (hence changes in transformative capacity) can be observed in settings both European and Asian is by means of the state building or extending its links with domestic power actors – both vertically and horizontally, as William Coleman (2001) has shown for France in the context of strengthening agricultural exports; and as Mark Lehrer (2000) and Cieply (2001) have demonstrated for Germany and France with regard to promoting high-technology entrepreneurship and its financing. Similar developments have been analysed in the case of neo-developmental states in East Asia (especially Korea and Taiwan) where the state's success in coordinating more complex industrial upgrading in the context of increasing openness has come to rely more heavily on participation of organized business in the policy process and on the coordination of inter-firm networks for product development. The Korean state's recent partnering with an IT consortium to create, *inter alia*, a domestic software industry is a case in point (Weiss 2003b). While the GI partnership for pursuit of joint projects may often occur by invitation of organized interests in civil society (as has occurred in Germany and Korea), GI is not present unless the rules of the game are established by the state.

There is evidence in other arenas as well that states may come to interact more closely with organized power actors – especially where systemic risk (and competitive rivalry) is strong (and perceived to be so). The US shift from a predominantly arm's-length towards a more collaborative approach to the regulation of financial derivatives, arguably the most globalized of markets with the greatest potential for system destabilization, appears to support this conclusion (Coleman 2003). Earlier parallels in America's formation of public–private partnerships in agriculture and high-technology also support the hypothesis – e.g. the formation of Sematech in 1987 to relaunch the US semiconductor industry. This and similar high-technology initiatives have meant the overthrow of an arm's-length approach to industrial change and the embracing of GI, impelled by fear of losing out to the Japanese, and legitimated in the strategic language of a threat to national security. Conversely, in markets with little systemic risk (or external competition) – e.g. in US telecommunications (cf. Tilton 2003) – one may expect preservation of an arm's-length regulatory style.

These examples, from Asia to Europe and the US, add flesh to the larger theoretical point that globalization does indeed impact on state power, but the impact is not *only*, or even *generally*, constraining. For globalization also contributes to the expansion of governing capacities through the transformation of public–private sector relations, by creating new pressures for social coordination. There is then a plausible case for studying globalization as a process with nationally enabling effects, not just constraining ones.

Mann's big picture perspective on globalization is highly attuned to incorporating such diverse logics. But his apparent acceptance of Keynesianism as the *sine qua non* of the state's economic role, alongside the reality of the 'financial capital constraint', leads him to avoid any consideration of globalization's *positive* (or enabling) impact on state activity in the sphere of *production*. Even in the sphere of welfare, where he links outcomes to cultural differences (much in the way I have linked them to institutional differences), he passes by that opportunity.

But what if 'globalization' is not only the common denominator behind higher-order *welfare* efforts, but also the driver of greater state coordination of *economic* change? This is indeed what I am proposing. To argue along these lines means of course that globalization would need to be disaggregated (something I do not do here), so that future research would need to consider both the 'global' character of markets (hence their potential for systemic risk as in the case of financial derivatives), and the intensity and character of international competition (measured, for instance, by the international exposure of particular sectors).

Conclusion

I began with the question raised by Mann's work as to how globalization was impacting on the state's usefulness to social life. We know from *The Sources of Social Power* that the biggest state transformation came with the leap into industrialism as states gained in penetrative reach and extractive capacity what they forfeited in despotic power over their subjects. Are we seeing a parallel trend with the leap into globalism? Is the state's infrastructural power being 'transformed' by global markets and international competition? Indeed it is, I have argued, but in some ways unanticipated by Michael Mann's work, or conventional theory. Mann makes two observations on this issue. The first is novel and important and suggests a link between the development of globalization and the growth of state power. While his earlier writing on globalization begins to explore that link, it disappears from his most recent work. Mann develops instead the more conventional observation, based on quantitative analysis of the relative importance of the domestic economy *vis-à-vis* the global one, that the economy is still largely national in scope and that the state still plays an important regulatory role, with variations according to different state characteristics.

I have indicated ways in which Mann's first observation could be developed further. This would lead not to finer and finer measurements of economic globalization, but to more historical and comparative analysis of the links between the various levels of globalization, the varying nature of its pressures, the changing perceptions of national vulnerability, and the corresponding character of state activity. In the context of industrial governance and state–economy relations examined here, I have proposed that contrary to the dominant 'constraints' view of globalization, a key tendency of increasing economic integration and the heightened risk to national economic security is to induce a shift from the more statist, top-down and rigidly arm's-length forms of rule to more collaborative and jointly coordinated forms of economic management (or new forms of governed interdependence). This is another way of saying that the state's usefulness to social life tends to be strengthened, not weakened, by globalization; that the state's infrastructural power remains robust and that it is being adapted to new tasks. Understanding more about the specific conditions under which globalization produces this effect is a subject worthy of further research. Mann's theory of infrastructural power and its evolution under new conditions of economic globalization remains central to that task.

Notes

* Work on this chapter was facilitated by support from the Australia Research Council's Discovery Grant Program.
1 Unless otherwise indicated, data in this paragraph are from Hobson (2003).
2 This paragraph is based on data from Swank (2003).
3 Arguments and references in this section are from Weiss (2003a).

References

Alamgir, J. 2003. Managing Openness in India: The Social Construction of a Globalist Narrative. In L. Weiss (ed.), *States in the Global Economy: Bringing Domestic Institutions Back In*. Cambridge: Cambridge University Press.

Boix, C. 1998. *Political Parties, Growth and Equality: Conservative and Social Democratic Economic Strategies in the World Economy*. Cambridge: Cambridge University Press.

Centeno, M. A. 1997. Blood and Debt: War and Taxation in Nineteenth-Century Latin America. *American Journal of Sociology*, 102(6).

Cieply, S. 2001. Bridging Capital Gaps to Promote Innovation in France. *Industry and Innovation*, 8.

Coleman, W. 2001. State Power, Transformative Capacity and Adapting to Globalization: An Analysis of French Agricultural Policy. *Journal of European Public Policy*, 9(2).

2003. Governing Global Finance: Financial Derivatives, Liberal States, and Transformative Capacity. In L. Weiss (ed.), *States in the Global Economy: Bringing Domestic Institutions Back In*. Cambridge: Cambridge University Press.

Doner, R., and A. Ramsay. 2003. The Challenges of Economic Upgrading in Liberalising Thailand. In L. Weiss (ed.), *States in the Global Economy: Bringing Domestic Institutions Back In*. Cambridge: Cambridge University Press.

Galbraith, J. K. 2001. Globalization Fails to Make the Money Go Around. *Sydney Morning Herald*, 26 July.

Garrett, G. 1998. Global Markets and National Policies: Collision Course or Virtuous Circle. *International Organisation*, 52.

Hall, J. A. 1985. *Powers and Liberties*. Blackwell: Oxford.

Held, D., A. McGrew, D. Goldblatt and J. Perraton. 1999. *Global Transformations: Politics, Economics and Culture*. Cambridge: Polity Press.

Hobson, J. 2003. Disappearing Taxes or a Race to the Middle? In L. Weiss (ed.), *States in the Global Economy: Bringing Domestic Institutions Back In*. Cambridge: Cambridge University Press.

Katzenstein, P. 1985. *Small States in World Markets: Industrial Policy in Europe*. Ithaca: Cornell University Press.

Lehrer, M. 2000. Has Germany Finally Fixed its High-Tech Problem? The Recent Boom in German Technology-Based Entrepreneurship. *California Management Review*, 42.

Lucas, J. 1998. The Tension between Despotic and Infrastructural Power: The Military and Political Class in Nigeria, 1985–1993. *Studies in Comparative International Development*, 33(3).

Mann, M. 1986. *The Sources of Social Power, Volume I: A History from the Beginning to 1760 AD*. Cambridge: Cambridge University Press.

1993. *The Sources of Social Power, Volume II: The Rise of Classes and Nation-States*. Cambridge: Cambridge University Press.

1997. Has Globalization Ended the Rise and Rise of the Nation-State? *Review of International Political Economy*, 4(3).

2000. Modernity and Globalization. Unpublished, given as the Wiles Lectures at Queen's University, Belfast.

2001. Globalization, Global Conflict and September 11. Paper presented at the Workshop 'Globalization and its Challenges', University of Sydney, 12–14 Dec., 2001.

Quinn, D. 1997. The Correlates of Change in International Financial Regulation. *American Political Science Review*, 91.

Steinmo, S., and C. Tolbert. 1998. Do Institutions Really Matter? Taxation in Industrial Democracies. *Comparative Political Studies*, 31.

Stoner-Weiss, K. 2002. *Local Heroes: The Political Economy of Russian Regional Governance*. Princeton: Princeton University Press.

Swank, D. 2003. Withering Welfare? globalization, Political Economic Institutions, and Contemporary Welfare States. In L. Weiss (ed.), *States in the Global Economy: Bringing Domestic Institutions Back In*. Cambridge: Cambridge University Press.

Tanzi, V., and L. Schuknecht. 2000. *Public Spending in the Twentieth Century*. Cambridge: Cambridge University Press.

Tilton, M. 2003. Ideas, Institutions, and Interests in the Shaping of Telecommunications Reform: Japan and the USA. In L. Weiss (ed.), *States in the Global Economy: Bringing Domestic Institutions Back In*. Cambridge: Cambridge University Press.

Weiss, L. 1998. *The Myth of the Powerless State*. Ithaca: Cornell University Press.

2001. Does Size Matter Less when Domestic Institutions Count? Paper prepared for the Conference on 'Small States in World Markets – Fifteen Years Later', Gothenburg, Sweden, 27–29 September 2001.

2003a. *States in the Global Economy: Bringing Domestic Institutions Back In*. Cambridge: Cambridge University Press.

2003b. Guiding globalization in East Asia: New Roles for Old Developmental States. In L. Weiss (ed.), *States in the Global Economy: Bringing Domestic Institutions Back In*. Cambridge: Cambridge University Press.

Weiss, L., and J. M. Hobson. 1995. *States and Economic Development*. Oxford: Polity Press.

Woo-Cummings, M. 2003. Diverse Paths towards the 'Right Institutions': Law, the State and Economic Reform in East Asia. In L. Weiss (ed.), *States in the Global Economy: Bringing Domestic Institutions Back In*. Cambridge: Cambridge University Press.

Zhu, T., 2003. Building Institutional Capacity for China's New Economic Opening. In L. Weiss (ed.), *States in the Global Economy: Bringing Domestic Institutions Back In*. Cambridge: Cambridge University Press.

Part III

European exceptionalism?

10 From theory to history: 'The European Dynamic' or feudalism to capitalism?

Robert Brenner

Introduction: Mann's post-modern enlightenment conception

Michael Mann's notion of 'The European Dynamic' lies at the heart, and is the ultimate payoff, of his enquiry into the sources of social power. It constitutes his account of the emergence of *both* the modern agro-industrial economy *and* the modern centralized state and international system of multiple states, *in terms of* what he understands to be the four networks and sources of social power. But, from the outset, one is obliged to confront a conundrum. There appears to be a yawning gap between Mann's explicit theoretical commitments and his practical historical account of the rise of the West.

In introducing his general theoretical approach, Mann delivers a stern warning of the dangers of attributing too much coherence to societies as a whole, the sort of jeremiad as to the perils of reification of concepts that has long been the meat and drink of post-structuralism fading into post-modernism. '[M]ost sociological orthodoxies', he asserts, 'mar their insights by conceiving of "society" as an unproblematic, unitary totality' (1986: 2). In fact, argues Mann, 'We can never find a single bounded society in geographical or social space' (1). Societies, he insists, 'are not social systems; they are not totalities' (1). 'Because there is no totality, individuals are not constrained in their behavior by social structure as a whole' (1–2). We therefore have no reason to expect, by way of the aggregation of the social-structurally constrained actions of the society's component individuals, the emergence of system-wide patterns of development. 'Because there is no social system,' says Mann, 'there is no "evolutionary" process within it' (1). The upshot, in Mann's view, is that society needs to be understood not as a unified whole, but in terms of four separate networks of social interaction (economic, political, military and ideological). These emerge autonomously as distinct 'organizations, institutional means of attaining [different, fundamental] human goals' and thereby constitute society as 'multiple overlapping and intersecting power networks' (2).

Nevertheless, when Mann comes to explaining the rise of the West, his interpretation could hardly go more directly against his advice on method. He makes no bones about conceiving of Europe as a whole from around the year 800 AD as a coherent totality – 'a single broad socio-geographical area' that 'possessed a social unity', 'contain[ing] a single set of interrelated dynamics' (1986: 373). Consistently with his conception of societies as 'consisting of multiple overlapping and intersecting power networks', Mann insists that the '*origins* of the European miracle were a gigantic series of coincidences' (505, emphasis added). But, he does not shrink from referring to what emerged from these coincidences as the 'medieval social structure' (374), nor attributing to it an inherent 'enormous dynamism' (374). This dynamism reflected the fact that '[a]ll the sources of social power – economic, political, military and ideological relations – tended to move in a single general direction of development', which 'it is conventional to describe ... as "the transition from feudalism to capitalism"' (373). 'European dynamism was systemic', he proclaims, and 'characterized Europe as a whole' (504), with the result that, although '[s]etbacks occurred ... the checks did not last long before the forward movement resumed' and 'the motor of development that medieval Europe possessed ... helped it move toward industrial capitalism' (373). '[W]e can discern movement toward this leap forward gathering force through the whole medieval and early modern period' (373), 'an essential continuity, perhaps from about 800 to the agricultural revolution of the eighteenth century' (400, emphasis added).

The outcome is perplexing. Mann professes great doubt in theory about the notion of society as a socio-geographic unity, with specific associated patterns of development. But he has no compunction whatsoever about embracing in historical practice a conception of Europe as precisely that – a 'single broad geographical area' that 'possessed a social unity' which evolved by way of 'a single set of interrelated dynamics' over the course of a thousand years, issuing not only in the agricultural and industrial revolution, but also the modern centralized, territorial state and the modern multi-state international system (373–4). Nevertheless, the fact remains that, in the end, Mann does not shrink from finding the ultimate theoretical lessons of the long-term unilineal evolution of Europe's economy and polity to be purely anti-holist – viz. that the state is autonomous and that the rise of the multi-state system took place in abstraction from, is inexplicable in terms of, the trajectory of the economy.

The object of this chapter is to get to the bottom of Mann's disconcerting combination of 'post-modern' anti-holistic social theory and classical, eighteenth-century unilineal evolutionary sociological history. In the first part of the chapter (I.), I will ask how Mann can present as his fundamental thesis that society is constituted by four 'overlapping and intersecting [social] power networks' that pursue their own distinct trajectories in separation from one another, yet, at the same time, grasp the rise of Europe as the ascent of a unitary totality in which these four separate networks of social power evolve together for a millennium. To provide an answer, I will present Mann's theorization of the sources of social power, limn out his interpretation of the 'European miracle', and specify the conceptual-cum-historical links that he has forged to connect the two. In the second part of the chapter (II.), I will ask how effectively Mann's theory prepares the ground for his account of the rise of the West and how well the latter gives credence to the former, while evaluating his historical interpretation in its own terms. To offer a critique and alternative, I will call into question the capacity of his theory to adequately incorporate property, force and class exploitation, show that this incapacity undercuts the theoretical presumption in favour of the separation of the economic at the core of his account of the European miracle, and, from that conceptual point of departure, by challenging his understanding of European economic development and the rise of the centralized, territorial state, cast doubt on his ultimate generalizations concerning the state.

I.   From anti-holism to the European Miracle?

1.   Mann's Theoretical Framework: the sources of social power

From function to power 'In its most general sense', says Mann, 'power is the ability to pursue and attain goals through mastery of one's environment' (1986: 6). Mann thus understands *social* power to find its source in the specialized organizations, called 'networks of social power', that people establish to get things done for society, carrying out the *division of labour in society* most broadly conceived (6–7). The four main *types* of network of social power arise in order to fulfil what Mann sees as human beings' four basic needs (14), or society's four basic *functional requirements* – the provision of meaning (ideological power), defence (military power), subsistence (economic power), and order and justice (political power). They do so by generating, respectively, the four main *sources* of social power – transcendent values and normative cohesion (or what Mann calls *immanent morale*), concentrated coercion, the capacity to extract, produce and allocate natural resources (or what Mann calls the *circuits of praxis*), and centralized, institutionalized, territorial regulation (14–15, 22–9).[1]

The four types of cooperative networks for getting things done thus *found* social power through constituting organizations that mobilize the four sources of social power for carrying out – ever more effectively – the four basic societal tasks or functions. Mann, following Talcott Parsons, terms this constitutive, *horizontal* form of power 'collective power', by contrast to 'distributive power', which refers to the more familiar form of *vertical* power, meaning 'mastery exercised over other people' (6).[2] Distributive power 'is the probability that one actor within a social relationship will be in a position to carry out his own will despite resistance' (6). It entails a zero-sum game, in contrast to the positive-sum game entailed by collective power.

From collective to distributive power Mann understands distributive power as deriving from collective power.[3] It emerges out of the hierarchy of supervision, coordination and control that Mann sees as inherent in the division of labour *within* the network of social power itself and indispensable to the latter's fulfilling its role within the societal division of labour. Vertical distributive power is, thus understood by Mann, no less than horizontal collective power, in terms of its functionality (1986: 6–7). As Mann explicates the emergence of distributive from collective power:

[I]in pursuit of their goals, humans enter into cooperative, collective power relations with one another. But in implementing collective goals, social organization and division of labor are set up. Organization and division of function carry an inherent tendency to distributive power, deriving from supervision and coordination. For the division of labor is deceptive: Although it involves specialization of function at all levels, the top oversees and directs the whole. Those who occupy supervisory and coordinating positions have an immense organizational superiority over the others. The interaction and communication networks actually center on their function, as can be seen easily enough in the organization chart possessed by every modern firm. (6–7)

As Mann memorably puts it, 'The chart allows superiors to control the entire organization, and it prevents those at the bottom from sharing this control' (7). The fact remains that those at the bottom are obliged to obey not just because they are subordinates within an organizational hierarchy inevitably controlled by those at the top, but because they have no place else to go (7), in view of the indispensable function performed *for them* by those at the top. Compliance will therefore be forthcoming, because those in authority 'set in motion machinery for implementing collective goals' that are shared by those at the bottom and because, for those at the bottom, 'opportunities are probably lacking for establishing alternative machinery for implementing [those] goals' (7). In deriving distributive from collective power, Mann actually puts most of the emphasis on the superior organizational position of those at the top *vis-à-vis* those at the bottom, at least rhetorically. 'The masses comply' because '[t]hey are *organizationally out-flanked*' (7, emphasis in original). But, at least as far as I can see, it is the functional indispensability of those at the top that is ultimately decisive in making for their domination over those at the bottom. Their organizational control alone is quite insufficient, for, unless those at the bottom depend on their superiors to carry out a crucial function for them, they can avoid their power simply by opting out of the organization.

Mann makes clear that, ultimately, '[t]he few at the top can keep the masses at the bottom compliant, provided their control is *institutionalized* in the laws and norms of the social group in which both operate' (7, emphasis in the original). But since '[i]nstitutionalization is necessary to achieve ... collective goals ... distributive power, that is, social stratification, also becomes an institutionalized feature of social life' (7). In other words, the legitimization of distributive power occurs in the process of legitimizing collective power, because the former emerges in the process of constituting and consolidating the latter. Strikingly, yet consistently, Mann neither needs – nor does he make – any reference to force in deriving distributive from collective power. Subjection to insti-tutionalized distributive power results from the functional dependence of those at the bottom on those in control of a common organization to generate collective power to realize shared goals.

Mann does not, it should be said, ever quite make explicit what is actually entailed by distributive power. When those at the top of a net-work of social power exercise their distributive power, what are they able to accomplish *for themselves* – i.e. beyond what they would already be able to accomplish by virtue of their authority within the organization in terms of the organization's own function(s)? Mann does not tell us what, if anything, they are enabled to *distribute* to themselves from those at the bottom by virtue of their distributive power, or precisely how they manage this. This is a major lacuna to which it will be necessary to return.[4]

> *Society as multiple intersecting, overlapping networks of social power* Mann's account of the sources of social power in terms of human requirements and societal functions is designed to provide the rationale for his rejection of the notion of society as a unified totality, to lay the basis for his alternative conception of society as constituted by autonomous, intersecting and overlapping networks of social power, and to pave the way for his interpretation of the European Miracle. According to Mann, in order for humans to fulfil their needs for 'material subsistence', 'to settle disputes without constant recourse to force', 'to explore the ultimate meaning of the universe', and 'to defend whatever they have

obtained and pillage others', they constitute, respectively, economic, political, ideological and military networks of social power (1986: 14). Since these networks of social power thus arise to fulfil separate and distinct functions, it stands to reason that they should, all else equal, take the form of separate and distinct organizations pursuing separate and distinct paths – rather than evolve in unison as they might do if they were bound together within a unitary social structure. 'Where is the necessity', asks Mann, 'for all these social requirements to generate identical socio-spatial interaction networks and form a unitary society?' (14). There is none. Rather, '[t]hose involved in economic subsistence, ideology, military defense and aggression, and political regulation possess a degree of autonomous control over their means of power that then further develops relatively autonomously' (15). As a result, 'Human beings do not create unitary societies but a diversity of intersecting networks of social interaction' (16). As Mann sums up, '*Societies are actually federations of organizations*' (52, emphasis in the original).[5]

Stability and change In the end, the networks of social power do have a tendency to unity, which derives, according to Mann, from the fact that the four major social power networks 'are not fully independent of one another'(1986: 14–15). As Mann asserts, 'all are necessary for each', with the result that 'the character of each is likely to be influenced by the character of all' (14–15). Ultimately, '[t]he more institutionalized these interrelations, the more the various power networks converge toward one unitary society' (15). Mann offers little indication of the actual mechanisms that accomplish and reproduce this convergence of networks of social power – or the relationship between convergence and the separation/autonomy of networks at the heart of his theory – and his reliance on the functional interdependence among them raises more questions than it answers. In the end, the interrelated issues of societal integration and stability, as far as I can discern, are only minimally confronted, with legitimation in terms of societal values and norms left, residually, to do most of the work.

In keeping with his idea of power as resulting from the autonomous creation of independent organizations to accomplish major societal functions, Mann sees social change as driven above all by organizational improvement through organizational innovation and as taking place through what he terms 'interstitial emergence'. People are always seeking to find better organizational means to achieve their goals. They use the 'invention of new organizational techniques' to construct more effective networks of social power. They nurture these 'rival configurations of one or more of the principal power networks' within the 'interstices' of the existing society, meaning alongside the already-existing networks.[6] Ultimately, the new improved organizations transcend their outmoded predecessors, the new networks of social power not so much transforming as replacing the old (2–3, 15–16). As Mann summarizes the process:

> History derives from restless drives that generate various networks of extensive and intensive power relations. These networks have a more direct relation to goal attainment than institutionalization has. In pursuit of their goals humans further develop these networks, outrunning the existing level of institutionalization.
>
> This may happen as a direct challenge to existing institutions, or it may happen unintentionally and 'interstitially' – between their interstices and around their edges – creating new relations and institutions that have unanticipated consequences for the old. (15)[7]

2.   *The link between theory and history: the separation of the political from the economic*

Mann's pivotal theoretical conclusion that the four sources/networks of social power tend to be not just conceptually but institutionally separate from one another constitutes the key conceptual link between his general theory of the sources of social power and his particular interpretation of the European dynamic. Because networks of social power emerge autonomously in relationship to the four fundamental societal needs, it follows that 'a broad division of function between ideological, economic, military, and political organizations is ubiquitous' (1986: 18). Given the premise that the institutional separation from one another of the four networks of social power is thus historically quite normal, if not necessarily the norm, Mann is able to proceed logically, with no need for further explanation, to find unremarkable the general proposition on which he founds his analysis of the Europe Miracle. In Europe from 800 AD onwards, as the outcome of a long and fortuitous historical development, the conceptually separate functions of the state and of the economy came to be carried out by quite institutionally separated organizations or networks of social power. As Mann puts it:

> Medieval European states ... redistributed very little of contemporary GDP. Their roles were overwhelmingly political. The separation between economic and political functions/organizations was clear and symmetrical – *states were political, classes were economic*. (17, emphasis added)

With the institutional separation of the political and the economic as his *point of departure*, Mann is enabled to provide a clear rationale for the unilineal evolution of the European socio-geographic totality:

(i) Autonomous networks of political power provided social peace and protection of property, but did not predate upon the economy;

(ii) Autonomous individualistic and competitive networks of economic power, unfettered and unburdened by political institutions, gave rise to self-sustaining agricultural, commercial and industrial growth;

(iii) Capitalist economic classes, arising from the networks of economic power, selected out modern nationally defined centralized states, which themselves emerged from inter-state conflict, as providing the best available political support for their own efflorescence, consolidating in the process the modern multi-state international system.

3.   The European Miracle

Political foundations of economic dynamism For Mann, *the* decisive factor making for the flowering of European economic and political dynamism was the putting in place in the period before 800 AD, as the outcome of long series of historical developments leading from the ancient empires of the eastern Mediterranean and Middle East through the Roman Empire to feudal Europe, of an historically unprecedented type of network of political power (1986: 409). 'Previous civilizations had provided infrastructure of extensive power [i.e. effective political regulation extending over large distances] but only at great cost, often through what I termed ... compulsory cooperation' (377). The latter were characterized by unitary states with a monopoly of power that were inextricably intertwined with the economy by virtue of their politically coerced mobilization of labour and heavy taxation. Although such states could bring about a certain degree of 'development', beyond a certain point they sapped an economy of its surpluses and its energy. But, in the wake of the disintegration of the eastern empires and with the fall of the Roman Empire, there emerged what Mann calls a 'multiple acephalous federation' (376) – a political network of social power that possessed none of the growth repressing effects of its predecessors.

Above all, a triumphant Christianity, the immediate legacy of historical developments within the Roman Empire, replaced compulsory cooperation and itself constituted networks of political power that were unprecedentedly cheap and effective.[8] 'Compulsory cooperation [was] swept aside by Christendom's normative pacification, and the European state never recovered it' (423). Christianity operated through two channels to provide the requisite political regulation. First, it offered transcendent values, which made possible a certain pacification of the Continent. These values legitimated, and thereby secured obedience to, social norms by the general population. They also gave the constituent local economic networks a feeling of identity and membership in a cohesive larger whole – i.e. Europe – that was essential in paving the way for their expansion. Second, Christianity reinforced what Mann calls the '*immanent* morale' of the ruling class of feudal lords that directly governed the society. It thereby made for an enhanced level of cohesion among its members, enabling them to offer cheap, but reasonably well-run de-centralized states, which did not monopolize political power (376, 377, 397). It was 'the combination' of virtually costless Christian ideology and inexpensive, weak, parcellized feudal states that depended upon that ideology that 'helped ensure a basic level of normative pacification, confirming property and market relations with and between the cells [of the economy]' (377). The outcome was that 'enough of [the infrastructure of extensive power] was provided by ideological means, by Christianity without a state, that expansion and innovation could burst out from the local intensive cell' (377; cf. 504).

From individualism and competition to self-sustaining growth The system of political regulation supplied by Christianity and the weak feudal state was able to unleash Europe's economic dynamism because it freed up the operation of an underlying economy that was itself constituted by individualistic economic units holding *de facto* private property which operated in competition with one another. From as early as 800 AD, the agricultural, commercial and industrial units of the economy were 'dominated by private property, in the sense of hidden and effective possession' (1986: 399). Their 'localism did not stifle an outward, expansionist orientation, but took the form of intense, regulated, class riven competition' (412). The result was in keeping with Adam Smith's expectations of the invisible hand – the unfettered growth of exchange and towns, leading to the growth of specialization and the division of labour, an uptick of investment, and, above all, the acceleration of technical change.

Europe's economic progress was built, according to Mann, upon the unique productiveness of Europe's individualistic agriculture. Although European civilization long trailed China in terms of a variety of extensive power networks, 'in another range of power achievements, intensive ones, especially in agriculture, Europe was leaping ahead by AD 1000' (378). 'The image [is] of small groups of peasants and lords standing looking at their fields, tools, and animals, figuring out how to improve them, with their back to the world, [able to be] relatively unconcerned with more extensive techniques of social organization [that through political regulation made possible exchange and assured their private property and social order] in the secure knowledge that these were already available' (413). Europe's individualist cultivators working fertile wet soils thus provided the main motor of growth. European lords and peasants were able, according to Mann, to take agricultural technology beyond that of any previous civilization. With their iron ploughs, they penetrated the soil more deeply. With their harnessing of draught animals, they tapped energy more effectively. With their sheep-corn husbandry, they struck a more productive balance between arable and pasture (403–6).

The outcome was epoch-making. '[Lords' and peasants'] economic praxis was enhanced, and this provided one of the decisive power reorganizations of world history' (412–13), especially as the growing output of European agriculture circulated, from the start, to growing towns, whose artisans and merchants served to facilitate the growth of urban industry and international commerce and, in turn, to stimulate the further growth of agriculture. Full fledged economic development was the order of the day for the first time in world history, manifested in the fact that, according to Mann, productivity rose continuously, as expressed in rising yields (402–3). This enabled an ever-greater part of the population to subsist off the land and, equally strikingly, allowed for the transcendence of the Malthusian dynamic, ensuring 'that with a hiccup or two, populations continued their upward movement right through medieval and early modern periods (402). The agricultural and industrial revolutions represented the ultimate outcome of the same, 1,000 year-long continuous process.

From economic dynamism to centralized state and multi-state system Finally, as Europe's economy expanded ever further beyond its initially mainly local, 'intensive', forms and became ever more 'extensive', indeed international, especially via the construction of ever broader and more complex commercial networks, it nurtured the need for new, broader forms of political organization to regulate it. Mann understands this process as an exemplification of his more general understanding of how societal change takes place by way of organizational innovation. 'European dynamism, now primarily economic, threw up a number of emergent interstitial networks of interaction for which a form of [political] organization that was *centralized* and *territorial* was distinctly useful. In the competitive structure of Europe, some states lit upon this solution and prospered. There the power of the state, centralized and territorial, was enhanced' (1986: 416, emphasis in the original).

Mann thus sees certain medieval states – functioning, by definition, as political networks of social power, to provide *central, territorial* institutionalized regulation – as gaining increased effectiveness by virtue of their increased centralization and territoriality, as they evolved 'interstitially' *vis-à-vis* other states, out of a process of intensifying inter-state competition, i.e. warfare. As Mann puts it, 'states and multi-state civilization developed primarily in response to pressures emanating from the geopolitical sphere' (65), and it was in this sphere that the autonomy and creativity of the medieval and early modern networks of social power were primarily asserted – specifically the construction of geopolitical territory. In Mann's words, 'The main reorganizing force of political power ... concerns the geographical infrastucture of human societies, especially their boundedness' (521), '[t]he outstanding example of [which] is in [medieval and] early modern Europe' (522).

As the economy meanwhile dynamically developed, its 'new characteristics' brought 'new pacification requirements' – specifically defending contracts, organizing markets and guaranteeing property (421, 422). Especially after 1200, above all merchants, who needed the protection and privileges that the state could offer and were prepared to pay for these (see 'the state–merchant alliance', 1986: 427–8), but also other social forces that hoped to gain either from protection of their property or from the spoils of war, threw their support behind the more centralized and territorial states that had emerged, especially by providing finance, thereby further strengthening it (423–4, 427–8, 430–2). Speaking more generally, as the economy expanded, it 'required an extensive infrastructure quite as much as an intensive one' (437). The latter could not be provided by the Christian Church, the scope of which was too broad. Nor could it be supplied by the older highly local feudal states, the range of which was too small and 'the multiple, particularistic obligations to which fettered private property' (399). The economy therefore came to 'select out' states whose borders fit its broadened scope. These emergent 'national' states were able to prosper, in turn, by providing coordination, especially in the form of justice, for the dominant groups of the dynamic economic order. Increasingly powerful, they came to win out in the field of geopolitical competition, constituting in the process what came to be the modern international system of states (444–5).

As Mann puts it, 'The precipitating factor of this secular trend [to centralized territorial coordinating states and corresponding international state system] was almost always the fiscal pressures on the state emanating from its international military needs. But the underlying *cause* of the extension of the state's coordinating powers lay more in the extension of class relations over a wider geographic terrain through the transition from broadly "feudal" to capitalist economics' (512, emphasis added). 'As the original dynamism of feudal Europe became more extensive, capitalism and the national state formed a loose but coordinated and concentrated alliance' (446).

To succinctly sum up the progression set in train by the establishment of separated political and economic networks of social power:

Unimpeded but protected by institutionally separate networks of political power, autonomous individualistic organizations of economic power, under pressure of mutual competition, drove self-sustaining economic progress. Meanwhile networks of political power pursued their own distinct trajectories towards centralization, territoriality and the coordinated national state in response to military competition, but were able in the end to survive and thrive only because they provided indispensable functions for the developing economy and its leading classes, who supported them financially and administratively. This bifurcated symbiotic evolutionary process ultimately issued in industrial capitalism, on the one hand, and the centralized territorial national state and multi-state system on the other. Mann's ultimate theoretical conclusions fall out – that the state is autonomous, especially with respect to international relations, and the developing economy could not and did not determine the multi-state framework that turned out to regulate it.

4.   The riddle resolved: coincidental capitalism from 800 AD

The resolution of the riddle of Mann's seemingly contradictory combination of an anti-holistic, anti-evolutionary theoretical standpoint – culminating in his view of society as constituted by multiple intersecting, overlapping networks of social power – and an Enlightenment interpretation of the European miracle – exemplified in the unilineal pattern of growth of the economy and parallel maturation of the centralized territorial state and multi-state system – should now be evident. Up to a point, Mann does follow his methodological cum theoretical programme. He therefore explains the *origins* of the European miracle as resulting from a long 'pre-history' of the development of what he believes to be essentially autonomous political and economic networks of social power, manifesting 'a gigantic series of coincidences'. Thus, Mann's 'argument is that without an understanding of more macrostructures of power – beginning with those in the eastern Mediterranean, continuing with those in the Roman Empire, and culminating with those in Christendom – we could not find in place both the intensive and extensive power preconditions of the European miracle' (409). So far so good.

But, it could hardly be more obvious that, with his subsequent account of the European miracle itself, he betrays his own methodological strictures. 'We can never find a single bounded society in geographical or social space' (1986: 1), he says. But from 800 AD, Europe constitutes just such a society in Mann's account. 'Societies', he asserts, 'are not social systems; they are not totalities' (1). But, what Mann actually argues is that the separation, from about the same time, of a political network of social power providing protection for but no predation upon an economic network of social power constituted by individualistic private property units in mutual competition provided exactly such a totality for little short of a millennium. 'Because there is no totality', Mann argues, it follows that 'individuals are not constrained in their behavior by social structure as a whole' (1–2). Yet, it is because the separation of the economic from the political constituted a structure of constraint upon the society's constituent members that the individual actors in Mann's story are, as he argues, persistently obliged to pursue quite consistent micro-patterns throughout the length of the medieval and early modern periods – what Mann terms 'rational restlessness', manifested in the ongoing search for more effective production so as to enable higher profits. Mann concludes that, 'Because there is no social system there is no "evolutionary" process within it' (1). Yet, it is because individuals did actually follow consistent micro-patterns against the background of a persisting social system that Mann is able to find what could hardly be a more classically unilineal evolutionary pattern, manifested in a thousand years of economic development and state building.

What is the European totality that forms the point of departure and constitutes the explanation for the European Miracle? It is, of course, nothing less than the classical capitalism defined by Adam Smith, in which a non-interfering state capable of providing peace, justice and security, on the one hand, will free up, on the other, individual private property so as allow, via the invisible hand, individuals to reap the rewards of their own effort and to bring, by way of competition, permanent progress. As Mann paraphrases the Glasgow sage, 'If you have peace, easy taxes, and a tolerable administration, the rest is brought about by the "natural course of things"' (406).

Mann could not be more explicit about the Smithian character of his account, even if he would not be entirely happy with the label.[9] Well before the turn of the first millennium, the European economy was made up of 'a multiplicity of part-autonomous, competitive, local economic power networks – peasant communities, lordly manors, towns, and merchant and artisan guilds – whose competition settled into that single, universal diffuse set of private property relations we know as *capitalism*' (510, emphasis added). Once the separation of the economic and political had been established:

[I]ndividual families and local village-and-manor communities were participating in a wider network of economic interaction under institutionalized norms governing property possession, production relations, and market exchange. They possessed the autonomy and privacy to keep to themselves the fruits of their own enterprises and thus to calculate likely costs and benefits to themselves of alternatives strategies.

Thus with supply, demand, and incentives for innovation well established, *neo-classical economics can take up the explanation.* (1986: 409, emphasis added)

More specifically, once the burden of compulsory cooperation was lifted, 'an extremely long-term persistence of a distinctively "European" peasant-plus-iron economy ... fits quite well into a *neoclassical explanation* of the European miracle' (408, emphasis added). At the same time, especially where they had decent access to major markets, 'the lords' estates became more like *capitalist* agriculture, producing commodities for exchange' (408, emphasis added). As Mann concludes, 'The transition that saw Europe leap forward was not primarily the late-medieval transition from feudalism to capitalism. That process was largely the institutionalization of a leap that had occurred much earlier. By 1000 AD that leap, that dynamic, was already taking western Europe to new heights' (412) – and would carry it through to the agro-industrial revolution of the eighteenth century. Mann takes it for granted that with the establishment of the separation of the political from the economic by 800 AD or thereabouts, instantiated by weak but effective non-predatory states and secure private property, capitalism had for all intents and purposes come into being. Henceforth, as a consequence, capitalist development could be assumed, it did not have to be explained; a *transition* to capitalism was therefore extraneous[10]; and capitalist development was a done deal.[11]

II.   Networks of social power or social-property relations?

A theoretical and historical argument that posits, and purports to explain, steady capitalist development from the end of the Dark Ages into the epoch of the agricultural and industrial revolutions is bound to raise eyebrows, of both conventional economic historians and traditional historical sociologists. The former tend to see self-sustaining economic growth as coming relatively late, in the early modern epoch at earliest. The latter are committed to viewing the movement from medieval to modern as entailing a transition from one sort of society to another – feudal to capitalist or traditional to modern – and of conceiving, in turn, of the separation between state and civil society as expressive, if not constitutive of, modernity. But, if we are to properly appreciate and fruitfully criticize Mann's novel conclusions, we must fully grasp the way in which he comes to them, closely examining each step in the argument.

The separation between the economic and the political, emerging at the start of the Middle Ages, constitutes, as has been repeatedly stressed, the key conceptual link between, on the one hand, Mann's theoretical understanding of society in terms of functionally defined networks of social power and, on the other, his socio-historical interpretation of the European Miracle in terms of the interconnected development of capitalism and rise of the centralized territorial national state. But both sides, so to speak, of this nexus are open to question.

(i) Mann's theory of social power provides the point of departure for his idea of autonomously developing organizations/institutions, and he moves smoothly in conceptual terms from the four separate societal functions or needs to the four separate networks of social power, to the notion of society as constituted by multiple overlapping intersecting networks, to the plausibility, even expectation, of a separation of the political from the economic in medieval Europe. But, in so doing, Mann leaves paradoxically undertheorized the issue of the economic reproduction of the agents that operate the autonomous organizations that for him constitute society, let alone the processes of economic appropriation via property rights, property differentials and class exploitation underpinned by force that figure so centrally in classical, and not just Marxist, historical sociology. The question that therefore imposes itself is how Mann can integrate these mechanisms within his theory of power and, in particular, whether, in so doing, he can sustain the separation of the economic and political as either theoretically plausible outside capitalist societies or empirically actual in most of medieval and early modern Europe?

(ii) The medieval separation of the political from the economic provides the premise or point of departure for Mann's interpretation of the European Miracle. This is, first, because he proceeds from Smithian premises about the automatic operation of the invisible hand under conditions where political networks of social power secure order and justice but do not fetter the economy and where private property is secure. It is second because, analogously to – if in a different way from – classical political economists from Smith to Marx, he sees the capitalist economy and capitalist classes as developing in the interstices of the old order and selecting out and buttressing the centralized, territorial state. Nevertheless, both these mechanisms – behind, respectively, self-sustaining growth and the rise of the modern state – find their rationale, in the first instance, in a theoretical argument that, as just suggested, may be faulty due to its difficulty in integrating the reproduction of property differentials and exploitation. More directly to the point, it may be asked whether Smith's assumptions concerning the inherent dynamism of unfettered individual property *per se* make sense and can grasp the actual path of the European economy. Could medieval peasants and lords really be expected to operate along capitalist lines? If not, is it possible to sustain the notion that the evolution of economic networks of social power during the medieval and early modern period, and the social classes that it precipitated, lay behind the rise of the modern state and international system of states?

1.   *From collective to distributive power? The question of property differentials*

Mann's approach distinguishes itself from those to be found in the Marxist, as well as the Weberian, traditions, in deriving distributive power from collective power, itself generated through the organization of networks of social power to fulfil a societal requisite. The 'translation' from horizontal to vertical power takes place, it will be recalled, by means of social power networks' organizational hierarchies – indispensable to the division of labour within the network of social power, essential in turn to the execution of their societal function/fulfilment of a need, and ultimately irreplaceable by those at the bottom – while simultaneously endowing those at the top with the coordinating and supervisory capacity to out-organize those at the bottom. As Mann succinctly sums up: 'The masses comply because they lack collective organization to do otherwise, because they are embedded within collective and distributive power organizations controlled by others' – that carry out functions required by all (1986: 7).[12]

Property, force, and material appropriation Nevertheless, the fact remains that Mann never specifies how those at the top – by making use of their distributive power – extract – *presumably without equal compensation* – what they need to materially reproduce themselves *qua* rulers, over and against the ruled. Nor does he tell us how, in terms of his theory, those at the bottom of the organization – or indeed all other members of society – accomplish economic appropriation. Networks of *economic* power carry out the tasks of extraction, allocation, transformation/production, and distribution required to make available a final product to society. But, Mann does not, within his formal theory, specify the mechanisms by which members of the society – either within or outside networks of economic power, dominant or dominated – actually gain regular access to that product, exploitatively or non-exploitatively.[13]

The issue of economic appropriation – of the structures or mechanisms behind the distribution of the economic product – is routinely answered, by both theoretical historical sociology and empirical practical history, by reference to property rights in general and exploitation in particular, leaving aside the complex and controversial question of what, precisely, is

entailed by each. The structure of property rights in the means of production, as well as in the social product produced by others, thus governs the
way in which the economic product is distributed so as to make possible
the reproduction of the members of the society. This structure is, in turn,
it is generally assumed, directly or indirectly, guaranteed/sanctioned by
force. In fact, in his practico-historical analysis, Mann has no trouble
acknowledging such commonplaces. This is indeed evident in an informal definition that he provides of stratification – which he takes to refer to
private property differentials in general and economic classes in
particular.[14]

Stratification involves the permanent, *institutionalized power of some over the material chances of others*. Its power may be *physical force* or the *ability to deprive others
of the necessities of life* [itself dependent on force, R.B.]. In the literature on origins
it is usually a synonym for private property differentials and for economic classes,
and so I treat it as a decentralized form of power. (1986: 38, emphasis added)

It remains the case that, in the course of presenting his formal theory
of social power, Mann makes no attempt to conceptualize and assimilate either private property, or private property differentials, or the
exploitation associated with the constitution of classes, or the force
required to sanction or support these. Private property differentials
do come up in Mann's discussion of *diffused* power, which he sees
as arising – in contrast to the *authoritative* power generated by formal
organizations – out of informal, unorganized cooperation, exemplified above all by market exchange. But though Mann sees unequal
property as a form of distributive power, he is unable to demonstrate
how it is derived from diffused collective power, but must treat it, though
implicitly, as a premise of the latter. As he puts it, market exchange
'*embodies* distributive power, whereby only some persons possess ownership rights over goods and services' (8, emphasis added). But since
market exchange obviously cannot itself explain the distribution of
ownership rights over goods and services among those who enter into it,
this is not to account for the distribution of ownership rights, but to take
it for granted.

As to force, Mann – consistently – has only restricted use for it within
his theory of social power. This is, above all, because he understands
distributive power, in the first and last instance, as accruing to those at the
top of networks of social power by virtue of their strategic position within
the organization and their irreplaceability in enabling those networks to
perform indispensable societal functions. Since those at the bottom of the
organization are out-organized by and dependent upon those at the top
for the execution of these functions – which they cannot themselves

organize to perform – there is no need for force to back up power. It follows that, within his theory of power, Mann allots a role for force in a clear and formal way only to *military* networks of social power, for the obvious reason that the execution of their function requires it by definition. He grants as well, if more informally, a role for force with respect to the operation of *political* power networks, apparently because it is essential for the administration and enforcement of justice (11, 14). But since, in his formal theory, Mann does not go beyond his derivation of distributive from collective power and seek to explain – presumably by recourse to the same analytical framework – the appropriation of the economic product by those at the top (or, for that matter, those at the bottom, or those outside) networks of social power, it is not so surprising that Mann has little place in his formal theory for property rights and thus coercion.

From collective power to exploitation? The question remains as to whether Mann's theory of power *can* – or does implicitly – account for the processes of economic appropriation made possible by property rights in general, their distribution, or exploitation in particular. In this respect, the definition of stratification that Mann puts forward in the course of presenting his formal theory of social power is not helpful, because it simply re-poses the question.

Stratification is the *overall creation and distribution of power in society*. It is the central structure of societies because in its dual collective and distributive aspects it is the means whereby human beings achieve their goals in society. (10, emphasis in the original) [15]

The problem confronting Mann would thus seem to be to comprehend his informal, practico-empirical garden-variety account of stratification (above) in terms of his formal theoretical account (here). But he never resolves this directly.

Mann's theory does, it must be stressed, offer a possible route to integrate economic appropriation by way of property rights/property differentials in general and exploitation in particular within his theory of social power: that is, to understand unequal economic appropriation as a species of distributive power, and thus to conceptualize it in the same way Mann conceptualizes distributive power more generally – as derivative from collective power. But, there is reason to doubt that this path is actually open to Mann, given his characterization of distributive power itself. Mann would thus presumably interpret unequal economic appropriation as he does distributive power, as resulting from the relationship of those at the top – executing the function of coordination and supervision in the hierarchy and thereby making an indispensable contribution to the organization's operation – and those at the bottom – out-organized by those at the top and dependent upon them to set in motion the machinery upon which everyone depends. In this case, the acquiescence of those at the bottom in any sort of payment by themselves to those at the top would be understood as an expression of the dependence of the former on the latter for the execution of a function necessary for themselves. Viewed from the opposite angle, any exaction by those at the top from those at the bottom would ultimately be ensured by the implicit threat of those at the top to refuse to carry out their role.

Nevertheless, this account seems problematic. The threat of defection by those at the top could ensure a payment from those at the bottom only if those at the bottom were unable themselves to assume their role; otherwise the organization's rulers' threat to renege would carry no bite. Mann takes it for granted that the ruled cannot perform the function of the rulers, but he does not explain on what basis. In fact, it is not easy to come up with a reason why those at the bottom could not take over the role of those at the top – unless, of course, it is that they lack the resources required to perform the role. Such resources might include instruments of force, means of production, or appropriate training or skill. But if economic appropriation by those at the top from those at the bottom were made possible only because those at the bottom were unable to assume the place of those at the top *due to the fact* that they lacked and the former possessed the instruments of force, or means of production, or appropriate training or skill required for the role, that economic appropriation would have to be interpreted as resulting from the 'background' distribution of resources, and not from the ability of those at the top to perform a function. In this case, we would be back to standard approaches to unequal economic appropriation, which view it as resulting from differential property rights in the means of production or the social product, backed up directly or indirectly by force, rather than polar positions and roles within an organizational hierarchy. For the same reasons that it is hard to see how position at the top of an organizational hierarchy, i.e. Mann's 'organizational' chart, can, in the absence of an unequal distribution of resources, favour those at the top or endow them with the capacity to distribute anything (non-reciprocally) from those at the bottom, it is difficult to see how it can constitute for those at the top the more general capacity to 'carry out [their] own will without resistance' *vis-à-vis* those at the bottom. Mann's derivation of distributive from collective power is in doubt.

Stratification in history If it is not easy to see how collective power can give rise to unequal appropriation in general and exploitation in particular, it is also difficult to grasp how the various social relationships and processes underpinning the latter that are found historically could find their roots in the former. This is above all because the structures of property rights behind unequal appropriation have been *about* – have been constituted in order to make possible – the economic reproduction of some collectivities at the expense or exclusion of others – and not to carry out a social function as are Mann's networks of social power. Because they are designed to make for exploitation and exclusion but not the execution of a societal function, it is difficult to see how they could find their foundation in the cooperation of the exploited and excluded, as does Mann's distributive power *vis-à-vis* collective power. Since, in their essence, these social relationships and processes are non-reciprocal, it is finally difficult to see how they could have their maintenance ensured by normative legitimation *alone*, as is Mann's distributive power, without the supplementation of an indispensable quotient of *force*.

Thus, as Mann himself puts it, private property differentials in general and class exploitation in particular involve the 'the permanent, institutionalized power of some over the material chances of others' (1986: 38). Historically speaking, as Mann says, this permanent institutionalized power has been exerted in two ways – by means of the direct application of 'physical force' or on the basis of the 'deprivation of others of the necessities of life', itself requiring the sanction of force (38).[16] The first of these, quasi-universal in pre-capitalist class societies since the rise of settled agriculture, was made possible by the self-organization of exploiters (lords) precisely so as to mobilize and monopolize the means of force. This enabled the take by pre-capitalist ruling classes, in the form of a coerced levy or tax (in the guise of labour, kind or money), from a class of peasant producers who possessed their means of subsistence, i.e. sufficient land, tools and labour to produce what they needed to maintain themselves. The second, most characteristic of capitalist societies, is enabled by the separation of the direct producers (workers) from their means of subsistence and production (both land and tools) and the monopoly of the means of production by a separate class of capitalists.[17] This structure makes possible the take in the form of a profit by a capitalist ruling class, by obliging the direct producers to sell their ability to labour to the latter for less than the former can sell on the market the product of the use of its labour, a relationship that must be ensured in the last analysis by the coercive powers of the state.

In each of these cases, it should be clear, economic appropriation depends on the emergence and maintenance, ultimately by force, of different systems of what I would call *social-property relations* – i.e. the relations among direct producers, among exploiters, and between exploiters and direct producers that, taken together, enable/specify the regular access of individuals and families to the means of production (land, labour, tools) and/or the social product *per se*. That is, the distribution of the economic product takes place in accordance with place in a social-property structure, not with position/role in an organization, or network of social power, defined by its function. The flow to pre-capitalist lords from possessing peasants did not follow from their mutual cooperation within a network of social-power, in which the former performed indispensable functions required by the latter. Peasants as possessors of the means of subsistence were, by definition, economically self-sufficient and, as a rule, fully capable of self-government. They had no need for lords to perform any task in order *for them* to carry out their economic reproduction or political functions. For this reason, pre-capitalist lords could not appropriate part of peasants' product by performing/withholding a necessary function, nor were they were required to perform such a function to effect their take. To reproduce themselves at peasants' expense, pre-capitalist lords were simply obliged to constitute a collectivity capable of applying sufficient force, with the performance of any economic or political function by lords for peasants or society literally *noblesse oblige*. Lords might, in fact, carry out major productive or governmental roles, but only as a consequence of, not as a condition for, their rights to the peasants' product.

Nor does the flow to capitalists from proletarians require their mutual cooperation within a network of social power, in which the former perform indispensable functions required by the latter. Workers are economically dependent upon capitalists, but not for the latter's performance of indispensable functions. From domestic industry through contemporary cooperatives, workers have carried out all aspects of what Mann terms the *circuits of praxis*, with no need for the intervention of capitalists. Capitalists cannot therefore appropriate part of workers' product by performing/withholding a necessary function for a network of economic power, nor are they required to perform such a function at all. To reproduce themselves at workers' expense, they are simply obliged to dispose of capital, in the form of money or means of production, under conditions where workers without such capital have no choice but to cede to them part of their product to survive – either in the process of working for a wage with capitalists' means of production, or working on equipment leased from capitalists for a rent, or working with 'their own' means of production purchased with money borrowed (against little or no collateral) at interest from capitalists. Capitalists might indeed organize production directly, but not as a requirement to appropriate part of workers' product, and only as a consequence of, not as a cause, of their monopoly of the means of production.

As Marx somewhere put it, a capitalist is a captain of industry because he is a capitalist, not vice versa. Similarly, a lord was a general, judge or policeman because he was a lord, not vice versa. By the same token, an emperor was operator of irrigation systems because he was an emperor, not vice versa.

2.   The merger of the economic and political in pre-capitalist societies

But given that, in pre-capitalist economies, economic reproduction depended upon appropriation via property rights in general and exploitation in particular that themselves required the institutionalized capacity to apply force, it is hard to see how the pre-capitalist economy could ever be autonomous from the polity, how the two could be anything but inextricably intertwined or merged. As Mann himself recognizes, 'In an agrarian economy it is difficult to exclude the peasant altogether from direct access to the means of production [and subsistence]: land. Once in possession, he or she was ... coerced directly' (1986: 151). Lords thus tended to find it difficult to derive an income from ownership of land alone – as, due to peasant possession, there were few tenants or workers to valorize it. They were therefore generally obliged, in order to reproduce themselves economically, to constitute 'permanent, institutionalized power' over the peasants that would enable them to apply force to gain access to the peasants' labour or product – via slavery, serfdom, or tribute in money or kind (152). In order to accomplish this, they had to organize themselves into a political community, the existence of which was premised upon the endowment of its individual members by the community with 'politically constituted private property' in the form of a right to a take from the peasants. This right might enable direct access to peasants' product in the form of de-centralized levies by the community's members (as with a fief). Alternatively, it might give community members indirect access to peasants' product via a share in a collectively appropriated centralized levy or tax (as with a state office). In either case, lordly political communities had to reproduce their members' rights by means of executing the quintessentially political functions of defence, or offence, against outsiders (military), settling disputes among their members concerning their rights (justice), enforcing the settlements of those disputes (police), and finally, of course, the point of the whole exercise, extracting part of the peasants' product ('taxation'). In sum, the property rights through which lords materially reproduced themselves (institutionalized, e.g. in a fief or an office) were politically constituted by a lordly community executing the functions that we normally associate with the state or the political – functions that had to be backed up by coercion. To reproduce themselves pre-capitalist lords had to form a state. By the same token, access to these politically constituted rights depended upon membership in the political community. Economic reproduction was therefore in its essence a political process. The economic and political, class and state, were merged.

At the same time, in pre-capitalist societies – as in every society – the institutions and personnel executing political functions – and thereby by definition constituting the state – had to have the capacity to wield sufficient force to overcome any resistance, if they were to be effective. The reason for this is that the fulfilment of every political function – military, justice, police, taxation – requires this. Given that in pre-capitalist societies the political communities making up the dominant class reproduced their members economically precisely by wielding the means of coercion to carry out political functions in the name of their members in order to forcibly exact either de-centralized or centralized levies from peasant possessors, it follows that the pre-capitalist state, to function effectively, had to incorporate the dominant class. Put another way, the pre-capitalist state had to largely overlap, in terms of institutional form and personnel, the pre-capitalist ruling class.

To come at the same point from the opposite direction: in pre-capitalist class societies any potential leader or leaders that wished to create, re-create, or expand the capacity to carry out political functions – to constitute a 'state' – could recruit military, judicial and police function-aries only by making those functionaries members of a ruling class, capable in material terms of self-financing a ruling-class form of life. Such a leader could actually accomplish this only by bringing these followers together in a political community capable of sustaining their allegiance by endowing them with 'politically constituted private property', providing rights directly or indirectly in the peasants' product. Put another way, any group capable of carrying out politico-military functions by virtue of its coercive capacity was virtually certain to use that coercive capacity to seek to create the conditions for materially reproducing itself and its members on a permanent basis by means of establishing rights in the peasants' surplus and the ability to redistribute wealth from other lords – for this was the only viable way to do so against the background of an economy dominated by peasant possessors. They could be expected, in other words, to plunder the peasantry and create the conditions for reproducing their predatory position, establishing themselves as an exploiting class. Simply stated, in the pre-capitalist context, to constitute and expand a state it was necessary to constitute and expand the ruling class, while any group capable of carrying out political or state functions would use its ability to exert force to make itself a class of exploiters.

It is true that, at times, pre-capitalist rulers sought to break the foregoing rule – that is to develop the administration of the state by appointing followers who were directly dependent upon themselves because they lacked the politically constituted private property, the powers and rights in the peasants' surplus, required for ruling class membership and, thereby, independence. But, equally routinely, such administrators did everything they could to secure precisely such property – in the form of offices, fiefs or land. The upshot is that the term 'bureaucracy' has at best limited applicability to pre-capitalist political systems, since state officials almost always were endowed with from the start, or came to possess, a certain autonomy from the administration by virtue of their politically constituted private property – fiefs, offices, land. As a consequence, the execution of public functions depended upon persons who saw their political position first and foremost as a private source of income. As Mann himself summarizes the process, '[the] State's recently acquired centralized powers were lost as its agents "disappeared" into "civil society", then were lost again, and so forth' (1986: 521). If reproduction of pre-capitalist ruling classes was dependent upon 'the political', the reproduction of the pre-capitalist state was dependent upon 'the economic'.

3.   European Miracle or feudal evolution?

Mann is able to establish a general theoretical presumption in favour of the normality of the separation of the economic and political that he claims to find in Europe at the time of the Dark Ages on the basis of his vision of society as constituted by autonomous intersecting, overlapping networks of social power, which themselves arise from the constitution of separate organizations to realize separate societal functions. That separation opened the way, according to Mann, for the European miracle by unleashing self-sustaining economic growth, which provided in turn the structural foundation for the inexorable rise of the centralized territorial state and multi-state international system. I have attempted to cast doubt on Mann's conceptual justification for the expectation of separate networks of political and economic power by arguing that it depends on his eliding, in his formal theory, of the process of economic appropriation on the basis of differential property rights and exploitation. Indeed, I have tried to show that his theory cannot in fact grasp differential property rights and economic exploitation because it cannot derive them as forms of distributive power from collective power. In this way, I have sought to prepare the ground for demonstrating that the requirements for pre-capitalist ruling classes to materially reproduce themselves against a background of peasant possession generally precluded the very possibility of the separation of the economic from the political, and enforced their merger. The question that therefore imposes itself is the relationship between these two divergent theoretical conceptions and the actual historical dynamics of economic and political development in the medieval and early modern period.

Weak autonomous state or predatory feudal state? Mann is able, in practice, to assert the separation of political from economic networks of social power in the medieval epoch not only by attributing an overriding role in normative pacification to the Christian Church, but also by picturing the medieval state *per se* as weak and minimally predatory. Since he defines the medieval state as 'the monarch and its creatures' (1986: 436) – presumably those in the monarch's immediate entourage who were directly dependent upon it – he has no difficulty making good his claim that it was quite feeble and accomplished little plunder, able to appropriate little of the economy's GDP. But Mann is able to characterize the medieval state in this way only by virtue of his peculiar – and theoretically inconsistent – definition of the state, which limits it to centralized, territorially based institutions executing government functions.[18] '[S]o decentralized were their political functions and so lacking territoriality were they' that 'in some ways it is misleading to call any of them "states"', especially since they 'had virtually no fiscal or economically redistributive powers' (392). But once we identify *all* of the forces carrying out political functions – not just those executing them from the centre – we are able to comprehend the medieval state in very different terms – terms with which Mann is ultimately obliged to concur. Like the vast majority of other pre-capitalist states throughout history, the medieval state necessarily encompassed the bulk of the feudal ruling class because the personnel and institutions of that class necessarily played such an overwhelming role in executing state political functions. As a consequence, it was neither so weak, nor so autonomous, nor so devoid of the capacity for predation as Mann contends – nor indeed so lacking in centralization or territoriality.

The medieval state and agrarian ruling class were obliged, like most other pre-capitalist rulers, to reproduce themselves in relationship to a peasantry in possession of its means of subsistence. Peasant possession was, in the first instance, like other forms of private property in this epoch, itself politically constituted – i.e. maintained by a political community for its members, in this case the peasant village, by means of its executing the political functions necessary to secure their rights – judicial functions to settle disputes among them concerning their rights, police functions to enforce judicial decisions, and military functions to defend against outsiders, including lords. As Mann puts it, 'Formidable as were the powers of lord, they were restrained by the fact that even the serf could find support from the village community and from customary law' (395). Peasant possession was sustained, it should be added, not only by the action of peasant communities, but also by the inability of individual members of the lordly class to find it in their self-interest to contest it. Because the agricultural economy was operated for the most part by peasants in possession of their means of subsistence, there tended to be only a restricted market in tenants or wage workers. As a consequence, individual lords had little motivation to expropriate their own peasants for, having done so, they would face major problems valorizing the land thus vacated either through renting it or farming it directly using hired labour.

Faced with producers in possession of their means of subsistence, medieval lords could sustain themselves economically only by constituting and maintaining the capacity to take a levy by extra-economic coercion from the direct producers. This was made possible by their constructing and maintaining the classically feudal political ties of interdependence which joined overlord to knightly follower and thereby constituted the feudal group, the ultimate source of lordly power, both leaders and followers. The overlord typically brought his vassals around him by endowing them with fiefs, which required their holders to provide him and his following with politico-military service, while endowing them with rights in the peasants' product (feudal rent), enforced by the feudal group.

Feudal lordship was able to successfully constitute itself – across much of Western Europe, from roughly around the year 1000 AD – by virtue of the ability of local lords to appropriate to themselves the right of the 'ban' – viz. political powers to make war, administer justice and levy taxes that had hitherto accrued to the Carolingian state and its members. This they were able to accomplish by gathering around themselves a political community of vassals, glued to the group through the obligations and benefits of the fief. What ultimately enabled these groups to amass the minimal coercive capacity to reproduce themselves economically by exploiting the peasantry and plundering other lords was their construction of castles as centres of military control and arming themselves as mounted warriors on horseback with coats of armour. With the benefit of their central fortresses and on the basis of their superior military resources, they were enabled to dominate a rather minimal territory, over which they exerted the judicial, police and military powers required to defend the rights of the members of the group so as to make it possible for them to levy exactions on the peasants and warfare on their neighbours.[19]

What the lords offered the peasants was a form of 'protection', in the classic sense. The peasants' payment was in no way recompense for 'defensive' functions performed for them by lords. Lords had little or no interest in risking life, limb or money for peasants' safety, and had no need to do so to exact their take. Like gangs everywhere, lordly bands simply made the peasants an offer that they could not refuse. The peasants paid up, not because of any function the lords carried out for them, but because the lords monopolized powerful coercive resources – castles, weaponry, armour, horses. To the extent that peasants could resist, they did so, and were able, during the early part of the feudal epoch, in important regions of Western Europe, to bring down rent so profoundly as to reduce many lords to poverty.[20]

It might be noted, in passing, that the rise of feudalism in the form of banal lordship, taking place out of the disintegration of Carolingian rule, had nothing do with lords offering protection to peasants from marauding bands during the epoch of the great invasions of Europe. The latter had essentially petered out before the former got off the ground. It is interesting to note in this regard that:

[I]n northern France, threatened by Viking raiders, a tradition of peasant resistance [to the invaders] ... continued despite the collapse of royal power. This tradition was codified in the capitulary of Meersen in 847, with the general call to arms of the Franks ... At the end of the century this practice was generally replaced by the selfish and ineffectual maneuvers of armed bands of aristocrats, with whose interests the levy often conflicted. In 859 the peasants between the Seine and the Loire came together to repel the Vikings, but their contingents were crushed by the princes' cavalry. Again in 884 the villagers formed guilds to resist those who pillaged them.

On the other hand, the 'growth in the number of castles ... cannot be related to the need for defense against invaders – the Viking raids north of the Loire ceased around 930 and in the Midi the Saracens of Freinet were wiped out in 972'. The emergent class of banal lords constructed the castles, roughly between 950 and 1050. They did so, not to defend themselves against external raiders, but as an indispensable precondition for the establishment of their dominance, the consolidation of their power.[21]

The feudal bonds of interdependence that enabled the constitution of a feudal band around a leading lord made possible the construction of what were in fact full-fledged states, even if highly localized ones, capable of dispensing justice, keeping the peace and waging warfare, though only over a very restricted area. But it remains the case that the *raison d'être* of the governments thus created was to constitute the dominant class of feudal society by establishing the instruments for extracting, redistributing and consuming the wealth upon which this class depended for their maintenance. State and ruling class were thus two sides of the same coin. The distinctive ties which bound man to man in feudal society (not only the relations of vassalage strictly speaking, but also the more loosely defined associations brought together by patronage, clientage and family) constituted the building blocks, at one and the same time, for the peculiarly fragmented, locally based and politically competitive character of the feudal ruling class and for the peculiarly particularized nature of feudal states. It was lords' feudal levies that provided the material base for the feudal polity. It was lords' capacity to create, expand and sophisticate their states that held the ultimate key to their material reproduction as individuals and as a ruling class.

In view of the essential merger between state and ruling class in medieval Europe, Mann's claims that the medieval state was autonomous, weak and only minimally predatory is difficult to accept. The fact is that Mann himself, when he comes to concretely describing the medieval state – as opposed to characterizing its role in the European Miracle – reaches the same conclusion, relinquishing in the process his initial definition of the state in terms of its ruler and immediate entourage and agreeing that the collectivity constituted by the ruler's lordly followers should be included. 'Most of the functions that [the ruler] exercised for the society', says Mann, 'were exercised through other autonomous power actors, the vassals' (1986: 391). Thus, '[h]is ritual functions and the infrastructure of literacy for his bureaucracy were controlled by transnational church; his judicial authority was shared with church and local [feudal and] manorial courts; his military leadership was exercised … over retainers of other lords; and he had virtually no fiscal or economically redistributive powers' (392). This is understandable, since 'the feudal state was an agglomeration of largely autonomous [lordly] households' (391). As he concludes, in symptomatically self-contradictory language, 'The weak state could not implement legislation without the local cooperation of the lords: *it was the lords*' (411, emphasis added). As the other side of the coin, feudal states, understood as made up not just of kingly or princely overlords and their immediate entourage, but the lordly groups that followed them, could not only appropriate major portions of the peasants' product, but were able, in the process – and in order to do so – centrally administer broad territories with impressive efficiency.[22]

Capitalist development or Malthusian stagnation? The significance for Mann's interpretation of the European Miracle of his weak, non-predatory, but nonetheless effective medieval state was its ability to unleash the inherent potential of unfettered but protected individualist private property. Once the founding separation of the political from the economic was secured, Mann stresses, the neoclassical logic of the invisible hand could take over the explanation. Implicit in Mann's reasoning are thus two assumptions, derived from Adam Smith. First, since by specializing, agriculturalists could secure gains from trade greater than from diversifying, they would naturally specialize, if only given the opportunity to secure the fruits of their labour by secure private property and freedom from predation. Second, since by specializing agriculturalists would leave themselves dependent upon the market for their inputs, they would have no choice, if they wished to survive, but to sell their output competitively and thus to produce at the lowest possible cost. But, both these premises are open to question, especially with respect to the peasant possessors in charge of most agricultural production in medieval and early modern Europe.

It should be noted first that, possessing direct non-market access to their means of subsistence, peasants did not *have* to seek the gains from trade. Because they were relieved of the necessity to buy their inputs on the market and thus from the requirement of selling their output, they had no need to produce competitively, so no need to maximize price with respect to cost, thus no need to specialize. Faced with the entry of lower-cost producers into their market, they would of course suffer reduced income from sales of their physical surpluses. But they would face no threat of going out of business, since their material reproduction did not depend on those sales.

Nevertheless, the fact remains that to point out in this way that peasants were not required to seek the gains from trade to survive is in no way to demonstrate that they did not, in any case, find specialization and cost-cutting more generally to be in their self-interest, as is generally assumed. Obviously, virtually as a matter of logic, peasants, like anyone else, wished to secure the gains from trade, to the extent possible, all else equal. But all else was not equal. The fundamental problem with the Smithian view therefore is that it fails to take into account the *cost* of specialization in terms of other peasant goals, what they would have to *give up* if they chose to concentrate in Smithian fashion on producing what they produced best, and bought everything else on the market. In fact, the *trade-offs* for seeking to secure the full gains from trade were too great, because specialization meant market dependence and subjection to competition, and the potential costs of the latter overrode the benefits of the former. As a consequence, peasants ended up choosing a whole series of 'rules for reproduction', or strategies for maintaining themselves, that ruled out specialization and maximizing the gains from trade.

Specialization conflicted, in multiple ways, with peasants' pursuit of the goal of economic security. Given the unpredictability of the harvest, to specialize was to risk disaster. In a bad harvest, food prices would rise, due to reduced supply. But having to pay high food prices would leave consumers less money to buy other goods, bringing down demand and thus the price for discretionary items. In this situation, specialized peasant producers would find themselves caught in a scissors, their returns squeezed by greater outgoings for food and smaller incomings from the sale of their non-food output. They might therefore have to go out of business, at a time when the costs of survival were at their height. But, since there was no welfare state for peasants, this might mean starvation and death, not an outcome that they could risk. Peasants could not afford to take a chance on this result, so they had to avoid the dependence on the market that comes part and parcel with specialization. Thus, they tended to adopt the rule for reproduction of 'safety first' or 'produce for subsistence', meaning diversify in order to directly produce everything one needs to survive, marketing only the physical surpluses left over.

Peasants' need to insure themselves against illness and old age also militated against specialization, because what they were obliged to do to secure such insurance was inherently non-economic. Specifically, parents had to have large families, in order to make sure that a sufficient number of sons survived to adulthood to take care of them. But, such a strategy would have been rendered unfeasible were the peasant family dependent upon the market and subject to competition, as it would have been had it specialized. This was because children were not cost-effective, since they cost more to support than they could bring in, and would have rendered non-competitive the peasant economic unit. The outcome was that to secure social insurance, it was necessary to avoid specialization in order to avoid having to compete to survive. Again, the sensible route was to 'produce for subsistence'.

Similar reasoning held with respect to peasants' strategy of subdividing holdings, the point of which was to provide material support for the male children who would provide them social insurance, while continuing the line. Subdivision, like having many children, was non-economic, because reducing the size of the plot normally rendered it less economically efficient, and thus less competitive. Since peasants needed to subdivide their holdings for indispensable goals, they had, on still other grounds, to avoid specialization, and to choose 'safety first'.

Finally, an extension of the foregoing point, peasants generally wished to respond favourably to sons' demand not just that they subdivide their holding to provide them a basis to form a family, but they do so as soon as possible, so that they could marry early. To make this economically feasible, peasants had to avoid market dependence, thus specialization.

In view of their choice for the foregoing rules for reproduction, pea-sants' private property, however secure and unfettered, could not bring about the pattern of self-sustaining unilineal economic growth assumed by Mann, following Smith, to result when the direct producers possessed politically unfettered private individualistic property. On the contrary, taken in aggregate, peasants' choices for production for subsistence, early marriage, many children and subdivision of holdings were all premised upon eschewing specialization and issued in a macro-pattern of demo-graphic expansion leading to declining marginal returns. Early marriage and many children made for population growth. Population growth brought extension of the area of settlement and subdivision of holdings. Extension of the area of settlement brought cultivation of worse land, while subdivision of holdings made for lower land/labour and capital/labour ratios. These two longer-term trends taken together made ines-capable, despite the once-and-for-all adoption of a number of new farm-ing tools and techniques, the defining tendency of medieval agriculture: viz. declining labour productivity. The latter manifested itself in rising food prices, declining wages and declining terms of trade (relative prices) of agriculture compared to industrial goods.[23]

The upshot was a developmental pattern quite the opposite of the self-sustaining growth that Mann sees highlighting the European Miracle. With agricultural output per producer declining, or at best kept stag-nant by increasing labour intensity, the urban population as a percentage of the total could not, *pace* Mann, surpass strict limits. European towns' population – driven upward, as Mann says, by the demand for urban military and luxury goods from the feudal lords of Europe – did not rise, therefore, as a proportion of European total population, above 12 per cent–15 per cent before 1700. Perhaps most definitive, with labour productivity declining, the growth of population past a certain point would issue in famine, disease and attempts to restrict the size of families. European demographic growth thus hit pretty much the same ceiling around 1300–1350 and again around 1560–1620, setting off the 'general crises' of the fourteenth and seventeenth centuries. One witnesses there-fore, between 1100 and 1750, not steady economic and demographic growth punctuated by a few hiccups, as Mann contends, but rather two 'grand agrarian cycles' (identified by Postan, Abel, and Le Roy Ladurie), marked by long phases of upward population growth and declining marginal output per person, more or less abrupt turnings of the trend, then long phases of population stagnation, decline or collapse, character-ized by the opposite trends. Reflecting pre-capitalist social property rela-tions dominated by peasant possession, the medieval and early modern economy of Europe was not Smithian but Malthusian.

The centralized territorial state: capitalist or feudal dynamic? The emergence of the centralized territorial states and the multi-state international system that together came to compose modern Europe was predicated, according to Mann, upon the ascent of the ever more dynamic networks of economic power and associated capitalist classes that drove the European Miracle – although the relationship was not quite direct. Exemplifying Mann's notion of 'interstitial emergence', ever more powerful and cohesive centralized territorial networks of political power tended to arise on the ruins of their international Christian and local feudal predecessors due initially to their superiority 'in their own terms' – i.e. in responding to the military and financial pressures arising from international warfare, especially by constituting geographical space through defining and strengthening borders. But they were able to prevail in the long historical run only because their ultimately national form 'was distinctly useful' to the increasingly extensive economy and its capitalist class representatives (1986: 416). As Mann puts it, 'Merchant and land-lord capitalists entered and reinforced a world of emergent warring yet diplomatically regulating states' (514) that had arisen out of autonomous processes in response to international pressures. Nevertheless, in view of what I have argued to be the evolution of an essentially feudal, not capitalist, political economy during the medieval and early modern period, both elements of this account need to be challenged in the same way. The centralized territorial state did not develop autonomously in its own terms as a self-developing network of social power either with respect to shaping space/creating boundaries or providing central regulation. Nor was it buttressed by capitalist development and capitalist classes. Its growth was driven, on the contrary, by the material requirements, the rules for reproduction, of the dominant class of feudal lords, who played a core and indispensable role in its construction at every step, since they constituted it at all levels, above all in its military aspect.

Like peasants, lords possessed direct, non-market access to everything they needed to survive, so were not subject to competition in production. Like peasants, too – though for different reasons – lords were unable to find it in their economic interests to pursue a capitalist strategy of cost-cutting by means of specialization, accumulation, innovation. The reason for this was that their dependence on coerced labour by peasant possessors made it very difficult for them to effectively improve production. Peasants had no incentive to work effectively on lords' land with lords' tools. Lords could not force peasants into line through threat of dismissal, because peasants possessed their means of subsistence. Deprived of the ability to fire, perhaps the best disciplinary device yet discovered to motivate careful and intensive labour in class-divided societies, lords found the supervisory costs of securing satisfactory work too high to justify much agricultural investment or innovation. Unable to profit by increasing the size of the pie through specialization, investment and innovation leading to higher productivity, lords could not, *pace* Mann, any more than could peasants, function like capitalists, but were obliged to rely either on *extensive growth*, extending their lands and cultivation, or *redistribution* of the existing pie by way of increasing their take from peasants and/or other lords, which required in turn building their lordly states.

Lords could increase the output from their estates by expanding production along already-existing lines through opening up and cultivating new lands. They might accomplish this on an individual basis via simple assarting, that is the local carving out of arable land from pasture, forest and waste, which took place throughout Europe, on a very large scale, during the early centuries of feudalism, when unsettled land was plentiful. Alternatively, they could do so collectively through pushing out Europe's borders through colonization, as exemplified in the great expansionary movements that ended up remaking the political face of the Continent between 1000 and 1300, largely by warfare and conquest – the lordly led trek beyond the Elbe to establish great estates in eastern Germany and in Poland; the crusades leading to the invasion of the eastern end of the Mediterranean; and the re-conquest of the Iberian Peninsula through centuries of warfare with its Arab occupiers.

In the absence of access to new land, decreasingly available over the long run, and unable to increase their income through productive investment in and increased productivity from their lands and peasants, lords had little means to increase their economic returns except by improving their ability to coercively redistribute wealth from peasants or other lords. This required the construction of lordly groups of sufficient breadth, strength and sophistication to prevail against both other lordly groups that were doing the same thing and their own peasants – who were not only increasingly well organized, but prepared, through mobility and the threat thereof, to take advantage of intra-lordly competition for peasant tenants. Lords were thus obliged to devote their surpluses to constructing larger, better-armed and more cohesive feudal states to increase their capacity to take the peasants' product and to plunder the lands and possessions of their lordly rivals.

It cannot be over-stressed that this turn by lords to what might be called 'political accumulation' – by analogy with its capitalist counterpart – is inexplicable merely in terms of its potential for increasing lordly income from peasants. It was *imposed* upon the majority of lords as a consequence of the structure of the trans-European feudal economy/polity as a whole. European feudal society was constituted from the start by a multiplicity of separate, initially localized, lordly groups organized for the purpose of exerting force so as to transfer wealth, not just *vis-à-vis* the peasantry, but also against other lords. Politico-military competition was thus an over-riding fact of life, which bore down on every feudal state. Mann is there-fore quite right to emphasize the way in which the multiplicity of states made for inexorably increasing politico-military stress on medieval states. He is also on target in bringing out that, in the field of natural selection thereby constituted, the more cohesive, centralized, territorially defined and militarily equipped would tend to win out – and to emphasize, in the process, the centrality of innovation in military organization and technol-ogy. He is correct, finally, in emphasizing the indispensable creative and strategic role played by the overlord and his immediate dependants at the centre of the feudal state in coordinating, disciplining and reorganizing its members in response to ever increasing politico-military pressure from without. But the problem with Mann's account is that the action of the lordly leader – king, prince or count – to build ever more efficacious national polities *vis-à-vis* other such polities could not proceed, with respect either to greater domestic centralization or to more precise terri-torial definition or to more effective military preparedness, without the conscious collaboration of the political community of lordly followers that collectively constituted his state. Mann's proposition that '[t]he only interest group that consciously willed the development of the national state was the state elite itself, the monarch and his creatures' (1986: 436) is thus the opposite of the case. The overlord's initiatives are simply incomprehensible apart from that of his lordly followers, especially the greatest feudal lords, since he depended upon them for counsel, admin-istration, finance and military backing. Indeed, the overlord could not be successful in maintaining his following, unless his state-building suc-ceeded with its primary task, improving the capacity of his political following to reproduce themselves economically, and this meant improv-ing not only the capacity to exploit peasants, but also – and especially – to wage war versus other lordly groups. Warfare was, for the lords of med-ieval Europe, a great machine for economic aggrandizement and state-building the key to warmaking. It was because not just the monarch and immediate dependants but feudal lords more generally had an interest in being part of an ever more effective state, that European monarchs, over time, were able to take the lead in building them.

The economic evolution of the feudal economy was thus marked not only by a cyclical Malthusian dynamic – driven by the tendency to popula-tion growth, subdivision of holdings, expansion of area of settlement, and declining agricultural productivity – but also by a unilineal dynamic to ever larger, better-equipped, more centralized and territorially defined states – driven by the requirement for ever more effective political accumulation to make possible lordly reproduction in a European world of competitive feudal groups. This is not the place to limn out, in any detail, this evolutionary process, but it may be possible to indicate something of its nature by mentioning the following successive phases.

(i) *banal lordship*: This was the initial, classical, small and highly localized form of feudal state, emerging throughout much of Western Europe around 1000 AD. It was instantiated in highly de-centralized political communities, organized around castellans and their mounted knightly followings, which made possible the redistribution of wealth to the lords who composed it from the peasants on their estates and the lordly groups they conquered in war. But its limited scope and internal incoherence left it vulnerable to peasant resistance and mobility, as well as politico-military pressure from larger, better-organized lordly groups. As a consequence, over the course of the thirteenth century large sections of the lordly class of France and western Germany suffered a crisis of seigneurial revenues.

(ii) *centralized national state/de-centralized individual exaction*: Emerging out of chronic intra-feudal conflict in northwestern France and ultimately the conquest of England, this form of political-class rule was perfected through the successive contributions of Norman, Anglo-Norman and Angevin lordly groups. It featured the achievement of ever greater group cohesion through the ceding by the groups' lordly members to their ducal and kingly leaders of rights to regulate their interrelations and to discipline them – exemplified in their relinquishing the right to wage private war within the group, their granting to the ruler the right to settle disputes among them (justice), their making him (not just their immediate overlord) their lord, and, above all, their support for the imposition of the common law. But, given the dependence of the Norman and English dukes and kings on their lordly followings for all aspects of their rule, this amounted simply to a major advance in the group's *self-organization* and *self-regulation*. The payoff of this centralized, cohesive state to the ruling class was enormous. It made it possible to re-strengthen lordship *vis-à-vis* the peasantry by bringing the weight and breadth of the state behind each of its lordly members in their conflicts with peasants who were not generally organized much beyond the village level – most spectacularly by institutionalizing serfdom within the common law. It also made it possible for the Norman, then English, lordly group to achieve hitherto unprecedented politico-military success against its less well-organized neighbours in the British Isles, Western Europe, and even Sicily and the eastern Mediterranean. This was highlighted, of course, by the conquest and parcelling out of England to the Norman lordly political community and the subsequent establishment there of what was, up to that time, by far the most highly advanced form of Mann's coordinated national state.

(iii) *centralized national state/collective extraction*: The basic condition for the rise of this type of state, classically in France, but also in west German principalities, was the politico-economic weakening of local lords, under assault by peasant communities. This opened the way for certain remaining great lords, in particular the Capetians and their successors – now under excruciating pressure from the much bigger and better organized English state/lordly class – to expand their power. This they accomplished through a process of 'concentric growth' (Perry Anderson) by which they built an ever more geographically extensive state by conquering and absorbing the jurisdictions of their smaller, weaker, localized rivals. But this was not, in essence, a question of state versus lords. The French monarchs were themselves a great lordship. The way, moreover, that they increased their power was precisely by expanding their feudal group in the classical manner by granting rights in the peasants' product – very often to the same lords whose jurisdictions they had absorbed. Although this process initially took place largely through the handing out of fiefs, over time it increasingly took a novel and epoch-making form – viz. the granting of offices in the army, judiciary and money-raising administrations that gave the holder politically constituted private property in part of an increasingly centralized take, royal taxation. This new form of state, and of the political organization of the lordly class, proved hugely more effective than its classical feudal predecessors in terms of its capacity to economically reproduce the lordly class through political exactions from the peasantry and plunder of other lords. The size and geographical scope of the state made peasant resistance, generally confined to a village or series of neighbouring villages, difficult; the unitary character of the take cut off the prospect of peasants' using their mobility to play one local lord off against another. As the state became ever larger and able to finance itself ever more effectively through never-ending warfare, it became militarily ever more potent. Already proving a serious foe for the English by the end of the Hundred Years' War, it emerged as the 'absolutist' war machine of Louis XIV in the seventeenth century, capable of supporting by taxation and plunder a gigantic apparatus of military officers, judges and revenue collectors – a dominant class that lived to a great extent off the returns to their privately owned offices in a kind of centralized feudalism.

(iv) *quasi-centralized national state/de-centralized exactions*: The lordly class of Eastern Europe, developing through colonization east of the Elbe, initially took a highly primitive, de-centralized form. It was therefore completely unprepared to withstand the stresses of the population collapse of the fourteenth century, and faced a profound crisis of seigneurial revenues. Over the long run, out of processes of intensive warfare, it ended up building a new form of quasi-centralized state, the estates-type state, whose lordly members represented themselves directly – in local diets and national estates. The point of this form – essentially a league of lords – was, by vastly increasing intra-lordly cooperation, to make it possible for the individual lordly members of the diets and estates to valorize their estates by successfully exploiting the peasantry – by controlling their mobility and cutting off the towns as a place for them to flee, imposing legal serfdom. The new form of state functioned quite well in reviving the economic fortunes of the East European lordly class in the sixteenth and seventeenth centuries, but it was too small and de-centralized to stand up to its better-organized, more centralized rivals elsewhere in Europe – and either had to increase its internal coherence by assuming an 'absolutist' form, as in the Prussian case, or find itself unable to resist external pressure and ultimately dismemberment, as in the Polish case.

The foregoing evolution, it seems to me, undermines both of Mann's major theses concerning the rise of the centralized territorial state. While medieval and early modern states developed, as he asserts, under the pressure of international politico-military competition in much the way he says they did, they did not do so autonomously. That competition represented the pressure on lordly groups throughout the system to adopt the rule for reproduction of political accumulation in order to reproduce themselves economically. The latter demanded ever more effective political redistribution of income and wealth from peasants and other lordly groups, so required, under the leadership of an overlord, the self-organization of lords into ever larger, more cohesive, more centralized, more territorially defined, and more militarily potent national political communities, or states. The rise of Europe's international system of national states organized for war was the inescapable by-product of that development. Mann rightly concludes that 'there is nothing inherent in the *capitalist* mode of production to lead to the development of class networks, each one of which is largely bounded by the territory of the state' (1986: 513, emphasis added). But the very constitution of the *feudal* mode of production led inescapably to precisely this outcome.[24]

Conclusion

The basic building blocks of society – the fundamental social groups that compose it – are, for Mann, *organizations*, networks of social power that are constituted to mobilize resources to realize social needs. Mann's notion of society as a 'federation of organizations' encapsulates this vision. But, there is a fundamental ambiguity in Mann's conception: viz. who is creating and operating these organizations and *for whom*? In developing his founding concept of collective power, Mann speaks as if there is a direct connection between function and fulfilment: those who establish social power networks do so to realize *their own* social needs and it is only by, in the process of, establishing them that they form social groups. But this would appear misleading. For to realize their needs people would seem to be obliged not so much themselves to create an organization to carry out the requisite function, as to gain access to such an organization's output, especially since the former can in no way be assumed to assure the latter. Mann asserts, for example, that, 'As humans need material subsistence they develop economic relationships, cooperating in production and exchange with others' (14). But, as has been argued, it seems more appropriate to argue that, to make possible the material appropriation that they require to reproduce themselves economically, people seek to constitute and sustain social groups that provide them property rights and/or the capacity to exploit that endows them in turn with access either to the means of production to fulfil their needs directly themselves or to appropriate the goods and services produced by others. In pre-capitalist societies peasants constituted political communities to defend their rights in the means of subsistence that enabled them themselves to produce what they needed. Lords, by contrast, rarely played any role in either Mann's local praxis (production) or more extensive circuits of praxis (production, allocation, etc.), but secured the income they needed to sustain a ruling-class form of life by building political communities that made it possible for them to establish rights in the peasants' product sanctioned by force.

The same point applies not just to networks of economic power, but perhaps even more clearly to networks of political power. Mann says that, 'As humans settle disputes without constant recourse to force, they set up judicial [and we might add police, military and tax] organization with a specified area of competence' (14). But, by their very nature, the political functions provided by states are to constitute the conditions to make possible the secure exercise of *other, non-political* functions – particularly economic reproduction, though not just that. It is therefore difficult to conceive of people establishing or maintaining state institutions for the execution of political functions except to fulfil the political needs of some *already-existing group* or *group-in-formation* – typically defence of property rights and military defence. Can we really conceive of people setting up and maintaining such organizations to fulfil political functions, *per se for themselves*, as Mann seems to do when he views medieval and early modern states as autonomously carrying out functions relating to domestic or inter-state relations – unless of course they already constitute, or are in the process of forming, a social group? As Mann ends up conceding, 'The first means of political power is territorial centralization. States are called forth and intensified when *dominant social groups*, pursuing their goals require social regulation over a confined bounded territory' (521, emphasis added).[25] From this standpoint, the dependence, not the autonomy, of the state would seem inescapable.

How then to understand the coming into being of the separation – in terms of both institutions and personnel – of the economic and the political, an indubitable, and defining, reality of many modern societies? What made for the widespread merger of the political with the economic in pre-capitalist societies was, of course, the indispensability of political organization to mobilize the capacity to coerce directly that was required by the ruling class to make possible economic appropriation from peasant possessors by communities of lords. By the same token, what enabled the separation of the political from the economic was the emergence of social-property relations that made possible economic appropriation in general and exploitation in particular, with no need for the direct application of force. These relations are, again, what Mann is referring to when he speaks of unequal property and exploitation made possible by 'the deprivation of others of the necessities of life' (18), which is, of course, instantiated where *capitalist* social-property relations obtain. Against a background in which the direct producers are devoid of the means of production – both land and tools – it is sufficient to possess capital (in the form of money or the means of production) in order to gain access to the fruits of exploitation and thereby membership in the ruling class. Since workers lack the ability to survive unless they are able to sell their labour power to members of a capitalist class *who* together monopolize the means of production, capitalists can depend on *economic coercion* in order to exploit. A state with a monopoly of force defends private property in general, so there is, as a rule, no need for capitalists themselves to wield force or to become members of a political community that does so. Indeed, from the standpoint of capitalists, the means of force are by and large a *faux frais* of production, to be relinquished to the extent possible, and there is no need for them to be members of the state in order to effectively exploit workers.

It is their capacity, in contrast to most if not all previous ruling classes, to exploit without the need to apply force – and therefore to find the means of force a cost to be minimized – that endows capitalist classes with an interest in a separate state that takes responsibility for carrying out political functions and that therefore monopolizes force. By the same token, it is the possibility of becoming a member of the ruling class without membership in the state or direct access to the means of coercion – and corresponding impossibility of using the state as an engine of exploitation by extra-economic coercion and in that way to politically constitute a ruling class – that 'frees' the state administration, for the first time in history, to function as a bureaucracy – by which I mean a governing group that cannot use its offices as private means of coercion to take an income and who are therefore at least to a degree capable of using them to 'objectively' carry out the specialized public functions that we associate with the state. But the question that immediately imposes itself is how, given the existence of such a state possessing a monopoly of force, capitalist classes can feel secure in their income. Why would not this state plunder the capitalists as did most previous states the direct peasant producers?

A full answer to this question is beyond the scope of this chapter, but two basic responses provide the necessary preliminaries, the first historical, the second conceptual.

A fully formed capitalist state that did not engage in predation upon capitalist producers could not, at least initially, emerge historically without the overthrow of the feudal-absolutist state. This was itself only made possible when and where there had emerged a capitalist class capable of accomplishing this, naturally bound up with the rise of capitalism itself. The latter was dependent upon the transformation of social-property relations entailed by the transition from feudalism to capitalism, a two-sided historical process in which the two fundamental constitutive features of the feudal mode of production were successively transcended – first, feudal exploitation by extra-economic coercion and, second, peasants' possession of their means of subsistence. The classic case is England where, first, peasant resistance and flight broke feudal lordship during the fourteenth and fifteenth centuries and where, second, feudal lords, unable any longer to take a surplus by force, asserted their rights to the land by separating the peasants from the means of subsistence in the fifteenth and sixteenth centuries. The class of capitalist tenants that emerged from this process had been rendered devoid of their means of subsistence, even if still possessing the means of production necessary to produce goods for the market. They were therefore rendered dependent on the market for a crucial input – land – so had to compete in order to survive and, for this reason, in contrast to their peasant predecessors, were obliged to adopt the rule for reproduction of maximizing exchange value/profits – meaning that they had to specialize, accumulate, innovate and move from line to line. The epoch-making outcome was a long-term tendency to rising labour productivity that brought in its train: the transcendence of the Malthusian trends that had hitherto confined the economy to secular stagnation and poverty; the reduction in relative prices for food compared to manufactures; the growth of the domestic market; the movement of the labour force out of agriculture into manufacturing – a full-fledged process of economic development, expressing the establishment of capitalist social-property relations.

In England, the rise of capitalism took place within a landlord shell: indeed, the landlord class, collecting competitive rents from commercial tenants, was the primary beneficiary of and ultimately the dominant force within the new social order. The capitalist landlords, as well as their capitalist tenants, had an overriding interest in a centralized state that would possess the coercive capacity to defend their property rights – but would *also* resist the temptation to use their monopoly of force to plunder them by sustaining or creating politically constituted private property, especially in office. By means of a long series of ultimately revolutionary conflicts, they succeeded in securing these goals through winning supremacy in the state of their class institution Parliament in 1688–9.[26]

Once capitalism was/is well-established, one could/can expect that the state would/will itself choose to defend private property and function for capital, *so long as vigorous capital accumulation had/has become the norm*. The reason is straightforward: in this situation the government is dependent upon the success of capital to achieve *its own* goals. That is, for a government to secure strong financial support for itself through taxation, to achieve high levels of employment so as to elicit political support, and to secure social order, it needs dynamic economic growth. To secure the latter, it needs healthy capital accumulation. To secure rapid capital accumulation, the state must, to the degree it is able, provide the incentive to invest of decent rates of profit. The upshot is that states in the presence of capitalist property and capitalist accumulation can be expected to make the creation of conditions in which capitalists make a good profit their top priority: so as to secure capital accumulation and economic growth. To do the opposite – i.e. attempt to use its monopoly of force to prey on capital – will kill the proverbial goose that lays the golden eggs. In sum, under capitalism, although the state is indeed separate from the economy and does possess a monopoly of force that allows it to take action independently from the capitalist class, the state can be counted on to act in the interest of the capitalist class. Only apparently autonomous, the state is dependent upon capital.

Notes

1 With respect to networks of *political* power, Mann deviates from his theoretical framework, neglecting to define and characterize them in purely functional terms, confining them to judicial/governmental regulation backed up by coercion that is *centrally administered and territorially bounded* (1986: 26). But his

justification for doing so – that political 'functions can be possessed by any power organization' – fails, because it could be applied to any of his four networks of social power. That a particular function could be carried out by a 'different' sort of institution, itself defined functionally, is a logical outcome of characterizing institutions in functional terms. It is indeed no defect, but rather a strength, of functional categorization for comparative-historical analysis. As an example, Mann himself goes out of his way to characterize, quite sensibly, the order-keeping function he attributes to the medieval Christian Church as political. More directly to the point, he is unable, in his concrete analysis, to restrict the definition, or scope, of the political to governmental/judicial functions executed by central institutional agents and must expand his definition to include all governmental/judicial functions whatever institutions/agents execute them, as is actually consistent with his theory. See also below (pp. 213–14).

2 See Parsons (1960: 220–1 ff.).

3 Cf. Parsons: '[P]ower is ... a facility for the performance of a function in, on behalf of, the society as a system', and only secondarily and derivatively 'a facility for getting what one group, the holders of power, wants by preventing another group, the "outs", from getting what it wants' (1960: 220).

4 See below (pp. 206–7 ff.).

5 Mann is ambivalent about his own fundamental assertion that the autonomous execution of separate societal functions leads to the institutional separation of social power networks. See, for example, his notion of the 'promiscuity of organizations' (1986: 17–18). But, he needs institutional specialization in order to derive and justify in theoretical terms his anti-holistic anti-evolutionary conception of society as constituted by multiple autonomous, overlapping, intersecting social power networks, so is ultimately obliged to stick with it.

6 Mann here proceeds explicitly by analogy with the Marxian idea that societal transformation is driven by the development of the productive forces, carrying with it new relations of production, which grow up in the 'interstices' of the old order and bring about its overturn and replacement (1986: 15–16).

7 Mann seems insufficiently clear on the central issue of the criteria by which superior effectiveness is identified – effectiveness in terms of what goals and whose goals? – and on the conditions under which an emergent network will transcend one already in place. In particular, does a new network of social power transcend an old one when it works better doing the same task – perhaps by way of a competitive process – or when it better serves another (increasingly powerful?) network of social power – perhaps because the leading representatives of that network have achieved greater power?

8 'I have singled out one [main power network], Christendom, as *necessary* for all that followed' (1986: 507, emphasis in original).

9 For Mann's own explication of his relationship to Smithian approaches, see 1986: 406–7. Mann points out that, in his own account, unlike that of Smith himself or latter-day Smithians, Durkheimian mechanisms, driven by Christianity – i.e. values legitimating normative pacification, the construction of European identity, and the enforcement of social solidarity of the feudal ruling class of lords – are invoked to account for the establishment of the Smithian preconditions that opened the way for the European Miracle – viz.

social peace, justice, non-predatory political institutions. But it must be said that the preconditions are no less Smithian for that reason.

10 As Mann concludes, '[T]he European miracle cannot be interpreted as "the transition from feudalism to capitalism" as the Marxist tradition has it' (1986: 506).

11 It might be noted in passing that Mann's explanation of the rise of the centralized, territorial state bears a family resemblance to the classical account of Adam Smith, in which the monarchy enters into alliance with the nascent urban bourgeoisie, granting them privileges of self-government in exchange for their support, so as to extend protection of private property and law and order at least to the towns, over and against the marauding nobility (*Wealth of Nations, Book III*, ch. 3). But, as Mann would emphasize, this account understands the development of the state only internally, in terms of civil society alone, leaving out the critical role of inter-state relations in general and warfare in particular that he brings out.

12 For the critical role of the organization's rulers' functional indispensability in accounting for their domination, see above (pp. 192–3).

13 Mann defines '[t]hose able to monopolize control over production, distribution, exchange, and consumptions' as constituting a 'dominant class' (1986: 24). But, what this implies, in Mann's theoretical framework, is no more than the proposition that those at the top of the hierarchy within networks of economic power, as in the case of any network of social power, are able to exert distributive power over those at the bottom. It does not tell us whether economic appropriation takes place within the network of economic power and, if it does, how it does. Nor does it tell us about economic appropriation that takes place outside, or beyond, networks of economic power, *vis-à-vis* other networks of social power.

14 I term this conceptualization of stratification informal, because Mann does not present it in connection with the presentation of his formal theory of social power in 'Societies as Organized Social Networks', the first (theoretical) chapter of *Sources of Social Power*, but rather in 'The End of General Social Evolution: How Prehistoric Peoples Evaded Power', the book's second (analytico-historical) chapter.

15 This definition of stratification is found in 'Societies as Organized Social Networks', the first (theoretical) chapter of *Sources of Social Power*.

16 Mann does not explicitly spell this out, but it seems to me more or less logically implied.

17 For the same formulation of capitalist exploitation, 1986: 374–5.

18 See note 1.

19 For the standard account of the origins and early development of feudal lordship, see Poly and Bournazel (1991).

20 See below (p. 223).

21 Poly and Bournazel (1991: 26–7, quotation from page 26).

22 See below (pp. 222–5).

23 Mann can reach the opposite conclusion because he takes yields as indicative of labour productivity, when, in fact, they expressed the productivity of the land. Yields tended to increase due to the ever-increasing number of people

per unit of land that resulted from population growth, i.e. due to the intensification of labour. But because each additional labour input per unit of land
yielded an ever smaller increase in output, rising yields could neither support a
decreasing proportion of the labour force off the land or put off demographic
crisis indefinitely.

24 Mann asserts, similarly, that 'Nothing in the capitalist mode of production (or
the feudal mode of production *if that is defined economically*) leads of itself to
the emergence of many [political] networks divided and at war, and of a class
structure that is nationally segmental' (1986: 515, emphasis added). But, the
problem with this formulation is that the feudal mode of production, requiring
the increasingly effective political organization of its dominant lordly class for
its very economic reproduction, cannot, without mischaracterizing it, be
defined economically.

25 It should be noted, for the sake of clarity, that networks of political power –
organization to fulfil political functions – can emerge to serve groups that are
not dominant – as, e.g., peasant communities (which in a few historical cases
have no lords) or relatively egalitarian tribes.

26 For a fuller explication of the economic and political processes briefly outlined
here, see Brenner (1993).

References

Brenner, R. 1993. Postscript. In Brenner, *Merchants and Revolution*. Princeton:
Princeton University Press.
Mann, M. 1986. *The Sources of Social Power, Volume I: A History from the Beginning
to 1760 AD*. Cambridge: Cambridge University Press.
Parsons, T. 1960. Distribution of Power in American Society. In Parsons,
Structure and Process in Modern Societies. Chicago: The Free Press of Glencoe.
Poly, J., and E. Bournazel. 1991. *The Feudal Transformation 900–1200*. New York:
Holmes and Meier.

11   The rise of the West

Stephan R. Epstein

The appearance in 1986 of the first volume of Michael Mann's trilogy (Mann 1986) brought to an end an extraordinarily fruitful decade, during which a heterogeneous group of economic historians (Mendels 1972; Jones 1981; Brenner 1982), economists (North 1981), and historical sociologists (Anderson 1974a; 1974b; Wallerstein 1974–80; and Hall 1985) jointly attacked, challenged and rewrote many of the established narratives of premodern European history. Mann's empirical range was greater, his theoretical ambitions broader and his analytical scope more encompassing and compelling than most; but he shared with this group the core aim of defining and explaining the mystery of the 'European miracle', and it is on this matter that Mann's thoughts are arguably most incisive and original.

Our understanding of the premodern (medieval and early modern) economy has changed significantly since 1986, not least thanks to the works I have just mentioned, which set in motion a more systematic use of cross-cultural comparison and more rigorous, social science-based analysis; other influential developments are more recent, like the rise of 'global history' and the irruption of southeast Asian economic history into European historians' consciousness discussed by others in this volume. However, many of the certainties about the premodern economy that writers in that decade took for granted have also now been challenged – certainties about the absence of cumulative, intensive economic growth and technological change; the causes of productivity gains in agriculture; the dominance of anti-market mentalities among the peasantry, and the origins of markets; the devastating consequences of harvest crises on mortality; and the pernicious economic effects of non-'democratic' political institutions. Now that premodern European historians are questioning the very definition of 'modernity', this is an appropriate time to take stock of Michael Mann's contribution to these debates.

Among the many powerful insights in *Sources of Social Power*, two stand out for theoretical originality and empirical substance. The first concerns the nature of coordination – the control by decision makers of interdependent

233

activities that jointly satisfy one or more constraints – as both the major source of social and economic power (Mann 1986: 537, 'collective and distributive powers'), and as a heuristic framework for a materialist history of premodern Europe. The second insight concerns the growth of social power over time and space.

Mann is particularly effective about the first phase of political coordination in medieval Europe, which he defines as a 'form of territorial federalism' shaped by the dialectic between national political regulation and local autonomy and dating to the period between 1155 and 1477, when the 'feudal' Burgundian state came to an end (1986: 416). He is on less sure footing after 1477, perhaps because he shifts focus to the highly centralized English monarchy and tends to forget the persistence of forms of 'territorial federalism' with their attendant political and fiscal tensions under the Spanish Habsburg, the Polish Commonwealth and the Holy Roman Empire of the German Nation. His discussion of differences in political coordination within constitutional and absolutist monarchies is enlightening (1986: 477–83), but it underestimates the difficulties that most pre-Napoleonic Continental states faced in overcoming 'feudal' or parcellized regulation. This may be because Mann prefers the better-informed neo-Weberian Perry Anderson to the neo-Whig Douglass North, but it also stems paradoxically from a lack of attention to the benefits of coordination for *economic* power.

Mann's blind spot towards the economics of coordination is notable particularly in light of his strong criticism of the neoclassical assumption that markets are 'natural'. To some extent Mann follows Douglass North in emphasizing the need for 'normative regulation' in markets, but he takes the argument further and is empirically more convincing. North's main weakness is that he lacks a theory of power and the state, which he replaces with public choice assumptions about state 'predation' mitigated by the virtues of English and North American constitutionalism. By contrast, Mann's theory of power as coordination gives us a well-defined template to assess the benefits and limitations of different *forms* of state. Thus, for example, his view that markets and regulated competition are 'a form of social organisation, a *mobilisation of collective and distributive power*', leads him to emphasize, in my view correctly, the efficacy and creativity of 'empires of domination [which] combined military concentrated coercion with an attempt at state territorial centralisation and geopolitical hegemony' (Mann 1986: 412, my italics).

For Mann, in other words, markets *are* coordination, and coordination – viewed as a combination of 'freedom' (market) and 'power' (hierarchy) – *makes* the market. This somewhat Hicksian claim has important implications that are not always fully or consistently pursued (Hicks 1969).

Mann, for example, implies that 'empires of domination' that do not face strong countervailing powers will do well at coordinating markets that enhance productive and commercial efficiency. This supports current opinion about the Chinese imperial economy and in part also the Mughal and Ottoman ones, but seems to conflict with his claim elsewhere that only medieval Europe develops 'capitalist' (e.g. competitive) markets. A more significant implication is that both old Marxist debates on the transition to capitalism (which posited a dichotomy between market (capitalist) and non-market (feudal) society, and assumed that markets would emerge fully fledged from the transformation to property rights to land; see Robert Brenner's chapter in this volume) and the neoclassical counterblast (that markets are natural so their origins can be ignored) are fundamentally miscast. Mann's theory suggests that we put in their place a – comparative and historical – political economy of markets, no longer premised on a specious opposition between regulation and non-regulation, and between hierarchy and market. In practice, Mann tells us, historical markets arise from different permutations of the two pairs. The claim frees us at a stroke from the institutional Whiggishness inherent in much neoinstitutional and historical economics, which posits a linear progression in institutional efficiency from ancient 'despotism' to modern liberal democracy based on *ex ante* claims about the economically optimal constitution. Instead, Mann invites us to enquire into the economic consequences of different forms of political organization – be they centralized or decentralized, despotic or absolutist, city-centred or territorial, federal, parliamentary or republican – without any prescriptive or preconceived views on their relative advantages and drawbacks at different points in time.

Mann's second major insight, which concerns the evolution of social power, consists of two distinct claims. On the one hand, Mann develops a materialist theory of the persistent growth in time of social power that recalls G. A. Cohen's recasting of Marx's theory of technological determinism. Compare Mann:

Human capacities for collective and distributive power have increased quantitatively throughout [history] ... A process of continuous invention, where nothing is lost, must result in a broadly one-directional, one dimensional development of power. This is obvious if we examine *either* the logistics of authoritatively commanding the movement of peoples, materials, or messages, *or* the infrastructures underlying the universal diffusion of similar social practices and methods.

(Mann 1986: 524)

with Cohen:

The productive forces tend to develop throughout history [because] men are ... somewhat rational. The historical situation of men is one of scarcity. Men possess intelligence of a kind and degree which enables them to improve their situation. Rational beings who know how to satisfy compelling wants ... will [therefore] be disposed to seize and employ the means of satisfaction of those wants ... When knowledge provides the opportunity of expanding productive power [men] will tend to take it, for not doing so would be irrational ... It is a [historical] fact ... that societies rarely replace a given set of productive forces by an inferior one ... yet [it is also a fact that] *productive forces* are *frequently replaced, by better ones.*

(Cohen 1978: 150–4; italics in original)

However, whereas Cohen is concerned with the accumulation of human knowledge in everyday production, Mann emphasizes that the major advances in human power come from the *movement of knowledge across space*. Historical change in Mann's view seems to arise from the dialectic between endogenous developments in the technologies of communication and their diffusion, through the unfolding of what he terms the 'marcher effect' or what Ernest Gellner called the 'doctrine of the essential periphery'. As we shall see further, peripheries play a critical role in Mann's theory in taking up the torch of leadership from the core: the 'new erstwhile recipients are also essential for further progress'.[1]

The marcher effect solves the conceptual and narrative problem of how configurations of social power are recombined in a materially progressive sense: in Mann's tale, Europe adopts the best of Near Eastern civilization via Christianity (and Rome), while northwestern Europe and particularly Britain benefit from their distance from the conflict between Christianity and Islam (Mann 1988: 17). The marcher effect also provides an elegant justification for Mann's strong emphasis on European institutional social, political and cultural unity, on the importance of geopolitical interaction, and on institutional cross-fertilization across the Continent, which sets him against the more traditional 'Eurocentric' emphasis on uniquely national 'paths' to capitalism adopted by several of the writers listed at the beginning of this chapter (Mann 1986: 508).[2] Mann's historical analysis (for example of British developments since the Norman invasion, which he describes as largely endogenous with the exception of foreign wars) is not always consistent with his theory, but the theory, as we shall see, is generally sounder than the history.

Mann's principal theoretical contribution for practising historians is therefore a materialist theory of history driven by two major sources of development: the intensification and extension of political power through technologies of coordination and communication, and the diffusion of these power forms from core to frontier societies through culturally replicable blueprints. The theory is inherently evolutionary, and as such is closer to Marx than to Weber. Indeed, Mann's main conceptual and analytical weaknesses stem from not applying this evolutionary materialism rigorously to the 'rise of the West', a question he frames in strictly Weberian terms as the problem of the European 'miracle'. Whereas Mann in materialist guise postulates the unity of mankind in a 'process of continuous invention ... [which generates] a broadly one-directional, one dimensional development of power', Mann in Weberian form postulates the distinctiveness and non-universality of Western history, its unique and 'miraculous' transition to modernity, and interprets the underlying heuristics of the two models quite differently. In the first, evolutionary, 'acorn-to-oak tree vision of humanity' as Gellner termed it (Gellner 1980a: 73–80; Mann 1986: chs. 1–11), Mann assumes that there will be many examples of a particular development and relies on the comparative method to identify causation. In the second, 'gatekeeper model of human progress' (Gellner), Mann describes the European historical path as fortuitous, for which reason general laws and comparative analysis do not apply and subjective interpretation and 'feel' take centre-stage (1986: 501–3).[3]

This theoretical inconsistency forces Mann into several analytical cul-de-sacs. One problem stems from the fact that Mann lacks a theory of economic and technological development. This means that he never fully justifies his materialist claims (how is new human knowledge produced?), and slips easily into a tautological definition of capitalism as a combination of free markets and growth that arose only in Europe (Mann 1988: 10–11, 13). Statements that premodern Europe was the economic 'prime mover' because only Europe had the right mix of normative regulation and individual freedom to dispose of privately owned resources (Mann 1986: 375, 506–7), and that European agriculture was vastly more productive than that of Asia (1986: 405–6), are not backed up with any evidence, and flatly contradict the broadly evolutionary postulate that economic development is universal. Mann admits to this failing with respect to analysing differences *within* Europe (1986: 450: 'a genuine theory would require both economic theory and a comparative methodology'), but the same point applies to differences between Europe and the rest of the world.

The conflation of capitalism with industrialization probably lies at the root of this difficulty. Mann does sometimes distinguish between capitalism defined in Marxian terms and industrialization (1986: 374–5), but mostly he suggests that the distinction is 'ideological'. As a result, he confuses two aspects of premodern development that are best kept analytically distinct: a Smithian process, based on slowly evolving technological practice and specialization of function in response to growing market demand (market integration), that occurred mainly in the agrarian sector; and a Schumpeterian process, based on endogenous patterns of training and labour mobility rather than direct market stimuli, which led to more rapid technological change mostly in the industrial and service sectors.

Recent research on premodern Southeast Asian economies has brought the distinction between the two processes into sharper relief. There is now enough evidence of long-run intensive economic growth outside premodern Europe to require some important revisions of older historical models. Intensive growth of the Smithian kind seems to have been ubiquitous in Eurasian agrarian societies, implying that Smithian growth did not require a full-blown capitalist mode of production in Marx's strong sense, although it may have required a form of capitalism in Mann's weaker, neoclassical sense. Smithian growth could be quite easily reversed, however, mainly due to a collapse of the power system that enforced the rules of trade as an effect of domestic conflict or outside aggression.

The logistical fragility of premodern systems of extensive, despotic power, and the high costs of socio-political coordination, meant that economic reversals could also be deep and long-lasting. On this account, Europe's political fragmentation and institutional pluralism may have been something of an advantage, because they allowed locally more appropriate reactions to major logistical and socio-economic setbacks like the late medieval and seventeenth-century 'crises'. Differences in institutional flexibility may explain why Europe after *c.* 1300CE seems to have generated more systematic patterns of Schumpeterian growth than Southeast Asian societies, where technological change outside agriculture became progressively muted. Indeed, it seems likely that the major and abiding differences between premodern European and non-European societies were the mechanisms for the generation and diffusion of technical knowledge, rather than the presence or absence of markets.

In sum, if we define capitalism in Mann's terms as an economic system based on free markets and individual, exclusive property rights, we are faced with two problems: first, premodern Southeast Asia becomes just as capitalist as premodern Europe, which makes it hard to posit any kind of European exceptionalism, and second, we are no closer to explaining the processes of *technological* innovation that led to the European Industrial Revolution. Mann's theory does not help us identify a solution, either, because it doesn't predict the impact of system traits (state and market structures) on economic and technological outcomes; this is where it would most clearly benefit from systematic comparison and counterfactual reasoning. Mann is aware of this limitation (1986: 450), but considers it an issue of empirical incompleteness; in my view instead it generates some serious blind spots in historical interpretation. Four of these stand out: the overestimation of Christianity as an autonomous historical force, and conversely the underestimation of the Papal Revolution; the underestimation of the law and of the greatest legal invention of the Middle Ages, the corporation; the overestimation of the independent role of war; and the absence of an endogenous theory of the state and of state 'efficiency'.

Christianity, norms and transaction costs

Mann views his main contribution to earlier narratives of the rise of medieval Europe as adding Christianity to the standard economic, political and military brew. Crucially, he uses the role of Christianity in the rise of the West to justify the claim that ideological power plays an independent role in historical change; so it is important to examine what evidence he brings to bear on the matter. This can be summed up in two testable claims: first, that the Christian ideology generated a kind of 'transcendence and immanent morale' among feudal lords (1986: 376–7) that underlay early European dynamism, and secondly, that Christianity generated the supra-local networks of trust necessary for long-distance trade to take off (Wickham 1988).

The first statement can be rephrased as the claim that Christian ideology and the Church solved problems of military and economic coordination in the early Middle Ages when secular forms of territorial coordination were weak. However, a few centuries earlier, Christianity had been unable to save the Roman empire from the barbarians or keep the eastern and western halves of the empire united, and nothing much had changed since; the pre-Gregorian Church was still ideologically and institutionally weak. Moreover, it seems inappropriate to date the starting point of European exceptionalism by dint of the substitution of secular rule by Christian ideology to the eighth century (Mann 1986: 413), since the eighth century coincided with the only prolonged period of almost unbroken Frankish unity 'which gave a powerful impetus to Frankish economic hegemony, as well as ... territorial expansion' (Wickham 1998: 347). Perhaps conscious of these problems, Mann turns to much later evidence, including the tenth- and early eleventh-century Cluniac and Cistercian movements – which however in economic terms mimicked the great eighth- and ninth-century Benedictine landlords, that in turn were modelled on the great Merovingian and Frankish aristocratic dispersed estates – and the Gregorian reforms and their aftermath in the eleventh and twelfth centuries (Mann 1986: 379–83). But he fails to question if the ideologically and institutionally aggressive Church of the twelfth and thirteenth centuries was an institutional and ideological prime mover, rather than a dynamic response to the growing claims of territorial monarchs amidst broader social and economic changes.

Mann objects to Anderson's description of the feudal core as a 'fusion of two prior patterns, the Germanic and the Roman', because it 'fits Christianity too easily ... as the transmitter, through Rome, of the "classical legacy"' (Anderson 1974a; Mann 1986: 505). However, by insisting on Christianity's independence as a historical vector, he ignores the question why only one out of many possible versions of that religion, medieval European Christianity, became so aggressively expansionist and institutionally dynamic. Conversely, he underestimates the importance of the Frankish empire in developing a 'unitary economic, military and ideological power' before the year 1000 (Mann 1988: 11; 1986: 376–7), which by 1350CE had been used to nearly double the size of Christian Europe by expanding into Iberia, Scandinavia, the Celtic periphery and east-central Europe (Bartlett 1993: 292).[4] On all these grounds, the independence of the *political* and the *military* effects of Christian ideology seem anachronistic and overstated.

Mann's second claim for Christianity is that 'normative pacification enabled more produce to be traded over longer distances than could usually occur between the domains of such a large number of small, often highly predatory, states and rulers' (Mann 1986: 383). In other words, as trade expanded and intensified over greater distances, social interaction become more complex and less predictable, and shirking and opportunism increased. In the absence of strong coordinating states (which only arose in the fourteenth and fifteenth centuries; see Mann 1986: 379), Christianity enforced the rules of the game by threatening divine punishment. The argument gives rise to two predictions: long-distance trade would develop first where secular extensive power was weak, and long-distance trade between Christians and Muslims would be under-developed compared to similar trade between co-religionists.

According to Mann, the first commercial networks linking northern and southern Europe arose in the eleventh century in a territory delimited by two lines in which French, English and German monarchical powers were absent: 'there is a correlation of economic wealth and dynamism and weak states' (1986: 408; but see *contra*: 402, on early growth in England). This however confuses the territorial size of states for their political and economic power, at a time when the two were still inversely related. At the start of the twelfth-century commercial revolution, the lands concerned – currently still Europe's economic heartland, its 'blue banana' – corresponded largely with the core of the old Frankish empire. At their two extremes were two regional 'prime movers', the County of Flanders and Lombardy, which established commercial and industrial leadership by energetically coordinating typically Carolingian modes of extensive power that included the enforcement of justice, a stable coinage and

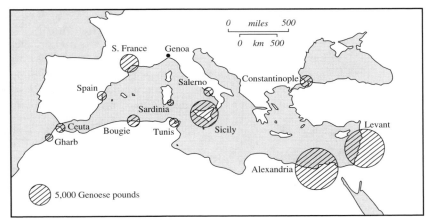

Source: Bartlett 1993: 186

Figure 11.1. Genoese investment in the Mediterranean region, 1155–64

measurements, the creation of new towns and markets, and canal building and drainage. The success of the Champagne fairs as the linchpin of
the commercial network was similarly based on strict political coordination and the provision of justice by a powerful regional count (Verhulst
2002; Epstein 2000b; Bautier 1953; Milgrom, North and Weingast
1990). Other important commercial institutions, like the Law
Merchant, were by-products of social coordination that arose endogen-
ously from the regular interaction of merchants with political authorities
(Greif, Milgrom and Weingast 1994). The specifically ideological role of
the Church in these developments is obscure, not least because it formally
remained largely hostile to trade well past the thirteenth century.

Evidence that at the outset of the commercial revolution the volume of
long-distance trade between Christian co-religionists was substantially
larger than that between Christians and infidels for ideological reasons,
rather than for reasons of distance, is instead inconclusive. Thirteenth-
century Genoese merchants, for example, seem to have traded more with
the Muslim Levant than with the French, Spanish and Italians (Figure 11.1),
and the same probably applies to Venice and Pisa in the same period.
The relative proportion of infra-Christian trade undoubtedly increased
over time, but most of this was over short and medium distances: right
up to 1600 the volume of infra-Mediterranean trade – a significant
share of which took place between Muslims and Christians – was
still far greater than north–south trade across the Alps (Bautier 1953;
Braudel 1972; Spufford 2000). There are two plausible explanations

why religious differences were apparently not a big barrier to trade. On the one hand, it seems likely that shared transcendental norms are not a *sine qua non* of trade (Wickham 1988); on the other, the higher level of political fragmentation in the early medieval West compared to Arab countries may paradoxically have made opportunistic behaviour easier between Christians than between Christians and religious aliens, because the commercial penalties for opportunism among Christians were lower.

The papal and legal revolutions

The 'Latin-Christian' identity was of course not a transcendental given, but was linked to the Gregorian institutionalization of the papacy as a universal and imperial authority. From the late eleventh century onwards the term *Christianitas* took on an increasingly territorial and 'western' meaning, partly because Latin Christians became increasingly aware 'that the rest of the world was not Christendom' (Bartlett 1993: 252–3). Mann has little to say about the rediscovery and reformulation of Roman law, which provided the intellectual and ideological underpinnings of the Papal Revolution and was instrumental in revolutionizing the sources of social power (see Mann 1986: 440–1 for a cursory reference). In the hands of the Church, Roman and canon law became sources of extensive and intensive power that harnessed Christianity to the expansion of social and territorial authority (Bartlett 1993: 243); law became a means for ideological, logistical and financial centralization, and helped transform the Patrimony of St Peter into the first 'ancient-modern state' (Berman 1983: 113–14; Prodi 1987).

The legal revolution had two additional, crucial ramifications for European development. Between the late eleventh and the early thirteenth centuries the law became 'disembedded', as an emerging class of professional judges and lawyers trained in law schools at universities established an 'autonomous, integrated, developing body of legal principles and procedures' (Berman 1983: 86). Moreover, universal law became the means by which Rome successfully developed the principles of political and legal pluralism against imperial pretensions. One of the effects of these two processes was what Mann calls 'autonomy' (Mann 1986: 397): 'the predominance of foreigners in a country's trade, the self-regulating powers of artisan and merchant guilds and banking houses, the political autonomy of urban communes against territorial princes, and the power of the merchant republics ... No single group could monopolise power; conversely, all power actors [lords, towns, peasants] had autonomous spheres.'

'Autonomy', however, was neither spontaneous, nor natural, nor somehow held together by the 'normative regulation ... provided by Christianity' (Mann 1986: 398); nor at this point in time did it yet relate specifically to the individual 'subject' in a modern sense. The concept – the outcome of a truly revolutionary 'fusion of the Germanic and the Roman' – is more accurately related to that of the *corporation*. Corporatism became central to most defining features of the 'West'. It was the basis for the incorporated town, borough and rural community, for the university, and for the international religious and military orders that organized the institutional consolidation and expansion of Latin Christendom. The theory of corporate personality made it possible to organize merchants and trading bodies into autonomous organizations, which could negotiate with the state for commercial privileges and military support because their existence extended beyond the lives of their members; it facilitated the dissemination of useful and practical knowledge by craft guilds, whose membership was individual and non-ascriptive and made it easier for artisans to migrate (Epstein 1998); and it legitimated the charters protecting 'proto-industrial' communities in the countryside from attacks by corporate guilds in the towns (Epstein 2000a: ch. 6). Western theories of political representation and corporate bargaining and the development of the Western state – including the peculiar tradition of 'small', urban-based states which survived side-by-side with the rising national states (Brady 1991) – all relied on the medieval principle that corporate groups do not derive their ultimate legitimacy and powers from superior authority. Corporatism turned into the West's most powerful 'vector of expansion' (Bartlett 1993: 309–10).

In retrospect, the major historical significance of Christianity was not so much the establishment of a European ideological *ecumene* between 900 and 1300, in the development of which it piggybacked on the Franco-Carolingian empire. Its main 'track-laying', world-historical achievement was the institutionalization of the Church, which from the twelfth century spurred the legal and political development of the self-contained, self-defining corporation, freed from legitimating authorization from above. If we drop ideology as an independent variable, the claim about European uniqueness that justified Mann's avoidance of comparisons with non-European societies becomes even more problematic, and the question posed by Gellner whether the European trajectory corresponds to a 'gate-keeper' (random and unique) or an 'acorn-to-oak tree' (functional and evolutionary) model of human history, gains new salience.

By downplaying the impact of religious ideology I do not mean to turn Roman law into an alternative *deus ex machina*, as Mann charges

Anderson with doing (Mann 1986: 398–9). Yet, by taking Roman law, which had been the law of a tributary state, and bending it to its own political requirements and to the needs of a decentralized society in which local rent taking and property rights were more important to lords than their relationship with the state (tax raising), the Church gave political legitimacy to European corporatism. Corporatism in premodern Europe became a social, economic and political vector of expansion through the combination of two historically contingent elements: political and social fragmentation, which kept corporate groups small, community- rather than territorially based, and non-ascriptive, and the corporate charter of Frankish ascendancy, which provided a flexible, infinitely replicable organizational matrix (Bartlett 1993).

Mann has more to say about the Roman law origins of private property in land, which he disputes. But his preferred explanation, that private property rights arose from the 'disintegration of an expansive [Roman] state [that] had enabled its provincial agents and allies to seize and keep its public, communal resources for themselves', and that 'as early as 800CE, European feudalism was dominated by private property, in the sense of hidden and effective possession' (Mann 1986: 398–9), stretches the point too far, not least because it implies that 'effective possession' was lacking in coeval non-European societies like the Chinese, Indian, Arab and Ottoman tributary empires.[5] It might be more useful to distinguish between 'effective' and 'direct' possession of land, a distinction expressed in feudal Europe as between direct and eminent domain. 'Effective' or beneficial possession, permitting free choice of crops, the disposal of harvests subject to customary tribute, and a degree of land transfer but not the eviction of the direct cultivators, seems to have characterized all advanced agrarian and tributary states. 'Direct' possession, which included rights of jurisdiction and disposal and thus the theoretical possibility of forced eviction, lay with the lord or state, but disposal rights were seldom exercised. By contrast, the concept of full possession, which implied the peasant's capacity to dispose freely of his land and thus also to become 'voluntarily' landless, seems to have emerged only in late medieval and early modern Europe out of underdeveloped and poorly understood Roman precursors (Johnston 1999). From this point in time, European property rights may have been unusual because title to land became exclusive and could be permanently alienated, rather than because title to land was secure.

Exclusive ownership established the legality of taking possession of surety for a loan. Thus, European lenders could protect their capital and returns through courts of law by evicting borrowers from their property if they defaulted, rather than relying on less certain social and moral suasion by friends and kin as seems to have happened in other agrarian societies (Pomeranz 2000). More clearly defined property rights may have increased the pool of capital available to European peasants, allowing them to borrow for longer and at lower rates of interest than would otherwise have been the case. In premodern China and India long-term debt seems to have been poorly developed, and rates of interest were no lower than 8–10 per cent (Pomeranz 2000; Deng 2003); by contrast, European peasants were able to raise long-term credit at rates that fell from 10 per cent on average in the thirteenth and early fourteenth centuries to 3–4 per cent in the eighteenth (Figure 11.2). Of course, if European rates began to fall significantly below Asian ones only during the fourteenth century, as the evidence suggests, we must also conclude that medieval Roman law – which had developed earlier – was at best a necessary but not a sufficient condition for sustaining well-working markets in land and capital.[6]

The extent to which differences in access to rural credit affected agricultural development and productivity in Europe and elsewhere is nevertheless still unclear. Recent work by Pomeranz, Allen and others suggests that Chinese and Indian agriculture at its best compared well with European averages on measures of calories produced per unit of land and worker; what effect a lower cost of capital made on setting European agriculture on a more intensive course through the greater use of drainage, livestock, enclosure and wage labour awaits further investigation.

War, taxes and the origin of the modern state

Taxes, as the means to assert the independent force of military power in the growth of the modern, national and nation state, are central to Mann's theory; and it is due in large measure to *Sources of Social Power* volume I's analytical *tour de force* on this issue that the political economy of taxation is now axiomatic in the study of the premodern state.

Mann takes the view that premodern states traded taxes for public goods. He focuses mainly on the state demand side, and argues through a detailed analysis of English taxation that a disproportionate share of tax receipts was spent on warfare (1986: 428–30, 511). By taking tax receipts as proxies for the size and growth of the territorial, coordinated state, and expenditure as an indicator, 'though not a perfect one', of the functions of the state (416–17), he infers that war was central to state formation. Although he qualifies these claims by noting that most domestic functions of the state (e.g. its fiscal supply side) do not appear on the balance sheet because they consisted of 'normative' services, he does not dwell much on what such services consisted of, what drove demand for them, or how they evolved over time.

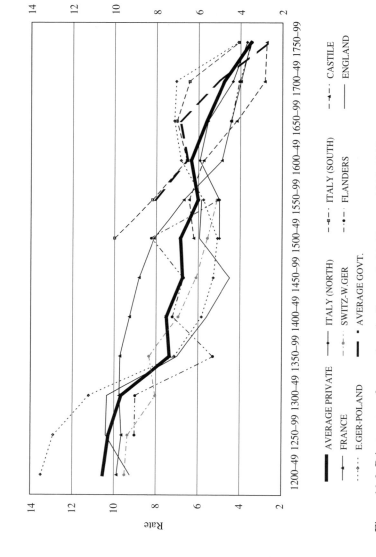

Figure 11.2. Private rates of return (nominal) to capital in Europe, 1200–1799

1200–49 1250–99 1300–49 1350–99 1400–49 1450–99 1500–49 1550–99 1600–49 1650–99 1700–49 1750–99

AVERAGE PRIVATE   ITALY (NORTH)   ITALY (SOUTH)   CASTILE

FRANCE   SWITZ-W.GER   FLANDERS   ENGLAND

E.GER-POLAND   AVERAGE GOVT.

Mann's lack of attention to the state's provision of public goods raises the question of what caused what. Did warfare drive subjects' willingness to pay taxes (Mann's proxy for state formation), or was it the state's political and technical capacity to raise taxes, its infrastructural power, that determined its capacity to wage war? Contrary to Mann's claim (1986: 424–5, 433, 451, 452–4, 457), evidence for early modern England and France suggest the latter. The English case poses the most serious problems for Mann's argument, for two reasons. First, the financial size of the English state did not grow substantially in real terms between the fourteenth and the late seventeenth centuries; expressed in per caput terms it actually declined (424–30).[7] Second, between the mid-sixteenth and the mid-seventeenth centuries England kept out of the major European wars; yet in the intervening period, the civil functions of the English state increased significantly and the sphere of public legislation on prices, wages and welfare expanded, taking over parts of the 'transnational power of the church' in the process. As England evolved 'from coordinated to organic state', 'centralising tendencies made state finances an incomplete guide to state activities' (Mann 1986: 458–61). Mann's explanation for the anomaly is *ad hoc* and begs the question of causation: 'England brought up the rear because the costs of its main armed force, the navy, did not escalate until well into the seventeenth century. Only when England and Holland supplanted privateering with empire building and encountered each other's naval power did their states take off ... The permanent war state arrived in England in two stages', the early Tudor period and the late seventeenth century (1986: 457).

On the evidence provided, therefore, claims about the independent function of military power must be strongly qualified. Tax receipts are at best an ambiguous measure of premodern state activities and power, because they leave out most of the public goods the state provided. Moreover, warfare was only one and perhaps not the most important among a variety of factors causing state activities to expand. There were endogenous social and political pressures that Mann disregards, which included the need to pay for a growing legal and regulatory administration and to meet the costs of interest on the public debt.[8]

Nevertheless, Mann's puzzle of finding a measure of state power remains. Can one distinguish between, and measure changes to, the state's military power – defined by its ability to tax – and its infrastructural power – defined by its ability to coordinate? In other words, can one distinguish empirically between the *fiscal efficiency* and the *economic efficiency* of the state?

Fiscal efficiency can be defined in simple terms as the capacity to maximize state income subject to political, economic and technical constraints.

Work by Mann, Patrick O'Brien and others suggests that between the thirteenth and the eighteenth centuries (when England managed to break through traditional, premodern barriers to fiscal expansion) the upper bound to what an advanced agrarian state in Europe and Asia could demand in tribute for purely military and administrative purposes was about 10 per cent of GNP, while the lower bound below which the state could no longer operate effectively was 3–5 per cent. The proportions are small, but the scope of variation was very large. Since economic and technical constraints to taxation were similar across European societies, the main constraints on states' tax-raising and war-making machinery must have been essentially political. Recent research on this topic suggests that three main sets of factors were at play (Bonney 1995; and 1999; Epstein 2000a: ch. 2).

First, a state needed to overcome the time inconsistency or commitment problem, which arises from the fact that the trade-off between taxes raised and public goods provided is not simultaneous. Subjects' willingness to pay was the result of repeated commitments of trust that the tax recipient(s) – the ruler(s) – would not renege on their promises. Trust could be enhanced, and the rulers' opportunism could be tempered, by aligning their interests with the taxpayers and by keeping the costs of monitoring the ruler low. One of the most effective premodern European states from this point of view was the republican city-state and federation, in which political elites were jointly taxpayers and tax recipients, and their actions in both roles were relatively transparent.

Second, fiscal efficiency was a function of state sovereignty and infrastructural power. More centralized tributary states faced lower negotiation, monitoring and collection costs than more decentralized and politically fragmented ones. This explains why the politically 'organic' and jurisdictionally integrated English state of the late seventeenth and eighteenth centuries could raise more taxes more cheaply than most nominally 'absolutist', but in practice decentralized, Continental states (Stasavage 2003). It may also explain the apparently high degree of fiscal efficiency in premodern China.

Third, fiscal efficiency was a function of the costs of monitoring taxpayers. Since sedentary peasants and their wealth were easier to oversee than mobile merchants, more highly centralized tributary states like China pursued policies favouring the former over the latter. The most sophisticated attempt at direct, moderately progressive taxation ever attempted in premodern Europe, the Florentine *Catasto* of 1427–30, failed after a few years because the republican city-state found the costs of administration impossibly high (Petralia 2000).

In early modern Europe, where states solved their financial shortfalls by borrowing against future income, long-term interest rates provide a measure of relative fiscal efficiency (non-European tributary states had no need to tap the capital markets, because their peasant tax base was sufficiently large, and warfare was less persistent and unpredictable than in Europe) (Epstein 2000a). In Europe, perceived differences in domestic regime determined the sovereign risk premium – the yield spread over the lowest prevailing rate – that individual states had to pay on long-term debt (Figure 11.3). There are three points to be made in this regard. First, the most salient regime difference was between city-states and monarchies, with the former generally paying lower rates of interest than the latter. Second, the risk premium was influenced by the borrower's financial competence and by the liquidity of its capital markets, as the consistently lower rates paid by Florence and Venice compared to north European city-states attest. Third, interest rates converged between political regimes in the long run, suggesting that the more severe constraints facing monarchies in terms of credible commitment and political fragmentation were relaxed over time. The links between borrowing costs, fiscal efficiency and regime structure are sketched in Figure 11.4.*

One final point deserves mention. A comparison between the early modern Dutch Republic and England suggests that the effects of military demands on fiscal efficiency were ambiguous. On the one hand, the Dutch Republic was forced to pay high rates of interest during its war against Habsburg Spain, even though it had one of the most sophisticated fiscal and financial systems in northern Europe. Creditors lacked faith in the Republic's ability to meet its obligations, whether because the fiscal system was actually less efficient than it now seems, or because they feared that the country would be defeated and would default on its debts; rates only fell sharply after the peace of Westphalia (1648). On the other hand, the sixteenth- and seventeenth-century-English monarchy paid the highest interest rates in Europe most probably *because* it kept out of the European military arena, as a result of which it faced few pressures to reform a still 'feudal' and inefficient system of taxation; most importantly, it only established a funded public debt in the 1690s, three-and-a-half centuries after the Italian city-states and about a century and a half after the major Continental monarchies. Fiscal reform, begun by Parliament during the first Civil War, only fully caught up with best Continental practice by importing more advanced financial methods from the Netherlands after 1689 (Epstein 2000a: ch. 2). In sum, although the long-term direction of fiscal change is clear, its direction over the medium term (which could last over a century!) was not clear-cut. On this evidence also, military power was a function of political power rather than an independent variable as Mann claims.

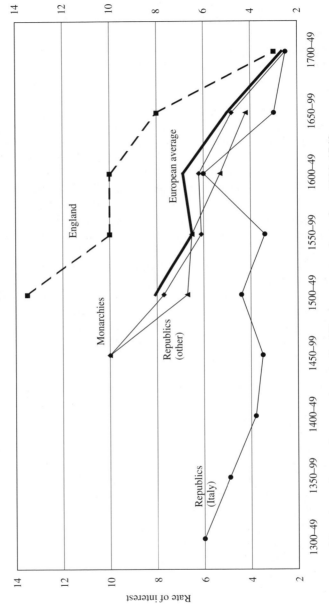

Figure 11.3. Long-term borrowing costs (nominal) of European states, by regime, 1300–1749

Borrowing
costs

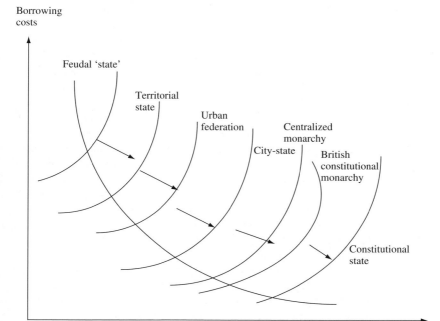

Fiscal efficiency = fn (Capital markets * Fiscal sovereignty)

Figure 11.4. Borrowing costs and fiscal efficiency

Political and economic efficiency

Mann postulates a strong link between European capitalism, a unique
kind of infrastructural power, and military competition between states.
However, he does not explicitly address the links between state and
economic efficiency, claiming that the correct unit of economic and
political analysis is the European network rather than its constituent
regions, and that in any case European state structures converged over
time (1986: 455). In other words, the geopolitical approach takes pre-
cedence over the state-centred, endogenous one. I have already mentioned the advantage of this stance for identifying how patterns of social
power migrate; but it also involves some serious drawbacks. If the main
geopolitical force, warfare, was not an independent vector of state formation, as I have concluded, other – most plausibly endogenous – forces
must have been at play. Perhaps more contentiously, many economic
historians would claim that geopolitical forces also played a secondary

part in the economic rise and decline of nations, and that other forces – primarily market integration and technological innovation – over which domestic policy and institutions had the dominant influence, were nearly always more salient. A theory of how power works *within* states is therefore essential – but Mann's view of individuals as largely reactive to state power seems to exclude this (1986: 436).

A geopolitical approach also glosses over the significant political differences between European states, and may underestimate their economic consequences. One of the most historically pregnant aspects of premodern Europe was its variety of political regime types, and the fact that economic leadership did not stay with one type of regime or country for very long. Mann's discussion of the slow 'migration' of power from southern to northern Europe is suggestive, but his explanations are vague, in terms of shifts from regions with more extensive power techniques to ones with more intensive power techniques (Mann 1988), or from 'weak states' to states offering 'most centralised order' (1986: 407–8). He also suggests that the dynamic equilibrium of the European multistate system was maintained by the ability of political rivals to 'copy in a more ordered, planned fashion' the 'new power techniques' that the 'leading power stumbles across' (1986: 456), but his detailed discussion of British state formation seldom refers to the country's many cultural, institutional and technological debts towards its neighbours. Thus, Mann's insight on the dialectic between advanced and peripheral societies gets lost because of his focus on state networks and his lack of comparative analysis.

Reformulating the problem of the 'European miracle' in more materialistic and comparative terms can solve many of these difficulties. Having questioned ideological and military power as independent explanatory variables, the crux of Mann's analysis of the rise of European capitalism can be summed up in two questions: what was the impact of power systems on economic outcomes (such as efficiency in production), and why did economically optimal power structures change over time?

Although Mann is mainly interested in the causes of state (rather than economic) growth, he assumes that a strong positive correlation holds between the two. His theory implies that some states are better for growth than others, and that infrastructurally 'strong' states generally grow faster than 'weak' ones because they coordinate more effectively between competing organized agents (we saw that Mann's apparent exception to this rule, the commercially dynamic 'corridor' between Flanders and northern Italy, actually confirms the rule). Medieval European states also offered protection to merchants; exploited economies of scale in warfare; leveraged domestic conflicts over fiscal distribution to expand their tax base; and generally stimulated economic expansion by helping to extend literacy, apply more effective management and communication techniques, and recover classical learning that included Roman law (1986: 422–3, 431–2, 436, 440–1).

Mann identifies two general causes of state decline or underperformance, both of which have strong Olsonian undertones (Olson 1982). The first cause is implied in Mann's thesis of the marcher effect, according to which latecomers – marcher or peripheral societies – benefit from being able to 'copy in a more ordered, planned fashion' the 'new power techniques' that the leading power had 'stumbled across' (1986: 456). By implication, leading societies decline as their power structures get entrenched and generate rent seeking by the elites.

The second, related cause is political and jurisdictional fragmentation, as a comparison of English constitutionalism and French absolutism reveals. 'Absolutist states [like France] were not infrastructurally stronger than constitutional ones'; absolutist despotism lacked the English 'power to co-ordinate civil society'; it was 'considerably less organic [e.g. politically integrated] than its constitutional counterpart, for it operated through a greater number of divisions and exclusions ... Whereas constitutionalism reinforced the development of an organic capitalist class, absolutism tended to block it or crosscut it with other political divisions' (Mann 1986: 477–9). Political fragmentation raised the costs of political and fiscal negotiation, search and enforcement. High political transaction costs – caused by contradictions between the heterogeneous segmentary and class interests of the ruling elites – produced coordination failures in Spain and France that weakened their powers to tax. The results were disastrous, for 'a state that wished to survive had to increase its extractive capacity over defined territories to obtain conscripted and professional armies or navies. Those that did not were crushed on the battlefield and absorbed into others' (Mann 1986: 490).

These institutional and materialist aspects of Mann's theory still seem to me very fertile; indeed, economic historians have barely begun to apply his ideas, and some of my attempts to do so are accordingly quite speculative. Combining Mann's insights about state formation, social coordination, and the growth and transmission across space of social power, with the views I have set out about premodern economic growth may give us a framework for answering the puzzle, or better, the set of puzzles known for short as 'the rise of the West'. We can sum up its main parameters in the following synthetic points (see also Figure 11.5).

1. The most remarkable feature of the premodern European economy was its sheer inefficiency. The gap between actual and potential agricultural output was frequently large; in eighteenth-century France,

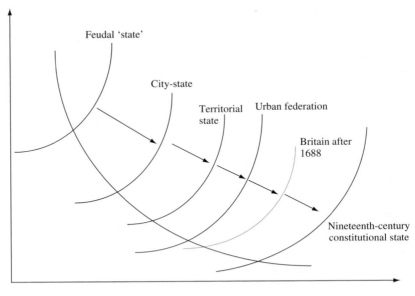

State sovereignty

PD: Prisoner's Dilemma; CF: coordination failure

(1) Feudal 'state': economic and political power (EPP) is parcellized among military elites, led by one *primus inter pares*; powers of coordination are weak
(2) City-state: EPP vested in the dominant urban elite, which establishes strong coordination with its 'country'; weak coordination with nearby/competing cities
(3) Territorial state: EPP vested in competing urban and rural elites; coordination by territorial ruler based on policy of 'divide and rule'
(4) Urban territorial federation: EPP vested in competing urban elites, held together by external military pressure; coordination through regional urban hegemons
(5) Britain after 1688: EPP vested in integrated national elite; legal/corporate affiliation in decline; strong centralized authority; strong coordination
(6) Constitutional state: EPP no longer derived from legal right/corporate affiliation; citizenship as a bundle of 'universal' individual rights; strong central authority; strong coordination

Figure 11.5. Political structure and institutional transaction costs (ITC)

existing technology could generate a 60 per cent higher output than was achieved in practice (Grantham 1993). However, some economies made use of their technological endowments more effectively than others. The main source of agricultural inefficiency and slack, and the main restrictions to premodern Smithian growth, came from the 'effective local possession of autonomous economic resources' (Mann 1986: 406), which gave rise to institutional impediments to trade, poorly specified property rights due to the parcellized sovereignty inherited from the 'feudal' past, and restrictions on rural proto-industrial growth. In sum, premodern economic inefficiency was caused by a lack of social and political coordination that generated multiple Prisoner's Dilemmas.

2. Smithian and Schumpeterian growth were not restricted to one region or political regime. However, large output gaps, sharp differences in agricultural productivity and in other expressions of growth like urbanization, and regular patterns of strong regional growth followed by long-term stasis or decline, point to weak convergence across regions. Although communication networks made it possible for new regional leaders to utilize the systems of knowledge and power developed by former leading regions (see paragraph 9 below), the lack of economic convergence, the existence of a variety of institutional equilibria and changes in leadership themselves suggest that knowledge still spread slowly and unsystematically. Changes in leadership also indicate that the optimal institutional context for growth changed over time, and that the crux of the changes lay in the interaction between political and economic power.

3. The interaction between political and economic power was most effective at the regional level, where the logistical 'tyranny of distance' was weaker and where urban and rural manufacture could benefit most from economies of agglomeration (Krugman 1991). However, economic and political power (EPP) in 'feudal' states was parcellized among military elites, led by a *primus inter pares*, and powers of coordination were localized and weak. By contrast, EPP in city-states in the Franco-Roman European core was vested in dominant albeit fractious urban elites, which established strong coordination with their 'country' (Figure 11.5). City-states combined to an unprecedented degree feudalism's *intensive* ability to coordinate trade and markets (because city-state elites sometimes included feudal lords and always included landowners), and the tributary Roman state's *extensive*, logistical capabilities (Epstein 2000b). A large proportion of the characteristically European intensive *and* extensive economic, administrative, military and ideological (both secular and religious) power technologies were developed between 1100 and 1500 by the Italian and German-speaking city-states (Mann 1986: 437). These tools diffused northwards from the Mediterranean, initially to the remainder of the Frankish core (northern France, Flanders and the Rhineland) and later to more peripheral states like England, the northern Netherlands and Scandinavia (Brady 1991: 146, 150, 155).

4. Up to *c.* 1450–1500CE the power of town over country was a source of dynamic growth, as towns deployed the most sophisticated legal, political, military and ideological powers of coercion yet invented to coordinate interchange with the countryside. However, city-states in the Roman-Frankish European core faced three long-run obstacles. First, city-based republics combined EPP in the rulers' hands, which led republican elites to confuse government by a class or party with the rule of state, and to systematically exploit their political power over the urban hinterland for economic ends. Second, city-states discriminated between citizens and non-citizens, which made it harder to coordinate power with other subject cities because coordination required the recognition of all citizen rights as equivalent, and became a further source of rent seeking in the countryside (most peasants were excluded *ex officio* from rights of citizenship). This may explain why European republicanism was unable to produce a general theory of the state as opposed to a theory of citizenship, and surely explains why no republican city-state became a successful territorial state (Koenigsberger 1988; Epstein 2000a; 2000b). Third, corporate affiliations in the Roman-Frankish core were stronger than in the more peripheral states (Brady 1991). Greater opportunities for corporate 'capture' may explain why the economies of the most advanced city-states slowed or contracted as the European economy emerged from the late medieval 'crisis' (Epstein 2001; 2006).

5. Territorial states and national monarchies adopted many of the technologies of power (tax and administrative structures, market networks and welfare structures) developed by city-states, most of which had a fixed cost base and displayed economies of scale. On the other hand, territorial and national states often weakened the jurisdictional powers of town over country, which helped rural proto-industry to grow. Proto-industry sought protection from urban guild monopolies in chartered, corporate villages or 'new towns', while depending at the same time on towns for skilled labour and services. This paradox explains why the most successful proto-industrial 'districts' in pre-modern Europe were situated in densely urbanized regions, and why proto-industry developed fastest during the late medieval and seventeenth-century 'crises', when centralizing states attacked urban EPP with the greatest determination.

6. Proto-industry contributed to Smithian growth by absorbing surplus agricultural labour. Consequently, the institutional freedoms from 'old' town prerogatives that were necessary to develop proto-industry in villages and new towns set basic limits to an economy's capacity to release agricultural labour, and, consequently, to raise the productivity

of agricultural labour. The greater ability of its urban sector to absorb excess rural labour by creating new urban centres gave seventeenth- and eighteenth-century British agriculture a critical institutional edge over Continental agriculture (Epstein 2001; Glennie 2001).

7. The efficiency of territorial and monarchical states was determined by the extent of cross-cutting political divisions (jurisdictional integration) inherited from the medieval past. In territorial and absolutist states, EPP was vested in competing urban and rural elites, corporate affiliations and prerogatives were still strong, and negotiation and coordination costs were high; territorial rulers had to adopt policies of 'divide and rule'. In the British constitutional monarchy, EPP was vested in an integrated urban and rural elite, corporate affiliations were in decline, and central authority and coordination were strong. Although the political similarities between absolutist and constitutional monarchies were greater than the differences (Mann 1986: 479, 482–3), absolutist states were politically *weaker* than a constitutional monarchy like England after 1688. England also benefited long before 1688 from an unusual degree of jurisdictional integration, which kept barriers to trade and the costs of market integration low (Mann 1986: 493–4).

8. A federated city-state like the United Provinces combined some of the advantages and disadvantages of city-states and monarchies. From the city-state, it took strong powers of coordination with the countryside and the alignment of elites' economic and political interests, which raised levels of social trust and kept borrowing costs low; from monarchies, it took a willingness to coordinate interests at a national level through the Stadtholder, who did not directly embody segmentary economic interests. EPP was however vested in competing urban and aristocratic elites held together by external military pressure (from Spain, England, France, etc.), corporate solidarity was stronger than national identity, and fiscal and economic coordination required costly negotiation ('t-Hart 1993).

9. Regional leadership shifted from the southern and central European heartland to northwestern Europe via Spain because the corporate, romanized institutions that wielded intensive power in south-central Europe resisted centralization (Brady 1991). The social costs of change in less romanized peripheral regions were lower. Those shifts were reflected in patterns of urbanization (Epstein 2001), of long-distance trade and, most critically, of regional technological leadership, which moved from northern Italy (*c.* 1100–1500) to southern Germany and the southern Netherlands (*c.* 1450–1550), then to the Dutch Republic (1580–1680), and finally to Britain (1700–1880)

(Davids 1995: 338). In other words, institutional efficiency was a necessary but not sufficient condition for marcher regions to forge ahead; they also needed access to outside sources of technological innovation, and they had to be able to create new ones. In pre-modern Europe, clusters of innovation could shift to new regions because skilled craftsmen could migrate freely where their skills were more highly rewarded, and because the costs of migration fell over time, with the late medieval and seventeenth-century crises marking major improvements in this respect (Davids 1995: 341; Epstein 1998). The link between technological migration and EPP was straightforward: regions with higher economic returns to migrants also enjoyed commercial leadership (Davids 1995: 339–40, 343–5), and commercial leadership was a result of more effective coordinating powers.

10. Although the migration of social power was a continuous process, major shifts in economic and technological leadership from 'core' to marcher regions were consolidated over relatively short periods of time. The most significant discontinuities occurred during the late medieval and the seventeenth-century crises, which are both best viewed as 'distribution crises' over the allocation of social surplus between producers, rentier urban and landlord classes, and the state (Steensgard 1978; Epstein 2000a: ch. 3). While elites in the core regions, most notably north-central Italy, sought refuge in rent seeking and caused their economies to contract (Epstein 2006), peripheral regions like the northern Netherlands and England benefited from greater political and jurisdictional integration to import and copy the core regions' fiscal, financial and manufacturing techniques. Europe as a whole benefited from the diversity of alternative political, legal and economic institutions, which increased the variety of options and created opportunities for improvement through 'mutual jealousy' (Hume 1994; Bernholz, Streit and Vaubel 1998).

11. The 'acephalous' and dendritic European state system (Mann 1986: 500–1) increased the costs of technological diffusion, most of which occurred randomly through voluntary and forced migration by individual skilled artisans. On the other hand, political disintegration may have diminished the likelihood of technological path dependence and may have generated a broader range of technological options than a more integrated political system. As the costs of migration slowly fell, the economy benefited from selection and recombination out of a larger knowledge pool. Inter-state competition had two further advantages: it generated a culture of technical

and consumer emulation within the elites, which made them keen to attract skilled craftsmen to produce for them, and it gave rise to institutional experimentation, diffusion and recombination, most notably in the sphere of war finance, where military success offered proof positive of institutional efficiency.

Notes

1 Gellner (1980b: 68–9) commenting on the Soviet Marxist Yuri Semenov (1980). See Mann (1986: 539): 'A regionally dominant, institution-building, developing power also upgrades the power capacities of its neighbours, who learn its power techniques but adapt them to their different social and geographical circumstances. Where the dominant power acquires the stable, specialised institutions of either an empire of domination or a multi-power-actor civilisation, some of the emergent interstitial forces it generates may flow outward to the marches, where they are less confined by institutionalised, antithetical power structures. Hence the bearers of interstitial surprise have often been marcher lords. The world-historical process acquires their migratory legs.' Mann seems to have been strongly influenced by Gellner and Semenov (see also note 2 below), although he does not cite them.
2 Mann's theory postulates the general unity of mankind, or at least of the inhabitants of the Eurasian landmass. See Gellner (1980b) for similar comments about Semenov's brand of Marxism.
3 Weber arguably believed more strongly in counterfactual reasoning than Gellner and Mann credit him with; see Ringer (2002). Decomposing complex historical processes into small-scale, recursive modules can solve Mann's problem of 'grand comparison'; see Roehner and Syme (2002).
4 European territorial expansion disproves Mann's view that blockage by Islam to the South and East was a necessary precondition for medieval growth (Mann 1988: 18; 1986: 406–7, 508).
5 It also seems to contradict the claim on the following page that 'unitary, exclusive ownership' was the result of the rise of the state (1986: 399).
6 On the other hand, the evidence also suggests that a fully fledged market of this kind emerged only during the 'late medieval crisis', which Mann denies marks the origins of the transition from feudalism to capitalism (1986: 500–11).
7 See Bonney (1999: 56) and the data provided by Patrick O'Brien for the European State Finance Database (ESFDB) (www.le.ac.uk/hi/bon/ESFDB). For the subdued effects of the sixteenth-century military revolution on French taxation, see Bonney (1999: 141), and the data published by Bonney for the ESFDB.
8 See Martin Körner's detailed breakdown of states' revenue and expenditure published by the ESFDB.
* I wish to thank Jan Leuten van Zanden and Maarten Prak for suggesting the graphic representation in Figures 11.4 and 11.5.

References

Anderson, P. 1974a. *Passages from Antiquity to Feudalism*. London: Verso.
1974b. *Lineages of the Absolutist State*. London: Verso.
Bartlett, R. 1993. *The Making of Europe. Conquest, Colonization and Cultural Change 950–1350*. London: Allen Lane.
Bautier, R.-H. 1953. Les foires de Champagne. Recherches sur une évolution historique. *Recueils de la Société Jean Bodin V: La Foire*. Brussels.
Berman, H. J. 1983. *Law and Revolution: The Formation of the Western Legal Tradition*. Cambridge, MA and London: Harvard University Press.
Bernholz, P., M. E. Streit and R. Vaubel (eds.). 1998. *Political Competition, Innovation and Growth: A Historical Analysis*. Berlin–Heidelberg–New York: Springer.
Bonney, R. (ed.). 1995. *Economic Systems and State Finance*. Oxford: Oxford University Press.
1999. *The Rise of the Fiscal State in Europe c.1200–1815*. Oxford: Oxford University Press.
Brady, T. A. Jr. 1991. The Rise of Merchant Empires, 1400–1700: A European Counterpoint. In J. D. Tracy (ed.), *The Political Economy of Merchant Empires*. Cambridge: Cambridge University Press.
Braudel, F. 1972. *The Mediterranean and the Mediterranean World in the Age of Philip II*. London: Fontana/Collins.
Brenner, R. 1982. The Agrarian Roots of European Capitalism. *Past and Present* 97.
Cohen, G. A. 1978. *Karl Marx's Theory of History: A Defence*. Oxford: Oxford University Press.
Davids, K. A. 1995. Shifts of Technological Leadership in Early Modern Europe. In J. Lucassen and K. Davids (eds.), *A Miracle Mirrored. The Dutch Republic in European Perspective*. Cambridge: Cambridge University Press.
Deng, K. 2003. Diandi. In J. Mokyr (ed.), *The Oxford Encyclopedia of Economic History*. Oxford: Oxford University Press.
Epstein, S. R. 1998. Craft Guilds, Apprenticeship, and Technological Change in Pre-industrial Europe. *Journal of Economic History*, 53(3).
2000a. *Freedom and Growth: The Rise of States and Markets in Europe, 1300–1750*. London: Routledge.
2000b. The Rise and Fall of Italian City-States. In M. H. Hansen (ed.), *A Comparative Study of City-State Cultures*. Copenhagen: Kongelige dansk videnskabernes selskab.
2001. Introduction. In S. R. Epstein (ed.), *Town and Country in Europe 1300–1800*. Cambridge: Cambridge University Press.
2006. I caratteri originali: l'economia. In S. Gensini (ed.), *L'Italia alla fine del medioevo*. Pisa: Pacini.
Gellner, E. (ed.). 1980a. *Soviet and Western Anthropology*. London: Duckworth.
1980b. A Russian Marxist Philosophy of History. In Gellner, E. 1980a.
Glennie, P. 2001. Town and Country in England, 1570–1750. In S. R. Epstein (ed.), *Town and Country in Europe, 1300–1800*. Cambridge: Cambridge University Press.

Grantham, G. W. 1993. Divisions of Labour: Agricultural Productivity and Occupational Specialization in Pre-industrial France. *Economic History Review*, 2nd series, 46(3).

Greif, A., R. P. Milgrom and B. Weingast. 1994. Coordination, Commitment and Enforcement: The Case of the Merchant Guild. *Journal of Political Economy*, 102(4).

Hall, J. A. 1985. *Powers and Liberties: The Causes and Consequences of the Rise of the West*. Oxford: Blackwell.

Hart, M. C.'t. 1993. *The Making of a Bourgeois State: War, Politics and Finance During the Dutch Revolt*. Manchester: Manchester University Press.

Hicks, J. R. 1969. *A Theory of Economic History*. Oxford: Oxford University Press.

Hume, D. 1994. Of the Rise and Progress of the Arts and Sciences. In D. Hume, *Political Essays*. Cambridge: Cambridge University Press.

Johnston, D. 1999. *Roman Law in Context*. Cambridge: Cambridge University Press.

Jones, E. L. 1981. *The European Miracle*. Cambridge: Cambridge University Press.

Koenigsberger, H. G. 1988. Schlussbetrachtung: Republiken und Republikanismus im Europa der frühen Neuzeit aus historischer Sicht. In H. G. Koenigsberger, (ed.), *Republiken und Republikanismus im Europa der Frühen Neuzeit*. Munich: R. Oldenbourg.

Krugman, P. 1991. *Geography and Trade*. Cambridge, MA: MIT Press.

Mann, M. 1986. *The Sources of Social Power, Volume I: A History of Power from the Beginning to AD 1760*. Cambridge: Cambridge University Press.

   1988. European Development: Approaching a Historical Explanation. In J. Baechler, J. A. Hall and M. Mann (eds.), *Europe and the Rise of Capitalism*. Oxford: Blackwell.

Mendels, F. 1972. Proto-industrialization: The First Phase of the Industrialization Process. *Journal of Economic History*, 32.

Milgrom, P., D. North and B. Weingast. 1990. The Role of Institutions in the Revival of Trade: The Law Merchant, Private Judges and the Champagne Fairs. *Economics and Politics*, 2.

North, D. C. 1981. *Structure and Change in Economic History*. Cambridge: Cambridge University Press.

Olson, M. 1982. *The Rise and Decline of Nations: Economic Growth, Stagflation, and Social Rigidities*. New Haven, CT and London: Yale University Press.

Petralia, G. 2000. Fiscality, Politics and Dominion in Florentine Tuscany at the End of the Middle Ages. In W. J. Connell and A. Zorzi (eds.), *Florentine Tuscany: Structures and Practices of Power*. Cambridge: Cambridge University Press.

Pomeranz, K. 2000. *The Great Divergence: China, Europe, and the Making of the Modern World Economy*. Princeton: Princeton University Press.

Prodi, P. 1987. *The Papal Prince: One Body and Two Souls: The Papal Monarchy in Early Modern Europe*. Cambridge: Cambridge University Press.

Ringer, F. 2002. Max Weber on Causal Analysis, Interpretation, and Comparison. *History and Theory*, 41.

Roehner, B. M., and T. Syme. 2002. *Pattern and Repertoire in History*. Cambridge, MA and London: Harvard University Press.

Semenov, Y. 1980. The Theory of Socio-economic Formations and World History. In Gellner, E. 1980a.

Spufford, P. 2000. Trade in Fourteenth-Century Europe. In M. Jones (ed.), *The New Cambridge Medieval History, VI: c.1300–c.1415*. Cambridge: Cambridge University Press.

Stasavage, D. 2003. *Public Debt and the Birth of the Democratic State: France and Great Britain, 1688–1789*. Cambridge: Cambridge University Press.

Steensgard, N. 1978. The Seventeenth-Century Crisis. In G. Parker and L. M. Smith (eds.), *The General Crisis of the Seventeenth Century*. London: Routledge and Kegan Paul.

Verhulst, A. 2002. *The Carolingian Economy*. Cambridge: Cambridge University Press.

Wallerstein, I. 1974–80. *The Modern World-System*, vols. I–II. New York: Academic Press.

Wickham, C. 1988. Historical Materialism, Historical Sociology. *New Left Review*, 171.

1998. Overview: Production, Distribution and Demand, II. In I. L. Hansen and C. Wickham (eds.), *The Long Eighth Century*. Leiden–Boston–Cologne: Brill.

12 A historical, not comparative, method: breakthroughs and limitations in the theory and methodology of Michael Mann's analysis of power

Jack A. Goldstone

Michael Mann's work ranges over such a vast array of periods and places – the prestate peoples of prehistory in the Old and New World; the ancient empires of Egypt, Assyria, Persia, Athens, Hellas, Rome; the varied states of Europe from the Middle Ages to the present; and excursions into India, China and the lands of Islam – that one's first reaction to my title might be: how could anyone claim that Mann's method is not comparative? Let me consult an expert who should know: Michael Mann. On p. 503 of the *Sources of Social Power*, Volume I (1986), he says: 'Historical, not comparative, sociology has been my principal method.' My purpose in this chapter is to explore the implications of this statement. I believe that this approach has allowed Mann to make several major breakthroughs in our understanding of states, their emergence and their development. For this, we will always be in his debt. At the same time, I wish to suggest that the limitations imposed by this choice have also led to problems in his theory of the emergence of the modern world.

Breakthroughs: Mann's theory of state formation and development

Mann's theory of state formation and development offers some of the most striking and significant advances since Weber. This advance does *not* lie in his four-fold typology of power, the now famous IEMP quartet: ideological, economic, military and political power. Although Mann is careful to trace his lineages to Spencer, and not Parsons, it is easy to recognize the lineaments here of the four-fold way; Parsons' boxes of systems in systems also rely on four basic types of social interaction (maintenance of values/ideology, adaptation to economic/environment settings, integration by conflict resolution and law enforcement, and goal setting via politics). Where Mann differs from Parsons, and this is such a radical difference that it is transformative in its implications for social theory, is in Mann's identification of *where* and *why* these types of social relationships are exercised. They are not exercised within self-sufficient, systemic (in the sense of holistic and contained), 'societies'. Rather, these various types of social relationships are exerted across networks that overlap, span, connect and differentiate multiple societies. Indeed, in Mann's theory, it is 'societies' that are convenient, approximate and subjective constructs; it is the networks of power that are real. In addition, these relationships are not exercised for the purpose of sustaining societies (e.g. for functionalist aims) – how could they be, since these relationships are generally not congruent with the boundaries of specific societies? Rather, actions in the various power networks take place in order to further the aims of power-holders: religious or other ideological leaders, controllers of modes of production, chiefs and monarchs, and generals.

Mann therefore does not offer an analysis of 'societies' in any general form. Indeed, he argues that efforts to do so pursue an illusion. Rather, he traces out how specific historical-social relationships emerge from the interaction of various networks of power, generating along the way various patterns of different political, territorial, religious/ideological and military units. Moreover, since the networks of power themselves develop historically, as new means of exercising power across time and space are developed, the outcome of the networks' interaction produces a succession of developing social patterns and units. Comparisons of 'societies' as if they were separate and individual 'cases' of some more general, pervasive and context-free general type is therefore simply misguided. What historical sociology must do, given this theoretical framework, is trace the development of social interaction over time as produced by the development, extension and interaction of various power networks.

This is a remarkable breakthrough in social theory, which had arguably previously been transfixed by the reification of 'societies' as the object of theoretical explanation. Shifting our emphasis from societies to the power networks that both constitute and extend beyond them is as radical as shifting the study of momentum from looking at the reactions of individual particles under forces to understanding the dynamics of the fields that constitute both the forces and the particles.

Yet this is not all. Mann's theory makes yet a further breakthrough by classifying the nature of power in two respects. First, Mann differentiates between *intensive* and *extensive* power (1986: 7–10). The former is the ability to concentrate power at a particular time and place. The ability to bring overwhelming military force to bear in a single battle, or to derive greater economic output from a single individual or group, are examples of intensive power. Historical instances include the Greek hoplite phalanx or the Roman legion in military power; the heavy iron mould-board plough and the steam-engine are examples in economic power. Extensive power, by contrast, is the ability to extend the reach of power over a larger spatial area. The ability of Roman emperors to extract revenues from regions spanning England and Iraq was extensive power; so too was the ability of the Pope to shape belief and church practices across continents. Although some power-wielders controlled high levels of both extensive and intensive power in some dimensions (e.g. Roman emperors had superior intensive military power and extensive political power relative to the Greeks), others varied. China, Mann seems to believe, had extensive but not intensive economic power in its peasant agriculture; feudal knights had intensive local power but little extensive reach.

So far, we are up to eight modes of power: each of the IEMP types could appear as intensive or extensive power. But Mann goes further. In addition, we can class power-wielders as to whether their power was high or low in regard to being *despotic* and *infrastructural* (Mann 1984; 1986: 94–8). The degree of despotic power corresponds to the latitude or lack of constraint in the range of actions available to the power-holder. Ottoman sultans had enormous despotic power; they were largely unchecked by other social and political actors in their choices. Modern presidents of developed states, by contrast, are hemmed in by laws and institutions that limit their options and punish them for transgressions; their despotic power is low. The degree of infrastructural power corresponds to the resources that a leader can command to pursue a goal. Egyptian pharoahs had considerable infrastructural power to bring the manpower and materials together that built the pyramids; but this is dwarfed by the economic and manpower resources available to modern states for prosecution of wars or domestic regulation and redistribution. Again, the two types of power are independent; high despotism can (and usually does) coincide with low infrastructural power, and vice versa.

Mann thus provides us with a 'power' field of great diversity and subtlety: four types of power, each of which can be graded along four separate dimensions (intensive, extensive, despotic, infrastructural). By tracing how these types of power developed, and how particular organizations and leaders increased or lost power of various types along these dimensions, Mann can generate a deep understanding of the earliest to the latest forms of religious, economic, military and state power.[1]

Mann's method in his works is therefore not comparative, in the sense noted by Skocpol and Somers (1980), of testing a theory by its ability to predict the common characteristics of specific cases from a limited set of information about those cases. Rather, Mann's method is detailed 'process-tracing' (Goldstone 2002c), a mapping of segments of the historical landscape by articulating the key causal relationships that produced specific, often unique, outcomes. The value of his theory of state formation and development as being the result of intersecting and overlapping power networks, changing in intensity, extensivity, despotic power and infrastructural power over time, is precisely that it gives a richer and more integrated mapping of how states develop over time than previous theories which treated states simply as the ruling elements of distinct 'societies', whose nature and power is determined by the systemic characteristics of the societies they ruled, whether those characteristics were unidimensional (Marx) or multidimensional (Weber, Parsons).

This method would seem highly appropriate to Mann's goal, which is not to explain 'societies' as such, but to explain the emergence and development of a particular kind of social formation: the modern industrialized nation-state. In Mann's work, this formation emerges not as the logical, evolutionary development of 'societies' as such, but rather as the outcome of a series of particular historical conjunctures or 'accidents' (1986: 531). The particular constellation of power characteristics that constitute the modern nation-state did not necessarily have to come together; that they did come together in a particular pattern was the result of collisions of various systems of beliefs, military technology, state expansion and economic improvements. In Mann's view, this novel pattern of power relationships created a situation in which the modern history of western Europe became quintessentially a history of classes and states, while the rest of the world remained mired in a more stagnant pattern of extensive imperial power, with weak classes and weak states held together mainly by ideological unification and compulsory cooperation of various elite factions and popular groups. Although the preceding statement is explicitly comparative, 'comparison' is not essential to Mann's argument, which is interested primarily in explicating the historical development of classes and states and their combination into what was unquestionably, by the twentieth century, the globally dominant power-formation: the modern industrialized nation-state. Mann thus focuses his account on the 'leading edge of power', that is, on those specific historical formations and developments that produced the outcome of interest.

I would accept almost all of the above insights. Mann is brilliant in mapping out how changing degrees of diverse types of power lifted the range of political control from villages to city-states to empires of domination to modern integrated states. He is equally insightful in showing how the contradictions among different kinds of power, arising within and spanning without particular social formations, could create crises that undermined empires and revolutionized economic production. But, the key question remains – has he identified the sources of modernity? That is, after all, the central goal of the entire enterprise.

To my mind, Mann falters in this respect. Not that his story is wrong, but it is limited and incomplete, precisely because it misses factors that can only be revealed by careful comparisons among different 'societies'.

Limitations: Mann's social theory and the emergence of modernity

Although Mann's volume seeks to focus on the 'leading edge' of power in history, there are some odd omissions if this is true. Although Mann points out that 'leadership' flowed in a northerly and westerly direction, from the Near East to Greece to Rome then to northern Italy, the Rhineland, and eventually to the constitutional states of Holland and England, there is almost no information on what were clearly the 'leading' economies and powers of Europe in the twelfth to seventeenth centuries, namely Byzantium, the republic of Venice, Medici Florence, the Habsburg empires, Holland and the Ottoman Empire. Rather, across the chapters on the 'European dynamic' (Mann 1986: ch. 12–14), the focus is, first, on the expansion of intensive agriculture using the iron-tipped mould-board plough in the wet-soil northwest of Europe, second, on the expansion of state power as demonstrated by the fiscal growth of the English state, and third, on the growth of national markets, again mainly in England.

Mann justifies this focus by pointing out that – even though Holland and France were close behind (1986: 450) – Britain was the first country to make it to the 'modern' formation of industrialized nation-state. Thus developments there deserve primary treatment. Indeed, Mann tells us that 'the probably proximate causes of the Industrial Revolution' can be traced to processes unfolding in Britain: agricultural improvement produced domestic surpluses, and 'the surplus thus generated was widely diffused in a large number of small amounts ... Thus a surplus was available to exchange for more varied household-consumption goods. [Therefore] the mass production of low-cost goods of all three types [clothing, iron goods, and pottery or leather] boomed ... The boost to its three main industries, cotton, iron and pottery; the stimulus to their development, which then turned into technological and scientific complexity; the generation of steam power; capital intensity, and the factory system' (1986: 495). Essential to this process was the growth of a large, integrated, national market for boosting demand and coordinating supply; this in turn was produced in large measure by the expanding role of the national state and its military and domestic roles in coordinating national authority.

This is a wonderfully coherent story, and it fits the general pattern of explanation of the Industrial Revolution that has dominated recent historiography. While at one time, the Industrial Revolution was seen as the product of an eruption of new knowledge and new technologies in the eighteenth century, spurred by the growth of modern scientific knowledge (Ashton 1948; von Tunzelmann 1978), in recent decades the story of the Industrial Revolution has been transformed by new scholarship. Quantitative studies by Crafts and Harley (1992) have shown that there was no sudden explosion of economic growth in eighteenth-century Britain; rather there is evidence of persistent and moderate growth from the mid-seventeenth century up to the early nineteenth century, and only thereafter does growth accelerate. Many of the technological advances behind this growth – introduction of fodder crops and reduced fallowing in agriculture, intensified use of water power in manufacturing, the cotton gin and spinning jenny, even the early cotton factory and rolling and puddling processes for iron – were not based on scientific advance but on farmers' and artisans' ingenuity (Mokyr 1999). In addition, as Mann notes, there is strong evidence of technological change and intensive growth during the Middle Ages – use of water mills, the heavy plough and new horse harnesses, the spread of iron tools – and thus of considerable expansion in population and resources. The story that Mann tells is fully consistent with this new scholarship: in the Middle Ages, northwest Europeans greatly increased their output from agriculture. Over the course of the thirteenth to sixteenth centuries, they therefore gradually increased their surpluses, while the growth of national states and their expenditure and authority created the demand and coordination to underpin national commodity markets. The growth of the market slowly drew after it further innovation and productivity increases. Everything else simply followed from the existence of this pre-existing momentum: as Mann states above 'development ... turned into technological and scientific complexity; the generation of steam power; capital intensity, and the factory system'.

While Mann differs from other current explanations of the emergence of modernity in the complexity of his argument – that it was the interweaving of four different types of power in transnational and subnational networks that, by something of a rare and accidental combination, produced the shift to modernity – he is following the same general lines of argument as such scholars as Brenner (1976), Wallerstein (1980), North (1981), Hall (1985), Crosby (1997), Landes (1998) and Levine (2001). All of these scholars agree that something changed relatively early in European history, between 1000 AD and 1500 AD, that imbued European 'society' or societies with a historically exceptional dynamism that led, in due course, to modern industrial societies. In all these stories, some factor unleashed early accumulation; this accumulation then provides the demand that leads to further growth. They differ only in arguing over what that 'something' was – a change in class relations (Brenner), the articulation of a new international division of economic roles (Wallerstein), a new foundation of security of private property and transactions (North and Hall), an exceptional concern with counting, machines and exploration (Crosby and Landes), or demographic and production shifts at the level of household and farm (Levine). Where Mann exceeds all of these competitors is in managing to incorporate all of their themes within a single, comprehensive view of the development of multiple, overlapping networks of power.

The problem with this accomplishment, however, is that the main precepts of the argument will not withstand careful historical *comparisons*, both within Europe and without. After all, as I have said elsewhere, even if one can trace the steps that lead from a point of origin to an outcome, *concatenation is not causation* (Goldstone 2000). It may well be true that the adoption of iron-tipped mould-board ploughs increased the productivity of labour in northeast wet-soil agriculture beyond anything seen before in those regions. But how do we know that the surpluses thereby produced were critical in producing later innovation and growth? Were those surpluses greater than those produced in other times and places? By how much? How much is enough?

To point to one critical comparison within Europe: consider Holland during the Golden Age. As de Vries (2000) has demonstrated, in the seventeenth century Holland intensified its agriculture beyond that found anywhere else in Europe, producing a level of real income approximately double that of England in the early seventeenth century, and remaining about 50 per cent higher all the way to 1750. For almost 150 years, in other words, Holland had more surpluses than Britain; its warehouses certainly served a large national and international market; and its manufacturing, transportation and military resources were the most intensively powerful in Europe. At the height of its power, in 1688, Holland successfully invaded Britain and replaced the British monarch with its own, and then used British financial and military muscle for the next thirty years mainly to defend and maintain Dutch independence and power on the continent.

Yet the ensuing process that Mann argues naturally unfolded in England – 'development ... turned into technological and scientific complexity; the generation of steam power; capital intensity, and the factory system' did *not* occur. In Holland, manufacturing and real incomes simply collapsed, falling by 40 per cent from 1740 to 1820 (although, admittedly, wages remained above English levels almost to the end of this period). There was no technological and scientific complexity introduced into Dutch society and manufacturing; instead, in the early eighteenth century the Dutch Reformed Church exerted itself to discipline thought, Newtonian science retreated into a few diminishing corners of Dutch universities, and steam power and factories came later to the Netherlands than to most other countries in Europe (Davids 1995; Feingold 1996). Surpluses led nowhere.

Similarly, it may be that the growth of the national state accompanied the development of modern industrial economies. But is that cause and effect? How much growth of state power is productive of modern economic growth – and how much is too much? Hall (1985) argued that despotic Eastern empires either were too arbitrary, or too extractive, or both, to permit modern economic growth. But Mann tells us that prior to the sixteenth and seventeenth centuries, European states were too tiny and too weak to coordinate national markets, integrate their societies and provide a spur to productive techniques. Apparently, sometime in the sixteenth to eighteenth centuries, some European states got it 'just right'. But how do we know this, except by attesting the coincidence of state and economic growth? Might it be that modern economies emerged *despite*, rather than because of, the growth of modern states?

After all, the state in Prussia and France seems modern, but Germany's economic modernization lagged a century behind that of Britain. Mann suggests that constitutional states, such as Britain and the Netherlands, had advantages for growth relative to absolutist states. But we have just seen that this did the Netherlands no good. Why Britain? For that matter, if the growth of the modern state and the modern economy are truly 'European' processes, and not the outcome of aberrant British exceptionalism, why does so much of Europe fail to develop modern national states until the twentieth century? After all, 'Britain' (with its imperial Irish possession of an ethnically distinct population, plus Scotland) was not a nation-state but a multinational empire that broke up with Irish independence in the early twentieth century. Germany and Austria-Hungary were run as empires until 1914, as was Russia until 1991. If we want to find an early case of the nation-state, providing nationally integrated markets, internal peace and a nationally unified elite, we would find it first in Japan after the Tokugawa unification in the early 1600s. And we do find considerable economic growth under the Tokugawa regime. But there is no trace of modern industrialization until after the Western introduction of new networks of power in the late nineteenth century.

Finally, if there is a solid foundation for the overall story that European modernization emerged in an unusual dynamic of accumulation and growth sometime from 1000 to 1500 AD, then there should be some evidence by 1800 or so of the effects of the dynamic. That is, the leading areas of the European economy should be showing greater levels of either consumption, or of surplus production, or of trade, or – if starting from a lower level than other regions – of rates of economic growth than other regions of the world. Yet in fact – and again, this is an empirical question hinging on historical *comparisons* – no such evidence can be found. I believe this calls into question *all* the theories of the emergence of modernity listed above, from North, Brenner, Hall, Landes and Mann. After all, if there is no evidence for any advantages to Europe either in rates of economic growth or levels of economic consumption or production as late as 1800, why bother with any arguments pointing to factors that supposedly set in motion substantial advantages accruing to Europe many centuries earlier?

The comparative method and evidence

Mann is quite correct that it is false reification to isolate separate 'societies' and compare them *as wholes*. Populations in various regions of the world were connected by trade, conquest and communication. Religions, commodities and empires moved across vast expanses of lands and population without much regard for natural or created boundaries. Yet we can still compare specific characteristics of the populations living in different areas in order to test the assertions developed from process-tracing undertaken in studies of one region.[2]

I mentioned above the emphasis that Mann places on the medieval expansion of productivity through harnessing animal power (using new harness and plough technology) and water power. He states 'in global terms, moreover, it probably gave western Europe a decisive agricultural edge over Asia and particularly over Chinese intensive rice-cultivation techniques'. Yet how do we know this is true if we do not compare?

First, how large was the increase in productivity? We can try to measure this directly, in terms of output per seed, or per acre, or labourer. Or we can try to measure this indirectly, in terms of the expected effects of accumulating an agricultural surplus: urbanization, or consumption of manufactured and/or imported goods.

Mann himself gives data in terms of seed ratios (yield in grains harvested per grains sown) for various times and places. He noted that in the second century AD, Roman agronomists offered the following estimates for yield ratios: from 8:1 to 10:1 in Sicily; from 10:1 to 15:1 in Etruria; and 4:1 for Italy as a whole (1986: 265). By comparison, England in the thirteenth century had a yield ratio of 3.7:1, France of 3:1. We do not know how representative these figures are for these regions as a whole – we are dealing with surviving records, not ideal random samples. But it seems that medieval yields were comparable to that of average Roman yields for Italy as a whole. By the seventeenth century, yields for England and the Netherlands are up to 7:1. In other words, they have roughly doubled in the period from 1200 to 1700. Is that evidence of exceptional dynamism? The yield level achieved is still less than the yield ratios reported for Roman Sicily – an area, I hasten to point out, as large as the Netherlands. Moreover, the growth rate is not impressive. If crop yields continued to grow at this rate – doubling every 500 years – we would still today be harvesting only 50 per cent more per seed sown than our eighteenth-century forebears. Hardly an adequate basis for modern civilization!

But perhaps what matters is that growth began – surely it could accelerate later? What of the urbanization and consumption effects of even modest increases in agricultural surpluses that could spur even more growth? Here again, comparisons are most illuminating.

Comparisons of Europe and China are often downplayed by Mann as comparing apples and oranges. After all, the Chinese emperors had vast *extensive* power. The displays that dazzled European visitors thus depended on the forcible extraction of very tiny local surpluses from a large and widely dispersed population. An imperial court that was opulent by European standards should not be taken to imply that Chinese society was any more than a vast collection of relatively isolated village 'cells' producing tiny surpluses which were stripped off for imperial and elite use, certainly insufficient to generate large market demand and economic dynamism through consumption. Where the European states and statelets might have less dazzling accumulations of wealth at their apex, they had far superior *intensive* production, spread over their populations, which produced a dynamic of ongoing growth. Or so the argument goes.

Yet comparative evidence simply will not sustain this argument. Recently collected evidence on consumption, production and trade in late eighteenth-century China shows not an involution of impoverished and overcrowded peasants prizing a bare living from the land (that is a late nineteenth-/early twentieth-century portrait). Rather, core regions of both China and India in the eighteenth century show levels of consumption, production, trade and urbanization to match those of the leading regions of Europe.

It is impossible here to summarize the last two decades of research on Chinese agriculture, urbanization, consumption and trade. Fortunately, I do not have to do so: other scholars have begun to provide such syntheses. What I have labelled the 'California school' of comparative sinologists (Wong 1997; Frank 1998; Lee and Wang 1999; Pomeranz 2000a;

2000b) have assembled considerable evidence of high living standards, urbanization and trade in China. Let us offer a few compelling comparisons: Pomeranz (2000a: 39) estimates that *for China as a whole*, calorie consumption in the early eighteenth century was 2,386 calories per adult equivalent per day (1,837 calories per capita per day). This is comparable to English estimates for the mid-*nineteenth* century. This estimate of adequate nutrition is confirmed by estimates of Chinese life-expectancy that are also comparable to English levels *c.* 1750 (Wong 1997: 28; Lavely and Wong 1998; Pomeranz 2000a: 37).

One might well ask how this was possible – certainly Chinese rice-cropping, with its multiple crops per year, was enormously productive in terms of yield per seed planted and per acre farmed, but the intense labour requirements to achieve such production surely would have meant a decreasing output per labourer and per capita; especially as China's population increased from 150 million or so at the mid-seventeenth century to 350 million in 1800 (Lee and Wang 1999: 6, 27).

In fact, estimates by Li (1998) for the Yangzi delta, the area of highest population density and urbanization, with a population larger than that of England and Holland combined *c.* 1750 (over 30 million), suggest that the application of labour to rice paddy land was virtually unchanged for several centuries. People were fed exactly as they were fed in Holland and England – by increasing the application of *capital* to the land to boost output, and by deploying labour in manufacturing (urban and rural) to produce commodities that could be exported in return for more capital and foodstuffs.

Agricultural output can be boosted by farming more land, applying more labour to existing land, or by applying more capital (in the form of irrigation, fertilizer, improved crops, etc.). In China, agriculture was already highly capital-intensive compared to European farming methods by the sixteenth century. Irrigation has long been cited as a major factor in Chinese farming, but in fact the key input in rice-farming in the lower Yangzi was the application of *imported fertilizer*, some 3.3 million tons of cottonseed, rapeseed and soybean cakes per year, *c.* 1750, or roughly 200 pounds of fertilizer *per person per year*.

This fertilizer was obtained in exchange for manufactured products, mainly textiles, produced in the Yangzi delta and exported all over northern and central China. Planting of cotton and mulberry trees (to feed silkworms) displaced local plantings of rice or were interspersed in multiple cropping regimes, greatly raising the value of output per acre. Women were increasingly diverted from adjunct tasks in farming to primary responsibility for the production of silkworms, cocoons and thread. In addition, the products of the Columbian exchange, chiefly potatoes and maize, lifted productivity in marginal regions of China just as they did throughout Europe (Wong 1997; Pomeranz 2000a).

Along with fertilizer and manufactures, grain exports and other bulk items flowed throughout China. Far from a host of isolated village cells with only state extraction to prize resources loose from villages, it appears that internal trade of all sorts in China exceeded that of Europe. Wu Chengming (cited in Pomeranz 2000a: 34) estimated that in the eighteenth century, the long-distance trade in grains annually involved sufficient produce to feed 14 million people; this is more than twenty times the Baltic grain trade in its heyday. And in the eighteenth century, China's largest item of foreign trade was tea, exchanged primarily for European silver. Yet all that tea was grown on land apparently not needed to produce foodstuffs, because the efficiency of Chinese agriculture allowed a large portion of land to be devoted to commercial crops. In fact, in the Yangzi delta c. 1750, Pomeranz (2000a: 329) has assembled acreage data by prefecture that shows that of roughly 52 million acres in cultivation, over 50 per cent were devoted to non-grain crops. Again, this is in a region with a population of over 30 million!

Trade and grain surpluses flowed to large urban markets. Many cities in China – and elsewhere in Asia – were larger than any European city before 1800 (Elvin 1973). In the mid-seventeenth century, when London is credited with beginning to spur a national market (Wrigley 1967), its population was 400,000. At the same time, the chief commercial city of the Yangzi delta, Nanjing, had over a million inhabitants, and Beijing, the imperial capital, perhaps 600,000. By 1800, another commercial city in southern China, Guangzhou (Canton), and its neighbouring sister city Foshan had a million-and-a-half residents (Frank 1998: 109). The Yangzi delta (today home to Shanghai) was in fact an urbanized zone similar to Holland or southwest England, dotted with major cities such as Hangzhou, Huzhou, Jiangning, Ningbo and many smaller towns in addition to Nanjing. As an aside, we should note that China was not unique in this respect. The core regions of India and Japan were also highly urbanized. In 1757, Robert Clive remarked regarding Murshidabad, the old capital of Bengal, that 'This city is as extensive, populous and rich as the city of London, with this difference: that there were individuals in the former possessing infinitely greater property than in the latter.' Much the same could have been said of Lahore, Agra and Delhi (Goody 1996: 13).

What we see in the Yangzi delta in the eighteenth century is a prosperous society, at its foundation propelled by the enterprise of peasant households in private markets, producing manufactured products for sale in national markets, and engaged in agriculture that was capital-intensive and dependent on imported purchased inputs.

Mann places considerable emphases on the dispersion of surpluses and demand to peasant households in England as creating the foundation for demand-led growth. So we should note that the consumption of Yangzi delta peasant households also matched or exceeded European levels, and that consumption was surging. While many peasants wore ramie and hemp garments in the seventeenth century, by the eighteenth century they had switched to cotton and silk; Pomeranz has shown that in the lower Yangzi cotton cloth consumption per capita *c.* 1750 was nearly as high as that in England in 1870 (Pomeranz 2000a: 141). Household furnishings – benches, tables, mirrors, beds, chests – also were comparable to that in Western European probate inventories (Pomeranz 2000a: 145). Consumption of non-necessities, such as sugar, tea and tobacco, also met or even exceeded advanced European levels.

It should also be recalled that heavy-ploughing of deep soils for wheat is in many ways an inefficient system of agriculture compared to rice (or even loess-soil dry) paddy farming. Deep ploughing requires lots of animal power – and those animals need to be housed and fed, using up valuable resources. Devoting large areas to pasture for horses and cattle and sheep was unnecessary in lowland China, where waterways gave cheaper and easier transport than the horse-drawn cart, something that England would only match after its canal craze in the late eighteenth century. Nor did absence of draft animals mean that Chinese families lacked protein in their diet or manure for their fields – keeping chicken and pigs and innumerable fish ponds meant more and higher-quality manure for fields and adequate protein for diets, at the cost of far less land and labour than keeping large field animals (Pomeranz 2000a).

In pointing to the origins of the Industrial Revolution, Mann emphasizes the role of demand and mass-consumption of three key commodities: cotton textiles, iron products and pottery. I lack data on Chinese iron production and consumption *c.* 1800, but for cotton and pottery the information we have is compelling. Of course, much Yangzi textile output was exported beyond the area, so the following figures are not all local consumption; but of course this was also true of British cotton output, and is all the more evidence of a mass-market demand to be satisfied by large-scale production. Pomeranz (2000a: 333), drawing on a variety of sources, estimates annual silk and cotton textile output in the Yangzi delta *c.* 1750 (not raw thread, but textiles) as 2 pounds per person per year of silk, and 14 pounds per person per year of cotton. This is rather more than the *total* per capita output of cotton, wool, silk and linen together for the United Kingdom in 1800 (12.9 pounds per year). Since the Yangzi delta's population in this period was about twice that of the UK, the total output in this region was far, far larger. Yet despite the size and growth of this market (recall that in the seventeenth century, hemp and ramie were dominant textiles, so that this market in silk and cotton was a newly emerging mass-production and export market roughly double the size of that in Britain), we do not find the further development of technology and power that is attested to flow naturally from the momentum of growth in Europe.

Similarly, in regard to pottery, Josiah Wedgewood's development of mass production for ceramics to supply English demand in the late eighteenth century is often remarked upon as a striking departure in the direction of market-driven mass production. But compare this description of the China's major ceramic works in the seventeenth century: the works at Jingdezhen imported vast quantities of refined cobalt oxide (to provide the blue colour) 6,000 kilometres from the Middle East, produced customized wares in patterns and shapes for Islamic lands, and shipped boatloads of ceramics to India, Europe and the Ottoman empire. Much of this development was prompted by Muslim merchants, who 'probably were responsible for the great investment of capital that transformed the privately owned kilns of Jingdezhen into well-organized industrial complexes controlled by commercial syndicates' (Finlay 1998: 155).

In sum, it is difficult to find substantiation in *comparative* evidence for the claims made in regard to early exceptional European economic momentum developed in the course of the *historical* process-tracing undertaken by Mann.

Another type of power

There is yet another type of power that I believe was responsible for the rise of the West, and it is hardly touched on by Mann's work. That is the power of knowledge. In his latest work on 'Modernity and Globalization' (Mann 2000) he does explicitly include as one element of the 'power institutions' of modernity 'Secular rational science' (2000: table 1). Yet despite this prominent mention, the rise of science plays only a minor supporting role in his longer-term story. It is simply one more kind of ideological power, arising out of the Enlightenment, grafted onto the already-surging momentum of economic growth swelling up from the Middle Ages and taken up by the emerging states and economic classes in their efforts to expand. At times, it disappears into the more diffuse process of 'rationalization' of organization, effort and thought noted by Weber. There is little appreciation of the special role of knowledge in differentiating the West from the rest. Of course, in Mann's view, knowledge simply couldn't play a key role, since he argues that economic momentum in the West became exceptional well before 1500, at a time when even Eurocentric scholars acknowledge that both the Orient and Islam far exceeded Europe in their knowledge of science and technology.

However, I hope the above comparative evidence makes it plausible that claims of exceptional European economic growth prior to 1800 must be greeted with considerable scepticism. It seems to me that we must look for some power effect that: (1) occurs after 1800; and (2) is geographically concentrated in Britain, in order to explain the rise of modern industrial society. I say this because there is no evidence of economic divergence between Europe and China before 1800, and because even after 1800 large-scale industrialization of all productive and transport processes develops in Britain at least a half-century ahead of its development elsewhere on the continent, even a century ahead of such clearly European regions as Iberia, Italy and Eastern Europe. Thus whatever happened to create the emergence of the modern world happened relatively late, and – at least on this Mann and I agree – it happened first in Great Britain.

I will not belabour what I feel is the answer to this problem here, as I have dealt with it elsewhere at length (Goldstone 1987; 1998; 2000; 2002a; 2002b). In brief, what happened was more a matter of *innovation* than of accumulation. Britain and Europe indeed experienced growth in the high Middle Ages; but so too did many other parts of the globe. Europe developed cities, large-scale trade, rising consumer surpluses and powerful states in the sixteenth to eighteenth centuries, but not as much as some other societies in other regions of the world. England developed the steam engine and applied it to mining, textile production, iron and steel production, and transportation from 1700 to 1800. No other society in any region of the globe or any era of history had ever done anything of the sort.

The steam engine was not just another technological innovation, like the spinning jenny or rolling and puddling process. It was different in at least three key respects. First, the latter inventions, like many others, applied to specific processes and industries. They were not generally transformative. Improve cotton-spinning and weaving technology all you like – it will not do much to improve the efficiency of agriculture or transportation. Steam engines, however (like water mills or windmills in this respect), were a general-purpose technology that could increase productivity in every aspect of production and transport. Steam engines pumped out coal and transported it, making heat energy more cheaply available to produce bricks for construction and tiles for draining lands; steam engines operated digging and hauling and transport machinery to move everything from fertilizers to finished products to market more cheaply than before; steam engines powered factory machinery to speed up production of products from iron to cotton.

Second, the steam engine allowed societies to tap a wholly new source of energy, or at least to do so in new ways (Malanima 2001). Prior to the steam engine, one could produce motive energy only by harnessing something else that already moved: animals, people, wind, water. One could burn coal, charcoal, or other fuels, but that only produced heat. The steam engine allowed one to take combustion energy (from wood, charcoal and, most usefully, coal) and convert that into *motive* energy. This was a breakthrough unprecedented in history. Wrigley (1988) and Pomeranz (2000a) have treated coal as valuable for providing an alternative heat source to wood/ charcoal, and thus saving forests. Millions of acres would have been required to produce the heat energy available from underground coal. But this is only part of the story – other societies that ran into fuel shortages have found other ways to manage their needs for producing heat energy, from conserving and replanting forests to burning other organic materials. It is not the heat produced by coal that made it critical to England's future, but the *motive power* produced by coal when harnessed to steam engines. Steam engines, in fact, were so inefficient that over 95 per cent of the heat energy of the coal was lost – Britain might as well have left its coal in the ground if 95 per cent of its heat energy was being wasted! But even that 5 per cent gave Britain an incredible mechanical advantage in *intensive* power, in the ability to concentrate large amounts of motive power, far beyond what water wheels or animal power could produce in a confined space.

Third, steam engines, and their efficient operation and deployment, were simply inconceivable without modern science. Knowledge of vacuums, measurement of pressure and hydraulic flow, the ability to calculate specific heats, the ability to calculate quantities of work produced from a given amount of fuel – all were essential to build, operate and efficiently deploy steam engines in production (Jacob and Reid 2001). It is no accident that our modern technical terms for power (watt), force (newton) and work (joule) are all named after Englishmen, for it was there that the science of power was first developed. Certainly, modern science was a pan-European development, with roots throughout the continent, and indeed more accurately a global development with roots in Indian and Islamic mathematics and astronomy as well as Greek philosophy. Yet the particular development of science into power engineering was only undertaken in Britain; in this respect we have the late and uniquely British advent of a new type of power (literally) that ushered in the modern industrial age.

Of course, there are complexities here that I am hurdling over: the marriage of science with entrepreneurship; the role of religious pluralism and toleration in conducing to innovation and entrepreneurial risk-taking;

the role of an emerging democratic society in spreading the aptitude and rewards for education and innovation. I have mentioned these elsewhere in my work (Goldstone 1987; 2002a; 2002b), but they deserve more extensive treatment. These elements are parts of the overlapping power networks of ideology and politics that Mann rightly features, and that remain important elements of the emergence of the modern world. I therefore would not claim that a focus on the emergence of knowledge as power, through science harnessed to power engineering, was sufficient to explain the emergence of modernity. However, I do believe it is a necessary element of any such explanation, and it is an element that Mann's theory largely overlooks.

In truth, one cannot contend that Mann neglects the power of knowledge in his work. Knowledge of agriculture, of how to smelt iron and craft iron weapons and tools, of how to capture water power for useful work, of how to increase the output of heavy soils, and how to structure state finances and credit markets, all play a role in the development of networks of power and the formation of states and economies. Yet such knowledge seems to come in somewhat at random, transforming power networks yet not being part of their dynamic. It may be that, prior to the scientific revolution, we can only treat such major leaps in knowledge as exogenous, episodic interruptions of prior equilibria.

After 1750, the power of knowledge no longer simply erupts periodically at random around the world. Modern science and engineering not only transform our understanding of nature and our ability to shape it; they transform the process of knowledge acquisition itself. Scientific enquiry – refuting common sense, and basing true belief on engines of measurement and testing of nature (Carroll-Burke 2001) – becomes a uniquely productive way of increasing and aggregating knowledge that provides useful power (Mokyr 2002). Indeed, as Mann seems to hint in his latest work, by the nineteenth century, the deliberate expansion and utilization of scientific knowledge is a critical characteristic of modern societies. This process may have its roots in medieval universities and artisanal tinkering. Yet by the nineteenth century it is no longer a mere general extension of rationalization and premodern thought. It is a new source of power that is inherent in modern societies – and a continuous power source that transforms military and economic, as well as ideological and political, power in the direction of modernity.

Conclusion

Michael Mann's theory of social power marks a major advance over many of its predecessors in decentring 'society', and in exploring the interactions of distinct types of power, and their historical development along several dimensions. In this regard, he has made a lasting contribution to social theory. His method of historical process-tracing of changes in the patterns of power deployment over time has provided valuable insights into the development of states, economies and stratification systems.

Yet this method is limited by its self-conscious choice not to test its findings through directed comparisons across cases. Such comparisons raise scepticism about some of Mann's assertions regarding key moments in the emergence of modernity. Combining historical *and* comparative methods may yield more clues to exactly how the modern world developed.

In particular, the old saw 'knowledge is power' may reflect more than just Mann's contention that manipulating ideological power in a social network is a source of power comparable to that wielded by military, economic and political authorities. Rather, the emergence of modernity seems to depend on a new kind of knowledge, and a new approach to the production and deployment of knowledge, that had no precedent. Modern scientific knowledge and its ongoing production and expansion seems to be a unique power in its own right, which played a critical role in the emergence and development of modernity.

Notes

1 Mann also provides yet another power distinction – between authoritative (consciously exercised) and diffused (spontaneous or background) forms of power (1986: 8–9). But Mann makes much less use of this in tracing the historical development of social relations, focusing much more on authoritative power in the military and political realms. However, in economic and ideological power, diffused power relations are more important, especially before the development of well-defined economic classes and religious hierarchies.
2 Indeed, I have argued that the virtues of comparative/historical sociology are best shown when both process-tracing and cross-case comparisons are brought to bear on problems of explanation (Goldstone 1997).

References

Ashton, T. S. 1948. *The Industrial Revolution, 1760–1830*. Oxford: Oxford University Press.
Brenner, R. 1976. Agrarian Class Structure and Economic Development in Pre-industrial Europe. *Past and Present*, 70.
Carroll-Burke, P. 2001. Tools, Instruments, and Engines: Getting a Handle on the Specificity of Engine Science. *Social Studies of Science*, 31(5).
Crafts, N. F. R., and C. K. Harley. 1992. Output Growth and the Industrial Revolution: A Restatement of the Crafts–Harley View. *Economic History Review*, 45.

Crosby, A. 1997. *The Measure of Reality: Quantification and Western Society 1250–1600*. Cambridge: Cambridge University Press.

Davids, K. 1995. Shifts of Technological Leadership in Early Modern Europe. In K. Davids and J. Lucassen (eds.), *A Miracle Mirrored: The Dutch Republic in European Perspective*. Cambridge: Cambridge University Press.

De Vries, J. 2000. Dutch Economic Growth in Comparative Historical Perspective, 1500–2000. *De Economist*, 148(4).

Elvin, M. 1973. *The Pattern of the Chinese Past*. Stanford: Stanford University Press.

Feingold, M. 1996. Reversal of Fortunes: The Displacement of Cultural Hegemony from the Netherlands to England in the Seventeenth and early Eighteenth Centuries. In D. Hoak and M. Feingold (eds.), *The World of William and Mary: Anglo-Dutch Perspectives on the Revolution of 1688–89*. Stanford: Stanford University Press.

Finlay, R. 1998. The Pilgrim Art: The Culture of Porcelain in World History. *Journal of World History*, 9.

Frank, A. G. 1998. *Reorient: Global Economy in the Asian Age*. Berkeley and Los Angeles: University of California Press.

Goldstone, J. A. 1987. Cultural Orthodoxy, Risk, and Innovation: The Divergence of East and West in the Early Modern World. *Sociological Theory*, 5.

  1997. Methodological Issues in Comparative Macrosociology. *Comparative Social Research*, 16.

  1998. The Problem of the 'Early Modern' World. *Journal of the Economic and Social History of the Orient*, 41.

  2000. The Rise of the West – or Not? A Revision to Socio-economic History. *Sociological Theory*, 18.

  2002a. Europe's Peculiar Path: Would the World be 'Modern' if William III's Invasion of England in 1688 had Failed? In N. Lebow, G. Parker and P. Tetlock (eds.), *Counterfactual History*. New York: Columbia University Press.

  2002b. Efflorescences and Economic Growth in World History: Rethinking the 'Rise of the West' and the Industrial Revolution. *Journal of World History*, 13.

  2002c. Comparative-Historical Analysis and Knowledge Accumulation in the Study of Revolutions. In D. Reuschemeyer and J. Mahoney (eds.), *Comparative Historical Analysis in the Social Sciences*. Cambridge: Cambridge University Press.

Goody, J. 1996. *The East in the West*. Cambridge: Cambridge University Press.

Hall, J. A. 1985. *Powers and Liberties: The Causes and Consequences of the Rise of the West*. New York: Oxford University Press.

Jacob, M., and D. Reid. 2001. Technical Knowledge and the Mental Universe of Manchester's Early Cotton Manufacturers. *Canadian Journal of History*, 36.

Landes, D. 1998. *The Wealth and Poverty of Nations*. New York: W. W. Norton.

Lavely, W., and R. B. Wong. 1998. Revising the Malthusian Narrative: The Comparative Study of Population Dynamics in Late Imperial China. *Journal of Asian Studies*, 57.

Lee, J., and F. Wang. 1999. *One Quarter of Humanity: Malthusian Mythology and Chinese Realities*. Cambridge, MA: Harvard University Press.

282   European exceptionalism?

Levine, D. 2001. *At the Dawn of Modernity*. Berkeley and Los Angeles: University of California Press.
Li, B. 1998. *Agricultural Development in Jiangnan, 1620–1850*. New York: St Martin's Press.
Malanima, P. 2001. The Energy Basis for Early Modern Growth, 1650–1820. In M. Prak (ed.), *Early Modern Capitalism*. London: Routledge.
Mann, M. 1984. The Autonomous Power of the State: Its Nature, Causes and Consequences. *Archives Européennes de Sociologie*, 25.
Mann, M. A. 1986. *The Sources of Social Power, Volume I: A History from the Beginning to 1760 AD*. Cambridge: Cambridge University Press.
    2000. Modernity and Globalization. Unpublished, given as the Wiles Lectures at Queen's University, Belfast.
Mokyr, J. 1999 (2nd edn). *The British Industrial Revolution*. Boulder, CO: Westview.
    2002. *Gifts of Athena*. Princeton: Princeton University Press.
North, D. 1981. *Structure and Change in Economic History*. New York: W. W. Norton.
Pomeranz, K. 2000a. *The Great Divergence: China, Europe, and the Making of the Modern World Economy*. Princeton, NJ: Princeton University Press.
    2000b. Re-thinking the Late Imperial Chinese Economy: Development, Disaggregation and Decline, circa 1730–1930. *Itinerario*, 22(3/4).
Skocpol, T., and M. Somers. 1980. The Uses of Comparative History in Macro-social Inquiry. *Comparative Studies in Society and History*, 22.
Von Tunzelmann, G. N. 1978. *Steam Power and British Industrialization to 1860*. Oxford: Oxford University Press.
Wallerstein, I. 1974. *The Modern World System*. New York: Academic Press.
Wong, R. B. 1997. *China Transformed: Historical Change and the Limits of European Experience*. Ithaca, NY: Cornell University Press.
Wrigley, E. A. 1967. A Simple Model of London's Importance in Changing English Society and Economy, 1650–1750. *Past and Present*, 37.
    1988. *Continuity, Chance, and Change*. Cambridge: Cambridge University Press.

Part IV

Promise and perils of modernity

13 The 'British' sources of social power: reflections on history, sociology, and intellectual biography[1]

Frank Trentmann

Britain performs a unique function in Michael Mann's presentation of the dynamics that made the modern world. It stands out, first, as the society that invented a modern state and modern capitalism in the eighteenth century, and then pioneered a viable model of modernization in the following century: a liberal-reformist system, fusing old regime and capitalist middle classes, and later complemented by welfarism. The British model in *The Sources of Social Power* anticipates the patches of light shed by the 'cultural solidarity' of the northwest European liberal democratic bloc in the twentieth century in the dark story of *Fascists* and *The Dark Side of Democracy* (Mann 1986; 1993; 2004; 2005). Through British history Mann traces what is to him the single most important source of the reordering of power in the modern world: the development of the fiscal-military state. It is the eighteenth-century fiscal-military state which produces the interdependence between the global and domestic dimensions of change. It is the state's international actions and the resulting tax burden that politicize people at home and which prestructure the old regime's liberal strategy of modernization. In the nineteenth century, it is a liberal state which drives the 'national caging' of social groups, and which preserves the military, diplomatic and financial power of old aristocratic and new financial elites, causing the crisis of 1914.

The story of the migration of power, away from ideological towards military and economic sources, that is at the heart of Mann's view of modernity is thus a heavily British story. Other societies contribute to the reorganizing of social power and arrive at different modernizing strategies, but Britain came first, not only in the sense of being the first capitalist society, but also in setting in motion a global–domestic dynamic of state expansion that would shape the formation of nation and class. There is also a link of a more immediate intellectual nature between British history and Mann's vision. For, I would suggest, this vision is not only indebted to a particular strand of British historiography, but has elective affinities with an older British radical tradition, that of Tom Paine and John Bright, who, like Mann, had strong roots in Manchester. Next to the obvious influence of Max Weber and Otto Hintze, then, it may be helpful to bear in mind the legacies of British radicalism with its analytical preoccupation with the state as an engine of foreign aggression, domestic overtaxation and corruption, and as a space for old elites to reassert their power.

A critical reading of Mann's use of Britain must not merely engage with historiographical or empirical aspects of British history but discuss these with a view to the more general theoretical ambition of his work and its intellectual sources. One appeal of Michael Mann's work, which has only recently been appreciated by the historical community, is the way in which the story of Britain is intimately connected to global and transnational developments. These connections in Mann's work will be explored in related stages. We shall begin by exploring the causal direction from international power to domestic politics, according to which the state's activities abroad create political culture at home and the national 'caging' of society. The view of the state is intimately linked to a strong 'radical' view of social and political relations, in which the state is less an autonomous institution than a space through which a united old elite acquire disproportionate historical agency, exercising power over a relatively impotent and divided people. It is a strong (and pessimist) version of a 'radical' vision of history, because it lacks the populist optimism of its radical ancestors who invoked a future in which 'the people' would emancipate themselves from statist oppression. It neglects civil society's internal generation of social power in the eighteenth and nineteenth centuries. The 'decline' of Britain in the twentieth century in Mann's work illustrates the contemporary legacy of the power crystallization of the old regime and the unbroken hold of elites on society (Mann 1988).

The explanation of British modernization exemplifies the strengths and weaknesses of Mann's organizational view of ideas (focusing on who controls literary communication) instead of a cultural understanding of ideas and values (concerned with meaning and sentiment) underlying collective identities and actions. A short discussion of the role of ideas and culture will return us to the spatial attraction of Mann's approach: the interdependence between international power relations and the national caging of societies. Curiously, the Empire plays only a marginal role in Mann's explanation of British modernization and European modernity more generally. Yet, the reshaping of social power within European societies did not merely play out a process first set in motion in global military struggles but was an intrinsic part of the simultaneous creation of imperial expansion and imperial culture.

In the last decade, the 'fiscal-military state' has become a central actor in histories of modern Britain, yet few cite Mann's work. Ironically, the reasons for the partial reception of Mann's conceptual insight reflect the very success of the term in eighteenth-century historiography. Such was the success of John Brewer's synthetic *Sinews of Power* (1989) – which popularized the term, partly drawing on Mann's essay on 'The autonomous power of the state' (1986) – that few historians since have bothered to engage with Mann's original and ambitious argument about the centrality of the fiscal-military state in the modernization of Britain. It is therefore entirely appropriate to use this occasion to accord Mann the recognition he deserves and to restore the fiscal-military state to its full meaning. Like Brewer, Mann emphasized the unique size and modernity of the British state, its efficiency and its administrative innovation. As opposed to earlier images of an archaic oligarchic system, an old elite here produced highly modern instruments of state power. Likewise, both studies highlight the inflationary fiscal-military cycle of foreign war leading to ever higher taxes and increasingly efficient modes of extraction as the main dynamic of state-building, a point first made by Otto Hintze before World War I. What is equally revealing are the differences. Brewer focuses on the century between the Glorious Revolution and the French Revolution. Mann traces the dynamic back to the high Middle Ages (1986: ch. 13). Furthermore, he sees the evolution of a powerful fiscal-military state in the eighteenth century as the engine of the transformation of domestic power relations, shifting the people from their apolitical everyday lives onto the track of popular politics, then pushing an old regime in crisis onto the liberal track of modernization, one rail laid by electoral reform and liberal constitutionalism, the other by the 'petite bourgeoisie' and its programme of liberal political economy. The British state now begins to order a very 'messy' society of overlapping and transnational group networks and identities, increasingly (though never perfectly) 'caging' it into nation and classes.

Much more so than in the now commonplace references to the fiscal-military state in the eighteenth century, Mann offers a master-narrative of the development of modern society. The state is the heroic agent of modernity – not class or nation as in earlier socialist and nationalist narratives. This is a welcome addition to the cast of historical characters. It avoids the economism that had characterized much social history, without falling into the originary trap of older national sagas. Similarly, our principal actor and the drama it unfolds is more complex and ambiguous than earlier populist master-narratives, be they socialist or Whig. Liberty and welfarism, far from being the result of a national elite's talent for liberty or the achievement of a working class, appear as products of the state's aggression abroad and the extraordinary and regressive fiscal extraction needed to fund it. Even the avoidance of genocide, Mann has argued more recently, was achieved only at the cost of Britain becoming a class society, in which class differences helped to cut across ethnic divisions.[2] This ambivalent picture of modernity can accommodate some of the criticisms levied against more monochromatic pictures offered in the 1980s, such as J. C. D. Clark's portrayal of Britain as an '*ancien régime*' (1985), which ignores the modernizing features of the eighteenth-century state and commercial society. Unlike conservative and socialist narratives of modernity, then, Mann's is attractive because it creates a conceptual bridge between the aristocratic and commercial world of the eighteenth century and the liberal industrial society of the nineteenth and twentieth centuries. It can be read as an institutional complement to the emphasis on continuities between the eighteenth and nineteenth centuries developed by historians of ideas and popular politics (Winch 1978; Stedman Jones 1983; Pocock 1985; Biagini 1992; Bevir and Trentmann 2002). Framing this development by putting international relations and domestic regime strategies together, moreover, considerably widens the scope of influences on liberal ideas. In this sense, Mann can be read as a statist complement to Tuck's recent argument (1999) that Western liberal notions of the sovereign individual played out earlier ideas about the sovereign state in an aggressive international climate.

How much of this interpretive burden can the British state bear? The significance of war and taxes in the decades after 1688 is beyond debate, and so is the unique efficiency of the British fiscal state and the uniquely high fiscal cost to eighteeenth-century Britons, especially consumers (O'Brien 1988). But what about the general primacy Mann has accorded to the state in the modernization of politics and society? Mann's strong argument about the state is underpinned by an equally strong view of the oligarchic, apolitical nature of British society between the Glorious Revolution and the French Revolution. Britain appears as a stable society ruled by an integrated ruling class, a nobility and gentry headed by a monarch. It is only in the late eighteenth and early nineteenth centuries that the expansion of the fiscal-military state finally pushed people to voice their grievances in a new language of politics. Before the late eighteenth century, the 'state and class had mattered little to most people' (Mann 1993: 116). Indeed, people in general, in Mann's view, are apolitical animals, preferring to be left alone: it is the state that forces them to demand political rights. In eighteenth-century Britain, they were mainly illiterate and incapable of organizing themselves. The vast majority of their actions, Mann insists, were spontaneous and 'apolitical', like most food riots (121). And even here, the roots of politics are in the state. 'Military-fiscal extraction drove forward a political and national class struggle' (Mann 1993). The whole battle over the franchise, Mann is confident, would have left the British people cold, if their economic lives as producers and consumers had not been trampled upon, and if working combinations had been granted (620).

The strong view of the fiscal-military state, then, combines an active view of an old regime elite, coordinating power relations through the state almost effortlessly, with a reactive view of politics, popular politics in particular. It presumes a long-term causation of state expansion (on the global stage of military violence) spilling over into domestic grievances, political unrest and the formation of nationhood.

Yet, politics and nationalism were active as well as reactive factors, both within and without Parliament. Surely, one dynamic driving the expansion of the British imperial state was a popular Protestant nationalism (Pincus 1996). By the 1740s, the language of liberty and patriotism had been welded together with a popular, masculine imperialism into a new kind of mass politics that turned Admiral Vernon (the victor of Porto Bello) and the Duke of Cumberland (the victor of Culloden) into popular heroes (Wilson 1995). In the late eighteenth century, loyalism was a mass movement (Colley 1992). In short, one reason for the tremendous success of the fiscal-military state was that many people (not all people, but not just elites either) supported Empire, Church and King. Popular politics was not a reaction to a state project, it was a constitutive part of it.

A similar process of interweaving can be found in the formation of the nation. Mann distinguishes between proto-nation and the genuine article, distinguished by its link to the state, which in the nineteenth century begins to cage a messy society into a class-nation. This distinction and periodization becomes complicated, however, once our focus shifts to Protestantism and how it defined national interests and fuelled the geopolitical activities of the state. The transatlantic civil war in the 1760s–70s, that led to the United States of America and a new British imperial state in the process, for example, can be viewed as conflict between rival forms of Protestantism, between Anglicanism and nonconformist denominations that acted as vehicles of different identities and traditions of authority (Clark 1994). By the eighteenth century, English national identity could draw on a long and diverse set of traditions – from medieval conceptions of dynasty and law to early modern Protestantism and ethnic conceptions of the colonized other (Spenser 1633; Canny 1998; Clark 2000). It was not a mere by-product of state formation.

Mann's use of the 'old regime' reflects the preoccupation of his larger sociological theory with secular modernity – and its blindspots. The geopolitical interest in a secular state blends out many other dimensions of state and government. Contemporaries would have been surprised to see it almost exclusively analysed as a secular state, rather than a confessional state which was, after all, created out of a popular rebellion against a king (James II) with Catholic ambitions; equally, dissenters would have found the link between their demand for religious toleration and civil liberties underemphasized. Mann's larger view of secularization as part of modernity is also at odds with the renewed centrality of religion in nineteenth-century Britain and continental Europe. A 'fundamental secularism [characterized] modern European civilization', we are told. Religion lost 'much of its capacity for social organization to secular power sources and to a predominantly secular European culture' (Mann 1986: 471). The indifference to religion is part of a larger abandonment of ideology by Mann as an analytical category of power in the modern period.

The distinction between despotic and infrastructural power was a tremendously simple but powerful insight of Mann's *Sources of Social Power*. The fiscal-military state is low on the first and high on the second, but only when it comes to waging war and financing it. This leaves an obvious question. Who or what agency holds power in domestic relations not touched by this geopolitically oriented state? In volume one, Mann noted in passing that the British constitutional and French absolutist regimes 'were subtypes of a single form of state: a weak state in relation to the powerful groups of civil society, but a state that increasingly coordinated those groups' activities to the point where we may begin to talk of an organic class-nation whose central point was either the court or the court/parliament of the state' (1986: 481). Recent historical research, by contrast, has moved towards a view of power in eighteenth-century Britain based on coordination between diverse social and political groups. Whereas Mann emphasizes the central state as the knowing agent which initiates and controls coordination, historians have viewed coordination partly as a sign of the vulnerability and dependence of state actors. Parliamentary and extra-parliamentary politics and public scrutiny offered significant arenas for a wide range of groups to criticize and control the workings of the state. If the Hanoverian state often managed to extract the resources it needed, then, this was partly because it was willing to listen to a growing volume of public voices (Hoppit 2002). An older view of eighteenth-century politics as an increasingly restrictive system dominated by an increasingly unrepresentative oligarchy has been toppled by studies finding reciprocity, mutual recognition, openness and high degrees of contestation in elections and local government (O'Gorman 1989; Rogers 1989; Goldie 2001).

The connection between 'old regime' and fiscal-military state moves Mann away from exploring the dynamics of power coordination. Mann's view of Hanoverian England is ultimately that of a top-down society, perhaps best summarized in his verdict that '[t]he nation *was* a class', a tiny elite meeting in the Houses of Parliament (Mann 1986: 469). This approach reflects perhaps the influence of two separate strands of British historiography: Plumb's argument of the return of stability (1967) and Namier's older view of self-interested elite politics (1929). It overrates the coherence and power of the old regime alliance of aristocracy, gentry and merchant oligarchy. To be fair, Mann is careful to introduce the 'old regime', 'the British ruling class in 1760', as a 'label [that] is not meant to indicate great homogeneity; its politics were factionalized' (Mann 1993: 97). Yet, as with Namier, old regime politics is personalized politics: it is about ins and outs. Little is heard here about urban politics, the conflict between Whigs and Tories or Court and Country, Jacobites and anti-Jacobites and the very different strategies of order and state expansion they were championing, such as the heated debates about Empire and the conflict between a Eurocentric and a navalist blue-water strategy. These conflicts had broad social dimensions to them, in which popular pressure was exerted on elites and in which elites tried to manage or court public politics.

Mann's view of the 'old regime' as a collective actor also structures the argument about its successful survival in the nineteenth century. After successfully adapting itself to capitalism in the early modern period, the 'old regime' masters the socio-economic and political challenges of the modern period by adopting a 'liberal' strategy of modernization in alliance with the 'upper petite bourgeoisie'. The old regime harnesses the twin forces of modernity: state and capitalism. In 'old regime liberalism' new bourgeois groups become their junior partners. Once firmly in place, the updated liberal version of the old regime sees a crystallization of earlier systemic practices and power habits. The Victorian period, and in many ways the twentieth century as well, is thus marked less by change of regime than by a change in personnel, as financial and mercantile elites (the City) come to complement older landed elites in positions of power. Just as with the old elites in the eighteenth century, so with the 'gentlemanly capitalists' in the nineteenth and twentieth centuries: it is their decisions which determine the structure of British society and economy and its global face of Free Trade and the gold standard. World War I, for Mann, is not an erratic accident but the systemic outcome of 'old regime liberalism'. Financial elites pursued their capitalist interests while an older elite monopolized diplomatic and military institutions and discourses of power. Note, this division of labour is again premised on the passivity and impotence of the people and on an exclusionary picture of party politics. The 'Liberal party', Mann emphasizes, 'was a party of notables, not a social movement' (Mann 1993: 620). The working classes only 'stumbled' onto a reformist path eventually because they were pushed by the action of state and capitalist elites, just as they had earlier stumbled onto the liberal demand for the vote because of the fiscal-military state. Even then, the politicization of the people retained traces of apathy, most notably, according to Mann, an inward-looking preoccupation with domestic affairs that left foreign politics solidly in the hands of an old elite.

From an analytical perspective, Mann's view of modern Britain here is distinguished by the parallel working of two sets of spatial and social power relations. One set illustrates his overall thesis of the ways in which geopolitical state actions create national societies. The other set is about how the British old regime manages to obscure the systemic linkage between global and domestic power relations and monopolize the control of the former by separating it from the latter. In a similar vein, the financial elite continues to get away with global economic policies that spell 'decline', poverty and unemployement for twentieth-century Britons (Mann 1988). There are, of course, good academic godfathers of this view, especially Joseph Schumpeter (1943), who highlighted the staying power of the aristocracy in imperial, military and diplomatic positions of power in Victorian Britain, a view developed further by Arno Mayer in *The Persistence of the Old Regime* (1981). Yet these academic sources are perhaps more secondary influences or amplifiers of a deeper, underlying 'radical' view of history in Mann's work that is more home-grown. The emphasis on the corruption of the old regime and how it travelled 'sideways' into the City, the instrumentalist view of elite politics, the ease with which the people are allegedly distracted from the realities of international politics, and, above all, the centrality of taxes as a litmus test of aggression abroad and injustice at home – all these are classic tropes of the English radical tradition. The 'feudal' link between an aggressive state, aristocratic culture and tax-based corruption had been the running theme of Tom Paine and followers. The Chartists believed that parliamentary representation would improve the conditions of the people by severing the connection between aristocratic privilege and tax-funded war and corruption. Manchester became the home of a Victorian extension of this critique. Richard Cobden and John Bright looked to freedom of trade to erase aristocratic control of international affairs and the feudal-militarist culture that came with it. Late Victorian and Edwardian 'new liberals' and radicals, like J. A. Hobson and E. D. Morel, located the springs of the new imperialism in the secretive influences of a few financiers in foreign policy dominated by their aristocratic cousins and in mass media and leisure which kept the people ignorant of their true internationalist interests. Enlightened public opinion and democratic control of foreign affairs continued to be twin aims of radical politics well into the twentieth century.

The principal strength of this tradition is its understanding of the geopolitical foundations of domestic social structures. This remains a fruitful line of enquiry, as, for example, work on the conjuncture between imperial expansion and an aristocratic reassertion of power in early nineteenth-century Britain has shown (Bayly 1989). Mann's radical account of Britain and modernity, however, has a distinctly pessimist flavour. Such is the configuration of power structures moulded by aristo-cratic and financial elites over centuries, and the deep-rooted lack of popular will to change them, that in the essay 'The Decline of Great Britain' (1988) he confronts readers with a catastrophic alternative: a comprehensive collapse of services and manufacturing, or commercial capital and multinationals 'able to go it alone' with unemployment at 20 per cent. Here is the voice of the 'radical' academic writing in the shadow of Thatcherism. This pessimism recalls Cobden at his gloomiest, as in *England, Ireland and America* (1835) where Britain, dominated by feudal elite and expensive interventionism, without the political will to produce a well-educated electorate, threatened to fall behind America. While Mann shares many of the same targets as his radical ancestors (the fiscal-military state, aristocratic corruption, the City), his pessimism arises from a theory of history which lacks their populist narrative of emancipation. Whereas Paine's critique of statism was complemented by a utopian civil society of small self-governing communities (Keane 1988), Mann's historical vision is one of the increasingly extensive and intensive institutionalization of power and the caging of societies – even globalization, he has recently remarked, does not reverse this trend, merely modify it (2000). Mann's, in short, is a 'radical' critique from above. There is no collective actor from below to put the critique into emancipatory practice.

Reading Mann in this intellectual context prompts several related questions. To what degree is the 'radical' view of the enemy (corruption, an old–new–elite nexus, liberal political economy) a helpful tool for analysing historical change? Second, how well does Mann's view of politics without the people map onto the history of modern Britain? Finally, how do we reconcile a vocal radical culture, which focused on the rights of the people and international justice, with Mann's insistence that elite hegemony was based on public indifference to politics and international affairs?

The first question moves us straight to the heart of the thesis that the old regime switched onto the tracks of liberalism in its hour of crisis in the 1830s. Of course, the First Reform Act happened, as did the reform of the poor law and the switch from mercantalism to Free Trade. But what was the dynamic of this switch, and what groups were involved? Here the 'old regime' perhaps suggests much more of a collective actor than most historians would be comfortable with. After all, the split of one socio-political elite formation (the Tories) over Catholic emancipation and Free Trade was a necessary condition for the triumph of liberal reforms. On the other side of the political spectrum, it has been argued, the reforms of the 1830s and 1840s were not triumphs of liberal politics but driven forward by a small coterie of Whig aristocrats who understood themselves as enlightened leaders in the historic mission of regaining public trust in government (Mandler 1990). The old regime was deeply divided, some turning to liberal modernization for survival (though no one envisaged a dynamic industrial growth society), others embracing imperial mercantialism or insular conservatism. New financial and mercantile elites were no less divided in their views on free trade and protection (Howe 1992). Perhaps the City benefited disproportionally from the global economic bias of Victorian and Edwardian Britain, but this does not mean that a 'gentlemanly capitalism' had privileged access to the state at the exclusion of industry, or that it could have functioned without a successful export industry (Daunton 1989; Offer 1999). It is problematic to map sociological groups or economic sectors onto an entire socio-political regime, let alone deduce a regime's historical origins and workings from their costs and benefits (Trentmann 1998).

Complicating our view of 'the old regime' opens an analytical space for popular politics. Earlier we noted the role of popular contestation and affirmation in eighteenth-century politics. Nineteenth-century politics carried echoes of seventeenth- and eighteenth-century ideas but now became a more regularized affair, witnessing the expansion of political mass movements and a new preoccupation with politics in national culture. Mann has a valid point when he repeatedly reminds us that it matters who has political power, and who has not. Yet his organizational concern with politics favours an instrumental concern with the formal control of institutions at the expense of other forms of political communication and contestation. Politics, to Mann, is a black box, or perhaps rather a transparent, neutral instrument coordinating previously existing resources and interests. It is not a process through which social groups, claims or problems acquire and contest interests, identity and legitimacy. Thus, the description of the Liberal party as 'a party of notables' distracts from its tremendous appeal to popular radicals and liberals, and from the political narrative of civil society and emancipation with which its members identify (Biagini 1992; Trentmann 2000/2003). 'So what?' it might be replied. Does an account of popular politics affect Mann's larger argument about old regime liberalism, its origins, sociological composition or policy preference? It does not strictly question the dis-proportionate power of old and new elites, nor does it dispute Mann's observation that the British regime was distinguished by capitalist and older elites' willingness to cooperate rather than enter into conflict with each other. What it does though, is to question the dynamics that gave birth to the liberal regime type and that helped to sustain it – and, in this sense, it points to the need to qualify the apportionment of responsibility and blame for the path of modern British developments. Let us briefly review the evolution of 'old regime liberalism' examining questions of its birth (1832), legitimacy (mid-Victorian fiscal reform) and hegemony (popular Free Trade).

Following standard accounts, Mann portrays the First Reform Act of 1832 as the conscious strategy of an old regime in crisis seeking 'to detach the petite bourgeoisie from the mob' (Mann 1993: 125). This is correct in as far as many Whigs recognized the claim of increasingly prosperous middling groups to representation and hoped to contain more democratic reforms. But this instrumental reading of politics misses the cultural contribution of political debate and mobilization in the formation of social and political interests and identities. For it was only in the agitation for reform that middling groups gradually came to define themselves as a collective actor: 'the middle class' (Steinmetz 1993; Wahrman 1995). Similarly, feminist studies have emphasized that after 1832 workers played an instrumental role in constructing new gender identities by adopting the language of the independent, responsible male citizen to justify their demand for enfranchisement (Clark 1995).[3] Politics, in other words, was not just a set of strategies initiated by the elite which rear-ranged an existing chessboard of players; it transformed the nature of the game, the identity of its participants, what could be said and what imagined to be doable.

This applies to the elite as well, and helps to explain the renewed legitimacy of an elite-dominated government in the mid-Victorian period. The survival of the liberal old regime in Britain in the 1840s – a decade of violence, revolution and famine elsewhere – is not sufficiently explained by the united front of new and old elite. It does not explain why the old regime was not confronted by a succession of systemic crises and attacks but, instead, managed to develop an unprecedented degree of legitimacy. A period of unprecedented tax-relief, as Mann rightly points out, was a lubricant of greater harmony. Yet, why did the elite suddenly choose this strategy, if a united aggressive stance had worked so well in defending its interests? And why a strategy of fiscal retrenchment and reform that ultimately closed the tap of the fiscal-military enterprise which had served the old elite so well in the past? Nor does a tax-cut fully explain why the people forgave the rather unpretty treatment they had received at the hands of a united regime. One answer to these questions centres on the concept of trust. A new generation of elite politicians had emerged (Huskisson, Peel, Gladstone) which turned against mercantilist traditions and privileges and towards a notion of political leadership as responsible for restoring and recycling trust between governors and governed. Fiscal equity became the basis of social trust. Taxes had to cease being seen to target certain classes and benefiting others (Matthew 1979; Daunton 2001). The reasoning of this new elite, moreover, rested precisely on the idea that fiscal politics could be used to give tax-paying citizens an enhanced, direct interest in the state of international affairs; Gladstone, in his budget of 1853, reintroduced the income tax with the argument that linking the income tax threshold to the franchise would make citizens support peaceful, and thus cheaper government. The success of this redefinition of leadership depended on the prior significance assigned to the fiscal-military sources of 'corruption' and political inequity by popular radicals (Stedman Jones 1983; McKibbin 1990). In other words, if radicals had seen their grievances as ultimately caused by capitalism, race, gender or any other set of inequality, tax-relief hardly would have generated the loyalty to the old regime it did.

Finally, liberal hegemony rested on popular support for Free Trade. Liberal political economy survived the great depression of the 1880s and the challenge of imperial tariff reform after 1903 because it was able to generate superior support across classes and regions. While sections of aristocratic and capitalist elites (including some financial-mercantile groups) looked towards protectionism or tariff bargaining, popular radicals and liberals, organized labour and women's movements mobilized to defend pure, unilateral Free Trade. To them it combined a vision of social emancipation and civic consumption with international peace and national identity that emphasized Britain's mission to civilize the world and perform its imperial trust. Free Trade was not just an instrument of self-seeking elites but a popular vision of civil society, however flawed we might think this to have been with hindsight. Moreover, the popular defence of Free Trade belies the argument that the geopolitical choices of the old regime were made possible because of public indifference to international affairs; rarely, in modern history, has popular politics been more engaged in international affairs than the radical and liberal interest in national freedom fighters after 1848, the Gladstonian campaign against the 'Bulgarian atrocities', the Congo reform movement, and Free Trade. The geopolitical thrust of the liberal system had broad roots in British society. To recognize this does not mean we have to abandon Mann's emphasis on the 'national' caging of metropolitan societies. In fact, we can use it to overcome a dangerously flawed but persistent binary that has structured narratives of British history. The battle between Tariff Reform and Free Trade was not a battle between a nationalist-imperial and a cosmopolitan project staged by producers (Birmingham) versus financiers and merchants (City, Manchester). Nor were the imperial costs and benefits of Free Trade unintended consequences. In the Victorian and Edwardian periods, Free Trade developed into a national ideology of 'transcendent' qualities (in the Weberian sense) shaping cross-class identities, partly because it became an increasingly nationalist project, extending notions of Protestant mission and national superiority into an imperial and international vision. This process of the national caging of what had earlier been a supranational cosmopolitan project of the Enlightenment was located in political culture, rather than directed by the state (Trentmann 2002).

The functional primacy assigned to the fiscal-military state in Mann's work overshadows the changing role of social power and self-organization in modern history. For a book about 'social power' there is remarkably little about its changing conception over time. In the course of the seventeenth and eighteenth centuries, the ancient concept of 'civil society' acquired new significance, simultaneously describing norms of civility and a growing network of clubs and associations (Keane 1988; Colas 1997; Morris 1990b; Trentmann 2000/2003; Clark 2000; Hall and Trentmann 2005). Britain was very much a frontrunner. By the turn of the nineteenth century the majority of Britons, including many women and workers, were active in some club or association, ranging from cultural clubs to friendly societies. Applying Mann's fiscal litmus test of social power reveals their significance: the combined budget of philanthropic societies in the late Victorian period exceeded the budget of smaller European states at the time (Prochaska 1990: 358). Associational life reorganized urban society and helped create new middle-class identities: it also created new boundaries of exclusion and new potential for authority and policing (Harrison 1982; Davidoff and Hall 1987; Morris 1990a; Trentmann 2000/2003). Mann uses the term 'civil society' throughout his writings, including for ancient and medieval societies. Yet in *Sources of Social Power* it denotes little more than a descriptive reference to society as such, while in his recent *Fascists*, it is used more narrowly to denote any kind of association; whether the militant *Stahlhelm* in Germany after World War I has enough pluralist or tolerant features to qualify inclusion into 'civil society' is debatable. This lack of analytical clarity reflects a relative methodological indifference to the configuration of power in society outside the state. Arguably, how power is reconfigured within social networks should be crucial to Mann's larger story of the migration of power, since it is premised on historical actors' reinterpretation of the purpose and nature of social life and its relation to political life. The roots of this omission rest in Mann's institutional, statist conception of politics. Yet, much of modern society is about collective organizations which were neither pre-occupied with the state nor defined by it. People create and define sources of social power when they get together to form a library, a working men's club, an evangelical reform movement, or private insurance societies. The relation between bodies rooted in civil society and the state is a historical variable that depends as much on conceptions of society and the internal dynamics of these bodies as on the position of the state.

This analytical blindspot points to the low interpretive weight Mann attaches to the role of ideas. For it is not only ideas of civil society that are neglected, his treatment of modern societies in the *Sources of Social Power* assigns to ideas a relatively minor part, more generally. Following Weber and Durkheim, Mann distinguishes between 'immanent' configurations of ideology (which reinforce the confidence of an existing social group) and 'transcendent' versions of ideology (which transcend existing groups and create new sacred forms of authority) (Mann 1986: 23ff.). The latter applies to the world-salvation religions, but it declines with the coming of a secular European civilization. Power now migrates from ideological to military and economic sources. His concern with power has by now become a question of organizational control of resources, especially literary forms of communication. Ideologues matter if it can be shown that they control and regulate the flow of ideas; this organizational treatment and scepticism of intellectuals recalls Gellner's theory of nation formation.[4] The emergent ideologies of conservatism, liberalism and romanticism, by contrast, do not seem to matter much.

There is a conflation here between ideas and communication, or, to be precise, literary infrastructure, that echoes Karl Deutsch's work on the formation of nations. Control over meaning systems and the production of meaning are, however, phenomenologically very different things; a binary presentation of the history of ideas as either about disembodied sequence of one great intellectual influencing another or about organizational networks controlled by ideologues is unhelpful and brackets the new history of ideas and discourse as well as cultural history (2004: 78). Mann analyses ideological sources of power as a separate category as if they can be separated from military, political and economic ones. The organization of political and economic resources, however, requires a prior idea and knowledge of the nature of these resources and the work they should be put to. Equally, the ideas that define projects of capitalist development and critique them are rooted in longer traditions of beliefs

(Bevir 1999; Bevir and Trentmann 2004). Ideologies are particularly powerful and ambitious combinations of ideas, and there are more or less ideological periods in history, but there are always ideas that inform the other sources of power. Liberal political economy, to take just one example, is read by Mann as an articulation of a prior capitalist transformation of socio-economic relations: 'By 1770, Adam Smith's "invisible hand" ruled civil society. Classical political economy arose to describe it.' Similarly, Free Trade gives expression to the existing interests of capitalists in the nineteenth century. This is debatable empirically and theoretically. How do people know of the social realities around them and what their interests are, let alone the interests of an entire regime? It can be argued that Smith's view of society was far removed from the realities of a free market, industrial growth society. He described what ought to be, rather than record what there was (Poovey 1998; Winch 1978). Similarly, popular support for Free Trade presumed it would foster more civic and less materialist social relations, a far cry from the common equation of Free Trade with free market materialism. In fact, it bears out Mann's general methodological defence of the 'unintended consequences' of history. Interestingly, Mann is reluctant to apply this insight to modern Britain as much as to other societies. Unlike old regime liberalism in Britain, the path to a modern industrial society in Germany, for example, is interpreted much more as the unintended consequence of an authoritarian incorporation to an industrial society (Mann 1993: 324ff.).

The role of modern Britain in his earlier work connects with Mann's recent work on the twentieth century. Mann has always distanced himself from any presentation of modern Britain in terms of 'peculiarity', presenting it rather as one point on a spectrum of modernizing paths. At the same time, Britain does not receive the same critical analysis as other countries. This, perhaps, results from the confident 'radical' focus on the state that withdraws energies from a critique of ideologies. But it also comes from an instinctive, underlying liberalism (or perhaps, rather, humanism) that smuggles in concepts of non-ideological normalcy. Mann's justification for moving away from ideas and ideologies when discussing modern Britain may be found in his recent study of *Fascists*. Family socialization and institutions 'normally insulate us from needing frequent recourse to general meaning systems ... [by] generat[ing] everyday routines which "work" and seem "normal". In times of crisis, however, traditional routines may no longer seem to work and we are thrown onto more general ideas in order to find new workable practices.' It is in such moments of crisis that intellectuals can offer new meaning systems. World War I and the inter-war crisis were such abnormal times. It is now that ideas are integrated again in the analysis, as in Mann's discussion of Carl Schmitt, who receives more attention than any other single thinker in his works on modern societies (2004: 75 ff.). But how 'normal' was a society, like modern Britain, where a popular and often fanatical evangelicalism shaped mass movements and perceptions of society and political economy in the late eighteenth and early nineteenth centuries (Boyd Hilton 1988)? The proliferation of moral reform associations, the density of popular political mobilization, and the spread of new ideas on race, gender and society suggests that most modern Britons were not content with the 'normal' routines provided by family and institutions of everyday life. The divide between a non-ideological normal society and an ideological crisis-ridden one is deeply problematic. Again, while Mann is surely right in his recent study of *Fascists* to include the languages of historical actors, his treatment of ideas remains imprisoned in an organizational materialism. His work on the biographies of fascists in several countries is groundbreaking and reveals whole clusters of social data, but the ideas remain instrumental. What fascists say is in the last analysis interesting for him because it gives voice to non-ideological social categories, such as age, social background, ethnic identities. Ideas and language do not shape social categories.[5]

Mann's secular, non-ideological rendering of modern Britain, then, is intimately connected to his organizational preoccupation with the infrastructures of power. This assessment requires one modification, however, and this will point us back to the spatial dynamics of power, which are the most original and stimulating dimensions of Mann's work. In his most recent work on ethnic cleansing (2005), Mann draws an interesting connection between liberal ideas and ethnic politics through which he links different types of liberal democracy in Western societies to the different treatment of their colonial subjects. In a liberal view of the state as internally stratified, as in Britain, where the state has the independent role of mediating between groups, ethnic cleansing is unlikely, for the state preserves diversity amongst its citizens. In a liberal view of the nation as an organic body, as in the United States, by contrast, there might be a temptation to purify the organic unity further, and such regimes have given rise to instances of ethnic cleansing (2005: ch. 4). But, what about Australia? Mann emphasizes that ethnic cleansing here was driven by colonial settlers, far away from the metropole which was unable to check this process (2005: 79–83). What is interesting from an analytical perspective is the introduction of an additional spatial dynamic to the geopolitical one in the *Sources of Social Power*. Then it was the geopolitical activities of the fiscal-military state at the stage of global conflict that set into motion a reconfiguration of social power at home. Now, Mann adds a reverse linkage: ideas about liberal democracy arising in the metropole spill over into ethnic policies in the colonies. No doubt, this argument will attract debate. The contribution of British/imperial history to this debate might be to raise a question about the analytical framing of this power relationship. Mann's work implies a certain linear cause-and-effect relationship that maps onto metropole and colony. Recent work in imperial and post-colonial studies, by contrast, has placed metropole and colony as mutually constitutive formations in one and the same analytical frame (Cooper and Stoler 1997). From this perspective, ideas and identities in Britain, including those of liberal democracy and citizenship, were always also shaped by colonial developments (Hall 2002).

British history plays a crucial role in Mann's account of the development of the modern world and the migration of power within it. Mann's use of modern British history, this chapter has argued, reveals the ideological context and theoretical ambition and tension of his work more generally. Our discussion has sought to produce a creative encounter between Mann and recent historical work to bring out those larger theoretical issues. In Mann's hands, the thesis of the fiscal-military state and a successful old regime liberalism reflect an organizational, instrumental and secular view of power that privileges elite actors and central-state institutions at the expense of popular politics, civil society and ideas. In the last decade, historical studies of the latter have complicated our understanding of the former. Starting his project during the Thatcher years, Mann emphasized the state as a powerful domestic and global actor and took a fairly pessimistic view of the creative potential and relative autonomy of popular politics and civil society – at the very time when many continental Europeans turned to a version of civil society that almost forgot the state and political power altogether. One principal contribution this allowed Mann to make was to raise a big question about the connection between the global and domestic reconfiguration of power in the modern world. This remains an enduring achievement. Historians of Britain and its Empire are increasingly turning to perspectives of culture, civil society and post-colonialism. If they are unlikely to find much sympathy with Mann's more organizational and instrumental approach, they will certainly be the poorer for not engaging with the larger questions of his work.

Notes

1 I am grateful to the editors, workshop participants and Frank O'Gorman for their comments.
2 Here is an interesting argument about class if there ever was one! As other chapters focus on class and fascism, it will suffice here to raise one

methodological issue. Why is class privileged as a form of identity that tends to scramble militant ethnic ones? Why is a range of other identities and forms of difference, such as gender, religion or age, for example, unable to perform a similar function of diffusion?

3 Cf. Mann, to whom the gendered identity of workers, like other identities and interests, are fully formed prior to their entrance into the political process: 'To struggle for his interests, the masculine collective laborer was forced into politics, where he encountered the existing crystallization of the state' (1993: 617). Other chapters discuss Mann's treatment of class and gender more extensively, so it will suffice here to point to one area of disagreement. The decline of class fervour in the course of the nineteenth century, in Mann's view, results from the shift from family to male employment (227). As most historians have now pushed forward the rise of class consciousness as a predominant identity into the late nineteenth century or have eliminated it altogether, Mann's argument becomes difficult. In fact, it could be argued, inversely, that the more gendered language of increasingly male-dominated labouring politics helped to consolidate a sense of working-class politics. Similarly, the gendered culture of evangelicalism and the gendered division of home and work has been seen as integral to the formation of middle-class identities in the late eighteenth and early nineteenth centuries (Davidoff and Hall 1987).

4 Ernest Gellner, *Nations and Nationalism* (1983: 123 ff.): 'these thinkers did not really make much difference' (1983: 124). It always struck me as odd that academics take such a low view of what is (or should be) their own business.

5 If we can no longer deduce class consciousness from workers' social characteristics, why should we be able to do this for fascists? Note the ambivalent treatment of anti-semitism. On the one hand, Mann recognizes that Hitler's contempt for Jews from the Pale had no connection to any social experience, given their small percentage in German society. On the other hand, he argues that the type of anti-semitism was a direct function of the socio-economic profile of haters and hated: in Germany 'Jewish dominance over credit and trade encouraged a materially-motivated antisemitism among poor peasants and (probably less frequently) among urban renters and consumers' (2004: 258).

References

Bayly, C. A. 1989. *Imperial Meridian: The British Empire and the World, 1780–1830.* London: Longman.

Bevir, M. 1999. *The Logic of the Histories of Ideas.* Cambridge: Cambridge University Press.

Bevir, M., and F. Trentmann (eds.). 2002. *Critiques of Capital in Modern Britain and America: Transatlantic Exchanges.* Basingstoke: Palgrave.

  2004. *Markets in Historical Contexts: Ideas and Politics in the Modern World.* Cambridge: Cambridge University Press.

Biagini, E. 1992. *Liberty, Retrenchment and Reform: Popular Liberalism in the Age of Gladstone, 1860–1880.* Cambridge: Cambridge University Press.

Brewer, J. 1989. *The Sinews of Power: War, Money and the English State, 1688–1783.* London: Unwin Hyman.

Canny, N. (ed.). 1998. *The Oxford History of the British Empire, Volume I: The Origins of Empire*. Oxford and New York: Oxford University Press.

Clark, A. 1995. *The Struggle for the Breeches: Gender and the Making of the British Working Class*. London: Rivers Oram Press.

Clark, J. C. D. 1985. *English Society 1688–1832: Ideology, Social Structure and Political Practice during the Ancient Regime*. Cambridge: Cambridge University Press.

1994. *The Language of Liberty, 1660–1832: Political Discourse and Social Dynamics in the Anglo-American World*. Cambridge: Cambridge University Press.

2000. Protestantism, Nationalism, and National Identity. *Historical Journal*, 43.

Clark, P. 2000. *British Clubs and Societies 1580–1800: The Origins of an Associational World*. Oxford: Clarendon Press.

Colas, D. 1997. *Civil Society and Fanaticism: Conjoined Histories*. Stanford: Stanford University Press.

Colley, L. 1992. *Britons: Forging the Nation, 1707–1837*. New Haven: Yale University Press.

Cooper, F., and A. L. Stoler (eds.). 1997. *Tensions of Empire: Colonial Cultures in a Bourgeois World*. Berkeley: University of California Press.

Daunton, M. 1989. 'Gentlemanly Capitalism' and British Industry, 1820–1914. *Past and Present*, 122.

2001. *Trusting Leviathan: The Politics of Taxation in Britain, 1799–1914*. Cambridge: Cambridge University Press.

Davidoff, L., and C. Hall. 1987. *Family Fortunes: Men and Women of the English Middle Class 1780–1850*. London: Hutchinson.

Gellner, E. 1983. *Nations and Nationalism*. Oxford: Blackwell.

Goldie, M. 2001. The Unacknowledged Republic: Officeholding in Early Modern England. In T. Harris (ed.), *The Politics of the Excluded, c. 1500–1850*. Basingstoke: Palgrave.

Hall, C. 2002. *Civilising Subjects: Metropole and Colony in the English Imagination 1830–1867*. Oxford: Polity Press.

Hall, J. and F. Trentmann (eds.). 2005. *Civil Society*. Basingstoke: Palgrave Macmillan.

Harrison, B. 1982. *Peaceable Kingdom: Stability and Change in Modern Britain*. Oxford: Clarendon.

Hilton, B. 1988. *The Age of Atonement: The Influence of Evangelicalism on Social and Economic Thought, 1795–1865*. Oxford: Clarendon.

Hoppit, J. 2002. Checking the Leviathan, 1688–1832. In P. O'Brien and D. Winch (eds.), *The Political Economy of British Historical Experience, 1688–1914*. Oxford: Oxford University Press, pp. 267–94.

Howe, A. C. 1992. Free Trade and the City of London, c. 1820–1870. *History*, 77.

Keane, J. (ed.). 1988. *Civil Society and the State: New European Perspectives*. London: Verso.

McKibbin, R. 1990. *The Ideologies of Class: Social Relations in Britain, 1880–1950*. Oxford: Clarendon.

Mandler, P. 1990. *Aristocratic Government in the Age of Reform: Whigs and Liberals 1830–1852*. Oxford: Clarendon.

Mann, M. A. 1986. *The Sources of Social Power, Volume I: A History from the Beginning to 1760 AD*. Cambridge: Cambridge University Press.
1988. *States, War and Capitalism: Studies in Political Sociology*. Oxford: Basil Blackwell.
1993. *The Sources of Social Power, Volume II: The Rise of Classes and Nation-States*. Cambridge: Cambridge University Press.
2000. Modernity and Globalization. Unpublished, given as the Wiles Lectures at Queen's University, Belfast.
2004. *Fascists*. Cambridge: Cambridge University Press.
2005. *The Dark Side of Democracy: Explaining Ethnic Cleansing*. Cambridge: Cambridge University Press.
Matthew, H. C. G. 1979. Disraeli, Gladstone, and the Politics of Mid-Victorian Budgets. *Historical Journal*, 22.
Mayer, A. J. 1981. *The Persistence of the Old Regime: Europe to the Great War*. London: Croom Helm.
Morris, R. J. 1990a. *Class, Sect, and Party: The Making of the British Middle Class, Leeds 1820–1850*. Manchester: Manchester University Press.
1990b. Clubs, Networks, and Associations. In F. M. L. Thompson (ed.), *The Cambridge Social History of Britain 1750–1950*. Cambridge: Cambridge University Press.
Namier, L. B. 1929. *The Structure of Politics at the Accession of George III*. London: Macmillan.
O'Brien, P. K. 1988. The Political Economy of British Taxation, 1660–1815. *Economic History Review*, 2nd ser., 41, pp. 1–32.
O'Gorman, F. 1989. *Voters, Patrons and Parties: The Unreformed Electoral System of Hanoverian England 1734–1832*. Oxford: Clarendon.
Offer, A. 1999. Costs, Benefits, Prosperity and Security, 1870–1914. In A. Porter (ed.), *The Oxford History of British Empire: The Nineteenth Century*. Oxford: Oxford University Press.
Pincus, S. C. A. 1996. *Protestantism and Patriotism: Ideologies and the Making of English Foreign Policy, 1650–1668*. Cambridge: Cambridge University Press.
Plumb, J. 1967. *The Growth of Political Stability in England, 1675–1725*. London: Macmillan.
Pocock, J. G. A. 1985. *Virtue, Commerce, and History: Essays on Political Thought and History, Chiefly in the Eighteenth Century*. Cambridge: Cambridge University Press.
Poovey, M. 1998. *A History of the Modern Fact: Problems of Knowledge in the Sciences of Wealth and Society*. Chicago: University of Chicago Press.
Prochaska, F. 1990. Philanthrophy. In F. M. L. Thompson (ed.), *The Cambridge Social History of Britain 1750–1950*. Cambridge: Cambridge University Press.
Rogers, N. 1989. *Whigs and Cities: Popular Politics in the Age of Walpole and Pitt*. Oxford: Clarendon.
Schumpeter, J. A. 1943. *Capitalism, Socialism, and Democracy*. London: G. Allen & Unwin Ltd.
Spenser, E. 1633. *A View of the State of Ireland Written Dialogue-Wise between Eudoxus and Irenæus*.

Stedman Jones, G. J. 1983. *Languages of Class: Studies in English Working Class History, 1832–1982*. Cambridge: Cambridge University Press.

Steinmetz, W. 1993. *Das Sagbare und das Machbare: zum Wandel politischer Handlungsspielräume, England 1780–1867*. Stuttgart: Klett-Cotta.

Thompson, F. M. L. (ed.). 1990. *The Cambridge Social History of Britain 1750–1950*. Cambridge: Cambridge University Press.

Trentmann, F. 1998. Political Culture and Political Economy. *Review of International Political Economy*, 5.

2002. National Identity and Consumer Politics: Free Trade and Tariff Reform. In P. O'Brien and D. Winch (eds.), *The Political Economy of British Historical Experience, 1688–1914*. Oxford: Oxford University Press.

(ed.). 2000/2003. *Paradoxes of Civil Society: New Perspectives on Modern German and British History*. Oxford and New York: Berghahn.

Tuck, R. 1999. *The Rights of War and Peace: Political Thought and the International Order from Grotius to Kant*. Oxford: Oxford University Press.

Wahrman, D. 1995. *Imagining the Middle Class: The Political Representation of Class in Britain, c. 1780–1840*. Cambridge: Cambridge University Press.

Wilson, K. 1995. *The Sense of the People: Politics, Culture and Imperialism in England, 1715–1785*. Cambridge: Cambridge University Press.

Winch, D. 1978. *Adam Smith's Politics: An Essay in Historiographic Revision*. Cambridge: Cambridge University Press.

14   Networks and ideologies: the fusion of 'is' and 'ought' as a means to social power

Jack Snyder

In the contemporary era, international politics is increasingly animated by the projects of ideology-infused transnational networks. In the wake of the attack on the World Trade Center, the attempt to squelch the Al Qaeda global Islamic terrorist network was the all-absorbing foreign policy enterprise of the advanced democracies. At the same time, trans-national networks, especially non-governmental activist organizations linked in what is styled a 'global civil society', have become a central carrier of liberalism's worldwide ideological project of promoting democracy and human rights.

The power of transnational ideological networks is hardly a new phenomenon in international affairs. The Comintern and the Christian missionaries were earlier examples. Nonetheless, some particular features of the contemporary era may be fuelling the current surge in the power of such networks, such as the creation of the Internet, the purported globalization of markets and culture, and the peaking of the United States' military-economic preponderance. Much of the research on contemporary principled networks has been done by enthusiasts who see the ideas as spreading largely because they are correct. They concern themselves with the short-run tactics of advancing the ideological agenda (Risse and Sikkink 1999). Only a few works have tried to understand this phenomenon from the standpoint of a basic theory of the sources of social power (Keck and Sikkink 1998; Boli and Thomas 1999). That is where the writings of Michael Mann may be able to help.

Mann's conception of the sources of social power arguably becomes most distinctive when analysing the confluence of networks and ideology. Making a self-consciously heretical move for a sociologist, Mann rejects 'society' as the basic building block of his analysis of social power. Instead, he thinks in terms of people linked in networks of social ties, networks that may sometimes cut across political and cultural boundaries or may lie in the interstices of official power structures. In his historical analysis, what he calls 'spurts' in social power tend to happen when interstitial and cross-boundary networks form around a powerful ideology that unleashes a qualitative leap in the mobilizing, organizing potential for social cooperation on a broader scale (1986: 3). Such episodes are the major engines of his two-volume history of social power (1986; 1993). His analyses of the rise of the world's major salvation religions and of the French Revolution are the two key examples that he himself points to in this regard (2004: 78). In particular, his comparative analysis of the power networks underpinning the rise of Christianity, Hinduism, Buddhism and Islam provides what is arguably the most methodologically focused moment in the two volumes. The nexus between networks and ideologies consequently offers an ideal opportunity not only to apply Mann's thinking to a set of central issues in contemporary international politics, but also to gain insight into the nature of Mann's enterprise as a whole.

I begin by reviewing some of Mann's more general remarks about networks, ideologies and social power, including his stance towards the classic arguments of Karl Marx, Max Weber and Emile Durkheim, as well as some of Mann's summary evaluations in *The Sources of Social Power*. I next turn to Mann's empirical analysis of the great religions and the French Revolution to assess which of his views seem best supported by these histories.

To help organize the analysis, I focus in particular on the relationship between 'is' and 'ought' in the efficacy of these ideas-based social networks. I mean this in two related senses. First, what is the relationship between the social facts of a given social arrangement and the nature of ideological concepts that gain power in it? Second, how are empirical and normative arguments related in generating persuasive ideological power? I will show that 'is' and 'ought' are closely related both in the content of ideological doctrines and in causing social outcomes in ways that are disturbing from widely accepted philosophical standpoints. Most people tend to accept as obviously true David Hume's dictum that one cannot properly derive an 'ought' conclusion from an 'is' premise, yet protagonists in Mann's stories do it all the time. Likewise, most people agree with Jürgen Habermas, John Rawls and American public opinion scholars that a social actor's principled arguments lack persuasive force when they have transparent origins in the actor's parochial social position, yet Mann's protagonists successfully deploy such arguments all the time. We know this from our daily newspapers, too: within Slobodan Milosevic's 'principled' network, it made perfect sense to argue that because of the fact that Serbians had died in a battle in Kosovo several hundred years ago, they ought to own it now. I want to use Mann's rich material to try to understand how this kind of miraculous transubstantiation of 'is' into 'ought' occurs.

Mann's stance on ideological power and social networks

Drawing on the concepts of the founders of sociological thought, Mann identifies three sources of ideological power: control over meaning, morals and ritual. Drawing on Weber, Mann argues that understanding the world and acting in it require 'concepts and categories of *meaning*' that cannot be derived from mere sense perceptions. Such meanings, which are 'necessary to social life', derive from 'social organization'. They provide answers to fundamental questions about humankind's relationship to nature, the origins of society, life-cycle transitions and the basis of legitimate authority. Those who control social meanings wield the power to mobilize collective activity and to distribute its benefits (1986: 22). Mann claims to go beyond Weber in stressing the role of ideology not just as a 'switchman' that determines on which of multiple possible tracks actors pursue their interests, but (together with economic, military and political power) as the 'tracklayer' that creates *de novo* a pattern of social action (28).

From Durkheim, Mann draws the argument that norms ('shared understandings of how people should act morally in their relations with each other') are necessary to sustain social cooperation based on mutual trust and collective morale. He who controls norms wields power (22). Mann goes beyond Durkheim, however, by pointing out that ideology does not simply 'integrate and reflect an already established "society"; indeed it may actually create a society-like network, a religious or cultural community, out of emergent, interstitial social needs and relations' (23, 369–70).

Drawing further on Durkheim, Mann stresses that ideological power encompasses yet a third dimension: aesthetic and ritual practices. This dimension of ideological power, he says, can have potent effects on collective action and distributive outcomes, and cannot be rebutted by rational arguments.

Whereas Marxian analyses imply that ideology gains its power by creating a false consciousness, duping its victims and masking the truth, Mann says that manifestly false ideas are unlikely to spread. Rather, effective ideology has power because it exists on a plane that transcends mere truth or falsity: 'It cannot be totally tested by experience, and therein lies its distinctive power to persuade and dominate' (23). In a social sense, however, Mann remarks that effective ideologies are 'true' insofar as the social world is ordered by their cosmologies and concepts of the sacred (369–70).

Expressing Mann's framework in terms of 'is' and 'ought', the first dimension of ideology, dealing with ultimate meaning (a kind of transcendental 'is'), exists on a plane that stands above the merely empirical

'is' and ethical 'ought'. The second dimension, morality, occupies the
plane of 'ought'. The third dimension, ritual, makes concrete the first two
dimensions. The three together constitute social reality, and in that sense,
create the social 'is'.

Mann makes little room in this framework for the purely factual and
causal aspects of ideology – that is beliefs about how the world works that
are in principle subject to empirical verification or refutation (the empirical
'is'). Bolshevism was rare, he says, in grounding its ideology in a scientific
theory that was vulnerable to empirical falsification. Other secular ideologies, such as that of the French Revolution, typically combined empirical
arguments inextricably with non-falsifiable moral ones (1993: 193–4). The
lack of a substantial, autonomous role for empirical beliefs is not too
surprising for the great salvation religions, but it is striking in a scheme
that also applies to the great secular ideologies, including not only Marxism
but also liberalism. This makes sense, however, in terms of Mann's notion
that successful ideologies do not simply describe the world, they remake
the world to fit their descriptions (1986: 369).

Mann contends that ideologies become powerful not because of the
content of their ideas *per se*, but because of the way they go about answering
basic questions of meaning and the consequences that this has for their
organizational potential. 'The answers that ideologies give to the "meaning
of life" questions are not all that varied', he asserts, and those answers are
non-falsifiable and riddled with contradictions (21). What distinguishes
then between the ideologies that succeeded in conquest from the also-rans?
Ideologies that are the engine for the expansion of social power are those
that 'argue that human problems can be overcome with the aid of *transcendent, sacred authority*' that cuts across existing social boundaries in a way
that makes possible the organization of a broader, more effective power
network (22). 'An ideology will emerge as a powerful, autonomous movement when it can put together in a single explanation and organization a
number of aspects of existence that have hitherto been marginal, interstitial
to the dominant institutions of power' (21).

The intellectual content of the ideology's 'explanation' plays an important role in this process. As we shall see more fully in discussing the
historical examples, it must address the substance of perceived social
problems or contradictions, it must fit the outlooks and concerns of the
actors that comprise the network-in-the-making, and it must do so cre-
dibly enough to be 'genuinely adhered to' (23). Network organization,
intellectual content and social opportunity must all dovetail to generate a
leap in social power. To explain how this works, I will invent some
terminology that I think is consistent with Mann's framework, though it
may not precisely reflect the way he talks about it.

One element in this mix is the *latent organizational potential* for the emergence of such a network. This depends on the available infrastructure, such as means of communication and on exploitable social contradictions. A second element is the presence of appropriate *suppliers* of ideology. While Mann is adamant that ideological power is much more than a matter of manipulation, entrepreneurs with a motive to supply the ideology play a large role in his stories. A third element is the *demand* for the suppliers' particular ideas, which typically must resonate with the social concerns of a potentially mobilizable constituency and also with that target constituency's existing conceptual apparatus. The fourth element is the dynamic of *competition and positive feedback* through which these three components accumulate social power and expand the domain of the power network that the ideology animates. I discuss and illustrate each of these elements in the following sections.

Structural potential

Mann's descriptions of the latent structural potential for a qualitative leap in ideologically based social power focus on two dimensions: the prior existence of an infrastructure of social ties and capabilities out of which a new network can be formed, and on social contradictions that prevent existing networks from maximizing their power potential.

Prior infrastructure: trackfollowing or tracklaying?

Mann pays considerable attention to the latent infrastructural potential for the creation of an ideologically motivated network. Ideas need a medium to facilitate their spread. In the case of the rise of Christianity, this medium was provided by widespread urban, elite literacy and by a broad network of pre-existing ties among traders linking urban areas throughout the Roman Empire and linking different social strata within particular urban areas (1986: 125, 313, 366). Even before the rise of Christianity, Roman authorities were fearful that such ties created a latent potential for the rise of a social network that could rival their authority. As in the case of the Falun Gong in contemporary China, what bothered the authorities was not so much the ideological content of such a potential rival's message but the mere fact of the independence of its network. Emperor Trajan, for example, objected to the formation of volunteer fire brigades on the grounds that the firemen, once linked in a group, might find political topics to discuss (324).

Mann notes that empires can play a big role in creating the infrastructural potential for the spread of universal salvation religions. As in the case of the Romans, imperial masters may not themselves attempt to homogenize the religious and cultural identities of their subjects, often preferring to preside over a live-and-let-live system of religious pluralism and tolerance. However, by creating a political framework for the movement of goods and people, the establishment of urban melting pots, and fostering literacy and some cultural contact, empires help create the conditions that facilitate the emergence of such ideological networks. In general, Mann contends that such developments are favoured when there exists some kind of mismatch between the geographical extent of a political system and its market or social networks. This may apparently take different forms, however, since the Roman Empire's arena of political control comprised numerous cultural areas, whereas the Hindu cultural area was larger than the area of control of any political entity. Mann implies that the mismatch of size created favourable conditions for the emergence of salvation religions in both cases, though ones taking different forms (1986: 352, 363–6).

Islam, however, inverts this pattern. The feuding tribes of the Arabian peninsula lay outside the networks of the Byzantine and Persian empires, though they were perhaps influenced by the model provided of these civilizations and by the example of existing monotheistic religions (344–8). Instead of animating a latent network created by an imperial precursor, Islam was a tracklayer that laid down a pattern of social organization that integrated a vast array of disparate societies. Muhammad's doctrine provided an ideological solution to the collective action dilemmas that had left the Arabian tribes divided and their disenfranchised younger sons discontented amid the growing trading wealth of Mecca. Ties of reciprocity based on belief rather than kinship, welded together by a simple doctrine and intensive ritual, created the morale that was needed for military victories and the openness to conversion that was needed for the network's open-ended growth. However, the extent of the growth followed a pattern that was the opposite of that of Christianity, which expanded only as far as the latent network that Rome had provided for it. Instead, Islam rolled up the areas that lacked any comparable ideology of mass collective action, but came to a halt when it reached the edges of civilizations that had already discovered such power techniques. Thus, Christianity reorganized an existing civilization, whereas Islam created a civilization mainly out of hinterlands. If useable theory is to come out of this analysis, it must evidently be of the kind that explains when and why such different patterns emerge.

Social contradictions: power through integrative synthesis?

Structural potential for an expansion of social power capacity may also be latent in social contradictions, whose resolution may allow an intensification of collective action. As in Marx's theory, a given mode of social organization can bring the development of social power only so far until its growing internal contradictions produce a deadlock of opposing logics. Mann's most elaborate example of this is the rise of Christianity as a solution to no fewer than five contradictions of the social order of Imperial Rome: the tension between universalistic ties of Roman citizenship and the particularistic ties of kinship, class, village and tribe; the tension between the equality implicit in citizenship and the hierarchical nature of the Roman state; the formal centralization of imperial rule versus the reality of local governance; the uniformity of official culture versus the multicultural reality of the empire's lands; and the tension between militaristic and civilizing methods for managing relations with barbarians at the edge of empire (1986: 306–7). Christianity's appeal, says Mann, was that it offered a solution to these contradictions by creating an effective ideological basis for 'a universalistic, egalitarian, decentralized, civilizing community' (307). The network underpinning this development was centred on urban middling strata, linked by ties of trade between cities and classes, who felt especially cross-pressured by the contradictions of Roman society. Initially, urban Jews outside Palestine and later urban Greeks were central to this network's growth.

Mann, like other contemporary authorities, argues that these contradictions did not amount to a *material* crisis of empire in the period of Christianity's expansion. In fact, living standards and material conditions were good, though Rodney Stark (1996) places more stress than Mann on the horribly crowded urban conditions and deplorable public health conditions that made cities ripe for epidemics. Rather, Mann says, 'their "suffering" was confined to their normative sphere, or deciding what community they belonged to' (1986: 309). Christianity's solution to this normative dilemma was in part doctrinal: it resolved contradictions by erasing them with its ecumenical formula for integrating the community. As Stark (1996: 209) puts it, 'Christianity served as a revitalization movement within the empire' by 'offering a coherent culture that was entirely stripped of ethnicity'. But doctrine was only one aspect of this. Mann points out that 'the contradictions of Rome were essentially organizational', and the normative solution was only effective insofar as it was also an organizational solution (1986: 310).

Stark's research is especially good at showing the effectiveness of Christianity in solving collective action problems. Christians had much higher survival rates during epidemics than pagans did, because Christians were much more likely to take good care of sick members of their community (Stark 1996: 74–5). Stark's rationalistic account also stresses selective incentives: women were disproportionately attracted to the Christian community, which preached relative equality between the sexes. Based in part on inferences from his theories of social ecology, he speculates that the expansion of Christianity was fuelled in part by conversions of men through marriage (1996: 95–115). Overall, Christianity was convincing because, relative to the alternatives, it produced tangible social results. Empirical demonstration (the 'is') established the credibility of the cosmological and especially the ethical doctrine (the 'ought').

This seems to be a common pattern. Mann argues similarly that the Hindu cosmology that gave meaning to the caste system 'was a plausible belief system because it led to results'. Brahmins controlled not only ritual, but also practical knowledge, including literate communications channels, and served to integrate social and economic networks that were politically balkanized. Caste doctrine worked both to 'mobilize a collectivity' and also 'authoritatively stratify it as well'. From the standpoint of both collective and distributive power, cosmology seamlessly accounted for compelling social facts (Mann 1986: 362). In the rise of Islam, the social demonstration effect of doctrine was even more direct: cavalry infused with Islamic morale won all its battles. On a more mundane level today, Islamic cosmology gains credibility because in Cairo and Istanbul, Islamist networks are good at filling gaps in the educational, health and public service infrastructure.

Nonetheless, as Mann notes, the power of the salvation religions to organize collective action was far from unlimited. Christianity, for example, failed to solve the fifth and ultimately decisive contradiction of empire, namely, how to manage relations with the barbarians. Christianity did not organize itself to convert these outsiders and instead left the problem to the secular military realm. Not only in this area, but even in the area of basic mass education, Christianity remained parasitic on the political and organizational structures of the pagan empire that had preceded it (1986: 334).

In sum, salvation religions produced a spurt in social power because they developed a doctrinally infused network that resolved social contradictions and unleashed collective action. Methodologically, one worry is that with the advantage of hindsight it is all too easy to describe any successful social movement in these terms. To save the argument from being a rather loose tautology, it is important to show in detail all the fine-grained causal connections among the pre-existing network ties, the micromotives of actors, the rise of ideas and the specific stages of growth of the movement. Stark's approach, which aspires to ground itself on deductions from explicit analytical assumptions and on rigorously positivist comparative testing methods, provides a methodological structure that helps us to gauge whether Mann's somewhat looser, inductive, historical sociology is merely telling of confirmatory 'just so' stories. In fact, Mann and Stark do advance similar arguments on most points, despite the fact that Stark makes no reference to Mann's work.

The supply of ideology

In an organization-centred account of ideological power such as Mann's, one might expect the theme of active persuasion to recede into the background. In its place, one might expect an examination of how ideas are reified as social facts that are so taken for granted, so embedded in social practice, that the question of persuasion to believe in them hardly arises (Berger and Luckmann 1964; Grafstein 1992). 'Immanent' ideologies, as Mann calls ideologies that legitimate the status quo, might endure because practical living presents no alternative; 'transcendent' ideologies, as Mann calls the utopias propounded by entrepreneurs in alternative interstitial networks, might prevail because they demographically or militarily out-compete their rivals (Stark 1996).

While Mann occasionally notes such dynamics, for the most part he does not go down this road. Instead, active purveying of ideas through social networks and active persuasion of converts is a central theme of *The Sources of Social Power*. Mann explains how Christianity was propagated in a two-step process in which elites disseminated written doctrine and persuasive epistles (the letters to the Corinthians, for example), which was subsequently transmitted orally to illiterate lower strata (1986: 316–20). Even in early Islam, where armed conquest played the initial role, religious conversion *per se* was meant to take place not by coercion but persuasion backed by the monopolization of literacy, law and ritual (347).

If persuasion is a key mechanism for generating ideologically based social power, who is doing the persuading, and why? Mann admits that 'ideologies always do contain legitimations of private interests and material domination' (23). On an institutional plane, he argues that fixed investments in economic and military assets create incentives to intensify social power to 'cage' people in networks that preserve those investments. On an ideological plane, he implicitly admits that much the same occurs. His accounts are populated by Brahmin priests who live well and have high status, and by Kshatriya secular leaders who promote Buddhism and Jainism precisely because it relegates religion to otherworldly pursuits and gets the Brahmins out of this-worldly ones (355). New ideologies bear the imprint of self-interest and social position no less than status quo doctrines. Christianity caught on first among urban, mercantile, Hellenized Jews who sought to distance themselves from the insular, militant identity of the tribal Jews of Palestine, much as Reform Judaism caught on with similar groups in the nineteenth century (Mann 1986: 317; Stark 1996: 53–4, 63).

Yet Mann insists that ideologies 'are unlikely to attain a hold over people if they are merely' justifications of private interests (1986: 23). The case where this is perhaps clearest is the emergence of a militant nationalist ideology in the course of the French Revolution, which centred on identifying and confronting internal and external 'enemies of the nation'. As François Furet (1992), Lynn Hunt (1984), and with reservations Mann (1993: 167–9, 188–9, 207) have convincingly shown, the content of revolutionary ideology cannot be understood mainly in terms of the parochial material interests of the bourgeoisie or any other social group. Rather, as Mann puts it, ideological 'principle was an emergent property of revolutionary politics, an unintended consequence of action' (1993: 197). Trying to maintain power with no established framework to institutionalize support from fickle, politicized urban masses, 'the ideological elite discovered its basic power technique: moral persuasion to evoke a grand declaration of principle, which then proved coercive and self-fulfilling' (196). In this fluid environment, says Mann, warhawks like 'Brissot did not win the support of the assembly by pragmatic arguments'. Indeed, pro-peace spokesmen argued more cogently and with greater foresight. Nonetheless, 'the assembly chose bellicosity as a statement of high emotional principle to unite disparate power factions' (204–5). Normative persuasion had its volatile reign, increasingly divorced from the empirics of underlying self-interest or plausible consequentialist reasoning.

In Mann's view, this peculiar ascendancy of a sociologically unmoored ideological elite reflects the unique political errors that characterize the French Revolution: 'as revolutions occur when regimes lose their powers of concentration on their interests, mistakes are *essential* to revolutions' (170). This perspective strikes me as unhelpful. Mann would have been better advised to draw on his own tracklaying metaphor. Far from being a unique situation, the French Revolution was an archetype of politics in conditions when political institutions are weak relative to high demands for mass political participation, a circumstance analysed in the seminal work of Samuel Huntington (1968). Precisely under these circumstances of institutional deficit, politicians are desperate to use ideology and cultural symbols to try to lay down some tracks in the institutionally trackless political desert. Ever since the paradigmatic French Revolution,

nationalist claims to rule *for* 'the people', despite the lack of institutionalized accountability *to* the people, are the nearly universal expedient
of political elites who face this dilemma. In this setting, over-baked
accusations of traitorous links between internal opponents and external
enemies are a ploy that allows hard-pressed political elites to shore up
their tenuous hold on power in the absence of institutional legitimacy.
Thus, the unmooring of political ideology from social networks in this
circumstance – the disconnection of 'ought' from 'is' – is neither unique
nor a mere mistake. Rather it is the typical outcome of a gap between
institutions and participation. In one form or another, this dynamic
has been a major engine producing the nationalist ideologies that have
been the most characteristic political doctrines of the modern era
(Snyder 2000).

The demand for ideology

In contemporary discussions of the appeal of nationalist elites' propaganda, the central puzzle is why do the followers follow (Fearon and
Laitin 2000)? The same question arises in Mann's discussions of the
rise of salvation religions and other ideologically powered networks.
Four answers seem possible.

The first answer is that an ideology is more likely to be effective if its
purveyors have an advantage in controlling the means of persuasion, in
the way that Milosevic controlled Belgrade television coverage of the
Kosovo issue in the late 1980s (Gagnon 1994–5). Throughout Mann's
case studies from the Brahmins to Brissot's newspapers, control over
media, information and education exerts a powerful effect in creating a
demand for ideology. When such resources remain in the hands of
established elites, the prospects of 'immanent' ideology are favourable,
but when such resources are found in the interstices of society, 'transcendent'
ideology has a chance. However, supply does not always create its own
demand. As we have seen, Christians left basic education in the hands of
the pagan Roman state, but they prevailed anyway.

The second answer is that the success of ideological persuasion may be
illusory: perhaps Milosevic did not persuade Serbs with his ideological
arguments, but simply created a self-fulfilling prophecy through *faits
accomplis* that provoked Serbia's enemies and consequently forced Serbs
to rally to him as their most plausible protector (De Figueiredo and
Weingast 1999). In such cases, one might expect ideology to tag along
behind behaviour rather than driving behaviour. This view of the
sequence is plausible for the French Revolutionary Wars. In order to
deflect Brissot's charges of treason, the French King threatened to attack

anti-revolutionary French émigrés in German border states, triggering Austrian deterrent threats which in turn provided further ammunition for Brissot's belligerent persuasion campaign. This cycle of provocation and reaction helps to explain how a revolutionary movement that initially saw itself as pacific could so quickly turn militant in its nationalism (Snyder 2000: 161–7; Walt 1996). However, such dynamics cannot account for the bulk of the success of the ideologies Mann discusses. In the Christian case, in particular, he shows that ideological persuasion was a central force in its own right.

A third answer is that ideological persuasion works best when it piggy-backs on familiar ideas, that is when it resonates with existing cultural preconceptions. Thus, the Serbs were arguably primed to accept Milosevic's ethnonationalist propaganda by the legacy of rivalry between Serbia and Muslim Turkey and by experience of Croatian fascist atro-cities against Serbs in World War II. Similarly, Mann notes that early Christian teaching included many elements that were familiar to its target groups of Hellenized Jews and Greeks, since it combined Greek philos-ophy and Jewish ethics (1986: 319).

The fourth answer focuses less on the familiar pedigree of ideas than on their social utility for the target group. Mann argues, for example, that there was an 'elective affinity' (to use Weber's term) between the needs of urban trading classes in the Roman Empire and the doctrines of Christianity. Official Roman dogma failed to provide an ideological legiti-mation for private activity outside authoritative hierarchies or an ethical basis for stable relations of reciprocity that underpin market transactions. Christianity, says Mann, filled that gap (1986: 312–13).

Pedigree and utility may be mutually reinforcing. Christianity appealed to Hellenized Jewish traders for both reasons. But which force is the more primary one? Does the basic motivation arise on the utility side, and then wordsmiths rummage through a toolkit of resonant themes to fit the need, or does the available stock of cultural meanings exert a more active force on ideological development?

Mann's discussion of the rise of Buddhism out of Hindu traditions suggests that the latter is sometimes true. In Mann's account, Hindu Brahmins had a worldly face as regulators of communal rituals, but also an otherworldly face towards transcendental meanings. Both were socially useful, the former because it put the Brahmins in control of much of everyday life, and the latter because it helped assert their status vis-à-vis mundane political and military elites. However, the otherworldly element, if taken too seriously, risked pulling Brahmin concerns out of the mundane entirely. Buddhism, says Mann, represented precisely this trend, which grew in part out of the logic of the earlier Hindu ideology: Buddhist and Jain asceticism resonated because of ideological echoes from Hindu cosmology. These offshoots then picked up support from non-Brahmin elites who perceived utility in a doctrine that would relegate religion to otherworldly matters, but in Mann's account this appears as a consequence rather than as the primary cause (1986: 354).

To get further leverage on the question of pedigree versus utility, the spread of the cult of Isis in the Roman Empire can be compared to the somewhat later rise of Christianity. The cult of Isis and Serapis emerged from Hellenized Egypt around BCE 200 and spread to numerous imperial cities over the subsequent five hundred years. Its cultural pedigree was pagan, not Jewish. Despite these dissimilar cultural origins, the correlation between the communities to which Isis and Christianity spread has been calculated by Stark at 0.67 (1996: 199). This implies that these 'interstitial' communities felt some demand for an ideology that would suit their needs better than that of official Roman doctrine. Score one point for utility over pedigree.

Christianity won out over Isis. Why? Stark speculates that this had to do with the intellectual content of their respective doctrines, but not because of their different pedigree. Rather he notes that Isis was a typical pagan cult, in which adherents would add Isis to their existing stock of deities in the hope that Isis would deliver private goods to the worshipper. In terms of sociological function and utility, this was not a qualitative break. In contrast, Christianity required exclusive conversion to a monotheistic community with high solidarity, creating normative bonds that effectively promoted collective action and the provision of collective goods within the group (Stark 1996: 205–8). Christianity was a doctrine whose intellectual content generated a leap forward in social power, whereas that of Isis did not. The substance of ideas mattered because of their different implications for utility, not because of their different pedigrees.

Mechanisms of expansion: competitive advantage and positive feedback

How is it that certain ideologies generate the leap in social power that allows them to expand their sway over territory and people? The principal set of mechanisms pertains to the ways that ideologies generate an increase in the effectiveness of mobilizing the power latent in a social network. A secondary set of mechanisms helps explain how the network becomes locked into a particular pattern, including some mechanisms that are not grounded in effectiveness advantages.

Socially effective ideologies can expand their scope of domination either by competition effects or demonstration effects. Early Christianity gained power in the Roman Empire in part, says Stark, because fewer of its adherents died in plagues. Early Islam prevailed over local cultural rivals because it defeated them in battle. Thus, they gained a degree of advantage through competitive fitness without having to persuade anyone. However, these social proofs of the efficacy of their doctrines also helped persuade on-lookers that their religious tenets were potent. Direct competition effects and secondary demonstration effects should normally go hand in hand, though in particular cases, one or the other may play the more central role.

How do ideologies increase the effectiveness of groups? The general answer is that they increase the effectiveness of collective action within the network by reducing shirking and opportunism and thus facilitating cooperation in power-generating tasks (Hechter 1987; Hardin 1982). I see two basic routes by which they do this.

The first route is that ideologies motivate individuals to contribute more towards achieving the network's goals. For example, if the ideology convinces believers that they will gain a reward in paradise if they die in battle for the cause, this purported selective incentive will reduce shirking. Mann argues that motivation for the enterprises of large-scale networks is dramatically enhanced when such networks can tap into the emotions generated by local and family ties: 'extensive classes and nations have possessed more moral fervor, more passion, when they can also mobilize the more intensive networks of the members' (1993: 227). People are willing to die for religious and nationalist causes because ideology links the stakes in them to hot-button, home-fires issues of blood, family, gender and identity. Consequently, it is good strategy to use religion as an ideological stalking horse for, say, class grievances that may have less inherent emotive content (228). The trick is to link the practical objectives to the high-energy motivators. For this reason, highly effective ideologies, like Hinduism's doctrine of caste, have come 'in a package that could not be easily unpacked', where sacred texts, for example, are also the sources of scientific, legal, social and economic knowledge (1986: 357–8).

The second route is that ideologies imbue cooperative norms with sacred force so that collective action dilemmas can be more easily solved. The deontic force of a sacred ideology is not necessary to solve all dilemmas of group action. Often, coordination based on custom, trial and error, or contractual institutions can do the job. This is especially true when cooperative arrangements have been in place for a while, and consequently have been able to generate expectations around which cooperation can converge. But almost by definition, such expectations are weakly formed in the tracklaying stage of the development of a social network's power to organize collective action. Cooperation needs a boost from charismatic ideology. Stark's account of the success of the early Christians in surmounting public health dilemmas is a good example.

This works not just by motivating individuals to incur costs or take risks for the collective good, but also by motivating them to engage in potentially costly sanctions against those who violate group norms. Mann points out the key role of ostracism in enforcing the caste system. Because India was politically decentralized, such culture-wide sanctioning norms had to be coordinated and enforced through ideology, not through external authority (1986: 357–8). Even so, it would be wrong to view this system as working simply through the psychological internalization of norms. Even in a decentralized system, individuals who fail to fully internalize the norms must behave as if they have done so as long as there is a good chance of being called to task by a true believer. Once India began to urbanize, and individuals' caste identity became difficult to verify, employers began to follow their pecuniary interest and stopped trying to enforce caste-based work norms, since the risk of being sanctioned for failing to sanction others had dramatically declined (Hechter 2000).

Normative solutions to collective action problems do not necessarily produce a highly efficient social equilibrium. While Mann sees Hinduism as in some ways the most effective of all ideological systems for organizing collective and distributive outcomes (1986: 342), its rigidly stratified system was in other ways inefficient and ultimately uncompetitive. Ideological systems have to be only as efficient as their local competitors. Given that proviso, expansion of an ideologically based network might happen not because of any great efficiency, but because of some other source of positive feedback.

Positive feedback can occur where there are increasing returns to scale. Minor, temporary or completely fortuitous advantages can establish a given competitor as the monopolist in a market niche, whose position gets locked in by increasing returns. VHS versus Betamax is the canonical example (Pierson 2000). Thus, Christianity may have been more efficient than the cult of Isis as a power-generating network, but it was not efficient enough to save the empire from the barbarians or even to sustain the scale economies that united its eastern and western domains. Christianity's ascendancy had something to do with its relative efficiency in generating collective action within its club, but it also had something to do with the positive feedback effects that were generated by virtue of the niche it was filling.

Other forms of positive feedback may result from the dynamics of rhetoric. In the French Revolution, for example, Mann observes that the ideological elite got trapped in the rhetoric of treason that it had adopted for transitory, tactical reasons. Lock-in occurred unintentionally when 'popular pressure ensured that later "betrayal" would risk dignity, position, even life' (1993: 196, 207, 234; Lichbach and Seligman 2000: 112–13). In the field of international politics, we call this 'blowback' (Snyder 1991: 41–2).

Another mechanism of positive feedback, already discussed above, is the *fait accompli*. This can create ideological lock-in by provoking an action by a competitor that fulfils the predictions of the ideology and makes its prescriptions necessary. In short, an ideology can entrench its hold and expand its domain either because it is more effective than competitors in organizing collective action, or through a variety of institutional, rhetorical, or behavioural positive feedbacks, or both.

The relationship of 'is' and 'ought'

What does the foregoing suggest about the relationship of 'is' and 'ought' in ideologically infused social networks? At a minimum, it is clear from Mann's historical accounts that the content of normative ideology typically mirrors social structure in much the way that Durkheim said it does, though not always for Durkheim's reasons. Mann (1986: 155) endorses Jacobsen's (1976) classification of the stages in the development of Mesopotamian religion, wherein the changing depictions of god and the content of social norms track closely with changes in the social distribution of political, economic and social power. Mann calls his own account of the rise of early Christianity in the interstices of the Roman Empire 'a very Durkheimian model' (1986: 309).

In terms of the rhetoric of ideological persuasion, Mann portrays normative and empirical claims as conflated and intermingled in every social network he discusses. His discussion of the late eighteenth century is typical. The Enlightenment is 'a fusion of religion, science, philosophy, and the arts' (1993: 194). Specialized science spilled over into 'generalist moralizing knowledge' (229–31). In the French Revolution, 'leaders mixed values and norms with fact' in 'Hunt's "politics of authentic emotions"' (193). In the New World, 'supposedly factual portrayals' of French and Huron behaviour 'were actually moral and political tracts'. The expansion of literacy spurred 'writing, reading, and oral assembly networks' that created 'links between the intensive and the extensive, between the secular instrumental and the sacred moral' (229). Hume's well-meaning prescriptive intervention evidently failed to straighten out the prevailing conceptual mess.

It is less clear from Mann's accounts precisely how 'is' and 'ought' come to be entwined in this way, or why people tolerate their indiscriminate conflation in argument. One possible answer is that, as social constructivists would have it, social facts, including identities and interests, are constituted of norms. In this view, 'is' is thoroughly suffused by 'ought' in its very bones. The opposite view is that social norms serve as a superstructure that rationalizes social facts and interest. Not only Marx believed this. Weber argued, for example, that shamans invented religion in their attempts to rationalize and obfuscate why their magic often failed to deliver the promised results. Taking a somewhat different tack, Edna Ullmann-Margalit argues that *de facto* coordination equilibria take on normative force on the grounds that it is wrong to frustrate convergent expectations that are beneficial to the group (1977: 85–9). In these various ways, 'ought' may emerge from 'is', whether Hume likes it or not.

Mann's view, as I understand it both from his general statements and from his historical accounts, is different. He sees neither 'is' nor 'ought' as having primacy over the other; rather, they are interactive and co-constitutive of social power networks. An ideologically animated expansion of social power depends on the coming together of a latent potential for collective action in a social network, the motivation of a group of entrepreneurs to organize that collective action, and their provision of a normatively infused ideology that effectively overcomes barriers to collective action.

The promotion of this ideology requires effective persuasion that conflates 'is' and 'ought'. Mann repeatedly shows this, but he does not explicitly show why this is the case. Boiling this down to its essence, my own explanation is as follows. Large-scale collective action in human groups inherently requires the effective invocation of transcendental meaning and deontic norms. Habit, force and direct reciprocity are simply inadequate to overcome the potential problems of shirking and opportunism that are endemic to any complex, extensive social network. Collective social action needs a boost from the sacred. Conversely, the claims of intellectual systems of transcendental meaning and normative obligation are inherently unverifiable on their own terms. Apart from a little man behind the curtain who can stage 'miracles' on their behalf, the only compelling proof that can be mustered for them is a social proof: namely, that groups that adhere to these doctrines demonstrate competitive advantages that make outsiders want to jump on the bandwagon. Thus, the sacred needs a boost from effective collective action. In this way, 'is' and 'ought' are necessarily bound together in social action as well as in social persuasion.

Implications for Mann's research programme

Mann's research programme on the sources of social power is fascinating and fertile. His historical interpretations are well grounded empirically and produce fresh insights on diverse conceptual issues. However, from the standpoint of a consumer in the field of international politics, unapologetic-ally mired in the search for deductively derived empirical generalizations, his research programme as presently constituted has some limitations.

One problem is the distracting focus on 'the four sources and organiza-tions of power': i.e. the political, military, economic and ideological (1986: 22). This typology labours under the dead weight of the history of socio-logical thought, especially the debate between the schools of Marx and Weber. But Marxism is obsolescent as an active social philosophy, and monocausal explanations based on political, military, or economic reduc-tionism are no longer the liveliest contenders in contemporary social science. Because of the debates sparked by social constructivists, it probably does make some sense to theorize about the relationship of ideological power to the other three, but to run politics against economics and against military power is a contest that even Mann does not seem to take very seriously.

The harm done by this classification scheme is mainly that it distracts from other schemes whose mechanisms and processes cut across these dimensions. I have in mind not only the rationalistic collective action theories that Stark, for example, invokes, but also culturalist arguments like those of Furet and Hunt. Mann brings in such themes episodically, but his research programme is not set up to theorize about them systematically.

This is a problem on methodological as well as substantive grounds. Methodologically, it would strengthen Mann's ability to prove his argu-ments if they were framed, like Stark's aspire to be, in terms of empirically testable deductive generalizations. The proof of this is in the pudding: Mann's arguments about the rise of Christianity are often similar to Stark's, but the latter's cleaner approach to stating and testing hypotheses often makes his account the more telling demonstration.

Substantively, abandoning the hoary four horsemen for a more pro-ductive categorization of power-generating mechanisms would increase the likelihood of finding the portable generalizations that Mann tells us just cannot be had (1986: 341). While it is unlikely that Mann himself will want to make this move, those in more positivistic fields who want to adapt his approach and insights would be well advised to attempt it. For those who want conceptual take-home points that can illuminate con-temporary circumstances, theory should offer a more clearly specified generative logic and a more specific list of potentially relevant hypotheses.

Implications for understanding contemporary networks and ideologies

Let me conclude with one brief example showing how these insights might be applied to contemporary issues. In the field of international politics, social constructivism has been one of the most influential research programmes since the end of the Cold War. Within constructivism, an especially strong research agenda has been advanced by those scholars who see social reality as constituted by ideas and norms 'almost all the way down' (Wendt 1999). In their view, culture, defined as shared knowledge or symbols that create meaning within a social group, determines whether behaviour in the absence of a common governing authority is bloody or benign. This has practical implications. If more benign ideas and identities can be effectively spread throughout the globe by cultural change and normative persuasion, they argue, then 'ought' can be transformed into 'is': support for warlike dictators can be undermined, perpetrators of war crimes and atrocities can be held accountable, benign multicultural identities can be fostered, and international and civil wars will wane.[1] This outlook is echoed by influential activist networks, such as Amnesty International and Human Rights Watch, who see themselves as the vanguard bearing a set of norms that has the potential to fundamentally transform the nature of world politics.

In contrast, sceptics about such transformations argue that anarchy, whether among states coexisting in a self-help system or among contending groups inside collapsed states, gives rise to an inescapable logic of insecurity and competition that culture cannot trump (Mearsheimer 2001; Posen 1993). These realist sceptics fear that a transformative attempt to supersede self-help behaviour amounts to reckless overreaching that will create backlashes and quagmires. Ironically, in this view, the idealist vanguard of the new world order will need to rely increasingly on old-fashioned military and economic coercion in a futile effort to change world culture for the better.[2]

Mann's perspective on the nature of social power might bring some valuable insights to this debate. His work should sensitize us to the power that value-infused transnational networks can generate. The realists are wrong to dismiss such prospects out of hand. However, Mann's approach should also alert us to the fact that the power potential of a network does not derive from ideas and persuasion 'all the way down'. Ideas thrive only if they find a social niche in which they resolve contradictions of meaning or organization for actors in the network. Some scholars such as Kathryn Sikkink make an effort to analyse the sociology of power in activist networks, but their sociological interest in the targets of persuasion and in the material preconditions of an effective human rights regime remains limited (Risse and Sikkink 1999). For both the scholars and the activist organizations, their principled idealist ontology makes them less attuned to these considerations than Mann's insights would recommend.

This is unfortunate, because of the key role of successful demonstration effects as a social proof in persuading targets to jump on a network's bandwagon. So far the liberal human rights and transitional justice agenda has at best a mixed record to report (Stedman 2001: 748). Democratic consolidations have gone most smoothly in South America, South Africa and East Central Europe, where past human rights abuses were not sternly prosecuted. Tribunals for the former Yugoslavia and Rwanda did not deter subsequent abuses in the immediate neighbourhood. In the Islamic world, liberal human rights approaches are for the most part anathema, as transnational networks based on illiberal principles of *sharia* and terrorism spread. Human rights successes, such as expelling perpetrators of ethnic 'cleansing' from Kosovo and bringing Milosevic to the Hague, may be attributable more to naked military coercion than to the power of human rights norms and networks. In short, social proof for this ideology remains to be demonstrated. Arguably, designing human rights strategies that are more attuned to the kinds of sociological dimensions that Mann explores might improve that network's effectiveness. As the world grapples with the volatile consequences of the rise of ideology-infused networks of various kinds, Mann's historical sociology provides an invaluable conceptual guidebook to such dynamics.

Notes

1 Finnemore and Sikkink (1998: 916); Risse and Sikkink (1999); Wendt (1999: 141, 377–8); Ruggie (1998: 199 and *passim*). These scholars adhere to the constructivist approach to the study of international politics, but not all constructivists are so clearly wedded to this transformative political agenda. For more qualified views, see Katzenstein (1996: 536–7) and Owen (1997: 232–5). For further analysis, see Snyder (2002).

2 Layne and Schwartz (1999). For a more positive assessment of the role of military power in support of a constructivist agenda of global transformation, see Ruggie (1998, 240–55).

References

Berger, P., and T. Luckmann. 1964. *The Social Construction of Reality*. Garden City, NY: Anchor Books.

Boli, J., and G. M. Thomas. 1999. *Constructing World Culture: International Nongovernmental Organizations since 1875*. Stanford: Stanford University Press.

De Figueiredo, R., and B. Weingast. 1999. The Rationality of Fear: Political Opportunism and Ethnic Conflict. In B. Walter and J. Snyder (eds.), *Civil Wars, Insecurity, and Intervention*. New York: Columbia University Press.

Fearon, J., and D. Laitin. 2000. Violence and the Social Construction of Ethnic Identity. *International Organization* 54(4) (autumn).

Finnemore, M., and K. Sikkink. 1998. International Norm Dynamics and Political Change. *International Organization*, 52(4) (autumn).

Furet, F. 1992. *Revolutionary France, 1770–1880*. Oxford: Blackwell.

Gagnon, V. P. 1994–95. Ethnic Nationalism and International Conflict: The Case of Serbia. *International Security* (winter).

Grafstein, R. 1992. *Institutional Realism*. New Haven: Yale University Press.

Hardin, R. 1982. *Collective Action*. Baltimore: Johns Hopkins University Press.

Hechter, M. 1987. *Principles of Group Solidarity*. Berkeley: University of California Press.

  2000. *Containing Nationalism*. New York: Oxford University Press.

Hunt, L. 1984. *Politics, Culture, and Class in the French Revolution*. Berkeley: University of California Press.

Huntington, S. P. 1968. *Political Order in Changing Societies*. New Haven: Yale University Press.

Jacobsen, T. 1976. *The Treasures of Darkness*. New Haven: Yale University Press.

Katzenstein, P. (ed.). 1996. *The Culture of National Security*. New York: Columbia University Press.

Keck, M. E., and K. Sikkink. 1998. *Activists beyond Borders*. Ithaca: Cornell University Press.

Layne, C., and B. Schwartz. 1999. For the Record. *The National Interest*, 57 (Fall).

Lichbach, M. L., and A. Seligman. 2000. *Market and Community: The Basis of Social Order, Revolution, and Relegitimation*. University Park: Pennsylvania State University.

Mann, M. 1986. *The Sources of Social Power, Volume I: A History from the Beginning to 1760 AD*. Cambridge: Cambridge University Press.

  1993. *The Sources of Social Power, Volume II: The Rise of Classes and Nation-States*. Cambridge: Cambridge University Press.

  2004. *Fascists*. Cambridge: Cambridge University Press.

Mearsheimer, J. 2001. *The Tragedy of Great Power Politics*. New York: Norton.

Owen, J. M., IV. 1997. *Liberal Peace, Liberal War*. Ithaca: Cornell University Press.

Pierson, P. 2000. Increasing Returns, Path Dependence, and the Study of Politics, *American Political Science Review*, 94(2).

Posen, B. 1993. The Security Dilemma and Ethnic Conflict. *Survival*, 35(1).

Risse, T., and K. Sikkink. 1999. The Socialization of International Human Rights Norms into Domestic Practice. In T. Risse, S. Ropp and K. Sikkink (eds.), *The Power of Human Rights: International Norms and Domestic Change*. Cambridge: Cambridge University Press.

Ruggie, J. 1998. *Constructing the World Polity*. London: Routledge.

Snyder, J. 1991. *Myths of Empire*. Ithaca: Cornell University Press.

  2000. *From Voting to Violence: Democratization and Nationalist Conflict*. New York: Norton.

  2002. Anarchy and Culture: Insights from the Anthropology of War, *International Organization* (winter).

Stark, R. 1996. *The Rise of Christianity: A Sociologist Reconsiders History*. Princeton: Princeton University Press.

Stedman, S. J. 2001. International Implementation of Peace Agreements in Civil Wars: Findings from a Study of Sixteen Cases. In C. A. Crocker, F. Hampson and P. Aall (eds.), *Turbulent Peace*. Washington, DC: US Institute of Peace.

Ullmann-Margalit, E. 1977. *The Emergence of Norms*. Oxford: Clarendon.

Walt, S. M. 1996. *Revolution and War*. Ithaca: Cornell University Press.

Wendt, A. 1999. *Social Theory of International Politics*. Cambridge: Cambridge University Press.

15   Mann's dark side: linking democracy and genocide*

David Laitin

The Dark Side of Democracy: Explaining Ethnic Cleansing was written by one of the premier macro-historical sociologists writing in the early twenty-first century. Through his two-volume study of *The Sources of Social Power*, Mann carries forward the great tradition of Marx, Weber and Moore with his vast historical knowledge, his conceptual innovations (portraying power in its separate military, economic, political and ideological components), and his compelling normative concerns (for social justice and the revulsion of violence). *The Dark Side* sparkles with the erudition and normative concerns that characterize his earlier writings. And his portrayals of murderous acts by states taken against their own populations – often in contradiction to approaches I have taken on the same issues – reflect an understanding of process, contingency and the popular social base of grisly perfidy. Much of the book is so well grounded sociologically and historically that both the complexity of the particular and the patterns of the general are retained.

Yet in regard to the principal set of theses, he uses his erudition and keenness of subtle argument to cloud social reality rather than to clarify it. This is a strong charge to hold against a scholar of Mann's stature. Yet I believe it is fully justified. Rather than enumerate the sub-theses that are cogently developed, or summarize his enlightening reconstruction of events, I will focus here on my critique of his principal theses.[1]

There are two separate points I will make to support my charge. First, from the book's provocative title on through the text, Mann associates the most grievous and murderous violations of human rights with democracy. Again and again the data compel him to back off from any causal story linking the two, but somehow he holds tenaciously to increasingly watered-down versions of an initially bold causal claim. Through his tenacious grasp on discredited hypotheses, Mann conjures the unwary reader into believing the book supports the claim embedded in the book's title – namely, that there is a systematic association between democracy and murderous ethnic cleansing.

Second, Mann designs a categorization of dastardly acts such that the modern form of state murderousness (genocide) appears, despite ambiguous evidence, as the very worst of a terrible genre. Nonetheless, Mann impresses his reader that it is both natural and obvious to view genocide as the highest stage of state brutality. It isn't. Perhaps Mann is driven to exaggerate the relative evil of genocide over other forms of mass murder because of his nostalgia for the snows of yesteryear (class politics). He is not apparently driven by any objective assessment of comparative state evil.

Point 1: the association of democracy and murderous ethnic cleansing

The book begins with a portrait of an Albanian couple in Kosovo – a 74-year-old Batisha Hoxha sitting in her kitchen with her 77-year-old husband, Izet. Several Serbian soldiers burst into the house, and beat the old man dead in search of information about the whereabouts of their children (2005: 1). One might ask in horror – is this book about the collapse of empire? Or is it about the excesses of nationalism? Perhaps it is a book about the implications of state failure? But no. This is a book whose title is *The Dark Side of Democracy*! What, the perplexed reader asks himself, does this violent vignette have to do with democracy?

This vignette serves as the segue into the principal theses of the book. The first one is that 'murderous cleansing is modern, because it is the dark side of democracy' (2005: 2). Note well this thesis does not say that murderous cleansing is modern and so is democracy, so that modernity has its dark side. Rather the 'because' logically implies that murderous cleansing is caused by democracy. In his explication of this first thesis, Mann begins backtracking. Democracy means rule of the people, he tells us; under certain conditions, however, 'the people' gets defined as an *ethnos*, and when this happens we see a rejection of citizen diversity. However, since Mann holds that 'citizen diversity ... is central to democracy', states that deny diversity are not by definition democracies (3). Already the initial association between ethnic cleansing and democracy is qualified. It seems that it is the denial of what is central to democracy that is the culprit.

We then move on to thesis 1(a), one that further qualifies the principal thesis. Here Mann theorizes that, 'murderous ethnic cleansing is a hazard of the age of democracy' (3). In the explication of this thesis, murderous cleansing is no longer caused by democracy, but it is a result of a perversion of democratic ideals (4). By thesis 1(c) the qualifications continue. Not democracy *per se*, but the process of democratization is the culprit, as this process unleashes forces that are not easily controlled by states in transition. By thesis 1(e) we see the principal thesis virtually abandoned. 'Regimes that are actually perpetrating murderous cleansing are never democratic,' he points out, 'since that would be a contradiction in terms' (4).

Qualifications and re-statements of his theses abound throughout the tome. In his account of the Rwanda genocide, for example, Mann concludes that the Hutus were motivated by a slogan of 'majoritarian democracy' (473). But here it is an ideological slogan, not democracy itself, which is implicated. Mann's culprit is not democracy, but a form of politics that uses democratic vocabulary, but in a different semantic sense. Elsewhere, we are told that 'democratization struggles' have their dark side (69). So it is the struggle for democracy rather than democracy itself that is the culprit.

In the final sentence of his penultimate chapter, Mann continues to water down his principal thesis. The sentence is a non sequitur, and doesn't follow from the data in that chapter on counterfactuals. 'For murderous ethnic cleansing', he writes, 'is the dark side of the would-be democratic nation-state' (501). I'm not sure what a 'would-be democratic nation-state' is, but I think Mann is saying that it is the dark side of states that are not democracies. And in the final paragraph of the book, we learn that ethnic cleansing will disappear 'when democracy is securely institutionalized' (529). Therefore the original notion that 'murderous cleansing is modern, because it is the dark side of democracy' now becomes something of the following: so-called democracies that really aren't yet democracies are dangerous.

Throughout the book, Mann elaborates on yet another thesis in regard to democracy, one that is not only watered down, but logically nonsensical – and as formulated, trivial. Mann implies that because democracy and genocide are both modern, they implicate one another. Logically, Mann is incorrectly linking two phenomena that are temporally but not causally linked. This type of reasoning would make democracy culpable for world war, AIDS and rap music. But the substantive claim, viz. that genocide is a function of the modern age, is trivially true. Students of nationalism and ethnicity have long known, at least since the LSE pathbreaking studies of nationalism, that social solidarity based on myths of common descent is a relatively modern phenomenon.[2] It is therefore unremarkable that state builders and revolutionaries in pre-modern times did not signal out descent groups as their enemies. Thus ethnically based killing is modern.

An unflattering summary of this rendition of Mann's principal argument might be this: in all periods in human history political leaders have ordered or tolerated the murder of subsets of their populations. In the modern era, while the percentage of the populations killed due to state-led violence may have been reduced, the targets have changed. While in the ancient world, *where* you lived was key; in the early modern world it was *what you believed*; and in the twentieth century, it has been *what descent group* you came from. That you cannot systematically murder groups that are not understood as groups is a true finding – but a trivial one.

Yet another rendition of the democracy→genocide thesis is the claim that in many contexts killing the ethnic/religious/racial other is popular, and therefore demagogues' 'mass appeal is a democratic one' (2005: 514). There can be no doubt that killing the other can have impressive mass appeal. That doesn't make the killing democratic. More important, it doesn't mean that democracies are more susceptible to killing ethnic others than are autocracies. As Reinhard Bendix elaborated in a classic study (1978), all modern rulers legitimate their domination in the name of the people. Both dictators and democratic leaders in the modern period seek to do things that are popular, and often succeed in manipulating information to make their own projects popular. What differentiates tyranny from democracy in the modern age are institutions such as fair elections and rule of law, factors that play almost no role in Mann's brief against democracy. Evidence for the popularity of (or even general partici-pation in) mass killing does not therefore implicate democracy as a causal factor in such killing.[3]

So much for the theoretical claims. What about the empirical evidence? It is almost astonishing that a book entitled *The Dark Side of Democracy* would have eleven of its seventeen chapters describe hideous killing of a variety of sorts perpetrated in non-democracies: Turkey and the Armenian genocide (two chapters); the Nazis and the holocaust (three chapters); the communist politicides, fratricides, callous or mistaken revolutionary projects, and 'classicides' ('Mann's neologism') in the Soviet Union, China and Cambodia (one chapter); the murderous ethnic cleansing in post-communist Yugoslavia (two chapters); and the geno-cide in Rwanda (two chapters). In nearly all of these cases, Mann makes the indirect and unconvincing claim that these events took place in a context of organic peoplehood (the nation, the tribe, or the class), and killing in the name of the people employs core words in the democratic vocabulary. But killing in the name of a people however named in non-democratic states does not implicate democracy in that killing!

Take the case of the Turkish genocide. Mann reports that Turkey up through 1915 was a 'semi-democratic system' (2005: 125). But it had 'effectively abandoned democracy' (2005: 129) before the Armenian geno-cide. Thus Mann assesses that this case does not support the core thesis of the book. The Young Turks had attempted a 'democratic transition', to be sure, 'but it was aborted well before the murderous cleansing began' (2002: 170). In the conclusion to his social history of the Armenian genocide Mann reiterates that in a 'direct sense' this was not a case of the 'dark side of democracy'. However, he asserts that the genocide 'could only have occurred in the age of democracy' (trivially true), and as a result of a 'perverted democratization process'. This last claim is odd because Mann quickly admits that democratization as a process was not taking place at the time of the genocide. So there could be no empirical link between the two.

Take now the case of the Nazis and their genocide. Mann correctly writes that the Nazis got to the brink of power through democratic elections. However, in the opening pages of the volume he asserts that 'of course' the Nazi regime was a dictatorship (2005: 4). Later he points out that the organic nationalism associated with Nazism will 'quickly ... lead' a polity 'out of democracy', because 'a state led by an elite or dictator claims to speak with a singular voice' (63). And in his full discussion of the holocaust he elaborates, pointing out that the consolidation of Nazi power was by violent means, and having 'immediately terminated democracy ... it was a party dictatorship that was to perpetrate the genocide' (184). Thus, the reader should conclude, these chapters will add no evidence in support of the principal thesis of the book. But at the very end of the three-chapter analysis of that genocide, Mann concludes that 'the ultimate tragedy of the Jews was also essentially modern: to be the main target of this cleansing organic nation-statism. In this way,' Mann writes, 'I have accommodated the Final Solution in a slightly indirect fashion into my first ethnic thesis: it was the dark side of the democratizing nation-state' (317). This is an odd conclusion since Mann agreed up-front that the genocide took place in a de-democratizing nation-state.

The subsequent analysis of communist cleansing (chapter 11) nearly (but not completely) abandons the principal thesis of the book, as Mann admits in its introduction that the states examined were 'not remotely democratic' (2005: 320). Since these polities viewed the people as a 'singular organic whole, not as stratified into plural interest-groups, as in liberal or social democracy', he reasons, 'this took them away from true democracy' (350). However, because the killing in these cases 'nourished *organic* conceptions of we, the people, the people as a singular ethnic nation or a single proletarian class' (350), Mann sees these cases as supporting his thesis (1a) that murderous ethnic cleansing is a hazard of the age of democracy. As I argued earlier, the 'age of democracy' argument has little merit. It would be like blaming the Yoruba civil wars on plutocrats because they took place during the Gilded Age.[4]

The most compelling evidence for a relationship between democracy and genocide is provided in Chapter 4, 'Genocidal Democracies in the

New World'. This chapter is a powerful and disturbing presentation of historical events that can only unsettle Americans, Australians, Spaniards and Germans. Their forefathers participated in a degree of human cruelty that is unimaginable to the twenty-first century liberal mind. That by today's standards, figures such as Thomas Jefferson should be seated next to Hitler and Milosevic as perpetrators of genocide is a gruesome idea, but one that Mann supports with stunning cogency. That settlers in these zones of European expansion not only gratuitously murdered indigenous suspects of attacks, but also envisaged and wholeheartedly supported solutions to the native problem that involved extermination is an undeniable fact of European migration and settlement. I continually sought to formulate mitigating circumstances to differentiate settler genocide from the Hitlerian holocaust – for example that indigenous peoples whose livelihoods were threatened by the settlers actually were threats to those settlers, in terms of raids and attacks, and this was clearly not the case of Jews in Germany – but these were failed patriotic attempts to vindicate the founding fathers of a liberal democracy in which I am a citizen. That American society is built on a foundation of genocide is blood that cannot be wiped clean from its hands.

Is this, then, the smoking gun linking democracy to genocide? I remain unconvinced. Take one of the more unsettling claims of the chapter – that Jefferson was a democrat and also a genocidal murderer. However unsettling, this is hardly evidence of such a link. After all, he was also a Christian, a wine drinker, an English speaker and a slave owner. We wouldn't say genocide is the dark side of wine drinking. There needs to be first a systematic relationship linking his democratic credentials to his genocidal policies, and second, there needs to be a mechanism theorized that shows the relationship to have causal properties.

In the conclusion to the chapter on settler democracy, Mann suggests (but does not demonstrate) a systematic relationship. He concludes (2005: 107), 'the more the settler democracy, the more ethnic exclusivity, the worse the treatment'. He subsequently stipulates that of four empires (two of which are not discussed in the text) the more democratic ones (the British and Dutch as compared to the Spanish and Portuguese) had more 'deliberate genocidal bursts'. He then adds that the German case is the exception. But a perusal of Table 15.1 below hardly gives support to the thesis. With $n = 4$, one exception weighs quite heavily. Moreover, Mann slips two cases of horrific ethnic cleansing by settlers (the Russian settlers in the Caucasus that 'almost amounted to genocide' and the Han settlers in Yunnan, in which an estimated 90 per cent of the local population were murdered (2002: 146)). If these cases were part of the dataset, and settler governance were coded as non-democratic for both of them, it would

Table 15.1. *Democracy and genocide in settler colonies*

Settler Colony	Democracy	Genocide
Mexico	Imperial centre not democratic; settlers not coded	Selective repression and ethnocide, but not genocide
Australia	Imperial centre democratic; settlers have some local democracy	Policed deportations, with 'unpremeditated genocidal bursts'
United States	Imperial centre democratic; settlers have considerable local democracy	Ethnocide, policed deportations, and common bursts of genocide
Southwest Africa	Centre highly authoritarian; lack of local democracy	Deportations and systematic genocide

become clearer that there was no relationship whatsoever between the level of democracy and the number of indigenous people murdered.

The evidence linking settler democracy to extermination remains confusing and inadequate. Mann provides some support to the idea that in the US, the more democratic the state (with California scoring highest), the more thorough the genocide. But this theme is not developed with any systematic data. The only case of settler expansion included in Mann's treatise where you do not get genocidal outbursts is Mexico, a case not coded on the independent variable. The text gives causal properties to such issues as Cortez's patience and the fact that settlement was largely by males, and thus the desire to take natives for sexual and/or marriage partners. These factors do not speak to the thesis at hand. Mann might have considered more recent cases as tests. A systematic dataset would surely include cases such as South Africa and Palestine, where settlers constructed democracies for their own ethnic groups, treated the indigenous populations inhumanely, but did not engage in genocide. In these two twentieth-century cases, to use Mann's formulation, *ethnos* and *demos* were deeply entwined, yet there was no genocide.

These new cases, along with those discussed in the book, suggest an alternative thesis, one raised by Mann. Under conditions where (a) native labour is not wanted, (b) settler land claims threaten the survival of natives, and (c) military power is more advanced among settlers, murderous ethnic cleansing is more likely, at times reaching genocide. Thus there is a logic of settler colonialism: settlers bring with them advanced agricultural techniques in a territory where the indigenous population lacks these techniques. When their labour is not needed by the settlers, these indigenous populations are seen as an unnecessary encumbrance on the advance of civilization. It is this logic, not the logic of democracy, which provides the incentives for extermination.

Throughout the book, as with the case of settler democracy, Mann is cavalier about disconfirming evidence. In his chapter on 'counter-factual cases', he examines the case of India, where the BJP, an ethno-nationalist party, 'came to power democratically'. Once in government, rulers realize, 'those who cannot keep order will fall' (2005: 483). This need ('here Mann is a functionalist') 'moderates their ethno-nationalist tendencies' (2002: 513). Mann does not ask whether the fact that India is a functioning democracy was part of the reason that BJP leadership felt a need to preserve order. Meanwhile, in Indonesia (far less democratic than India), Mann exhibits worry that its prospects for murderous cleansing are far worse than in India. Mann does not infer from these examples that democracy puts some constraints on murderous cleansing (as he did otherwise with weaker data for the western United States in regard to native Americans). To his credit, however, he provides the evidence that allows his reader to discredit the book's core claim.

By the end of the book, Mann's principal thesis is barely hanging on a thread. Indeed, to keep the narrative moving, the vast bulk of the book steers clear of the claim of its title and its principal thesis; only occasional oblique references to democracy – mostly at chapter's end – pay obeisance to the book's advertised message. But he returns to the democracy theme in the concluding chapter, where he calls for us in the 'North' to 'show more realism in our views of ethnic cleansing' (2005: 522). Here he suggests that we in democratic states are no more immune to ethnic cleansing than are citizens of less democratic states. The notion that organic national-ism or religious fundamentalism can hit all populations, democratic or authoritarian, is surely a worry. With this in mind, Mann concludes in his penultimate chapter that, there is 'no simple relationship ... between democracy and ethnic cleansing' (498).[5] On this last point (without the 'simple') I agree; it is astonishing that Mann persistently implies otherwise.

Point 2: genocide as the highest form of ghastly murder

Mann's categorization of appalling acts is laid out in his table I-1 (2005: 12). On the x axis, Mann distinguishes 'Types of Cleansing' and this axis has three values, going left to right: 'none', 'partial' or 'total'. This variable is continuous. On the y axis, the variable is called 'Types of Violence', and from top to bottom it goes from 'none' to institutional coercion, policed repression, violent repression, unpremeditated mass deaths, and finally premeditated mass killing. On the bottom right corner, the confluence of 'all' on the x axis and 'premeditated mass killing' on the

y axis constitutes genocide, and the table points to it as the highest form of violent cleansing.

The logic behind this table is biased. Take first the distinction on the x axis between 'partial' and 'total', with the implication that the latter is morally worse. For the case of genocide (which is total), Mann examines the percentage of the targeted ethnic population. But for the case of politicide and classicide (which are partial) Mann assesses not the percentage of political enemies killed but the percentage of the total population lost. And so, the killing of all gypsies in Nazi Germany is the highest form of state murder; whereas the killing of all supporters of Lon Nol by the Khmer Rouge doesn't reach the pinnacle of murderousness, even if more Lon Nol supporters were killed than were gypsies.

Now take the y axis, where premeditated mass killing is a higher form of state murder than callous war, mistaken revolutionary projects, and ethnocide (e.g. killing entire populations through the transmission of disease or through callous labour practices). In mass murder these are difficult distinctions to uphold. First, while state leaders might be excused for the first wave of deaths in a mistaken revolutionary project (such as the forced collectivization in Ukraine), the lack of murderous intent for the first round of deaths doesn't excuse the persistence in fulfilling the project. Second, as Mann cogently demonstrates through his processual accounts of actual genocides, the degree to which state murderers were following a single plan – even in the case of the Nazis in regard to Jews – is historically quite low. In most cases, as Mann shows, there was a 'Plan A' to address the problem of ethnic others that was incompletely successful. This induced a 'Plan B', somewhat harsher. The actual genocide occurs with 'Plan D', hardly in the minds of the killers when 'Plan A' was devised. Mann's processual approach to mass killing undermines his own categorization on the y axis of table I.1. He undermines his own categorization scheme by criticizing rival accounts of genocides as 'over-premeditated' (2005: 112).

Not only is table I.1 logically flawed, but it is also not an uncontested barometer of evil. Ethnocides, callous warfare, and other atrocities that do not reach the pinnacle of evil are not self-evidently less grievous than genocides. I do not have strong priors on the comparative dastardliness of murderous state projects. I would even admit that the bile in my stomach reading about what Mann calls 'callous warfare' is far less upsetting than for the chapters on genocide. Rather, I am criticizing the objectification of this feeling into two apparently Guttman-like scales. These scales allow Mann to make normative comparisons without clear moral argument.

Furthermore, elementary arithmetic suggests that the stomach some-times betrays reality. Take Mann's claim that the callous warfare of pre-modern periods fell short of genocide. But the extent of the killing (for examples the percentage of the targeted population killed) may (we don't know) be larger in earlier periods. Consider further Mann's discussion of the thirteenth-century war in France against the so-called Cathar heresy. Chroniclers report that when the Cathar stronghold of Beziers was stormed, 'most of its 8,000 or so inhabitants were slaughtered – men, women and children'. Consider as well the Thirty Years' War in Germany and Bohemia, in which 3–4 million people, constituting some 15–20 per cent of the population of the Holy Roman Empire, were killed. This in Mann's schema is also callous warfare. For Mann's rhetorical purposes, the siege of Beziers and the atrocities of the Thirty Years' War need to be less gruesome than Rwanda (a true genocide). In parenthesis Mann reduces the reader's horror by noting that the thirteenth-century chronicler 'may have been exaggerating' about the extent of killing in Beziers. (Note well, they may have underestimated the gore, but Mann does not speculate on a possible upwards revision of estimated deaths.) And the brutality of Magdeburg (a Protestant stronghold that was stormed by Catholic forces in 1631, killing some 30,000 men, women and children) is somewhat mitigated because it was not premeditated (2005: 48–9). Mann's categorization scheme codes this siege as 'callous warfare' falling one diagonal box towards multicultural toleration and away from genocide. Thus portrayed graphically, we get the impression that it wasn't all *that* bad. But what was the scale of the death? It may not have qualified as genocide (by definition), but it may not have been less systematically brutal.

The modern age, even with genocides, may well have been less brutal to individuals than earlier periods. Most datasets show a declining probability of dying a violent death in the modern as opposed to the pre-modern era. Perhaps pre-moderns specialized in generalized callous brutality while moderns specialize in more targeted brutality. But murder of *people* by those claiming political authority surely is declining (as a percentage of the world's civilian population) as murder of *peoples* (defined as ethnic entities) increased. The pictorial image in table I.1 of the modern form of massacre to be the highest stage of brutality is therefore arbitrary.

Mann believes that class conflict is a more civilized, less dangerous, form of conflict than ethnic/national conflict. The oft-repeated clause 'when class trumps ethnicity' is invariably followed by some favourable social outcome as compared to the alternatives. Cromwell's contribution to the killing of about 15 per cent of the Irish population (2005: 51) was mitigated by the fact that class politics dominated the secular realm (54). Nineteenth-century British politics were, according to Mann, less violent because class conflict was supreme.[6] However, when it is the reverse, that is when 'nation trumps class', we are led to expect some ghastly human horror. This becomes nearly a mantra, and it reads like nostalgia for the good old storms of *The New Left Review* as opposed to today's snows, that only drop blood.

Here again, chapter 11 on communist cleansing is instructive. Mann pulls no punches in counting the dead as a result of communist factional wars, communist-induced famines, communist purges of class enemies, and communist forced resettlement of peoples. But this chapter has a sub-theme that is consistent with these cases' placements on table I-1, which are less extreme than genocide. After toting the victims of Stalinism, some 8–10 million innocents killed (2005: 329), Mann reassures us that this does not constitute genocide. '*At its worst*', he concludes, 'this amounted to deliberate classicide/politicide' (330, my emphasis). The phrase 'at its worst' makes sense if and only if the logic of table I-1 is accepted, and that classicide/politicide is fundamentally less hideous than genocide.

At the end of this chapter, Mann suggests that communist killings may have had a silver lining, even assisting economic development (350). This conjecture also makes classicide/politicide perpetrated by communists to be less bad than the genocide of settler democrats. But even though Mann acknowledges that today's liberal democracies rest on a foundation of genocide, he does not use evidence of the long-term consequences to in any way exonerate the perpetrators. Of course, in the settler massacres there weren't economic benefits to the murdered autochthonous populations; but neither were there benefits bestowed on *kulaks* as a result of Stalinist brutality. Mann insidiously lessens the moral weight of politicide as compared to genocide not by moral argument but through an apparently objective table comparatively evaluating the scope and range of murderous practices. And this is designed to emphasize the pluses (and diminish the minuses) of class warfare.

In conclusion, Mann's principal set of theses linking democracy to genocide is massively misguided. His categorization of 'Types of Violence and Cleansing in Inter-Group Relations' (table I.1) designed to lessen the moral weight of murderous class warfare is equally misguided. Mann repeatedly (and correctly) shows that projects that began with idealistic goals have gotten revoltingly perverted when initial results were disappointing in meeting those goals. Yet there is a parallel here. In a sense, Mann's project to expose the dark sides of democracy and nationalism ran up against powerful evidence to the contrary. The brilliant research that went into the book's making fell victim to Mann's unwillingness to adjust his findings to the evidence – and led ultimately to a ghastly perversion of his historical sociological project.

Notes

* *Editors' note*: With Professor Mann's approval, the editors assured Professor Laitin that the typescript they sent him in 2002 would be final, and that he could base his review entirely on that version. Substantial changes, however, were made in the course of the publication process. To retain the integrity of Laitin's critique, several quoted passages that were cut from the 2005 published version have been retained herein and cited with their 2002 page reference. To meet publication schedules, Laitin was unable to read fully the published version, and in consequence takes responsibility only for correct representation of the content of the 2002 typescript.

1 I write 'principal' because there are other theses on the causes of murderous ethnic cleansing, relating to need for labour, fragmentation of states, and balance of power among social forces that get considerable support from the case studies. If Mann had made these factors his principal theses, the book would have stood as a major contribution to our understanding of state-led terror. It remains so, but now you need to overlook the leitmotif of the book in order to appreciate its positive contributions.

2 Kedourie (1960) and Gellner (1983) are the principal proponents of this view; Hobsbawm (1992) develops these themes in a series of provocative lectures.

3 Mann (2005: 3) adds several sentences (from the 2002 version I reviewed) to his explanation of his first hypothesis that acknowledges this problem, and resolves it in a rather confusing manner. The majority, he writes, 'can rule "democratically" but also tyrannically'.

4 In this chapter on communist regimes, Mann slyly slips in a reference to the 'contemporary phase of murderous ethnic cleansing in Chechnya ... perpetrated by an elected democratic regime' (2005: 355). But if Mann wanted to know whether there was any correlation between democracy and insurgent warfare in the post-World War II world, he would learn that there is no association whatsoever (Fearon and Laitin 2003).

5 In Mann (2002: 526) there is no ellipsis.

6 See e.g. claims to less brutality when 'class trumps ethnicity' (2005: 5). In the 2002 manuscript, this point is reinforced on pp. 68, 79, 80, 81, 82 and 98.

References

Bendix, R. 1978. *Kings or People: Power and the Mandate to Rule*. Berkeley: University of California Press.

Fearon, J., and D. Laitin. 2003. Ethnicity, Insurgency and Civil War. *American Political Science Review*, 97.

Gellner, E. 1983. *Nations and Nationalism*. Ithaca: Cornell University Press.

Hobsbawm, E. 1992. *Nations and Nationalism since 1780*. Cambridge: Cambridge University Press.

Kedourie, E. 1960. *Nationalism*. London: Hutchinson University Library.

Mann, M. 2005/2002 typescript. *The Dark Side of Democracy: Explaining Ethnic Cleansing*. Cambridge: Cambridge University Press.

Part V

Response

16 The sources of social power revisited: a response to criticism

Michael Mann

I feel honoured by this volume and indebted to the contributors for their praise and their criticism. Having long avoided reflecting on my methodology, I thank Joseph Bryant for revealing it to me and then defending it. Randall Collins gives an incisive account of the substance of my model of the four sources of social power (ideological, economic, military and political) and its location amid other sociological theories. As he says, my power sources are distinct in not being abstract but embodied in real networks of people. These have emergent properties giving them some causal autonomy, though they do not amount to 'logics of development', since they are also closely entwined. I do not focus on power resources held by individuals – unlike Bourdieu's model of economic, cultural, political and social forms of power. I focus on differences between the four networks, unlike most forms of 'network theory' (e.g. mathematical modelling or Castells' 'network society'). The closest parallel, as Collins observes, is with the new economic sociology emphasizing networks of economic connection. As he says, the same job could be done on ideological, military and political power. I also retain my distinctions between 'collective' and 'distributive', 'intensive' and 'extensive', 'diffuse' and 'authoritative', and 'infrastructural' and 'despotic' power, and I use them below.

I reject sociology's foundational notion of 'society' because the boundaries of the four power sources rarely coincide. Despite the increasing 'caging' of people within modern nation-states (noted in *Sources*, Vol. II), these have never been powerful enough to constitute whole 'societies'. Human activity comprises multiple, overlapping, intersecting networks of social interaction. This model has become widely accepted since I initially advanced it. It enables us to identify the root of social change, since plural power organizations can never be entirely institutionalized or insulated from influences coming 'interstitially' from cracks within and between them. Social change results from a dialectic between the institutionalization and the interstitial emergence of power networks.

I oppose all systems theory, all holism, all attempts to reify 'societies'. These make the 'totality' of social interaction into an actor in its own right.

But there is no totality. So Robert Brenner is right to pick me up for my remarks in Volume I of *Sources* suggesting that Europe in the Middle Ages was a single society. All I actually demonstrated was that Christendom was then a real network of interaction (though I did underestimate its links with Islam and Asia). There is no singular 'world system', no singular process of globalization; no multi-state 'system' dominated by a singular 'realist' logic; no logic of patriarchy. History is not the history of class struggle, or of modes of production, or of 'epistemes' or 'discursive formations', cultural codes or underlying structures of thought governing the language, values, science and practices of an era, underpinned by a singular process of power enveloping all human activity.[1] These systems theories succeed in capturing theorists not social reality.

I also oppose mono-causal theories. Explicit ones are now rare, though implicit ones abound, the unintended consequence of academic specialization. Economists tend to elevate the economy (though today many also embrace 'institutions' which are obviously more diverse), political scientists politics (though today often embracing economistic models). Many sociologists are also surprisingly economistic. In analysing globalization, many content themselves with analysing changes in the structure of capitalism, assuming these will change social life as a whole. Conversely, since 'the cultural turn' many confine themselves to ideological and cultural analysis. This is no better. Globalization involves economies, cultures, and also nation-states (there are now over 190 of them) and organizations dedicated to mass destruction. Globalization involves all four types of network and is therefore a plural and 'impure' process.

Ideally, any sociologist analysing macro-topics would always discuss all four sources of social power. If sociological theory is to be of any use at all, it must be both empirically based and cover the breadth of human experience. Of course, juggling four balls at once through world-history is ludicrous over-ambition, and I drop one of them from time to time (most of my critics say I am prone to fumble ideology).

I begin by discussing general criticisms of ideological, military and political power. Then I turn to more empirical issues, beginning with ethnic cleansing and then at greater length discussing Europe's 'miraculous' economic development and brief global dominance, focusing on comparisons with Asia/China. Finally, I offer some theoretical and normative conclusions.

Ideological power

My view of ideological power is said to be too materialist, too instrumental and too rationalist. Though in principle my model is none of these things, my practice has sometimes faltered. I prefer the term 'ideology' to 'culture' or 'discourse' not because I view ideologies as false or a cover for interests, as materialists tend to say. By ideology I mean only a broad-ranging meaning system which 'surpasses experience'. 'Culture' and 'discourse' are too all-encompassing, covering the communication of all beliefs, values and norms, even sometimes all 'ideas' about anything. When used so generally, they presuppose a contrast between only two realms, the 'ideal' and the 'material', leading to the traditional debate between idealism and materialism. The material might be conceived of as nature as opposed to culture, or the economic base versus the super-structure, or joint economic/military interests (as in IR 'realism'), as opposed to 'constructivism', or even as 'structure' as opposed to 'agency'.

These dualist debates are perennial but sterile. After a period dominated by materialist theories of everything, we now have cultural theories of everything. In my recent work I have noted how 'nation' and 'ethnicity' have largely replaced 'class' as objects of research; they are said to be 'cultural', whereas classes are said to be 'material'; they are usually discussed without any reference to classes; and 'cultural' and 'ethno-symbolist' have largely replaced 'materialist' theories of nations and ethnicities. Thirty years ago fascism was explained in relation to capitalism and classes; now it is seen as a 'political religion'. My books *Fascists* and *The Dark Side of Democracy: Explaining Ethnic Cleansing* suggest that this is not progress, but a shift among equally one-sided theories. Since I offer a four-sided theory, I win 4–1.

I have occasionally given the impression of being a materialist by (1) using the word 'material' when I should have written 'concrete' or 'real' (critics quote some of these passages); (2) endorsing John Hall's and Perry Anderson's description of my theory as 'organizational material-ism'; (3) emphasizing the 'logistics' and 'infrastructures' of ideology; and (4) declaring (1986: 471–2; 1993: 35) that ideological power had declined during the long nineteenth century, and that the extensive power of religion had continued to decline since, in the face of rising secular ideologies like socialism and nationalism.

Having now researched twentieth- and twenty-first-century fascism, ethno-nationalism and religious fundamentalism I disown the second part of (4) above, and accept that these centuries have so far been highly ideological. I accept Gorski's criticism that religion has not generally declined in the world. I was generalizing only on the basis of traditional Christian faiths in Europe, which still are declining. Edgar Kiser is also right to see me moving towards greater recognition of value- and emotion-driven behaviour. I have sometimes been too rationalistic about earlier periods. Joseph Bryant rightly says I give early Christianity too rational a content, at the expense of its mysticism, its superstitions and its prejudices. A universal doctrine of rational salvation cannot alone explain why 3,500 Christians chose martyrdom under the Emperor Diocletian – nor the conduct of Islamist or nationalist suicide bombers today. And Frank Trentmann is right to say I neglected the religious content of eighteenth-century English politics.

Yet John Hobson is wrong to see me as a materialist in the realist sense, as opposed to the idealist 'constructivism' he advocates. I have no objection to 'constructivists' whether in International Relations or sociology repeating that inter-subjective ideas, norms and values are important influences on human action, that actors' identities and interests are socially constructed, and that structures and agents are mutually constructed (Reus-Smit 2002: 129–34; cf. Brubaker 1996: ch. 1). Yes – but some human constructs then become reified as institutions and social structure, socializing and constraining later actors. Sociologists from Peter Berger and Thomas Luckmann to Anthony Giddens have called this the duality of action and structure. Idealist and materialist theories are equally simplistic by comparison.

My model abandons the distinction between ideas and materiality in favour of one between 'ideas-and-practices combined' (or 'action and structure combined') in each of four power networks. Yet one, the ideological, is clearly more idea-heavy than the others. It comprises networks of persons bearing ideologies which cannot be proved true or false, couched at a sufficient level of generality to be able to give 'meaning' to a range of human actions in the world – as religions, socialism and nationalism all do, for example. They also contain norms, rules of inter-personal conduct which are 'sacred', strengthening conceptions of collective interest and cooperation, reinforced, as Durkheim said, by rituals binding people together in repeated affirmations of their commonality. So those offering plausible ideologies can mobilize social movements, and wield a general power in human societies analogous to powers yielded by control over economic, military and political power resources.

Hobson and Reus-Smit say this is too instrumental, since it is concerned with power as means not ends and so neglects the content of ideologies. Trentmann says I emphasize control over meaning systems at the expense of the production of meaning. These accusations puzzle me. When I discuss Sumerian or Christian religion, or nationalism, fascism, 'Hutu Power' or American neoconservatism, I do discuss their content, since powerful ideologies are those whose content gives plausible meaning to people's lives. I do not claim to discuss *all* ideas, values, norms and rituals, only those mobilized in macro-power struggles. Ralph Schroeder gives my defence of this neglect: ideas can't *do* anything unless they are

organized. This is why the label 'organizational materialism' still seems
apposite, for ideas are not free-floating. Nor are economic acquisition,
violence or political regulation – they all need organizing. This is all
I mean by the term organizational materialism.

Since ideologies surpass experience, they provide a bridge between reason,
morality and emotion. Successful ones 'make sense' to their initiates but also
require and evoke a leap of faith, an emotional commitment. There must
be a truth content, since an ideology would not spread otherwise, but the
perception that it makes sense tugs morally and emotionally as well as
scientifically. Science alone lacks this power, being 'cold' and subject to
cold refutation. Jack Snyder succinctly explains in this volume why
groups infused with ideological fervour are more powerful than those
who lack it. I find his analysis accurate and impressive.

I distinguished two main types of ideology, 'transcendent' and 'immanent'.
These terms were taken from theology, where they indicate two types of
divine presence or spark. I wanted in fact to suggest that an ideology can
have a presence or spark capable of moving human beings to act outside,
and then defining, instrumental means–ends calculations.

Transcendent ideologies are the most powerful, with a more universal
appeal, capable of breaking through divisions between established power
networks – and across classes, genders, regions and states – by appealing
to interstitially emergent common identities, interests and emotions
generated by social change. The world religions did this most of all. More
recently socialism, fascism, nationalism and religious 'fundamentalism'
have also claimed transcendent visions and have drawn into an emergent
collective network people from across the boundaries of different institutionalized power networks. Socialist movements helped create broader
class identities than had hitherto existed, nationalists helped create nations
bridging existing class and regional divisions. This also helped give both
types of collectivity a moral belief and emotional confidence in their own
world-historical role.

Immanent ideologies strengthen the moral and emotional solidarity
and force of existing power networks. This is not merely 'ideological
reproduction' as Althusser and the early Bourdieu used to say. For it
may be the enhanced morale given by an ideology which enables an army
to be victorious (as Gorski suggests was so of Cromwell's New Model
Army), or it may enable a movement claiming to speak for a class to effect
a revolution.

Since these are ideal-types, ideologies may be more or less one or the
other. Influential ones tend to contain elements of both. At election times
most politicians attempt 'the vision thing' (in the inimitable words of
President Bush the Elder), though (like him) their vision tends to be

minimal and pragmatic. But even the most visionary ideologies are not born immanent or transcendent. They become so after complex social processes involving coalition-building and instrumental perceptions of what will work as well as more intuitive or principled elements.

I now add a third residual type, *institutionalized ideologies*, indicating only a minimal presence of ideological power. These are conservative and pragmatic, endorsing ideas, values, norms and rituals which serve to preserve present social order. They believe that emerging conflicts can be mediated successfully by compromises embedded in present institutions. At the borderline are ideologies like Thatcherism and social democracy, which (as John Hall says) are mildly transcendental. Though they work through present institutions, they have a vision of a better society. The essence of institutionalized ideologies is recognition that progress lies through compromise and pragmatism, so that 'dirty' back-stairs dealing must compromise their values. That is what most politicians in democracies know above all else (and what they cannot quite openly admit before their supporters and electorates). But in parallel fashion, the masses comply less because they believe the existing social order is morally right than because they live in it and habitually reproduce it through their actions. This is their *habitus*, as Bourdieu says: they have internalized cultural dispositions to act, think and feel in certain ways which lie below formal consciousness. Institutionalized ideologies are closer to the anthropologists' conception of 'culture' as the ideas, values, etc. that pervade everyday social practices.

I embrace as a virtue Hobson's accusation that my treatment of ideology is 'sporadic' – in the sense that the importance of ideological power fluctuates greatly according to time and place. Though Trentmann stresses the significance of religion in eighteenth- and nineteenth-century England, I doubt he denies my main point: religious ideologies were most intense (being genuinely transcendent) in the seventeenth century, then they declined through the eighteenth, nineteenth and twentieth centuries. Institutionalized ideologies are 'thin', in Hobson's sense, immanent ones are moderately thick, giving actors powers they would otherwise not have possessed. Transcendent ones are the thickest, constituting collective actors and interests and achieving major structural changes. Their construction is not an everyday occurrence, of course, at least not at the macro-level.

Emerging interstitial networks generate an explicit search for meaning. This happens where crises threaten the everyday routine of institutionalized networks and ideologies. In response, institutionalized elites begin to divide. Liberals may urge compromises with emerging discontented groups, conservatives intensify traditional values mixed with pragmatic repression. If crisis deepens, radical ideologists emerge, developing, through struggles, more general meaning-systems surpassing practical experience and claiming to be able to solve the present crisis. If institutionalized elites remain divided, radicals may achieve more intensive and extensive popular mobilization. This happens interstitially, since many people from different social networks are now forced into conscious reflection on the *impasse*, coming to similar conclusions. As Jack Goldstone (1999) has said of revolutions, while initial opposition to the institutionalized order may be largely explicable in terms of narrow instrumental interests, the creation of an alternative order requires general ideological visions going beyond direct self-interest and presenting a plausible way of overcoming the existing crisis.

One classic example comes from Marxian and Weberian interpretations of the rise of Protestant capitalism. Marx stressed the rise of the bourgeoisie, a new class emerging interstitially from diverse backgrounds. Some began as prominent merchant families, others as gentry, yeomen or even peasant farmers, engaging in more capitalistic farming, others were traders and artisans taking goods between producers and consumers. Though their behaviour was converging, they did not initially conceive of themselves as being the same sort of people at all. Weber focused on the common problems of meaning they faced, making moral sense of lending and borrowing, establishing rational accountancy practices, and socializing labour discipline. He noted how the ideology of Calvinism gave religious meaning and virtue to these practices, though he recognized in principle that this was a two-way process, with capitalistic practices also encouraging Calvinism. Through this mixed transcendent–immanent process a new collective actor emerged: a self-conscious Protestant bourgeoisie, pioneering capitalism, fighting for its political rights, even fighting revolutions and civil wars. Often it had higher morale than its opponents, derived from religious commitment.

In *Sources* I added geopolitics, adding the princes of Northwest Europe as interstitial power actors. They had been hitherto marginal, dependent actors in European geopolitics, yet their economic and naval power resources were growing. Removing religious legitimacy from Rome meant release from the power of France, Spain and Austria. This is why the moment that Luther nailed his defiant theses to the door of Wittenberg Church, the Elector of Saxony sprang to protect him – and the Thirty Years' War became inevitable. Thus the Protestant/Catholic divide across Europe resulted as interstitial economic, political and military power resources were (originally unintentionally) mobilized by divines grown ideologically discontented within the Church – a brief example of my model in action.

Fascists seeks to explain the emergence of the first mass fascist movements in response to the European crisis generated by World War I. This was less severe in countries where liberal representative government was already institutionalized before 1914. Their elites could absorb post-war crises, blending centre-left pragmatic reformism and centre-right ad hoc repression. They gradually adapted their institutionalized ideologies with elements of social and Christian democracy. Here institutionalized ideologies held the upper hand.

It was different in the semi-authoritarian monarchies destabilized by the war and the brand new states created out of the ruins of collapsed Empires. These were all 'dual regimes' (half-constitutional, half-authoritarian), lacking the routine institutions and mass compliance for coping. Both proved more vulnerable to emerging fascist movements. These were distinctively classless, their original core forming from soldiers of all ranks demobilized in 1918. They confronted the crises with plausible ideological solutions drawn essentially from their experience of military power during the war. They saw discipline, comradeship and national unity as the keys to modern social progress. This was the kernel of fascism, a transcendent nation-statist ideology. In Germany, Italy and Austria fascists could mobilize more mass emotional commitment and violence than could conservatives, liberals or socialists. But where conservatives maintained firmer control of military and political power, they were able to suppress the fascists, though taking the precaution of stealing fascist ideological clothing. The authoritarian regimes of Antonescu (in Romania) and Franco (in Spain) purported to be 'traditional', but actually their fascist-derived corporatism was a new immanent ideology of the right. Here we see institutionalized, transcendent and immanent ideologies struggling against each other in one period and continent.

Too much optimism pervaded some of my earlier discussions of ideologies. I dwelt on 'progressive' ideologies that improved the world, stressing their creation of collective more than distributive power, as Gorski and Bryant observe. Early Christianity was levelling and universal; medieval Christianity brought normative pacification; nationalism transcended classes. Gorski (drawing on Foucault) instead emphasizes the distributive disciplinary power of Calvinism. He suspects 'discipline' also loomed larger in the normative pacification provided by Christendom. He may be correct. With fascism, communism and ethno-nationalism in mind, I now see clearly that world-transforming ideologies contain both collective and distributional power, and do both good and harm. On the whole I prefer mildly transcendental ideologies, offering a vision of a better, though limited and not ideal future. I return to this later.

Political and military power

Gianfranco Poggi criticizes my separation of military from political power, cleverly forcing me into considering them together. He refines arguments voiced in his book *Forms of Power* (2001). He notes that the separation makes me a deviant among theorists, though perhaps my real deviance is to discuss military power at all. Poggi says that since 'force and fear' underlie political power, it is redundant to identify a separate military power deploying exactly these resources. I will flatly reject this, arguing that the two have diametrically opposed qualities.

In *Sources* I defined military power as 'the social organization of physical force in the form of concentrated coercion'. Reflecting on Poggi's criticism, I realize that 'coercion' was not strong enough. Webster's dictionary allows 'coerce' to mean 'compel to an act or choice', or 'bring about by force or threat'. This could refer to workers threatened with dismissal, or priests cowed into silence by their bishops. I should have defined military power as *the social organization of concentrated lethal violence*. 'Concentrated' means mobilized and focused, 'lethal' means deadly. Webster defines 'violence' as 'exertion of physical force so as to injure or abuse', or 'intense, turbulent, or furious and often destructive action or force'. These are the senses I wish to convey: military force is focused, physical, furious, lethal violence. This is why it evokes the psychological emotion and physiological symptoms of fear, as we confront the serious possibility of agonizing pain, dismemberment, or death. Poggi and I agree that this is a distinctive and important experience of power in human societies.

Poggi, however, relates it to politics, drawing on Popitz and Schmitt for support, though they were discussing the extremely violent politics of inter-war Germany. Schmitt became a Nazi, of course. He feared that mass (working-class) parties would vote *en bloc* in disciplined military fashion (his metaphor) and be unable to engage in constructive debate and compromise. With the example of the Bolshevik Revolution before him, he concluded that liberal democracy could not survive the onset of mass society. Politics required an authoritarian centre as protection against class warfare. Schmitt embraced steadily more militaristic models of politics, since force must be met by force. So his definition of politics as 'dividing friend from foe' reflected not the essence of politics, but its descent into militarism.

Military power holders say, 'If you resist, you die.' Such a lethal threat from armed persons is terrifying. The very unpredictability of who will end up as a corpse adds its own terrors. Though bombing or storming a city never kills everyone, the inhabitants all fear they might be one of the victims. Military power is not confined to armies. Lesser organized, lethal violence comes from gangs of paramilitaries, criminals or youths. I have written this chapter in two cities, Los Angeles and Belfast. In both of them lethal armed gangs remain active. Since 1980 about 25,000 people in the US have died in gang warfare, over twice as many as in the Afghan war of 2001–2002. 'Only' 3,700 have died in the conflicts in Northern Ireland over the last three decades, though many more have been beaten up or knee-capped.

Very few rules govern the deployment of military power. The 'rules of war' are precarious in all ages – as we have recently seen in Afghanistan, Iraq and Guantanamo Bay. The paucity of rules or norms is unlike economic or ideological power – and especially unlike political power, as we see in a moment. Military power also has distinctive internal organization. It combines the apparent opposites of hierarchy and comradeship, intense physical discipline and *esprit de corps*. This is so that soldiers will not respond with flight when they face the prospect of terror themselves. Only where social movements actually begin to physically fight do they develop such intense and peculiar solidarity. This is what made fascists tougher than their socialist rivals. Alcohol and drugs are often also administered, to dampen down combatants' own terror. They are not administered to political officials. Power exercised within military organization tends to be somewhat despotic and arbitrary, though tempered by shared comradeship and morale. And military power wielded over outsiders is the most despotic and arbitrary power imaginable.

I continue to define political power as centralized, territorial regulation of social life. Only the state has this centralized-territorial spatial form. Here I deviate from Weber, who located political power (or 'parties') in any organization, not just states. Most sociologists have ignored him and used the term only for state-oriented activity, though recent use by political scientists of the term 'governance' revives Weber's viewpoint. Governance may be administered by all kinds of bodies, including feudal manors and guilds, and modern corporations, NGOs and social movements. I prefer to keep the term 'political' for the state – including, of course, local and regional as well as national-level government. In feudalism, it becomes difficult to identify where states end and class organization begins, which Brenner makes some play of. But states and not NGOs and others have the centralized-territorial form which makes its rules authoritative for anyone within its territories. I can resign membership of an NGO and so flaunt its 'rules'. I am absolutely required to obey the rules of the state in whose territory I reside, and changes of citizenship are uncommon and rule-governed. 'Governance' is increasing in the world, but I prefer to discuss its non-state aspects in the context of ideological, economic and military organizations (with some geopolitical exceptions I mention later).

Weber said the modern state possessed a monopoly of legitimate violence, though I prefer a monopoly of institutionalized violence. Political rituals and routines, rather than normative legitimacy, makes actual violence minimal. They go together with institutionalized ideologies, occurring when violence, like ideology, is minimal. Regulation exercised from centre through territories, rather than either legitimacy (ideology) or violence (military), is the key function of the state. Its key apparatuses concern law and rule-governed political deliberations in centralized courts, councils, assemblies and ministries. But as Linda Weiss emphasizes, the state is not only laws and rules but also informal coordination between officials and representatives of domestically powerful groups. As she says, the most effective states generate the intense infrastructural and collective power she terms 'governed interdependence'. Infrastructural power is the essence of the routinized powers of states, while the exercise of despotic power is a sign of a weaker state. The part of social life which is intensely, routinely regulated and coordinated in a centralized and territorial fashion concerns networks of political power. In these senses political is the very opposite of military power.

I now confront two objections: behind law and coordination lies physical force; and states deploy armies, especially abroad in space which is not nearly so rule-governed. Both obviously contain some truth. Behind law does lie physical force, but in most states it lies well back and is not usually mobilized into lethal action. Political force is usually evoked first as a ritualized, machine-like, rule-governed and non-violent constraint. I reject Poggi's notion that when facing the state and its force we normally feel 'vulnerability to death and suffering'. I start with the easiest case for my argument, contemporary Western states. Here politics are overwhelmingly pragmatic, ritualized and non-violent. Regimes change with ceremony, not force.

True, crime and dissent may bring more forceful retribution in the form of ritualized coercion. But as Durkheim noted, our law is more restitutive than repressive, and it allocates punishment along agreed sliding scales. If found guilty of minor offences, we may receive only a probationary sentence or a financial penalty. For more serious offences punishment escalates, and we may be coercively deprived of our liberty. But unless we physically resist, incarceration remains ritualized and non-violent – we are handcuffed and placed in a locked cell. Our main fears are of public shame, of being trapped in an oppressive judicial machine, of losing wealth, or of being coercively confined. Terror is not the most appropriate word for our sentiments, unless perhaps we face the death penalty or a life sentence. A Republican or Loyalist activist in Belfast may feel terror when confronted in the street by the Irish Republican Army, the Ulster Volunteer Force, the paramilitary Royal Ulster Constabulary (now the PNSI), or the British Army, but after being arrested, different emotions will be aroused by the police and judicial authorities (unless torture is feared). This is the force of rules, not furious violence.

Strikes and political dissent sometimes invoke rough stuff from paramilitary and police forces. But Los Angelenos typically feel more fear when straying into unfamiliar 'ghettos' with alien gangs supposedly lurking nearby, than when picketing factories or marching against war; similarly for Belfast Republicans straying into Loyalist areas, or vice versa. They feel they understand and so can play around the edges of the rituals of police violence more easily than with those of gang or paramilitary warfare. You can't play games with the IRA or the UVF, but you can (much of the time) with the British or Irish governments.

States sometimes repress more violently, but usually in graded escalations. In the first, the police employ non-lethal riot tactics, causing injuries but rarely deaths. In the second stage, mixed police, paramilitary and army units will escalate shows of force. They broadcast threats, shoot in the air, and make demonstrative advances armed with low lethality weapons – riot armour and clubs, tear gas, rubber bullets, the blunt edge of cavalry sabres, carbines rather than automatic weapons, etc. In the third, military, stage the armed forces take over, exacting exemplary repression by killing as ruthlessly as they consider necessary, in order to terrorize the others. Here we see the escalation from political through mixed to military power relations.

Many states are more violent and/or despotic. Nonetheless, most still try to institutionalize their power. Royal prerogatives were exercised most effectively when they were not arbitrary, but predictable, conforming to established norms in consultation with the main regional power-brokers. Royal courts, baronial councils, city-state oligarchies, estate assemblies, etc. had their rituals and norms. The prevalence of rules among those who counted politically means that truly despotic power was usually mitigated by more routinized infrastructures. Despotism was a term of abuse, meaning power was illegitimate because arbitrary. The main institutional weakness of monarchy was well understood – a disputed succession or an erratic, incompetent monarch, either of which *in extremis* might lead to civil war – a move from political to military power. Of course, many historic states dealing with crime or dissent used violence more routinely, but this was usually against the lower orders, not politically recognized personages. Public beatings and limb amputations were part of this sliding scale, while police and state paramilitaries often tortured, sometimes in public. But for persons of substance, such punishments usually followed after legal forms or consultations were followed – either a trial or an inquisition with rules or a deal struck with families of substance.

Of course, the most violent and arbitrary states leap right over any divide between political and military power. Nazis, Stalinists, Maoists and Catholic Grand Inquisitors killed large numbers of people whose only crime was being defined as possessing an 'enemy' identity (as Jew, kulak, landlord, heretic, etc.). Any legal forms were phoney. An Ivan the Terrible or a Timur raised terror to an art-form. These cases blur political and military power. But all the power sources sometimes blur into each other. Economic and political power blurred in the Soviet Union. Many African states straddle the borderline between the two: state officials control most of the economy but operate under corrupt capitalist principles, while control over the para-statal economy generates much political struggle, being an important cause of the Rwandan genocide of 1994, for example (see *Dark Side*, ch. 15). But these cases do not negate the utility of distinguishing between political and economic power. Nor do very violent states negate the division between political and military power.

The second objection is that states deploy armies, which are often the most powerful armed forces. Nonetheless, civil and military administrations are normally separated, military castes and coups are distinctive phenomena, and many armed forces are not state-organized. Most tribal military federations were stateless; while most feudal levies, knightly orders, private merchant armies (like the British East India Company) and most insurgent and guerrilla forces were substantially independent of states. Some modern paramilitary formations have had closer links to political parties than the state, like the Hutu Interahamwe or the Nazi SA, while the Italian fascist party emerged out of a paramilitary. Most terrorists are stateless, as are bandits and criminal and youth gangs. Such military formations are widespread across the world today, enjoying great success in challenging the armies of states. Only rarely since World War II have the latter defeated guerrillas. Poggi is trying to merge political and military power precisely when most warfare is not between states. Since 1945 inter-state wars have declined, and intra-state wars – civil wars – now form the majority of wars, causing the majority of victims. Some call this 'the new warfare', but actually it is a revival of very old human social organization. All the military groups I have identified deploy arbitrary terror against outsiders, and within they cultivate discipline, comradeship and *esprit de corps*. Moreover, as Schroeder says, military power conquers new territories, whereas political power can only rule within.

A state may wield different military and political capacities. Germany has much more political than military power, the United States has the reverse. The US is the greatest military power in the world. In 2003 it conquered the whole of Iraq within twenty-four days. Its generals used the typical strategy of armies enjoying superior offensive fire-power: concentrate it on the enemy's command-and-control centres, seize and hold strategic communications routes and then take the capital. The US did this very effectively, even without significant allies on the ground. Give-or-take a siege or two, it is how the European empires also conquered their colonies. But American political powers are puny by comparison with theirs. The US lacked international political allies, but more critical was its failure to find political allies within Iraq. Apart from Kurdish forces in the north, it lacked allies who could mobilize patron–client networks on the ground. Ignoring the experience of past empires, it has relied for pacification and policing on its own soldiers, and so its apparatus of control remained highly lethal. Its 'police' are soldiers armed with M-16/M-4 semi-automatic weapons, calling in tanks, artillery and air-strikes. Such weapons produce mayhem, mangled and maimed bodies, and male, female, infant and elderly victims. This is the way to conquer armies and terrorize peoples, but not to police them or establish the rule of law (or to win them over ideologically). Here the distinction between military and political power is critical to an understanding of the abject American failure in Iraq. I see my book *Incoherent Empire* as a policy pay-off from my model, for I predicted the disasters which would ensue if an occupation and restructuring of Iraq (or Afghanistan) were attempted by a United States deploying massive military offensive fire-power, stingy economic budgeting, and wholly inadequate political and ideological power resources.

John Hobson says that I have tended to equate international relations with geopolitics. Initially I did, but not since introducing two refinements. First, I distinguished between 'inter-national' and 'transnational' relations. Inter-national relations (always with a hyphen) are relations between states or between groups organized within each state – like national football associations organized into FIFA, for example. Transnational relations transcend the boundaries of states, passing through them without reference to state power. I used the distinction mainly when discussing globalization, which blends both. I could have usefully deployed them when analysing earlier multi-power actor civilizations like Sumer or Greece. Their individual city-states shared in a common 'civilization' which was predominantly transnational, and they also conducted inter-national relations, including going to war with each other (though the word 'national' would be strictly anachronistic before modern times).

Second, I distinguished 'hard' from 'soft' geopolitics. 'Hard geopolitics' are matters of war and the avoidance of war; 'soft geopolitics' are inter-state agreements concerning non-lethal matters like law, the economy, health, education, the environment, etc. If the essence of political power is author-itative rule-making and enforcement, while that of military power is rule-light lethal violence, then hard and soft geopolitics must be separated into, respectively, military and political power. Soft geopolitics involve agreements between states often setting up inter-governmental organiza-tions (IGOs) which write the fine print, police conformity and punish breaches. Soft geopolitics politicize inter-national space, i.e. to submit it to routinized regulation, whereas hard geopolitics militarize it.

True, inter-national space is rarely as rule-governed as national space (though it is not anarchic, as realists sometimes say). We use the term 'trade war' to indicate a rivalry, in which, for example, in 2002 the US arbitrarily slapped tariffs on foreign steel imports, and the EU responded – as it was entitled to do under WTO rules – with counter-tariffs on a range of US exports. But while the WTO legal machinery ground slowly, it did grind towards fining the US millions of dollars for its tariffs. In this case the US evaded the fine by abolishing the offending tariffs in 2004. Since the WTO is ultimately a voluntary body, the US could refuse to pay and withdraw from it, but the advantages of membership are too great. Of course, some agreements are not enforceable at all. The Kyoto Treaty on Global Warming may be reneged on without punishment. It involved norms rather than laws, a much weaker level of political power. But overall, IGOs are part of politics.

In contrast, the 'hardest' of geopolitics involve wars or deterring wars, which are expressions of military power relations. So too are threats of war, and sanctions and blockades which inflict death and suffering, and so are alliances to build up one bloc's military strength against others. Alliances to preserve peace may blur the difference, though since they are characteristically insecure and changeable, they are less rule-governed than soft geopolitics. Once again, politics is about rules, routinization and the relative dominance of infrastructural over despotic power, whereas military power is rule-light, arbitrary and essentially despotic.

But concepts are only valid if they help explain the real world. Are there military, as opposed to political, phenomena? At the beginning of the twenty-first century, despite IGOs and NGOs and a supposed 'transnational civil society', the world remains lethal. One in six states are riven by civil wars, and there are purportedly twenty million

Kalashnikovs in use around the world. The US has military bases in over one hundred countries and has invaded two countries in the last three years. Over eighty countries collaborate in its 'war against terrorism' – because international terrorists have killed the citizens of over eighty countries. The US has 1.4 million men and women in its armed forces, though this is smaller than the 1.6 million employed in the US private security industry – a disproportion found also in Britain. There are 'no-go' areas for the police in many supposedly advanced and pacified countries. Isn't it time more social scientists studied organized, furious, lethal violence? We are human beings, mobilized into social groups, perennially prone to attack each other violently. Not everyone can sublimate violence into academic polemic.

Explaining murderous ethnic cleansing

Which brings me to David Laitin's polemic against my treatment of ethnic violence. My provocative title, *The Dark Side of Democracy*, seems to have enraged him, since it is the only possible source for his main claim that I say democracies commit murderous ethnic cleansing. On pages 2–4 of the book I explain my title in the form of one principal thesis and five sub-theses. The last two of these say that institutionalized democracies do not commit murderous cleansing, except for some settler states, and that by definition a democracy cannot murder a large number of its own citizens. So I *never* simply say that democracies commit murderous cleansing. Nor is it correct that 'on through the text, Mann associates the most grievous murderous violations of human rights with democracy'. Since I do not say such things, I *never* retreat to a 'watered-down version' of them. I do think there are connections between the two, or I would not have chosen this title. So let me explain what they are.

The book lays out eight principal theses (as well as the five sub-theses) which proceed successively from the most general causes to the most concrete processes of cleansing. After presenting them, I acknowledge (on pages 9–10) that they are only empirical tendencies, with exceptions. Nor do I present a large sample of cases. This is thick analysis of a few cases, able to bring out the unique features and causal processes of each.

My first thesis says that murderous ethnic cleansing is modern because it is the dark side of democracy – it does not say that democracies commit murderous ethnic cleansing. I go on to explain what this means. First, cleansing is modern, rarely found in large-scale human groups in former times. It does seem to have occurred in some conflicts between the kinds of small and simple human groups studied by anthropologists, and there was a larger exception perpetrated by a certain type of conqueror-settler, to which I will return. Laitin says my overarching claim is 'trivially true', showing he is not familiar with the literature. Most writers on genocide see it as a perennial feature of the human condition. I quote some of them. I also have some local news for him from LSE, where present scholars Anthony Smith and John Hutchinson have overturned the old LSE (Kedourie/Gellner) orthodoxy (which Laitin and I apparently share). They say that ethnic solidarities and conflicts are not exclusively modern, but 'perennial'. I quote them too. I expect some of these scholars will criticize my book. If they do, they will regard my argument not as trivial but important – and false.

The main reason I give for my modernist position is that ethnicity, though present in all eras, was much less important to power relations in former times than was class. Rulers and ruled were so divided by class that this outweighed any common ethnic identity they shared (most shared none). This invokes my second thesis: murderous ethnic cleansing only occurs where ethnicity dominates class, with class-like sentiments of exploitation channelled into ethno-nationalism. Atrocities were rarely committed by one ethnic group against another. I show, for example, that the Assyrians' worst atrocities amounted to 'exemplary repression' not 'genocide', as many have said. Thus, for example, some Jews or Babylonians were killed in order to get the majority to comply with Assyrian rule. Even Assyrian deportations had pragmatic economic and political goals, with no desire to 'cleanse' whole ethnic groups from their homelands. They killed and deported many people, but for different purposes.

My historical argument continues through a pre-modern phase of mid-level religious cleansing generated by ideologies of 'democratization of the soul but not the body'. Then came the crunch: modernity in Europe brought the notion of (political) 'rule by the people'. This ideology transcended class divisions once it referred to 'the whole people'. It did not initially do so in the liberal countries. There 'the people' initially meant only adult male property-owners, and so the emerging nation was 'stratified' and diverse – again nation did not transcend class. This happy accident meant that representative government was gradually extended class by class and from men to women, so that the whole of an ethnic group (or of multiple ethnic groups) was admitted to a common citizenship only after liberal democracy was already substantially institutionalized. Major 'cleansing' happened in some of these countries (I instance Britain and France), but generally through more peaceful, institutional means.

Yet through the nineteenth century the ideal spread of rule by the 'whole people', which is really what we mean by democracy. But this might confuse two different root words of 'the people', the Greek terms *demos* and *ethnos*. In multi-ethnic contexts, rule by the whole people might mean only rule by a dominant or majority ethnic group. This became especially problematic in the authoritarian Romanov, Habsburg and Ottoman empires, where insurgence might be in the name of rule by either all citizens or the locally dominant *ethnos*. I then trace the latter notion into 'organic' nationalism, which sees the people as one and indivisible and demands 'Poland for the Poles', 'Ukraine for the Ukrainians', etc. This I say was the root of the evil that followed.

So Laitin is wrong to say that I am imprecise about how modernity causes ethnic cleansing. Most scholars have concluded that it involved the rise of nationalism. This is true, but insufficient. I add first that the root of nationalism was the demand for rule by the people; and second murderous ethnic cleansing resulted where organic nationalism appeared in the bi-ethnic contexts explained in my theses 3–5. It is in this sense that ethnic cleansing is the dark side of democracy. More precisely, it is the perversion of democracy – not usually of institutionalized democracies (I will say why later), but of democratic ideals and processes of democratization. Nor is this a mere abstraction, for in my case studies I show that almost all the eventual perpetrators of murderous ethnic cleansing started their political careers seeking 'rule by the people', and then perverting their own initial ideals. These are quite close connections, operating through both broad historical processes and individual careers. Are the connections 'logical', as Laitin seems to require? I don't quite know what 'logic' would look like in history. But Laitin seems to have been dealing so long with static correlations between variables, dealing with process through lagged variables and cohort analysis (which he does brilliantly) that he cannot recognize processual historical arguments when he sees them.

In the case of the settler colonies I make the most direct connection. This is the only type of case where I say that still-functioning representative governments (for the colonists, not the natives) perpetrated massive murderous ethnic cleansing, and were more likely to do so than less representative governments. To support this, I do make brief comparisons between different colonial powers, and Laitin criticizes this brevity. He does not mention that the bulk of my comparative analysis concerns not place but time and agents. I compare colonies and states in North America and Australia before and after settlers acquired *de facto* and formal self-government. Murder increased after these changes. I also compare settlers, the colonial government and churches, and find that settlers favoured murder most, churches least.

I locate the underlying cause of such cleansing as the arrival of settler-conquerors who want the natives' land but not their labour (and such had probably formed most of the exceptions in earlier history). Laitin says my economic argument makes democracy causally redundant, but he is wrong. Where authoritarian colonial governments and churches had the power to restrain the settlers, cleansing was less serious. Both causes – settlement for land but not labour, and settler representative government – were required for murderous ethnic cleansing.[2]

There were two partial exceptions to my colonial argument, occurring between the 1860s and the 1900s: the atrocities perpetrated by Imperial Russia in the Caucasus and by Germany against the Herero in South West Africa in 1907. Only the Herero case is sufficiently documented to perceive the role of settlers.[3] Coding *de facto* reality on the ground as democratic or authoritarian is also more complicated than Laitin seems to think. This governor formally ruled the colony, and he was more moderate than most settlers, but they controlled the law-courts and most land acquisition, so provoking the Herero revolt which was suppressed with massive force culminating in genocide. But in both cases, settlers (and the civilian part of the state) played only minor roles in the culmination. The main perpetrator was the army high command, who in this period came with distinctively modern and technocratically ruthless war-plans. I suggest this might be a generic exception, providing a secondary contribution of modernity, at least in this period. I discuss what I call military 'tactical lures' towards murderous cleansing, instancing General Sheridan's tactic (during the same period) of attacking Native American villages in winter, which committed the braves into a war of position (in which his fire-power had the advantage) instead of a war of movement (to which the Native Americans were better suited). This was intended to force the braves to return to the villages to defend their women and children. It worked, and the result was general slaughter of Indian civilians as well as braves. I suspect similar lures existed in the Caucasus. Later I instance Milosevic's falling-back on the more ferocious paramilitaries when his army, the JNA, proved ineffective as a 'constrained lure'. But ultimately I did not sufficiently integrate military power into an argument that centred most on political power and then on ideological power.

In my non-colonial cases the relation between democracy and murderous cleansing was not so direct. Yugoslavia contained the closest relations. Elections were held in all the republics only weeks or months before the ethnic wars started. Ethno-nationalists, including those who (apart from Milosevic) became the leading perpetrators, won them all. These were free elections except for Serbia, where Milosevic exerted some controls over the process. He won the largest number of votes, but more extreme nationalist opposition parties got the second-largest share – and then provided the main paramilitary perpetrators. Ethno-nationalists now controlled every government in Yugoslavia (there were three rival groups in Bosnia), and they mutually escalated into organic nationalism and war. Among them, only Milosevic had not spent most of his political career favouring democracy.

Ottoman Turkey held free elections, with a limited franchise in 1908, seven years before the genocide. Independent centrists won the most seats, though the Young Turks did respectably, in alliance with the minority nationalist parties who later became their victims. At this time they favoured extending representative government, with democracy as their ultimate goal. Then a succession of military defeats interacted with coups and ethnic conflict pushed them towards 'organic nationalism', away from democracy. Formerly the leading advocates of reform, they were the perpetrators of the 1915 genocide, not the reactionary Sultan's party or the conservative centrists. In Rwanda, elections had followed independence during the 1960s. Hutu nationalists won them and their notion of 'majoritarian democracy' became less and less tolerant of the Tutsi minority. A military coup led to a Hutu-led dictatorship under President Habyarimana, which lasted twenty-one years until the eve of the genocide. Most commentators believe that the Habyarimana regime restrained ethnic violence. However, it was destabilized by a Tutsi invasion, economic difficulties and international pressure for the restoration of elections. It was in the run-up to these elections that Hutu Power factions radicalized and began to take over most of the new parties. Since most Hutu politicians expected them to win the elections, they were jumping on the bandwagon. The Hutu Power factions perpetrated the genocide.[4]

So almost all the leading perpetrators began their political careers demanding the creating or deepening of representative government. Then they perverted their own ideals. I take pains to describe their political trajectories. This means that Laitin can give as evidence of their anti-democratic stance my descriptions of the later stages of their careers, when they had abandoned their earlier ideals. He takes some statements from when they were actually murdering, when they were not remotely democratic. But I am describing a process, which begins with attempted democratization and then, when *demos* and *ethnos* increasingly entwine, goes into reverse.

The Nazi movement is the only one that started anti-democratic. Nazi leaders endorsed the leadership principle, attacked a Weimar democracy they claimed was corrupt and ineffective, and were violently brawling from early on. Nazism does not fit. But their major foreign collaborators whom I discuss do largely fit. Seven nationalist movements of eastern Europe began as democrats, then embraced organic nationalism, involving some murderous cleansing (though full-scale participation in Nazi genocides required other causes too).

Finally, India and Indonesia contain less serious conflicts. In India (Kashmir and 1947 apart) most ethnic conflicts involve 'riot cycles', in which further escalation is eventually stopped by government repression of rioters. Laitin says this is because India is a democracy, so this is a counter-case. My own argument is more complex. I repeat others' research finding that murderous riots occur less frequently in periods of martial law, when democracy has been suspended. I also say that government repression of riots comes from India being a stable institutionalized state, so that political elites see their own interests as resting more on the preservation of order than pursuing ethno-nationalist goals. I say that Indian democracy exercises a particular restraint on ethno-nationalism, for caste politics act like class politics elsewhere to lower the transcendent appeal of ethno-nationalism. Congress and the parties of the left express lower-caste grievances, undercutting the power of Hindu nationalism. Even the nationalist BJP is forced to respond to these, since it is vulnerable to the charge that it expresses high-caste interests. Caste/class partially undercuts nation. Laitin also claims violence is worse in Indonesia than in India because it is less democratic, though I emphasize that its state is less stable. Chua's (2004) case studies suggest that democratization generally worsens ethnic violence in developing countries, including Indonesia.[5]

This raises the broader links between political and ideological power. My thesis 1(c) says that democratizing regimes are more dangerous than stable regimes, whether these are democratic or authoritarian. My fifth thesis adds that going 'over the brink' into actual murder occurs when a state has been factionalized and then radicalized amid unstable geopolitical conditions. Putting these together reveals the differences between the types of ideology which I sketched earlier.

On the one hand, stable, institutionalized regimes generate 'institutionalized ideologies', strengthening pragmatism (including pragmatic repression), and routines which reproduce existing institutions. Politicians and police chiefs in India, despite often having strong Hindu biases themselves, eventually intervene to impose order since their careers ultimately depend on it. This lowers the attractions to them of 'immanent' or 'transcendent' ethno-nationalist ideals – whether the state is democratic or authoritarian. Tito's regime operated similarly in Yugoslavia. On the other hand, democratization is more likely to generate some domestic instability and faction-fighting. If it is also linked to unstable geopolitics, radicals can mobilize popular support around immanent and transcendent ideologies. Laitin thinks I am resorting to a weaker argument if I invoke ideals rather than practices. Both have

their distinct power. If practices are stable, generating routine pragmatism among elites and a routine *habitus* among the masses, they are strong.
But if practice is unstable, then ideals matter. Some ideals may have very
unpleasant consequences. I hope this is all now clear. Next time I might
choose a more boring title.

Laitin's second complaint concerns my typology of violence and
cleansing contained in Table 1.1. Its main purposes were to distinguish
the main types of violence and cleansing, to distinguish the focus of my
research – the shaded areas in the table which are high on both criteria –
and to indicate stages of escalation. That I say the intention to kill large
numbers appears late in the process does not 'undermine' my categories,
as Laitin says. Quite the reverse: it enables me to better identify the stages
of escalation. Throughout the book I describe many countries and
sequences with what I hope is a consistent terminology. I think this
table generates the most useful typology available in the literature.

Yet I do concede some ground to Laitin. My typology is not a pair
of Guttman scales, since types and degrees of violence and cleansing
mingle. There are actually elements of three scales: proportion of a total
population cleansed, proportion of a total population dying, and extent
of intended killing. I attempt to distinguish between unintended
deaths, intentional killing and the half-way category of 'callous' deaths
(behaviour which unintentionally caused deaths, but was not quickly
rectified because the perpetrator cared little for the victims' fate). That
is why genocide is below ethnocide in the violence typology and why
callous projects rank above merely mistaken projects in the cleansing
typology. This third element is confusing, I admit. If it were possible to
devise accurate statistics on all these dimensions, I might devise a better
schema.[6] But murderous ethnic cleansing does not allow that kind of
precision, and the table is adequate to its purposes. It is also true that
I occasionally compound the problem by saying that x is 'a worse' case.
This seems to indicate a moral stance, though I only intended to indicate
a relative position in the table. I share Laitin's doubts about the status
of 'genocide' as the 'worst evil', as opposed to other forms of inhumanity.
I say this in the text, when dealing with General Krstic's trial. It only
makes a legal difference whether he is convicted of conspiracy to genocide
or crimes against humanity – equivalent to most of my shaded areas. He
did command mass murder.

But I reject Laitin's further accusation that I show leftist bias in excusing
class more than ethnic atrocities. I do say that class conflict usually
generates fewer deaths than ethnic conflict. I give reasons for this – classes
are more inter-dependent than ethnic groups and tend to form less total
identities. But I say that post-revolutionary Marxist regimes differ.

The whole point of my long chapter on 'communist cleansings' is to precisely categorize them (as no one has previously done) and to analyse similarities and differences in violence and cleansing between conceptions of democracy that became perverted by ethnic or class organicism. Of leftists I note their distinctive evils, 'classicide' (killing classes) and 'fratricide' (killing comrades), which fascists tend not to commit, plus the infusion into class of 'ethnic' (hereditary) elements, supposedly with no place in Marxism.

My book focuses on process, and my thesis 6 says that intentions to murder only appear very late in cleansing sequences. Clear intent to commit mass murder does eventually appear in my cases, including communist ones, especially in Cambodia. Laitin says I excuse leftists because they intended to kill less often. This was not true of the Khmer Rouge, while classicide once begun was fairly systematic. However, famine deaths resulting from forced collectivization in China and the Soviet Union were not intended. They fit my category 'callous wars, civil wars and revolutionary projects'. They were callous since once the lethal effects of policy were known, the regimes were slow to change them. They did not care much for their victims. I also say that these callous acts resulted in the deaths of truly vast numbers of people – in fact much more than the intended deaths in either the Soviet Union or China. These are all precise and, I believe, correct statements. I excuse no one. Since I say similar things about the Franciscan missions in California and the British government during the Irish famine (lower absolute death numbers but these were higher proportions of the total populations), perhaps it is these comparisons which really bother Laitin.

We like to think of perpetrators being quite alien from us – 'primitive peoples' (like Hutus or perhaps Serbs), Nazis bringing a supposedly unique Holocaust, and communist dictatorships. More recently 'failed states' have entered the category of 'the Other'. I had not thought much about good and evil until writing this book, but that I know now that they are not things set quite apart from each other or from everyday life. They emerge together out of the problems confronting each generation in each place. Representative democracy is a major improvement for large-scale societies (more direct forms of democracy were always available for small ones), but it brought evil where *ethnos* and *demos* entwined. This is a problem of *our* civilization. That is what I mean by *The Dark Side of Democracy*.

Economic versus political power: the European miracle

Two chapters in this volume, by Stephan Epstein and Robert Brenner, discuss the remarkable rise of Europe to global leadership in the early modern period. I will respond, beginning within Europe and then broadening out to comparisons between Europe, especially Britain, and Asia, especially China. The latter also gives me the opportunity to comment on a debate which has erupted since my first two volumes of *Sources*. I finished Volume I twenty years ago and would now change various arguments in the light of subsequent scholarship. I also know more about basic economics. So I recognize my mistake in persistently using the rising productivity of land (rather than labour) as a measure of development – and now I can at least understand Brenner's accusation that I am a 'Smithian', though I reject it.[7] I also object to Brenner's assertion that mine is a functionalist theory of stratification. I do not say that those who hold power perform 'indispensable functions' for subordinates. I do say that distributive power derives originally from collective power, i.e. that stratification derives from social cooperation. So did Marx and so have many others.

Yet Brenner has a point when he says that my depiction of the European dynamic sometimes appears too 'systemic'. My remark that the crises of the fourteenth to fifteenth centuries and of the seventeenth century were mere 'hiccups' in an overall upward trend needs toning down (millions died). Brenner's argument that feudal lords and peasants were locked into relations which tended to stifle development also has some force. There were numerous obstacles and many inefficiencies and contradictions. Those who narrate development find it difficult to avoid an onward-and-upward tone. I did distinguish different geographic rhythms and I would now also distinguish more clearly several phases of economic development. First came the somewhat hidden and localized intensive development of the acephalous, backward and overwhelmingly rural networks of the early Middle Ages, in which Christendom and (over a certain space and time) the Carolingian Empire provided a minimum of more extensive integration. Then came more extensive 'Smithian' development towards markets, towns and states, still largely subordinated to local, feudal relations of production; then further development of commodities, markets, towns and states into Smithian 'high equilibrium' agrarian economies; then the surges into capitalism and industrialism that I will describe below. In each phase, there was a tendency for the institutionalization of social relations which had helped early development to block further development. As I described in *Sources* – and as Epstein also argues – these were not so much overcome as outflanked, as regions marginal and interstitial to previous phases pioneered new development. The ultimate 'secret' of such extraordinary yet uneven development in Christendom-becoming-Europe was its combination of intensive and extensive power relations, localism plus connections to a wider world.

Brenner sees his most fundamental argument as concerning the relations between economic and political power in feudalism. His discussion raises a dilemma confronting all analysis, but especially mine. I wish to make analytic and institutional distinctions between the four sources of social power, while also recognizing that they are mutually entwined. Since Brenner ignores ideological power and integrates military and political, he deals only with what he calls the economic and the political. He says I separate them too much. He says that the reproduction of the feudal ruling classes depended upon the political, while the reproduction of the state depended upon the economic. He adds that the *raison d'être* of feudal government was to enable the dominant class to extract the surplus labour of the peasants. This *is* a functionalist statement, since he is saying that not merely did government help the dominant class extract, but also this was the reason the government existed in the first place. The needs of the system (the mode of production) determined more particular social relations. I favour much more political (and military and ideological) autonomy than this. Medieval states performed multiple functions, and so they performed none of them perfectly.

He says the peasants physically occupied the land and knew they could live perfectly well without the lords. So the lords need their manorial courts, their armed retainers and the ultimate force provided by the central state in order to extract their own means of subsistence. This is quite unlike capitalism, he says, in which surplus labour can be extracted through purely economic means, since the workers do not possess the means of production. In fact, he says the distinction is between capitalism and all prior historical modes of production, practising a similar reductionism on all of them. I am sceptical of this familiar Marxist distinction. What happens to workers today who occupy their factories and deny access to the owner is rather similar to what happened to peasants withdrawing their labour from the feudal manor. They get repressed by force. Peasants were also economically trapped by the lords' organizational control of the mill and the market, just as workers today are by comparable economic power organizations. The differences are of degree not of kind.

But Brenner gets into more difficulties when he uses the same explanation for violence between feudal lords, that is in explaining wars. Medieval wars, he says, derived from 'the material requirements, the rules for reproduction, of the dominant class of feudal lords'. Indeed, he says that the eventual emergence of a Europe divided into national states is the inescapable outcome of the feudal mode of production. The ultimate driving force of wars was that lords could not derive higher productivity from their present lands. So they 'had to' either extend the cultivable part of their lands or extract more from the peasants or other lords by force.

This is surely a statement of alternative possibilities not just for a feudal regime but for any agrarian regime which has reached the limits of available technology on its presently cultivated lands.

But the question is whether any regime *could* do these things. If it could not, or if the cost of doing so was too high, then it might not even attempt them. In Europe some regimes could do this, cheaply. That is the decisive point, and that is not given by any definition of the class relation between lords and their peasants. In fact Brenner shows us how they could do this. He takes us on two brief tours of territorial expansions, one by lordly states into the pagan east, into Muslim Iberia and into Celtic lands, the other of expansions of kingdoms like France at the expense of smaller local lordships. But these two types of expansion did not derive from 'the rules of reproduction of feudal lords'. They derived from the geopolitical opportunities presented within Europe by the combination of the collapse of the Roman Empire, the barbarian invasions, and an era of local defensive warfare by knights with castles and armed retainers. Europe then presented the spectacle of much virgin land, many small states and some areas which were populated but almost stateless. Brenner here rightly emphasizes that some peasant communities were capable of mustering determined military resistance against the neighbouring lords. But scattered among these relatively weak statelets and stateless communities lay some more powerful states, for whom the opportunities for conquest were therefore unusually great. Some took their chance and the rest is European history. They would have probably taken their chance whatever their relationships to the peasants, whether or not these were feudal.

The consequence was the military/fiscal route of state modernization charted for Europe by Charles Tilly and myself. Epstein raises some pertinent questions about this, including that I give insufficient attention to the actual form of medieval and early modern states. What I have to say about this actually derives from the puzzle that this European route has not been followed in those other continents which developed multi-state systems. Miguel Centeno (2002) has shown this for post-colonial Latin America, and Jeffrey Herbst (2000) has shown this for post-colonial Africa. They produce suitably nuanced explanations for this, but these begin from the absence of serious inter-state warfare in those continents. Europe turns out to have been an unusually warlike multi-state system. However, another continent had experienced comparable levels of warfare, and with an initially similar trajectory of development. During the Spring–Autumn and Warring States periods in China (BC 770–221), there was repeated warfare among many small states. The outcome was political consolidation, penultimately into four great states, and then, finally, into one state conquering the others. Since then, China has remained one imperial realm (except for periods of civil war). Until this final stage, there developed fiscal-military, patrimonial/bureaucratic states, recognizably 'modern', resembling in many ways European states, though much earlier in time.

Scholars tend to describe the earlier phase of this process in both continents as 'feudal'. But to explain their propensity for warfare and then for consolidation, they focus on a different aspect of feudal relations: the ties of vassalage, relations of loyalty and service between lord and vassal. Combined, they exploited the peasantry (as Brenner stresses), but the incentives to war and consolidation did not come from that exploitation, but from the power vacuums and the power disparities that resulted from initially highly decentralized lord/vassal configurations. The power vacuum meant this was not a zero-sum game for those who could mobilize a significant number of vassals. They were likely to win wars.

Since the word 'feudal' has to do double-duty, referring to rather different class and military/political relations, it leads to much confusion. Perhaps it would be better to give a different term to the latter at least in Europe and China, one that reduces them neither to the feudal nor the capitalist mode of production, allows for some political autonomy, while also conveying their distinctive military and ideological power relations and a dynamic towards consolidation and 'modernization'. I suggest 'mini-imperial', since the big states were absorbed by conquest and intimidation of smaller states and stateless areas, beginning to rule them either highly repressively or 'indirectly', buttressed with ideologies of their own civilizational superiority, but with successful mini-empires then culturally assimilating the conquered and integrating them into common state institutions. These are all characteristics of empires, though many were rather small empires, and they were multiple. 'Mini-empires' will serve well. I will reintroduce the concept in my discussion of the Europe/ China debate, for they figure large there.

Yet we have not grasped all of the power structures of medieval Europe, or even begun to account for the different eventual outcome in the two continents. Brenner reduces Europe to the villages and manors of feudal-ism. I have added the lords, vassals and levies of feudal mini-imperialism. But what about the autonomous towns and guilds and the 'brotherhoods' of medieval Europe, and what about the Church? Epstein also recognizes their importance, calling them 'corporations'. Brenner says nothing about them. In *Sources* I say that the medieval period mobilized intensive, local forms of power within extensive normative solidarities, the com-bination being necessary for the development of market-based econo-mies. In earlier periods I stressed the extensive normative pacification provided by Christendom. Epstein is uneasy with this, and wants to add a

Carolingian political legacy and a Church revival of Roman law which then turned into a powerful corporate legal profession. He adds more political power (and more complexity) to my mainly ideological argument. He may be right. But he and I agree that such institutions held some autonomous power *vis-à-vis* states and lords. For their part, states attempted to play off lords against merchants, the Church and other corporations. It is difficult to find much that is comparable in China. I trace a substantial part of the deep-rooted dynamism of Europe to the diversity of local power actors. I said that in a sense there was 'private property' in the sense of 'hidden powers' long before that term came to have specifically capitalistic connotations. Now I turn to the 'Miracle' itself.

Economic power: the European Miracle versus Asian revisionism

Here I respond not only to critics in this volume, but also to a more general debate which erupted since I wrote the first two volumes of *Sources*. Writers who stress the 'European Miracle' of development tend to emphasize the deep historical roots of the rise of Europe and especially Britain, hitherto back-waters. *Sources* put me in this camp since my explanation went back centuries and largely stayed within Europe.[8] Brenner (with Isett 2002) argues that Britain overtook China by virtue of a deep-rooted transition from a feudal to a capitalist mode of production, though breakthrough came only in Britain, and fairly suddenly, in the late seventeenth and eighteenth centuries (since feudalism was blocking development before then). All this has been contested by a group of 'Asian Revisionist' scholars, comprising the 'California School', which includes Jack Goldstone (2002, and his chapter here), and an 'anti-Orientalist' group, which includes John Hobson in a recent (2004) book. They and writers like Pomeranz (2000), Bin Wong (1997) and Gunder Frank (1998) make the following arguments about the power sources.

Economic power

This is where most focus. They deploy two main arguments.

(1) Only in the nineteenth century did the European economy – more specifically, the British economy – overtake the Asian economy – specifically that of China's most advanced region, the lower Yangzi. In the eighteenth century, they say, the two continents and regions were broadly level. Before then, Asia and China had been much more advanced, but then

Europe had experienced 'Smithian development'. In the eighteenth century both were similarly caught in the Smithian 'high equilibrium' trap of agrarian economies. 'Smithian development' could extend the division of labour and markets, but without major technological or institutional breakthroughs no further surge of development was possible. Only the technology and institutions of the industrial revolution, acquired first by England from 1800, enabled first Britain, and then Western Europe to surge forward into global dominance.

(2) Overtaking occurred only because of two 'happy accidents'. First, Europe/Britain (unlike China) happened to have coal nearby its industry, reducing the costs of industrialization and enabling technological virtuous cycles to develop between its industries. Second, Europe/Britain forcibly acquired New World colonies which happened to provide sugar, timber, cotton and silver, which boosted its domestic economy and living standards and enabled it to trade with Asia. Revisionists reject the view that Europe and Britain possessed a deep-rooted dynamic which more persistently led towards breakthrough. Of course, Euro/British advocates (including myself) also note accidents, especially of ecology (soils, minerals, indented coastlines allowing lower transport costs, etc.), but alongside a deep social dynamic.

Ideological power

Goldstone says that the decisive reason for the eventual overtaking was the autonomous role and dynamism of British science. This is also implicit in the writings of some other revisionists. It is unclear whether we should regard this as a third happy accident. But, conversely, Hobson stresses the dependence of European on Chinese science.

Political power

They deny that the Chinese state was a growth-choking, anti-capitalist bureaucracy or even a major restraint on private domestic markets. It probably left trade more alone than European states, while the multi-state system of Europe also had inefficiencies.

Military power

The overtaking also involved military violence, in which Europeans excelled. Their military power also enabled eventual domination.

To discuss these issues it is helpful to distinguish two phases of economic development, one to a Smithian high-equilibrium agrarian society, and a second resulting from a breakthrough into an economy of more permanent growth. It is also helpful to distinguish the period of European/British economic *overtaking* from a later period of European power *domination* of Asia/China. On economic issues I focus on the comparison between Britain and the lower Yangzi.

I start with the demographic and economic measures of the 'moment' of economic overtaking (the Chinese data are mostly in Lee and Campbell, 1997, and Lee and Wang, 1999). The revisionists say that these measures indicate that China was at least level with England through the eighteenth century and into the beginning of the nineteenth century. They show that China had achieved over the previous few centuries a massive population growth with no apparent rise in mortality rates. China also practised population controls, and not only the notorious female infanticide. Since there was a surplus of males, many men were celibate while even the luckier ones tended to marry late. Couples also delayed the first child longer than couples in England did and they ended childbearing over six years earlier, so family size was smaller. There was also widespread adoption, which enabled parents to cope with the gender imbalances that often resulted from such practices. This is a picture of an agrarian society able to expand population when resources expanded, and restrict it when they didn't. Only in the nineteenth century, Lee and his collaborators argue, did the system break down, with famines resulting.

Nonetheless, for England we have the far more comprehensive dataset of Wrigley and Schofield (1989). Interestingly, these data derive from parish records, that is from the implantation within each village of an ideological power organization, a nationally organized church. There was no parallel, organizationally or in terms of records, in China. These data cast doubt on the revisionist argument. They show a steady English population rise from the 1690s, then a dip in the 1730s and then an astonishing rise, a doubling of the English population in only eighty years, from 1740 to 1820. There is not consensus on its causes. Razzell (1998) emphasizes mortality decline, Wrigley and Schofield stress fertility rises. Hart (1998) links the two by tracing a large decline in the stillbirth rate during the eighteenth century, and therefore an improvement in female nutrition (confirmed by Wrigley 1998), suggesting women were particularly better off in England than China. But the most important differences are that by 1750 infanticide was unknown in England and mortality crises attributable to famine had disappeared. By 1700 the relationship between food prices and mortality rates, already weak, had disappeared. In contrast, Lee and Wang (1999: 45, 110–13) admit both to famines in eighteenth-century China and to a continuing strong relationship between grain prices and mortality rates. Though any eighteenth-century differences between the most advanced regions of the two continents cannot have been great, it does seem that Malthusian crises had been banished in England and not in China.

Indeed, Kent Deng (2003) believes that fluctuations in the Chinese population were still those normal to traditional agrarian societies. Growth was possible, he argues, only where new land or new crops could be worked, and neither produced growth which could be sustained. He sees the Chinese economy as stuck within normal 'Smithian' agrarian cycles. On demographic grounds he dates the 'great divergence' between Europe and China as occurring before 1700. The revisionists respond to this by saying that without subsequent industrialization England would have reached the high point of a Smithian agrarian cycle, and then slipped back again as over-cropping and environmental degradation put a brake on living standards, nutrition and fertility. They point to Holland, which had surged ahead in Europe in the seventeenth century, and then slumped well behind England in the eighteenth.

But Brenner and Isett (2002) answer this with data on British labour productivity. These show fluctuations in earlier centuries, but a massive increase above these levels of about 60 per cent starting from somewhere just before 1700 to 1750. This enabled overall population growth, but there was also a doubling of the urban population, without any apparent decline in national health. Both these trends were unparalleled anywhere else in the world, though Holland saw a less dramatic rise. Brenner sees this as the crucial shift out of Smithian cycles, the fruits of a capitalist revolution in agriculture, with farmers treating all factors of production, including labour, as commodities. China's only expansions at this time were into virgin lands or new crops, neither of which increased labour productivity. In fact, say Brenner and Isett, Chinese labour productivity was declining. Britain could expand agriculture yet also release labour. The Smithian limits were being breached, since a breakthrough in labour productivity had occurred.

But was there yet industry to absorb the released labour? The conversion of coal into steam power proved to be the energy core of the English industrial revolution. Revisionists (following Wrigley) say that coal was a happy accident, abundant near the emerging industries, whereas in China coal was abundant but far from the areas which might have potentially industrialized. The facts are contested. But even if this were so, Britain's good luck had come early. Even by 1700 England produced five times as much coal as the rest of the world put together, and fifty times as much as China. Moreover, while Chinese coal output was declining through the eighteenth century, in Britain it was growing steadily, boosting the release of population to the towns and boosting the growth of metal-working. As we see later, this linkage between coal and metal-working also generated technological invention. So, if coal was a happy accident, it came early, in steadily greater quantities, and with 'virtuous' linkages elsewhere.

Nonetheless, economic historians now place less weight on particular 'leading' industries like coal mining, metal-working and cotton. They say that growth diffused fairly evenly across the whole English economy (Crafts 2000). Temin (1997) measured the efficiency of early nineteenth-century English industry in terms of its ability to lower prices of its exports in relation to imports. Substantial lowering occurred across most industries, not just coal and cotton, but also 'hardware, haberdashery, arms and apparel' indicating generally rising productivity. He says this reveals that a general entrepreneurial, innovative economic culture was already in place by 1800. Capitalist economic institutions also existed in China, but they now dominated England. An institutional breakthrough had also occurred. Brenner wants to attribute this all to changes in agrarian class relations, but that seems too narrow. Entrepreneurs emerged out of a variety of social backgrounds – landlords, yeoman and tenant farmers, peasants, merchants, artisans. Something much more diffuse was occurring.

It is true that trade relations were still more developed in Asia. The revisionists have demonstrated that Asia still dominated long-distance trade. Capitalist commerce had existed in coastal areas all over Asia well before 1700, with Chinese traders in the lead. At the beginning of the nineteenth century Europe still contributed a much smaller proportion of world trade. Frank observes that Europe had essentially nothing China wanted, except silver, whose export from the Americas to Asia was the only product enabling the Europeans to receive the many Chinese goods they desired. So Immanuel Wallerstein was much too Eurocentric when he claimed that there was a European 'world economy' existing by the seventeenth century.

If Europe's colonies were a 'happy accident', had they yet made much of an economic difference? This remains controversial, but they obviously made some difference. They brought silver to Europe, enabling Europe to trade with China, and they brought new crops, impacting somewhat on diets and calorific intake. O'Brien (forthcoming) says that inter-continental trade before the industrial revolution was limited. He estimates that trade with the New World boosted British resources by (at most) 1 per cent of GDP. Of course, cumulatively 1 per cent per annum might provide quite a boost, and this trade had been proceeding since the early sixteenth century. From about 1650 the price of goods traded internationally had been slowly though consistently falling, suggesting improvements in efficiency.

All this suggests trade and colonies did make a difference. But only from the mid-nineteenth century was there substantial convergence in commodity prices, suggesting the emergence of integrated global markets. They then centred in Europe and its colonies, though including parts of Asia by the end of the nineteenth century (O'Rourke and Williamson 1999; 2002). Colonies did eventually make a big difference, but not by 1800. There was as yet no single 'world economy'. There was not a European world economy, but nor was there an Asian or a Chinese world economy (as Frank claims). Only the market for silver can be said to have been genuinely tri-continental, linking Asia, Europe and the Americas. Regardless of whether British productivity had 'overtaken' that of the Lower Yangzi, they were not in competition, let alone involved in relations of dominance. They were still separate parts of the world. Of course, that was not so for the Americas. We should not lose sight of the obvious: that colonies are not primarily about 'overtaking' or 'economic efficiency'. They are about domination, extermination and economic expropriation by a force more naked than feudalism had ever seen.

So I have tended so far to uphold the traditional view of European/ British overtaking, of Asia/China. It happened well before 1800 – though dominance was not yet achieved. There were no longer Malthusian cycles in Britain, there was a surge in both labour productivity and capitalist institutions. The other vital factor in economists' models is technological innovation. To discuss this will take us out of the purely economic realm, however. It will take us especially into ideology. Of course, I argue that the European Miracle has to be explained in terms of all four sources of social power.

Science also played a major role in European development, one that I mentioned but did not stress sufficiently in *Sources*. Goldstone and others have shown that the new technologies of the industrial revolution can be traced back to the English 'scientific revolution' of the seventeenth century. Though (as I noted) most of the major inventions did not come from scientists, but from the 'micro-technologies' of engineers and artisans, it has now been shown that they had absorbed the general principles of scientific theories, and they shared a common technical vocabulary and method. They had imbibed the ideology that natural phenomena were orderly and predictable, mastered by means of a scientific method of exact measurement and reproducible experiment. Not absolute truth, but instrumental, incremental knowledge was their goal (Mokyr 1992; 2000). After about 1650, everyone agrees that Europeans, not Chinese, were making the important scientific and technological breakthroughs.

However, science was not as autonomous as Goldstone implies. Nor was it accidental. It was embedded in broader networks of ideological power, being a central thrust of the part-Protestant, part-rationalist reaction against the theology dominating science in Europe until the sixteenth or seventeenth centuries. Scientists believed that the laws they discovered were God's laws. Leibnitz, Boyle and Newton embedded their theories amid Protestant theology. In Catholic Europe science blossomed later, embedded in the anti-religious rationalism of the Enlightenment. Margaret Jacobs (1997; 2000) notes that many of the scientists, entrepreneurs and engineers of the English industrial revolution were Protestant Dissenters, committed to values of probity, order, and faith in both religion and science. Even in Charles Darwin's time in the mid-nineteenth century, most researchers defined their work not as 'science' but as 'natural theology'.

But science also responded to demand from political and military power holders. Representative governments in Holland and Britain, and 'enlightened absolutism' elsewhere, opposed what they viewed as the particularism of old regimes, which had developed science as a closed, somewhat esoteric caste, often in holy orders. They favoured a more public science. Leibnitz, Newton, Boyle and others were members of the English Royal Society, subsidized from public funds. King Charles II himself granted permission for Newton to uniquely remain a Fellow of Cambridge University without taking holy orders (Newton would not accept the dogmas of the Church of England). States in competition with each other appreciated the utility and ideological lustre of science. So did militaries. Naval and artillery competition spurred discoveries in metallurgy, chemistry and the precise measurement of time and space. Biology, botany and geology were boosted by colonial expansion. French and British warships carried scientists like Jean-Charles de Borda, Joseph Banks and Charles Darwin around the world, and ships were often stuffed with plants and animals on both legs of their voyages to the colonies, with a massive influence on the agriculture and diet of the people of Europe.

There were reverse influences too. Science was also 'democratized', not only by Protestant or Enlightenment influences, but probably more importantly by changing economic and political power relations. Old class and status divides were breached as entrepreneurs and scientists mixed together in clubs and reading-rooms. Members of Parliament and artisans shared some knowledge of contemporary scientific theories. Free communication of invention is crucial to economic development. Newcomen's first steam engine of 1713 was for pumping water out of flooded coal mines. Hundreds of people added piece-meal improvements over the next 150 years. Early eighteenth-century craftsmen were perfecting small instruments like clocks, telescopes, eye-glasses, guns and naval sextants and their metal-working improvements were adapted into bigger industrial machinery. Economic historians emphasize that technology made a slow but cumulative impact on growth in England. England's crucial technological resource lay less in initial invention than its subsequent diffusion, boosted by demand for industrial products from a competitive market, including large military customers, but also dispersed middling consumers.

Goldstone also says science retained autonomy after the industrial revolution. Scientific institutions may be distinct, but do they also exercise power over the four power sources? In Britain most university scientists/natural theologians remained in holy orders until the 1870s. Others found employment in commercial colleges like the East India Company College or the School of Mines. A few were gentleman-scholars with private incomes (like Darwin). Not until the late nineteenth century did they collectively congregate in secular universities, a caste apart. But by the mid twentieth century they needed research funding which only government, especially the military, and big corporations could provide. The leading edge of science (by now American) was servicing the demand of the military-industrial complex. Modern scientists have never been as autonomous as were earlier alchemists and astrologers. The problem with Daniel Bell's (1976) famous assertion that a post-industrial society moved power from capital to knowledge was presented by his own data: 75 per cent of R&D funds came from the government, mostly for military purposes. Science's main role was to contribute to the rationalization of ideological power in the modern era – science as ideology.

Goldstone is right that I neglected the role of science in the industrial revolution. I have remedied this not by making science a fifth source of social power, as he suggests, but by putting more science into my four sources. This especially puts more ideological power into my explanation of the later stages of the European breakthrough, as Gorski urged. But science was also stimulated by inter-state competition culminating in military and naval revolutions entwined with the (long-maturing) rise of northwest Europe, where it was reinforced by Protestantism and representative states. All this culminated in an agrarian capitalism/commercial imperialism, first in Holland, then more persistently in Britain, whose mass markets and communication infrastructures encouraged competitive industries to slowly invent and develop. I am also reluctant to accept Goldstone's emphasis on autonomous science as the crucial difference between Britain and China, since most of these broader stimuli were also absent from China at this time.

John Hobson (2004) has presented an impressive list of early modern European scientific and technological inventions which were imported from China or adapted from Chinese prototypes. Thus he seeks to expose the Eurocentrism of most accounts of the European breakthrough. I plead guilty to downplaying earlier Arab influences and trade (as Epstein notes). Hobson accepts that most of the crucial last steps inserting machines in factory or mass production were added by Europeans. But the main issue raised for my model of power organizations by the inter-continental flow of science is whether such ideas are more 'free-floating' across the world.

Knowledge is communicated through social networks which are always logistically constrained. But a single traveller in an alien land who notices a machine which might be useful back home can take home a drawing or model of it. Hobson shows that some merchants and missionaries were doing so over centuries of contact between China and Europe. Anyone with some knowledge of European work practices might be the carrier. A Jesuit might see the utility of a threshing device.

Yet such communication still had power preconditions. From perhaps 1600 parts of Western Europe were reaching up toward Chinese levels of economic development, while facing very different political and military problems. So Europeans were more interested in Chinese economic than political or military techniques. We must also explain why Europeans were, by about 1600, much more eager to copy and modify foreign machines than were the Chinese. In fact, by then Europeans were unusually outward-going and curious. Today the world faces comparable conditions, but with a very different result. Economists note that contemporary conditions should have enabled poorer countries to acquire and adapt Western technology, especially since their elites are often educated in the West. East Asia did so, but much of the world has not. The main explanation given by economists is that their economic and political institutions have not been supportive.

So there are several preconditions for what first seemed like 'free-floating ideas'. Provided human beings widely separated in space face similar problems, are somewhat outward-oriented, and possess favourable institutions, then the diffusion of technical knowledge may float across the world. The global diffusion of broader ideologies, like religion, seems at this time to have been much more variable. Neither the Chinese nor the Europeans were much interested in each other's religions, yet elsewhere natives converted readily to Islam or Christianity when they identified it as the key to acquiring all forms of power, recognizing that the foreigners were vastly more powerful than they were. Ideology is a source of power, but it is closely entwined with the other power sources, and it probably diffuses more when it combines reason with morality and emotion, which science does not do.

I move on to political institutions. The revisionists concede signs of political decline in the Chinese (and in the Mughal and Ottoman) empire from about 1600 onward. These formerly great states now seemed less able to provide order or dominate their region. China had reined in its long-distance trading fleets in the mid-fifteenth century. Thereafter, not even Chinese merchants and settlers in nearby Taiwan received serious aid from the imperial court. The Chinese state had turned inward, even though Chinese merchants continued to trade across Asia.

Economists find a strong correlation between economic growth and the rule of law in the world today (e.g. Barro 1997). They stress the political underpinnings of markets and private property. Economic historians note the excellence of the British political underpinnings during the early modern period (North and Weingast 1989). Revisionists say the same about the Chinese imperial state: China had enforceable property rights, they say, with even fewer restraints on property sales (and on labour mobility) than in Europe. However, Stephan Epstein's (2000) figures cast considerable doubt on this. Europeans could borrow more and at longer-term and lower rates than the Chinese. Whereas Chinese interest rates were typically 8 per cent–10 per cent, European rates were at this level by the fourteenth century, and down to 3 per cent–4 per cent by the mid-eighteenth century. This suggests that Europe had more clearly and securely, legally defined property rights. In this volume Epstein also generates a typology (which is also a rough historical sequence) of states' ability to solve coordination problems and lower transaction and borrowing costs – feudal 'states' did worst, then territorial states, then urban federations, then city-states, then Britain after 1688, then nineteenth-century constitutional states, which were the most efficient of all. This is formidable historical sociology, backed by data on long-term borrowing costs by states, down to under 3 per cent by the early eighteenth century.

The British state provided its paradoxical mixture of the rule of property law (which enabled violent dispossession of peasants from the land) and the rule of laws providing freedom from arbitrary power, due process, and freedom of association, including business association. Both sides of the paradox seem different from China. On the one hand, during the eighteenth century the Dutch and British parliaments represented major property-owners and limited the powers of their monarchs. These states *were* the major propertied classes, whereas in China the imperial state was to some degree *above* class structure. The English state exercised more *collective power* through the major property classes. It was already more of a capitalist state.

On the other hand came political struggles also unparalleled in China. In *Sources*, I said that the second half of the eighteenth century in England saw a revival of older seventeenth-century struggles over legal rights, taxation and representation. Trentmann criticizes me for neglecting similar struggles during the first half of the century. I expect he is right (the period 1600–1760 tends to slip between the cracks between my two volumes). But during the eighteenth century, emergent, interstitial forces sought further reform through parliament, the law-courts and the streets. Under pressure, the old regime divided. As Trentmann says, both conservatives and reformers mobilized mass support – 'King and Country' and 'Protestant Defence' against 'Reform' mobs (I had neglected the former). I stressed that these struggles were fuelled by a great expansion of the discursive media of ideological communication – literacy, newspapers, pamphlets, coffee-houses, etc. They mobilized to successfully extend freedoms and representation, coupled with rational-bureaucratic state reform over the period from 1760 to 1832. I am surprised that Trentmann thinks I give a uniformly top-down account of British politics, since my emphasis shifts in different periods. I emphasize that most political power actors (not just insurgents) stumble their way to success, under pressure, rather than plan it in advance. But by 1832 the state comprised *all* property-owners. China saw neither comparable political struggles during the eighteenth century, nor a similar result. The British state was more helpful to capitalism from the early eighteenth century, and then it was riven by class conflicts specific to capitalism.

Finally, I come to military power. Europe contained many states in lethal rivalry with each other for centuries. These originated as the 'mini-imperial' states I identified earlier, swallowing up their non-Christian and statelet neighbours, a game that was not zero-sum for the stronger. The game lasted for centuries, transitioning smoothly into imperialism overseas. Iberia, parts of Eastern Europe, Wales and Ireland saw plantations of settlers. Granada, the last Muslim province, fell to Ferdinand and Isabella's forces on 2 January 1492. Eight months later, on 3 August they saw off Columbus on his voyage of 'discovery'. Britain moved smoothly through Ireland into North America and the Caribbean, with settler colonies modelled on Conway and Londonderry. In the twilight of European imperialism, Germany and Italy sought overseas colonies almost as soon as they had absorbed the last local statelets into their domains. Existing imperial ideologies of civilizational superiority only needed fine-tuning. From the early sixteenth century Europe was Christianizing the Americas and sub-Saharan Africa. Thereafter European colonialism retained its self-righteousness, able to regard its most terrible atrocities as the workings of 'divine providence', or the necessary triumph of civilization over barbarism – and later as the triumph of the white race over inferior races. Conviction in its own moral superiority was deep-rooted, improved morale, and so contributed positively to imperial triumphs, for the reasons given in this book by Gorski and Snyder.

For centuries victorious armed states, merchant associations and settler militias expanded, while the defeated decayed or disappeared in Darwinian processes of the survival of the fittest. From the seventeenth century, Holland, France, and then Britain – and their merchants associations and settlers – became the main winners in this process. Fiscal pressures from their colonial/commercial wars led the states toward devising modern financial institutions like the Bank of England, bond markets, stock exchanges and financial derivatives. It also led countries which were naval powers towards more representative government, as I explained in *Sources*. Abroad, these states not only allowed their merchants autonomy (as also did the Chinese state), but they also gave them economic and military support where necessary. Tariffs and taxes could be kept low where mercantilism involved seizing market share by military power. Associations of merchants like the British East India Company and the Dutch VOC deployed their own private armies, and so did settlers. Such organizations were devised less to accumulate capital than to conquer, expropriate and so monopolize economic resources. The Dutch and British states were aggressively promoting commerce abroad, unlike the contemporary Chinese state, sometimes doing the fighting themselves, sometimes merely giving political privileges to armed bands of merchant capitalists and settlers.

Persistent military market competition among states, trading companies and settlers had perfected concentrated offensive fire-power. Europeans had very small armies and ships compared to those of China and other big Asian states. But the edge in European warfare since the sixteenth century had gone to fire-power, and European states invested heavily in this. Small high-tech armies and navies triumphed. There were no 'Smithian cycles' in military power, but steady progress. Europeans became better and better at killing people and overcoming their civilizations. European army and naval forces became more and more difficult to overcome in battle. Skilfully inserted into disputes between native princes, they could conquer land empires, as in America and India, where musketeers were proving their superiority over native levies from the early 1700s. But before the nineteenth century, European forces were mostly confined to sea-coasts which their naval guns could rake. By 1750 they dominated most sea-coasts, though China and Japan were still beyond their logistical reach.

European wars were costly, often draining the economy – a major cause of the decline of Holland, for example. Perhaps more of the European than the Chinese surplus was frittered away on war, cancelling out the waste of Chinese female infanticide or Chinese neglect of foreign trade. All human groups operate well below utility maximization. I do not neglect the economic inefficiency of war, but I do note that economic efficiency is not its principal goal. The 'efficiency' of war is military: achieving victory rather than defeat.

But the point is that victory can then change the parameters of economic efficiency. This is what militarism has done from ancient times right up to the successive expansions of Europe, Japan and the United States. Militarism generated an international economy not of free trade but of trade and land monopolies won by lethal violence. This had been nurtured by competition in countless battlefields and shipping-lanes. Militarism helped bring global domination, and with it the power to restructure the international economy. Exterminating the natives in colonies in the temperate zones, and replacing them with white settlers, brought economic institutions which boosted per capita GDP there – so say modern economists. This is a very macabre calculation. 'Per capita' means by each surviving person's head – the heads measured did not include dead native ones.

So Pomeranz, Frank and Hobson are right to emphasize the importance of military power to European dominance, and – to an extent depending on the economic importance of colonies and imposed terms of trade – to European overtaking. There was also a military reason for the inward-turn of the Chinese state. It did not result from any 'innate' conservatism of the imperial state, but from perception that its greatest threat came from the barbarians on its northern land frontier. Therefore China concentrated its resources and its trade there, and not in the sea-lanes. Its military posture on its northern frontier was defensive, geared to containing mobile, dispersed enemy forces. It had less incentive than Europeans to intensify aggressive fire-power against concentrated forces, since it did not face them. But this meant that in the long run the Chinese empire would disintegrate in face of the fire-power of European ships and marines.

But if revisionists wish to argue that lethal violence and colonies contributed substantially to European overtaking and/or dominance, they must recognize that this was neither accidental nor late. It was very deeply rooted in European social structure, and it had been repeatedly exercised, first against other Europeans, then against the relatively weakly organized peoples of the Americas and Africa, then into South Asia – and finally subordinating the Chinese Empire itself. Its rhythms were those of the centuries – of feudal mini-imperialism transitioning into the mini-imperialism of expanding national states and then into overseas colonial imperialism. By the eighteenth century the forms of European militarism were well-suited to an age of naval/commercial rivalry.

In 1750 China was still the world's greatest power, with the greatest share of its trade. Millions of Chinese still enjoyed the living standards to which only thousands of Britons could aspire. But Chinese powers were by now stagnant, even in the lower Yangzi, whereas England's were surging. I have identified in each of the four sources of social power distinctive surging rhythms, each entwined with the others, though each also somewhat autonomous. Somewhere between 1660 and 1760 these surges began to cumulatively take Britain beyond Smithian cycles of even a high-equilibrium agrarian society. It was not a sudden 'take-off' (as in the Rostow theory of the industrial revolution, now largely discredited), but a cumulative process of sustained slow growth of at first about 1 per cent per annum, eventually rising to nearly 3 per cent (and never higher) in the mid-nineteenth century (Crafts 1998). There could have been no single 'moment of overtaking', for the different sources of power had different rhythms. But it was a cumulative, entwined set of surges. Then in the nineteenth century it spread to much of Western Europe and to Britain's white settler colonies.

If we want a purely symbolic 'moment of overtaking' the year 1763 will do, since it involves important moments in the development of at least three power sources. After success in its war against France and Spain, Britain acquired dominion over a large part of three continents under the terms of the Treaty of Paris. It also meant that some settlers, especially in North America, no longer needed protection by British forces. Their independence and greater extermination of the natives was now on the cards. In the same year James Watt began to tinker with a Newcomen engine, leading to the first modern steam engine; and John Wilkes MP was charged by the English Crown with seditious libel, provoking massive riots leading into a great political reform movement. But no single moment would adequately capture such a long-drawn-out process.

Revisionists have underestimated the deep-rooted, entwined nature of European economic, ideological, political and military dynamism. This undermines their 'moment of overtaking' and 'happy accident' arguments. I have stressed here the different and sometimes conflicting temporal rhythms yet inter-penetration and long-run cumulation of ideological, economic, military and political power development. But I dissociate myself from some of the notions of European/British 'superiority' evinced by writers like David Landes (1998) and Eric Jones (2002). In this overtaking, efficiency was subordinated to power, and virtue played no part. Natives across much of the world would have been better off without the British Empire; while Manchester, my own birthplace, became the hell-on-earth which Engels described so graphically in 1844 in his book *The Condition of the Working Classes in England*. Most of the British themselves barely benefited for another hundred years.

This moment of overtaking was not global dominance. Not for a century after 1763 did the Western Powers begin to dominate East Asia, as symbolized by the unequal treaties imposed on Japan and China, and the colonialism imposed elsewhere. China continued to stagnate, though Japan responded, for it shared many parallel power resources to England's. China needed communism to adequately respond, almost another hundred years later, and two hundred and fifty years after the English surge. Western leadership may last little more than two centuries from the moment of overtaking, and only one century from the moment of dominance. The recent resurgence of Japan and the Little Tigers of East Asia, and the present resurgence of China and India (a similarly uneven yet cumulative process), seems to be shifting the balance of global power away from an over-extended United States and a toothless Europe. But this hundred years was actually the only period in history in which any single region of the world has been globally dominant.

To explain all this, I still feel that we must go back in time and further eastward and southward across the European continent – and also, of course, further afield. This began as a Mediterranean surge in contact with the Muslim world and Asia. Then it took a northwesterly swerve, through the network of trading cities and into the larger Catholic states, then into the Protestant lands, and then into England (before departing elsewhere). The deep ploughing of heavy, rain-watered soils in northwest Europe was not in itself of world-historical significance (as Goldstone observes with some acerbity). Its immediate significance was local, contributing to significant 'Smithian' growth. But since this locality later acquired world-historical significance, this plough played a part in the European Miracle, in conjunction with many other forces and relations of power. Explaining the emergence of all these required starting early. No one has persuaded me I should have started any later, or that a proper explanation should ignore any of the four sources of social power.

Conclusion

I began my project by asking the 'Engels question' – whether one of my four power sources was of decisive, final causal power in the structuring of social relations (he said economic power was, and so does Brenner). My answer is probably the Weberian 'no', but because of what Bryant calls my 'emergent' rather than 'foundational' view of power. The economy, the state, etc. do not possess given structures, exercising steady, permanent influence on social development. They instead prove to have emergent properties, as new assemblages of bits and pieces of them emerge as unexpectedly relevant for more general social development, and are appropriated as part of a new interstitial force. There seems to be no general, single patterning of these processes. All I have managed so far are period-specific generalizations, some of them arguable. More usually, I give multi-layered explanations like the one just presented – tentative, controversial and somewhat vulnerable to the empirical research of the next decade.

However, I make two general observations about causality. First, the causes of the development of one power source (other things being equal) mostly lie within its own antecedent condition, because its organization has some degree of autonomy. If we want to explain the industrial revolution, we look more at late agrarian economies than at religious or scientific discourse or at the practices of militaries or states; yet all are necessary for a full explanation. If we want to explain the rise of the modern state, we must look first at antecedent politics, which derived more from struggles over fiscal-military exploitation than, say, from exploitation deriving directly from the mode of production. It is obvious that new military organizations and strategies arise primarily to counter prior ones, and that Luther developed his theology primarily in response to disputes within the Catholic Church – though he became of world-historical significance only with the addition of economic and political power relations which led into wars of religion.

Second, when we refine our explanation by including the influence of other power sources, we rarely stress their core qualities. More often we bring in peripheral aspects which come to have particular (usually unexpected) significance for the power source we are trying to explain. To explain the rise of the modern state, we must introduce economic power relations, but most crucially those which were especially relevant to states, like taxes and expenditures bearing differently upon economic classes, i.e. the state's own economic infrastructure. Conversely, to explain why twentieth-century capitalism is divided into nations as well as classes, we focus less on the major political struggles of the nineteenth century – which concerned class, religious and regional movements – than on the unintended consequences of the pressure for them all to organize themselves at the level of the state in order to further their collective interests. Such analysis takes us further away from the prospect of any simple theory of 'ultimate primacy'.

Yet we can generalize about the sources' distinctive power capacities. Ideological power tends to be diffuse rather than authoritative, flowing informally and interstitially through networks of communication, relatively unimpeded by authoritative power centres like states, armies or class boundaries. The logistics of communicating verbal, then written and then electronic messages are less daunting than they are for armies, goods or law-enforcement. I stressed this in earlier historical times when writing about the spread of salvation religions, iron ploughs, cavalry and coinage. I returned to it here when discussing inter-continental flows of scientific and technical knowledge. Transcendent ideology also plays a distinctively discontinuous historic role, erratic in its manifestations, relatively sudden in its major eruptions. Yet such eruptions require conjunctions with long-maturing tendencies in other power networks, reaching crisis point through more contingent events like wars, recessions or fiscal crises.

Economic power is the most deeply entrenched in everyday life. Its routines involve half our waking lives and energies; it yields subsistence without which we would not survive. It combines diffuse markets with authoritative production units. Its rhythms are characteristically slow. The metaphor of economic 'revolutions' misleads, as we saw in Britain's industrial revolution, which took over a century. The great post-1945 economic 'boom' in Western Europe was also more persistent than sudden (Eichengreen 1999). Depression and inflation can impact more suddenly, but they do not, unaided, generate major social change. Political revolutions may transform distributive power relations, though they seem to also require combinations of war defeat, political crises and emergent ideologies. Economic networks exercise the most massive impact on collective power in the cumulative long term. Industrial capitalism may have changed the whole population's lives more completely than any other power process in human history. Yet gradualness means that the other power sources have time to adapt, often without great discontinuities in power distributions, as I showed in the case of nineteenth-century England in *Sources*. Trentmann criticizes my stress on top-down rather than bottom-up pressures on nineteenth-century politics. He exaggerates this, though my central argument does concern divisions within the working class. Economic conflict generated three competing types of working-class movements: class, sectional and segmental. Only where political exclusion of all workers thrust all three willy-nilly together did ostensibly revolutionary politics result. In Britain, in contrast, the regime was admitting male workers into political citizenship strata by strata and this produced a divided and then a reformist 'lib–lab' outcome. I still think this holds up.

Military power is essentially authoritarian and tends to provide the most disjunctive impact on social structure. The European Union remains a decentralized decision-maker, and so remains a military minnow. In the past, the enormous power of each European colonialism – exterminating native peoples, overturning native states, property rights and sometimes religions in the tropics – resulted most directly from superior military power. The two world wars of the twentieth century generated communism and fascism among defeated and dislocated countries and shifted patterns of technological development across the world. The effect of World War I was to disrupt processes of globalization, the effect of World War II was to boost them. Wars have great emergent powers, especially of destruction, but also sometimes of construction. The small guerrilla wars of today degrade their local environment but often also generate their own local modes of production, dependent on coercive control of goods which are high in value–weight ratio, like diamonds or cocaine.

Political power is predominantly authoritative and 'conservative', in the sense that it regulates, institutionalizes and stabilizes social structures over given territories. It also usually changes quite slowly and pragmatically. The law does this above all. However, economic cycles, shifts in class power, war and emergent ideologies may entwine in broad political crises within these territories, crystallizing diverse forces onto broader, more confrontational political struggles resulting in the extreme in coups, revolutions or ethnic, religious or other civil wars. But the question today is whether 'soft' geopolitics can help soften external relations, lessening wars and gradually filling those spaces which IR theorists used to call 'anarchic' with institutions.

The entwined effect of these power relations is complex and changeable, making sociological explanation very challenging. A central theme of my third volume is to assess long-term economic power *vis-à-vis* the short-term deflective power of wars, political crises, revolutions and ideologies. Did they actually re-direct the development of modern capitalism or merely temporarily, sometimes catastrophically, disrupt it?

Moving to John Hall's challenge, I conclude by being more explicit about the normative and supposed pessimistic implications of my model (emphasized also by Trentmann), and this also enables me to comment on Linda Weiss's view of globalization.

Distinguishing between four distinct power sources generates a model which is in some ways pluralist. Ideological, economic, military and political power, though entwined, are not normally merged. Capitalism, states, ideologies and militaries are not normally staffed by the same people, serving the same interests, mobilizing the same emotions. That is a good thing. I am sceptical of all those fused, systemic and often rather pessimistic views of the modern world as dominated by a 'rationalization process' leading to an 'iron cage' (Max Weber), by a 'capitalist system' now looking rather 'eternal' (pessimistic Marxism), or by epistemic disciplined power (Foucault) – or all theories of globalization as a singular process, even though some of them use metaphors of diversity – 'liquidity', 'hybridity', 'de-territorialization'. These still see globalization imposing a singular quality on all social relations. All these visions are greatly exaggerated. Even when there are tendencies in these directions, we see reactions against them.

Normatively, I oppose attempts to fuse together economic, military and political power in the service of some grand transcendent ideology promising attractive but chimeric ideals of perfection. If implemented, these fusions increase despotic power and then bring disaster or ossification. We recognize the despotism and disasters that ensued from the attempt to impose state-centred fusions in the name of fascism and socialism. Nazism, Stalinism, the Great Leap Forward and the Khmer Rouge brought some of the worst disasters in human history; though Mussolini, Franco and subsequent Soviet and Chinese regimes managed milder, less destructive despotisms. Currently, China and Vietnam may be working their way towards decent futures. More recent attempts at theocratic fusion have brought despotism to some Muslim countries – and mildly threaten it in Hindu India. The Taliban and Sudanese Islamists brought disaster, the Iranian Ayatollahs brought a more conservative despotism.

A neoliberal, capitalist-centred fusion, modelling all social life on the power of economic markets, now presents another potential despotism – by capital, since the ownership of capital is the greatest power within markets. This refers to the bundle of Thatcherite, neoliberal, 'rational-choice', 'cost-accounting', 'let markets rule' ideologies recently prominent in the West (including its academe), and especially in the US. They conceal trends towards monopoly and rule by big capital. In the US, for example, if current tendencies in disenfranchising the poor, campaign financing, and media concentration continue, democratic politics and ideologies might be overwhelmed by capitalist power (maybe they already are). Where neoliberal 'structural adjustment programmes' are let rip across the world's poorer countries, they rarely have much impact on growth, but inequality widens and foreigners grab more of their economies (*Incoherent Empire*, ch. 2). We should remember one former *laissez-faire* disaster, the Irish famine, where intervention to feed the Irish was opposed on the grounds that it interfered with the natural workings of essentially beneficent markets. Unchecked market powers might be later followed by stagnation, since more resources must go into maintaining that power against resistance from below. As John Hall notes, my empirical analyses reveal that despotism generates revolution. The way to revitalize leftist ideology across the world would be to let neoliberalism rip. However, the world need not go through such suffering. Far better to deconcentrate power. Freedom and social dynamism require erecting fire-walls between different sources of social power, protecting their relative autonomy. Different groups should control the power resources. Freedom and democracy rest on this separation of powers.

Reforms are desirable within the individual sources of social power. Though both collective and distributive power are necessary to social life, better to maximize collective at the expense of distributive power, so diffusing power more equally between social actors. That leads to three further preferences, for democracy, decentralization and competition, historically a liberal preference, though too often confined within the realm of political power. Political democracy is desirable. Even my consciousness of the dangers of confusing the *demos* with the *ethnos* means that the checks and balances normal to liberal models may demand confederal and consociational methods of power-sharing between ethnic groups (though this is a complex matter).

But the struggle for ideological and economic democracy may be equally important as political, and liberals have been less prominent here. Ideological democracy has been best explored by Habermas (1990: 116–18). He sees it mainly as a 'communicative structure' embodying a rational discourse whereby all contributions are equally heard and the better argument alone determines the 'yes' or 'no' responses of the participants. This 'ideal speech situation' would indeed be a truly egalitarian, democratic and collective ideological power. At present, he says, it is subverted by capitalism, the state and other power organizations which embody a rival strategic/instrumental rationality favouring their interests (what he calls 'the logic of the system'), which triumphs over the human 'lifeworld'. This might seem utopian, for it would involve radical curtailments of present distributive ideological powers. But that so much of our media, even its content, is controlled by authoritarian corporations, even individual persons, is inimical to genuine democracy. And therein lies a necessary struggle.

Marxists criticize a liberal democracy confined to the political sphere, seeing it as overwhelmed by the economic power of capitalism. They advocate workers' control to democratize and decentralize economic power. Of course, Marxists subverted this ideal when they reached power, fusing state ownership and control of economic power resources. In fact they left all the power sources more concentrated than under capitalism. The abject failure of state socialism forced most leftists to endorse weaker 'social democratic' forms of economic democracy, involving freedoms of speech and association for workers, rights of bargaining and consultation, and a de-commodification of basic living-standards through the welfare state. This has been substantially achieved in numerous countries, though maintaining it requires struggle, and changing conditions require changing ideological solutions. Social democracy was until recently a mildly transcendental ideology. Then some of its adherents retreated to a more institutionalized ideology, from which they merely defend existing achievements. So arises another necessary struggle.

In contrast, liberals uphold the freedom and social creativity involved in competition between many economic units, each enjoying only limited powers. Liberals endorse capitalism as long as it is decentred, fearing only centralization and concentration. In his later work Robert Dahl saw capitalist concentration as subverting democracy. There are further economic problems with liberalism – neoliberalism in the South, and in the North evidence that the 'liberal' or 'Anglo-Saxon' regimes of political economy are widening inequality, unlike the social democratic, Christian democratic or Asian 'developmental' regimes which dominate most of the advanced world (Mann and Riley, 2004). Liberalism now seems to be more of the problem than the solution to the concentration of economic power in the hands of a few.

I welcome Linda Weiss's addition of 'governed inter-dependence' (GI) to my 'infrastructural power' (IP). GI captures what the most effective states do – like eighteenth-century Britain or Prussia, or the Chinese imperial gentry-scholar state ruling an agrarian society, or the contemporary regimes she instances. She does not mention these earlier states and they did differ. Organizations representing the masses were not a part of GI in them, but they are in contemporary instances, in the shape of organized labour, populist parties and religious pressure groups, generating welfare states, redistribution of incomes and intervention in labour markets. Weiss focuses on business/state relations, yet even South Korean GI in the 1960s (with powerful *chaebols* and a semi-authoritarian state) sponsored low inequality and housing and education subsidies. This leads to a distinction between class-divided (earlier cases) and populist GIs (her own examples), which helps qualify her statement that GI characterizes modern states. States attracted by neoliberalism, like Britain and the US, may coordinate with business groups (though presumably less than elsewhere), but are returning to more arm's-length legal controls over labour unions and the welfare state – a regression towards class-divided GI.

But this difference is dwarfed by the fact that many Southern states, like those of most sub-Saharan Africa, have never enjoyed much infrastructural power, let alone governed inter-dependence. On independence, they inherited power networks which radiated less from territory to centre than from the colonial mother-country to their port-capital, which had little contact with most of the colony's hinterlands. Today the main power networks still radiate abroad from the port-capital, but now they reach to Northern-dominated capitalism. It is too simple to say that these countries are 'excluded' from global capitalism, as Weiss and I have both written. Their political and economic elites are not excluded. They are the 'gate-keepers' between the world and the country, but with the masses excluded. Weak infrastructural powers force elites to fall back on violent, less effective despotic powers to rule their countries (Herbst 2000; Cooper 2002). They may first attempt to rule through corrupt patrimonialism (half-despotically), but if this generates faction-fighting, they rely on repression which typically fails because of low infrastructural powers, generating revolt from regional warlords excluded from power, and the civil wars ably dissected by Laitin and colleagues. Latin American countries seem in a half-way position, with more effective and quasi-democratic states, though with infrastructures weakened by enormous social inequalities, *comprador* bourgeoisies and enclave economies – examples of faltering class-divided GI. But most of the South sees rather little GI.

High infrastructural powers coupled with low despotic powers give us populist GI. High infrastructural powers with more despotism moves towards class-divided GI, and this may then further reduce despotic powers. Low infrastructural powers push more towards despotism and the absence of any GI. This suggests that level of infrastructural power may be more causally decisive than level of despotic power. Support for this comes from the higher correlation of contemporary economic growth with measures of state capacity, like the rule of law and efficient Weberian bureaucracy, than with levels of democracy (Barro 1997: chs. 1 and 2; Evans and Rauch 1999).

Weiss is optimistic about the impact of economic globalization on Northern countries. She is correct that I have previously been rather defensive about the continuing powers of nation-states *vis-à-vis* globalization, and that this derived from social democratic Keynesian bias. I also agree that contemporary pressures may enable as well as constrain. But globalization itself neither constrains nor enables, since it is not an agent. Globalization is plural (economic, ideological, military and political), and so contains multiple agents. Some of these may constrain, as for example our economic pollution of the planet. In the future this may be viewed as the high-equilibrium trap of industrial societies, constraining further development, leading to economic cycles comparable to the Smithian cycles of agrarian societies. But I see few constraints on the North coming from globalizing capitalists. They live here, after all. Indeed recent writing on economic globalization (including those of Weiss and Hobson) has downplayed such constraints, while my own research with Dylan Riley reveals the variety of macro-regional responses to recent pressures. I am pessimistic about the Anglo-Saxon macro-region, especially Britain and the United States. In that limited sense I am flattered to be described by Trentmann as a John Bright gone sour (and not only because we both lived in Rochdale).

Substantial pressures are felt on all Northern states. Lesser ones are capitalist though not global in origin. European populist GIs rested on compromise between capital and labour, and organized labour has weakened. Since it is now disproportionately based in the public sector, unions have lost some of their GI capacity to coordinate state with private sector workers. High unemployment and marginal employment among less skilled workers also seems structural in contemporary capitalism. But according to recent welfare state literature, the main pressures come not from globalization or capitalism, but from demography and life-styles. Over the last decades Europeans have been spending more years in education, retiring earlier, and living longer while requiring more health care. The burden of welfare is growing, the working population financing it is shrinking. The burden is higher the more generous the welfare state, the more populist the GI. Most states will have to slash welfare, unless they choose to exploit non-citizen immigrant labour. So far their cuts have maintained existing levels of class and gender equality. Though pressures on classes and genders vary, the biggest difference may be between the private and public sectors, the latter enjoying better retirement and pension schemes. This would also have the consequence that organized labour would be less crucial to reducing inequality. This reinforces Weiss's criticism of traditional Keynesian social democracy but indicates that populist GIs must find new solutions to new problems of economic power.

Military power differs. Its main defect is not distributive power within, but lethality towards those outside. Thus the question of internal military democracy does not so greatly trouble me. Though in earlier history I sometimes saw order, and even economic development flowing from the exercise of military power in large-scale societies, that is not true today, except in the direst, the most Hobbesian of local circumstances. Organized violence is now much too lethal to bring much good to anyone. There are alternative sources of order available today to the militarism wielded by local warlords, rival states or the enraged Superpower. We can potentially strengthen a dense web of soft geopolitical arrangements which can ritualistically mediate and institutionalize conflicts, relegating lethal violence to marginal and infrequent roles in social interaction. That may also be utopian, but it generates another necessary struggle.

John Hall suggests I have become more pessimistic as tension has grown between my empirical work and my values. I remain attached to a mildly transcendental leftist ideology, which now must make revisions to twentieth-century social democratic Keynesianism. Progress has many facets – living-standards, more intensive and extensive power networks, wealth, democracy, security, etc. Any achievements in them bring new problems and many bring their own dark sides. The European Miracle brought dynamism and growth, alongside much increase in suffering. Seventeenth- and eighteenth-century English people developed more constitutional government, especially in the settler colonies. Yet these most murderously cleansed the natives. Many highly educated young men and women in advanced European countries converted to fascism for what they saw as principled, moral reasons. Then many of them committed terrible atrocities. The liberal democracies fire-bombed the people of Dresden and Tokyo. In *Incoherent Empire* I depict Al Qaeda militants as being genuine anti-imperialists who kill innocent civilians. Freedom-loving Americans aerially assault Afghan and Iraqi settlements, killing civilians and terrorists alike. Good and evil in human affairs are usually closely entwined.

I suppose this is a mixture of pessimism and optimism. We must face up realistically to our social propensity to do both good and evil. The struggle for social betterment never ends. Democracy and freedom are not achieved states but processes, and each generation is set new challenges in reconfiguring the sources of social power.

Notes

1 Though Foucault does intermittently distinguish between three power agencies – class (or caste), command economics, and the state.
2 I qualify these arguments with careful discussion of the callous use of native labour causing high death-rates and of unintended ethnocide, especially through disease.
3 In the version Laitin saw, I instanced a third possible case, by China in Yunan in the same period. I relied on a single article which revealed little about the actual processes, so I dropped it.
4 I omit the three major communist cases from this discussion, since they did not pervert democracy in the way I have discussed. For what it is worth, all three parties had in principle favoured both political and economic democracy, but they soon betrayed these ideals.

5 I do not accept all Chua's arguments. She is less knowledgeable outside South-East Asia and she emphasizes the economic causes of conflicts which I think work better in explaining ethnic rioting than more sustained murderous cleansing.

6 Laitin's examples of 'elementary arithmetic' are too elementary. The figure of 3–4 million dead in the Holy Roman Empire as a result of the Thirty Years' War is not those 'killed' (by other humans), but mostly deaths through malnutrition and disease. After the storming of Beziers in the Albigensian 'Crusade', I said not that '8,000 or so' but 'most of its 8,000' inhabitants were slaughtered, according to one chronicler. I say not that he 'may have been exaggerating' but that 'most scholars believe the chronicler ... exaggerated'. I do not know of one who believes this is an underestimate.

7 I am no more Smithian than Marxian. In *Sources* (1986: 409), when my analysis of the 'Miracle' is mostly complete, I say that the difficult part of the explanation is now over, since *both* neoclassical and Marxian orthodoxies can kick in, with both markets and class actors in place. Brenner says I 'paraphrase' Smith's famous remark about markets being natural, but I was actually quoting Ernest Jones, and my next sentence is 'But this approach misses several important preconditions' (1986: 406–7). Nor do I say that the requirements for capitalism were in place by the end of the first millennium. In that passage I say (1986: 510) that 1477 was the symbolic date when various power networks 'were beginning to develop into ... a capitalist multi-state civilization' (1477 saw the collapse of that most feudal of states, the Duchy of Burgundy). Only half-a-millennium out!

8 Because I focus on Europe I figure as one of the eight characters in the title of Blaut's *Eight Ethnocentric Historians* (2000). Two other contributors here, Robert Brenner and John Hall, are also among the eight, and so is Max Weber. Karl Marx should obviously be the ninth. This is good company.

References

Barro, R. 1997. *Determinants of Economic Growth: A Cross-Country Empirical Study*. Cambridge, MA: MIT Press.

Bell, D. 1976. *The Coming of Post-Industrial Society: A Venture in Social Forecasting*. New York, NY: Harper.

Blaut, J. 2000. *Eight Eurocentric Historians*. New York, NY: Guilford Press.

Brenner, R. and Isett, C. 2002. England's Divergence from China's Yangzi Delta: Property Relations, Microeconomics, and Patterns of Development. *The Journal of Asian Studies*, 61.

Brubaker, R. 1996. *Nationalism Reframed*. Cambridge: Cambridge University Press.

Centeno, M. 2002. *Blood and Debt: War and the Nation-State in Latin America*. University Park, PA: Pennsylvania State University Press.

Chua, A. 2004. *World On Fire*. New York, NY: Bantam Doubleday.

Cooper, F. 2002. *Africa since 1940: The Past of the Present*. Cambridge: Cambridge University Press.

Crafts, N. 1998. Forging Ahead and Falling Behind: The Rise and Relative Decline of the First Industrial Nation. *Journal of Economic Perspectives*, 12.

2000. Development History. Department of Economic History, LSE Working Paper No. 54/00.

Deng, K. Fact or Fiction? Re-examination of Chinese Premodern Population Statistics.*LSE Economic History Working Paper Series*, No. 76.

Eichengreen, B. (ed.). 1999. *Europe's Postwar Recovery*. Cambridge: Cambridge University Press.

Epstein, S. 2000. *Freedom and Growth: The Rise of States and Markets in Europe, 1300–1750*. London: Routledge.

Evans, P., and Rauch, J. 1999. Bureaucracy and Growth: A Cross-National Analysis of the Effects of 'Weberian' State Structures on Economic Growth. *American Sociological Review*, 64.

Goldstone, J. 2002. Efflorescence and Economic Growth in World History: Rethinking the 'Rise of the West' and the Industrial Revolution. *Journal of World History*, 13.

1999. Ideology, Cultural Frameworks, and the Process of Revolution. *Theory and Society*, 20.

Gunder Frank, A. 1998. *Re-Orient: Global Economy in the Asian Age*. Berkeley and Los Angeles, CA: University of California Press.

Habermas, J. 1990. *Moral Consciousness and Communicative Action*. Cambridge, MA: MIT Press.

Hart, N. 1998. Beyond Infant Mortality: Gender and Stillbirth in Reproductive Mortality before the 20th Century. *Population Studies*, 52.

Herbst, J. 2000. *States and Power in Africa: Comparative Lessons in Authority and Control*. Princeton, NJ: Princeton University Press.

Hobson, J. 2004. *The Eastern Origins of Western Civilisation*. Cambridge: Cambridge University Press.

Jacobs, M. 2000.Commerce, Industry, and the Laws of Newtonian Science: Weber Revisited and Revised.*Canadian Journal of History*, 35.

1997. *Scientific Culture and the Making of the Industrial West*. New York, NY: Oxford University Press.

Jones, E. 2002. *The Record of Global Economic Development*. Cheltenham: Edward Elgar.

Landes, D. S. 1998. *The Wealth and Poverty of Nations: Why Some Are So Rich and Others So Poor*. New York: Norton.

Lee, J. and C. Campbell. 1997. *Fate and Fortune in Rural China: Social Organization and Population Behavior in Liaoning 1774–1873*. New York, NY: Cambridge University Press.

Lee, J., and W. Wang 1999. *One Quarter of Humanity: Malthusian Mythology and Chinese Realities*. Cambridge, MA: Harvard University Press.

Mann, M., and D. Riley. 2004. A Macro-sociological Explanation of Macro-regional Trends in Global Income Inequalities, 1950–2000. Paper presented to American Sociological Association Annual Conference, August.

Mokyr, J. 1992. *The Lever of Riches*. Oxford: Oxford University Press.

2000. Knowledge, Technology and Economic Growth during the Industrial Revolution. In B. Van Ark and G. Kuper (eds.), *Technology and Productivity Growth*. The Hague: Kluwert.

North, D., and B.Weingast. 1989. Constitutions and Commitment: The Evolution of Institutions Governing Public Choice in 17th Century England. *Journal of Economic History*, 49.

O'Brien, P. forthcoming. Economic Growth: A Bibliographic Survey. In B. Stuchtey and E. Fuchs (eds.), *Writing World History*. Oxford: Oxford University Press.

O'Rourke, K., and J. Williamson. 1999. *Globalization and History: The Evolution of a Nineteenth-Century Atlantic Economy*. Cambridge, MA: MIT Press.

2002. After Columbus: Explaining the Global Trade Boom 1500–1800. *Journal of Economic History*, 62.

Poggi, G. 2001. *Forms of Power*. Oxford: Polity Press.

Pomeranz, K. 2000. *The Great Divergence: China, Europe, and the Making of the Modern World Economy*. Princeton, NJ: Princeton University Press.

Razzell P. 1998. The Conundrum of 18th Century English Population. *Social History of Medicine*, 11.

Reus-Smit, C. 2002. The Idea of History and History as Ideas. In S. Hobden and J. Hobson (eds.), *Historical Sociology of International Relations*. Cambridge: Cambridge University Press.

Temin, P. 1997. Two Views of the British Industrial Revolution. *Journal of Economic History*, 57.

Wrigley, E. A. 1998. Explaining the Rise in Marital Fertility in the 'Long 18th Century'. *Economic History Review*, 51.

Wrigley, E. A., and R. Schofield. 1989. *The Population History of England, 1541–1871: A Reconstruction*, 2nd edn. London: Edward Arnold.

Wong, R. B. 1997. *China Transformed: Historical Change and the Limits of European Experience*. Ithaca, NY: Cornell University Press.

Bibliography of Michael Mann's Writings

1970. The Social Cohesion of Liberal Democracy. *American Sociological Review*, 35: 423–39.

1973. *Consciousness and Action in the Western Working Class*. London: Macmillan.

1973. *Workers on the Move: The Sociology of Relocation*. Cambridge: Cambridge University Press.

1975 (with R. M. Blackburn). The Ideologies of Non-skilled Industrial Workers. In M. Bulmer (ed.), *Workers' Images of Society*. London: Routledge and Kegan Paul, pp. 131–61.

1975. The Ideology of Intellectuals and Other People in the Development of Capitalism. In L. N. Lindger, R. Alford, C. Crouch and C. Offe (eds.), *Stress and Contradiction in Modern Capitalism*. Lexington, MA: D. C. Heath, pp. 275–307.

1977. States, Ancient and Modern. *Archives Européennes de Sociologie*, 18: 262–98.

1979. Idealism and Materialism in Sociological Theory. In J. W. Freiberg (ed.), *Critical Sociology*. New York: Irvington Publishers, pp. 97–120.

1979 (with R. M. Blackburn). *The Working Class in the Labour Market*. London: Macmillan.

1979. State and Society, 1130–1815: An Analysis of English State Finances. In M. Zeitlin (ed.), *Political Power and Sociological Theory*, Vol. I. Greenwich, CT: JAI Press, pp. 165–205.

1980. The Pre-industrial State: A Review Article. *Political Studies*, 28: 297–304.

1981. Socio-Logic. *Sociology*, 15: 544–50.

1983. Nationalism and Internationalism in Economic and Defence Policies. In J. A. G. Griffiths (ed.), *Socialism in a Cold Climate*. London: Allen and Unwin, pp. 184–206.

1983 (ed.). *A Student Encyclopedia of Sociology*. London: Macmillan.

1984. Capitalism and Militarism. In M. Shaw (ed.), *War, State and Society*. London: Macmillan, pp. 25–46.

1984. The Autonomous Power of the State: Its Nature, Causes and Consequences. *Archives Européennes de Sociologie*, 25: 185–213.

1985. *Socialism Can Survive: Social Change and the Labour Party*. London: Fabian Society, Tract No. 502, 21 pp.

1986. *The Sources of Social Power, Volume I: A History of Power from the Beginning to 1760 AD*. New York: Cambridge University Press.

1986 (ed. with R. Crompton). *Gender and Stratification*. Cambridge: Polity Press (includes co-authored 'Introduction' pp. 1–10, and essay 'A Crisis in Stratification Theory? Persons, Households/Families/Lineages, Genders, Classes and Nations', pp. 40–56).

1986. Work and the Work Ethic. Chapter in Social and Community Planning Research, *British Social Attitudes*. London: SCPR, 25 pp.

1987. War and Social Theory: Into Battle with Classes, Nations and States. In M. Shaw and C. Creighton (eds.), *The Sociology of War and Peace*. London: Macmillan, pp. 54–72.

1987. Ruling Class Strategies and Citizenship. *Sociology*, 21: 339–354.

1987. The Roots and Contradictions of Contemporary Militarism. *New Left Review*, No. 162: 35–50.

1987. The European Miracle: A Historical Analysis. In J. Baechler, J. A. Hall and M. Mann (eds.), *Capitalism and the Rise of the West*. Oxford: Basil Blackwell, pp. 6–19.

1988. *States, War and Capitalism*. Oxford: Basil Blackwell.

1990. (ed.). *The Rise and Decline of the Nation-State*. Oxford: Basil Blackwell (contains Introduction 'Empires with Ends', pp. 1–11).

1992. The Emergence of Modern European Nationalism. In J. A. Hall and I. C. Jarvie (eds.), *Transition to Modernity: Essays on Power, Wealth and Belief*. New York: Cambridge University Press, pp. 137–66.

1992. After Which Socialism? A Response to Chirot's 'After Socialism, What?' *Contention*, 1: 183–92.

1992 (with A. Kane). Class Struggle and Agrarian Politics in Europe and America at the Beginning of the 20th Century. *Social Science History*, 16: 421–54.

1993. *The Sources of Social Power, Volume II: The Rise of Classes and Nation-States, 1760–1914*. Cambridge: Cambridge University Press.

1993. Nation-States in Europe and other Continents: Diversifying, Developing, Not Dying. *Daedalus*, 122(3): 115–40.

1994. In Praise of Macro-sociology: A Reply to Goldthorpe. *British Journal of Sociology*, 45: 39–52.

1994 (with R. Crompton). A New Introduction. In *Gender and Stratification*, 2nd edn. Cambridge: Polity Press, pp. vii–xxiv.

1995. A Political Theory of Nationalism and its Excesses. In S. Periwal (ed.), *Notions of Nationalism*. Budapest, London and New York: Central European University, pp. 44–64.

1995. Sources of Variation in Working Class Movements in Twentieth Century Europe. *New Left Review*, No. 21: 14–54.

1995. As the Twentieth Century Ages (review essay of Hobsbawm's *The Age of Extremes*). *New Left Review*, No. 214. Nov.–Dec: pp. 104–24.

1996. Authoritarian and Liberal Militarism: A Contribution from Comparative and Historical Sociology. In S. Smith, K. Booth and M. Zelewski (eds.), *International Theory: Positivism and Beyond*. Cambridge: Cambridge University Press, pp. 221–39.

1996. Neither Nation-States Nor Globalism (a reply to Peter Taylor's 'Embedded Statism and the Social Sciences: Opening up to New Spaces'). *Environment and Planning A*, 28: 1960–64.

1996. The Contradictions of Continuous Revolution. In I. Kershaw and M. Lewin (eds.), *Stalinism and Nazism: Dictatorships in Comparison.* Cambridge: Cambridge University Press, pp. 137–57.

1997. Has Globalization Ended the Rise and Rise of the Nation-State? *Review of International Political Economy*, 4(3): 472–96.

1998. Is there a Society Called Euro? In R. Axtmann (ed.), *Globalisation and Europe: Theoretical and Empirical Investigations.* London: Cassell/Pinter, pp. 184–207.

1999. The Darkside of Democracy: The Modern Tradition of Ethnic and Political Cleansing. *New Left Review*, No. 235: 18–45.

1999. Some Long-Term Trends in the Multiple-Boundedness of Societies. In C. Honegger, S. Gradil and F. Traxler (eds.), *Grenzenlose Gesellschaft?* Opladen: Leske & Budrich.

2000. Were the Perpetrators of Genocide 'Ordinary Men' or 'Real Nazis'? Results from Fifteen Hundred Biographies. *Holocaust and Genocide Studies*, 14(3): 331–66.

2000. Democracy and Ethnic War. *Hagar*, 1(2): 115–34 (longer version appears in T. Barkawi and M. Laffey (eds.). 2001. *Democracy, Liberalism and War: Rethinking the Democratic Peace Debates.* Boulder, CO: Lynne Reinner Press, pp. 67–85).

2001. Explaining Murderous Ethnic Cleansing: The Macro-Level. In M. Guibernau and J. Hutchinson (eds.), *Understanding Nationalism.* Cambridge: Polity Press, pp. 207–41.

2001. Globalization, Global Conflict and September 11. *New Left Review*, 2nd Ser., 12 (Nov/Dec): 51–72.

2001–2. Globalization is, among Other Things, Transnational, International and American. *Science and Society*, 65 (4, Winter 2001–2002): 464–9.

2003. *Incoherent Empire.* London/New York: Verso Books (paperback edn with added preface forthcoming 2005).

2004. *Fascists.* Cambridge: Cambridge University Press.

2004. The First Failed Empire of the Twenty-First Century. In D. Held and M. Koenig-Archibugi (eds.), *American Power in the Twenty-First Century.* Cambridge: Polity Press.

2004. La crisis del estado-nacion en America Latina. *Desarrollo Economico: Revists de Ciences Sociales*, 44 (174 July–September): 179–99.

2005. *The Dark Side of Democracy: Explaining Ethnic Cleansing.* Cambridge: Cambridge University Press.

Index

Romania, 350
Romanov empire, 360
Rostow, W. W., 383
Royal Society, 376
Runciman, W. G., 36, 136
rural credit, 245
Russia, 42, 45, 270, 360, 361 *see also* USSR
Rwanda, 330, 331, 337, 355, 362

Schmitt, Carl, 8, 300, 351
Schofield, R., 372
School of Mines, 377
Schroeder, Ralph, 346, 355
Schumpeter, Joseph, 292
science and technology, 8, 237–8, 257–9,
    276–80, 371, 375–8, 376 *see also*
    industrial revolution
secularization, 120, 127–8, 289–90
sedimentation, 80
Sematech, 182
settlers and ethnic cleansing, 333–5, 360–1
Sheridan, General, 361
Sikkink, Kathryn, 324
silver, 374, 375
Simmel, Georg, 105
Skocpol, Theda, 2, 19, 36, 158, 265
Smith, Adam, 49, 197, 201, 203, 217,
    219, 299
Smith, Anthony, 359
Snyder, Jack, 14–15, 347, 381
social democracy. *see* democracy, social
social disciplining, 110–11, 350
social movements, 10, 29–31, 34, 35, 42
    see also civil society
social-property relations, 208–9 *see also*
    property rights
social trust, 296
socialism, 10, 42–6, 45, 51, 122, 347, 388,
    389–90
society
    unitary, 189–91
    as unit of analysis, 24, 25, 343
sociology, classic, 19
sociology, comparative, 269–76
sociology, historical, 19–20, 21, 71, 94–5,
    151–3, 154–5, 160–4
Socrates, 137
Somers, M., 265
sources, use of, 81–6
South Africa, 334
South Korea, 390
Soviet Union. *see* USSR
Spain, 112, 113, 114, 234, 253, 350, 368,
    380, 388
Sparta, 154

specialization, 217–19
Spencer, Herbert, 263
Stalin, Joseph, 338, 355, 388
Stark, Rodney, 312–13, 314, 318, 319,
    320, 323
states, 78–9
    autonomy of, 172
    and civil society, 3–4, 11–12
    fiscal-military, 285–97
    formation of, 11, 107–17, 156, 198–200,
        220–5, 228–9, 245–9, 263–7,
        287, 289
    functions of, 2–4
    and geopolitics, 2–3, 21–2
    and globalization, 170–1, 174–83
    and infrastructural power, 7–8, 11,
        167–75, 182–4
    and law, 353–4
    medieval, 213–16, 220–5, 367–70
    and military power, 139–40, 141–8, 245–9
    and political power, 139–40, 141–8,
        352–3
    rise of modern, 27–32, 385
    and social movements, 10
    structure of, 23–7
    theory of, 162
statism, 168–9
steam engines, 14, 277–8, 376, 383
Stevin, Simon, 115
stratification, 205, 206, 208–10, 366
structuralism, 151
Sudan, 388
Sumer, 356–7
Sweden, 113, 114, 178

Taiwan, 179, 182
Taliban, 388
tariff reform, 296–7
Tarrow, Sidney, 19
taxation, 175–6, 245–9, 287, 295–6
tea industry, 274
technology. *see* science and technology
Temin, P., 374
tempocentrism, 151, 154
textiles, 275–6
Thailand, 179
Thatcher, Margaret, 43
Thatcherism, 348
Thirty Years' War, 337, 349
Thucydides, 154
Tilly, Charles, 2, 13, 19, 27, 29, 107, 137,
    158, 368
Tito, General, 363
Tocqueville, Alexis de, 7
Touraine, Alaine, 38